Major Theories
of Media Effects

This book is part of the Peter Lang Media and Communication list.
Every volume is peer reviewed and meets
the highest quality standards for content and production.

PETER LANG
New York • Bern • Berlin
Brussels • Vienna • Oxford • Warsaw

W. James Potter

Major Theories
of Media Effects

Analysis and Evaluation

PETER LANG
New York • Bern • Berlin
Brussels • Vienna • Oxford • Warsaw

Library of Congress Cataloging-in-Publication Control Number: 2019020982

Bibliographic information published by **Die Deutsche Nationalbibliothek.**
Die Deutsche Nationalbibliothek lists this publication in the "Deutsche
Nationalbibliografie"; detailed bibliographic data are available
on the Internet at http://dnb.d-nb.de/.

ISBN 978-1-4331-6952-6 (hardcover)
ISBN 978-1-4331-6951-9 (paperback)
ISBN 978-1-4331-6953-3 (ebook pdf)
ISBN 978-1-4331-6954-0 (epub)
ISBN 978-1-4331-6955-7 (mobi)
DOI 10.3726/b15812

Peter Lang Publishing, Inc., New York
29 Broadway, 18th floor, New York, NY 10006
www.peterlang.com

Table of Contents

Tables

Preface

The field of media effects has exhibited enormous growth in terms of empirical studies and theories. More than a decade ago, it was estimated that there were over 6,000 published empirical studies (Potter & Riddle, 2007) as well as at least 150 media effects theories (Potter, 2009), and the number of existing theories at that time might have been as high as 600 (Bryant & Miron, 2004).

Despite the great number of theories identified as being useful to guide media effects research, the empirical literature has always been—and continues to be—largely atheoretical, that is, only a small proportion of the vast literature of empirical tests of all kinds of media effects has been guided by any theory. Content analyses of the growing media effects literature typically find that only about one third of all studies designed to examine media effects even mention a theory and that less than 10 % of those empirical tests acknowledge the use of a theory to formulate hypotheses or guide their operational decisions (Bryant & Miron, 2004; Kamhawi & Weaver, 2003; Potter, 2018; Potter & Riddle, 2007; Potter, Cooper, & Dupagne, 1993; Shoemaker & Reese, 1990; So, 1988; Stevenson, 1992; Trumbo, 2004). Furthermore, only a handful of media effects theories are mentioned in more than several studies (Potter, 2009), which means that there are a few core theories that account for most of the mentions and the rest of the theories stretch out on a very long tail of only a few mentions each.

These patterns indicate that programmatic research is rare as a way of extending knowledge about media effects, that is, a very small percentage of the empirical work tests a claim in a theory or builds to general theoretical statements. Furthermore when programmatic research is undertaken, those lines of research are fairly short—only a few studies—with the exception of a handful of well-known theories. This fragmentation of research efforts across a wide range of exploratory topics provides the field with enormous breadth. But the cost for developing this breadth has been a limitation on depth. Thus the field has been much slower in developing depth where particular explanations are tested over a course of dozens of empirical studies and thereby progressively refined into confidently elaborated knowledge structures about the effects of the media.

In the scholarly field of media effects, which is now almost a century old, why are theories used at such a low rate in the development of the field? This is the central question of this book. In order to generate a good answer to such an important question, I present a strategy composed of a sequence of four steps. In the first step, the potential role of theory in guiding the design of individual empirical tests is clarified. I will show that theories offer the potential for high value in guiding the design of research studies that will make a difference to the development of a scholarly field.

In the second step, the most prominent media effects theories are analyzed. This step emphasizes depth over breadth so the scope of the analysis is limited to the six most cited theories of media effects. Each of these six core theories is carefully examined along 14 analytical dimensions in order to identify their essential characteristics. The analyses are presented in enough detail so that readers who want to apply it to any of the other hundreds of theories of media effects will learn how to do so.

In the third step, the six theories are evaluated by comparing and contrasting the theories along five basic evaluative dimensions (scope, precision, heuristic value, empirical validity, and openness) and one summary evaluative dimension (overall utility). This process results in a display of the relative value of each of the six theories arrayed on each of the five base evaluative dimensions as well as the summary dimension of overall utility.

In the fourth and final step, the results of the analyses and evaluations are used to construct a "big picture" pattern about how the major theories of media effects have helped—and failed to help—generate knowledge. These "big picture" patterns are then used to address questions about the value of this knowledge to various publics as well as to media effects researchers themselves.

Organization of the Book

Following from the structure of four steps outlined above, this book presents 12 chapters arranged in four parts. The first part lays the foundation for the book with two chapters. Chapter 1 shows how scholarly fields in general develop over time and the role that theory can play in that development. Chapter 2 applies the ideas in the first chapter to the development of the field of media effects.

The second part of the book focuses on analysis with seven chapters. Chapter 3 lays out the analytical dimensions that structure the examination of the six major theories—each of which is analyzed in Chapters 4 through 9. The six theories are Cultivation, Agenda Setting, Framing, Uses & Gratifications, Social Cognitive Learning, and Third Person.

In the third part of the book, the theories are evaluated by comparing and contrasting them along six dimensions. Chapter 10 describes the evaluation structure in detail, then the evaluation itself is displayed in Chapter 11.

The book concludes with a chapter that moves your attention away from the details of the theories and onto big picture issues. Chapter 12 uses the findings from the analysis and evaluation to reveal broad patterns about how knowledge is generated in the field of media effects. This chapter concludes with a discussion of the most pressing challenges facing these six theories—as well as all theories of media effects—in order to overcome problems that have arisen in the past and especially because of the enormous changes that have been taking place with the field's focal phenomenon.

Axioms and Stipulations

Scholarship is never an objective, mechanical presentation of facts. Instead, it is a series of arguments that are shaped by the author's axiomatic beliefs. By "axiomatic beliefs," I mean that authors work from a foundation of beliefs that guide their choice of topics, the way they construct arguments, how they use evidence to support those arguments, and even what they consider as evidence. When readers share the same beliefs as an author, then readers can more efficiently follow those arguments, that is, there are fewer barriers to understanding. However, where there is a difference in beliefs between readers and an author, readers will find themselves frequently lost or confused at best, and more typically they will find themselves arguing against the author whose work they will judge as trivial, wrongheaded, or out of bounds.

Because I want to make the reading experience as transparent as possible, I begin by laying out a series of seven foundational beliefs that guided me when writing this book. The more you—the reader—understand what these beliefs are, the more efficiently you will be able to read this book. I present these seven beliefs in two categories: beliefs about scholarship and philosophical beliefs. It is not my purpose here to convince you to hold these beliefs yourself. Instead I present them so that you have a better context for understanding the arguments I present throughout this book.

Beliefs About Scholarship

While writing this book, I came to realize that I have four strongly held beliefs about scholarly fields. I want to explain what these beliefs are up front so that you can understand the foundation for the thinking I present in this book.

The first of these beliefs is: The primary function of a scholarly field is to generate and communicate knowledge about its focal phenomenon. There are, of course, other important functions of scholarly fields; however, I argue that all other functions are secondary to this primary function. For example, one function of scholarly fields is to provide a community of like-minded scholars. If our scholarly field were a social club, then this function could reasonably be regarded as its primary one. But if we believe that the purpose of scholarly fields is to generate and communicate knowledge, then the scholarly community has more value as a tool that enables scholars to learn from one another rather than simply as a means of interacting with people who share one's interests. Also, if a research field attracts an increasing number of scholars, this growth *could* serve as an indicator of an increasingly valuable scholarly field. But it might not. If the growing number of researchers and greater number of research studies do not translate into a widespread sharing of lessons learned about methodologies and an integration of research findings, then the field devolves into fragmentation and moves away from—rather than toward—achieving its primary function. Therefore the growth in the size of a scholarly field can serve as a contributing factor to—but not evidence of—a field's evolution as it strives toward its primary function.

The second belief is: The key indicator of the growth of a scholarly field is its progression in generating and communicating knowledge that is *useful*. Usefulness has a slightly different meaning depending on who is consuming the knowledge. We need to consider two different kinds of consumers of this knowledge— researchers who want to contribute to the generation of knowledge and publics (such as teachers, students, parents, policy makers) who want information about the media so they can make better decisions about media use for themselves and others.

The third belief is: Theory is potentially the most valuable tool in helping scholarly fields achieve their primary function. Thus, theories are useful to the extent that they guide the generating and communicating of knowledge about the field's focal phenomenon. Theories guide the generation of knowledge by focusing scholars' attention on particular ideas and the theorized relationship among those ideas. Theories delineate the cutting edge of knowledge and provide a perspective on what the most important next steps are. Good theories document the evolution of their key concepts from an initial fuzziness toward increasing clarity. And good theories provide a more efficient context to structure reviews of the literature so that readers can more easily keep up to date with the growth of knowledge and thus avoid getting lost in trying to process thousands of micro findings from hundreds of individual exploratory studies.

The fourth belief is: Scholarship progresses through a hermeneutic process. This is the process whereby scholars make sense of an individual empirical finding in the context of broader patterns in the literature. And broader patterns cannot be constructed without individual findings. Thus the hermeneutic process is composed of two cycles: (1) downward movement generating more narrowly designed reductionistic research studies that dig deeper into each narrow topic; and (2) upward movement where the findings from individual studies are evaluated and synthesized into broader and broader patterns at higher and higher levels of generality. Thus, reductionistic research should not be regarded as having low utility; this is an essential step in the hermeneutic process. However, if a field produces only reductionistic studies while ignoring the need to continually collate, evaluate, and synthesize those findings into larger knowledge structures, the field stays in an exploratory phase where the scattered findings from thousands of individual studies have little stand-alone value. Both cycles of the hermeneutic process are required for a scholarly field to generate useful knowledge about its focal phenomenon.

This hermeneutic process illuminates why it is so difficult for a scholarly field to make progress when it is new. Scholars have no guidance as to where the cutting edge is because there are no big picture patterns. Scholars expend almost all their effort in attempting to identify key concepts, trying out different definitions for those concepts, and exploring which concepts are related to one another. Scholars must rely on speculation and be comfortable with designing reductionistic studies with little guidance. This is the nature of the exploratory phase.

Over time as the results from individual exploratory studies accumulate, patterns begin to emerge. Scholars develop a better sense about which concepts are most important, which definitions are more clear and valid, and how those concepts are related to one another in an overall system of explanation. Scholars see a clearer big picture pattern to their focal phenomenon, and this knowledge helps them design studies that focus on more important topics, employ more valid measures, and conduct the kinds of analyses that can better explain the nature of the phenomenon.

Big picture patterns are important to social sciences. "Science is about mapmaking. It's about taking a complicated world and reducing it to some sparse set of markings on a map that provides new guidance across an otherwise incomprehensible, and potentially hostile, landscape. A good map eliminates as much spurious information as possible, so that what remains is just enough to guide our way" (Miller, 2015, p. 1). "Science has proceeded by developing increasingly detailed maps of decreasingly small phenomena. At the heart of this reductionistic strategy is a hope that once we have detailed maps of the smallest of parts, we can paste the mosaic together and have a useful map" of everything (p. 2). However, reductionistic research alone is not enough because even if we know everything possible about the individual pieces that compose a system, we know very little about how those pieces interact with one another as they form the system as a whole. Detailed knowledge of a single piece of glass does not help us see, and appreciate, the image that emerges from a stained-glass window.

The hermeneutic process requires the continual sorting through the results from empirical studies to find the most valid pieces, then to use those pieces to construct a vision of broad patterns displaying a field's findings as knowledge.

Philosophical Beliefs

This book is based on three philosophical beliefs: ontology about human beings, ontology about the media, and epistemology about scholarship.

The first philosophical belief is: Humans are interpretive beings who are also governed by mechanisms. In the 1980s there was a prominent debate in communication about what scholars referred to as paradigms, which referred to fundamental beliefs about humans. Social scientists were characterized as positivists, which typically meant that they had a mechanistic view of human beings. In contrast humanists were characterized as actionalists or interpretists, which usually meant that they believed that humans exhibited important differences in the way they encountered experiences and interpreted their meanings. While the rhetoric has subsided somewhat, there is reason to believe that this perception of a difference between two forms of scholarship still exists.

My position is that it is useful to regard human beings as both interpretive beings and also governed by mechanisms. While humans are alike in many ways (e.g., as organic physical systems), humans are also unique from one another in other ways. And most typically, humans are a mix of the two where they exhibit profound differences from other humans while at the same time sharing some characteristics with other humans (e.g., inborn trait differences and broad-scale socializing influences). Stage theories of human development are evidence of this mix of differences and similarities. For example, Piaget's stage theory of cognitive development regards all children at age 3 as having the same cognitive capabilities but that there are also important differences across children by each age cohort. The research in all social sciences exhibits a belief about a mix of differences and similarities. For example, when researchers test for the influence of demographic characteristics (sex, age cohort, socioeconomic status, educational level, income level, etc.), they are acknowledging that important differences exist. Thus testing for biological sex indicates that a researcher believes that males are different from females in some important way but that all males are relatively the same and that all females are relatively the same.

The rhetoric in the paradigm debates is useful only if it continually reminds us that humans are both biological machines and creative interpretive beings. The key to making scholarly contributions does not lie in taking the "right" path; instead, the key challenge is in recognizing the ways that humans are uniformly hard-wired and using appropriate methods to generate data and analyses to increase our understanding of that part of the human experience while also recognizing the ways in which humans are different—from the subtle to the profound—and using very different methods to observe and document the nature of those differences.

A second philosophical belief is: The media constitute a dynamic phenomenon. Distinctions by media channel that used to be so important have eroded such that it is now very difficult to determine what is television, a film, a recording, a newspaper, a magazine, or a book. Also content distinctions have eroded so that news, entertainment, and advertising all blend together. And with the rise of digital technologies and interactive features, the distinction between content producer and audience member has eroded. Theories that do not adapt to the changing phenomenon by altering their definitions of key terms and their systems of explanation lose their ability to generate useful knowledge about media effects.

The third philosophical belief is: All scholarship is value based. While this belief is widely discussed in nonscientific areas of scholarship, it also holds in scientific areas. These values are revealed when we look at assumptions that underlie what we do as scholars. If we pretend that values do not exist or that they do not shape what we do, then we greatly limit our understanding of scholarship. Scholars need not be *advocates* of their beliefs in all their publications, but they should be *transparent* about their beliefs so readers can understand and even appreciate the value of authors' perspectives. The value of scholarship grows out of each scholar's ability to communicate a deeper understanding of a field's focal phenomenon.

Stipulations

Finally, I need to present two stipulations. These are the assumptions I have made to limit this project to make it manageable and still useful to readers.

First, I limited the focus to the scientific literature. While the field of media effects has attracted a wide range of scholars, the majority of the writing and research has been conducted from a scientific point of view. I am not arguing that empirical science is the only way—or even the best way—to generate knowledge about media effects; instead, I focus on scientific theories because the literature in this field is dominated by empirical studies of a scientific nature. Therefore, this is a good place to begin.

Second, I limited the analysis to six theories. While content analyses of the media effects literature have shown that there are several hundred theories mentioned (Bryant & Miron, 2004; Potter, 2009), almost all of those theories are mentioned in only one or two publications. This is truly a long tail pattern with very few theories being mentioned more frequently than several dozen times across the entire span of publications dealing with media effects.

Conclusion

You have now seen the foundation for this book by reading through these seven assumptions and two stipulations. I am not foolhardy enough to expect readers to agree with my perceptions of patterns or beliefs about scholarship. My purpose is not to try converting everyone to my way of thinking (although that would be great!). Instead my purpose is to stimulate discussion about important issues that have been influencing the growth (or lack of it) of the scholarly field of media effects by challenging some of our practices and beliefs. There have been too few discussions of this type in the past century and this neglect has left our field more fragmented, less organized, and less vital than it could be. As long as we keep the focus so strongly on the micro, the payoff from our enormous research energy will result in more and more tiny pockets of tentative findings where each scholar becomes more and more expert in a narrower and narrower sliver of the media effects phenomenon. While the demands of research require scholars to become more and more expert as they dig deeper into their narrow topic area, the hermeneutic process also has a second cycle that needs to motivate scholars to look for patterns across studies and transform the scattered piles of research results throughout the field into a meaningful structure of knowledge. The purpose of this book is to illustrate both of these cycles by breaking down theories into their essential parts then to put those pieces together in novel ways to show big picture patterns.

The essential contribution of this book is to present both an analysis and an evaluation of the six most prominent theories of media effects. By analysis, I mean to provide a detailed examination of each theory along 14 analytical dimensions. Thus this analysis exhibits more depth and detail than typically found in most reviews of theories. By evaluation, I mean to demonstrate the relative merits of the six theories by comparing and contrasting them along six evaluative dimensions in a way that invites readers to make their own judgments about which of these theories has the most value to a scholarly field focused on creating knowledge about media effects.

References

Bryant, J., & Miron, D. (2004). Theory and research in mass communication. *Journal of Communication, 54*, 662–704. doi:10.1111/j.1460-2466.2004.tb02650.x

Kamhawi, R., & Weaver, D. (2003). Mass communication research trends from 1980 to 1999. *Journalism & Mass Communication Quarterly, 80*(1), 7–27.

Miller, J. H. (2015). *A crude look at the whole: The science of complex systems in business, life, and society*. New York: Basic Books.

Potter, W. J. (2009). *Arguing for a general framework for mass media scholarship*. Thousand Oaks, CA: Sage.

Potter, W. J. (2018). An analysis of patterns of design decisions in recent media effects research. *Review of Communication Research, 6*, 1–29, doi:10.12840/issn.2255-4165.2018.06.01.014

Potter, W. J., Cooper, R., & Dupagne, M. (1993). The three paradigms of mass media research in mainstream journals. *Communication Theory, 3*, 317–335.

Potter, W. J., & Riddle, K. (2007). Profile of mass media effects research in scholarly journals. *Journalism & Mass of Communication Quarterly, 84*, 90–104.

Shoemaker, P. J., & Reese, S. D. (1990). Exposure to what? Integrating media content and effects studies. *Journalism Quarterly, 67*, 649–652.

So, C. Y. K. (1988). Citation patterns of core communication journals: An assessment of the developmental status of communication. *Human Communication Research, 15*, 236–255.

Stevenson, R. L. (1992). Defining international communication as a field. *Journalism Quarterly, 69*, 543–553.

Trumbo, C. W. (2004). Research methods in mass communication research: A census of eight journals 1990 to 2000. *Journalism & Mass Communication Quarterly, 80*(2), 417–436.

I

Foundations

CHAPTER ONE

The Role of Theory in Scholarly Fields

Scholarly Fields

Fundamental Purpose

The primary purpose of any scholarly field is to generate knowledge about the field's focal phenomenon, then to communicate that knowledge. In order to understand this purpose statement, we need to clarify the meaning of knowledge and focal phenomenon.

In any scholarly field, knowledge is not simply a finding from one study nor is it a listing of findings from multiple studies. Instead, knowledge is a structured, detailed description about what is believed to be known about a field's focal phenomenon. While the building blocks of knowledge are the findings from individual studies, those building blocks by themselves are not knowledge; they need to be evaluated for validity and usefulness, then assembled into a meaningful structure in order to attain the status of knowledge. The evaluation involves scholars assessing the validity of findings so they can discard the claims that are found to be faulty. Then the valid findings need to be calibrated for importance so that the most important findings can be used to form a solid core when assembling those findings into a system of explanation.

A field's focal phenomenon is the entity that scholars in that field are trying to understand and explain. For example, the focal phenomenon of the field of chemistry is physical matter that is studied by examining atoms and molecules. The focal phenomenon of the field of biology is living things that are subdivided into botany (the study of plants) and zoology (the study of animals). The fields regarded as social sciences are concerned with human thinking and behavior. Within the broader field of the social sciences, the scholarly field of psychology is focused on the focal phenomenon of the human mind; the field of sociology focuses on human interactions in groups; the field of economics focuses on the exchange of resources; and the field of media effects focuses on how the media exert an influence on individuals and aggregates.

Development of Scholarly Fields

Scholarly fields are generated when scholars become attracted to a phenomenon and are driven by curiosity to learn all they can about that phenomenon. As more scholars are attracted to studying a phenomenon and as they begin speculating about the nature of that phenomenon, they form a community to share ideas in articles, books, conference papers, and websites.

The speculation about the focal phenomenon reveals scholars' ontological beliefs, which are beliefs about the nature of the phenomenon, such as its size, its components, its processes, and how it interacts with other phenomena in the social and physical worlds. Researchers begin testing those speculations to find out which are most useful. These tests reveal researchers' epistemological positions, which are beliefs about the ways in which humans can come to know the phenomenon and the limits of that knowing. Because scholarship is a community endeavor, researchers publish their findings in scholarly outlets so their ideas about the phenomenon as well as their research findings can be shared with other scholars in the field.

Scholarly fields begin in an exploratory mode, where assumptions dominate. There are many assumptions that must be made early in the history of a scholarly field in order to answer questions such as: What are the most important concepts that can be used to explain the phenomenon? How should those concepts be defined? How can those concepts best be measured in research studies? How are those concepts related to one another? When a field is new, these questions have no existing answers or the answers are not very useful, so researchers must speculate about possible answers. Those speculations are evaluated by other scholars so that the faulty speculations can be weeded out.

The development of knowledge in a field always involves a hermeneutic process. This means that scholars try to leverage the result of an individual research study to argue that the result indicates a general pattern; scholars then use that speculated general pattern to explain an individual result. When a field is well developed, it is relatively easy to use this hermeneutic process because scholars have a well-articulated big picture of their phenomenon that allows them to easily understand any individual research finding. However, when a field is new, the big picture is fuzzy, so scholars rely on speculations based on what they think are reasonable assumptions at the time. It is rather like trying to solve a huge puzzle with thousands of pieces without knowing what the picture of the puzzle will reveal when all the pieces are assembled. Scholars must make reasonable guesses about what the picture is in order to start placing pieces in what they hope will be useful positions so that all the pieces go together in a way to reveal a coherent big picture. That is, scholars use their assumptions about what the big picture of the phenomenon might be in order to design their research studies. If their assumptions about the phenomenon are faulty, then the design of their research studies will produce findings of questionable value, that is, those results will be difficult to interpret or those results will not seem to make sense.

The hermeneutic process follows a circular procedure of using assumptions to support other assumptions. In many fields, scholars will attempt to break open this circular process of pure reasoning by introducing empirical tests that can be used to generate tests of those assumptions. Over time, those assumptions that have been found to generate support evolve into trusted empirically based findings, while those assumptions that fail to generate sufficient support from a program of empirical tests are regarded as faulty and are replaced with alternative assumptions.

The typical growth pattern in scholarly fields is by gradual evolution of ideas as scholars debate speculations and test them for empirical support. Gradually over time, scholars coalesce around certain ideas as being better descriptors of the field's focal phenomenon. These ideas become institutionalized as the accepted knowledge about the focal phenomenon. Scholars take these foundational ideas for granted as they try to build knowledge beyond this core.

In contrast to *evolution* as a growth pattern, some fields experience a *revolution* where scholars grow tired of accepting the foundational core ideas and challenge them as being outdated, too limiting, or faulty in some way (Kuhn, 1970). Growth through revolution occurs suddenly after a period where thinking is stuck, and the growth of knowledge slows down and might even stop. Scholars keep doing the same kind of scholarship over and over until the marginal utility of each new study approaches zero. Then a creative scholar introduces a new way of thinking about the phenomenon typically by strongly challenging an assumption then altering it in a way that suggests a fresh way to build understanding about the field's focal phenomenon. If that fresh thinking attracts enough scholars and if the new scholarship does indeed result in new insights about the phenomenon, then the revolution is successful and alters the direction of how scholars explain the field's focal phenomenon.

Theories

What Is a Theory?

The word "theory" has many different meanings in everyday language. Reynolds (1971) says that it can refer to "(1) vague conceptualizations or descriptions of events or things, (2) prescriptions about what are desirable social behaviors or arrangements, or (3) any untested hypothesis or idea" (p. 11). Thus we often hear people say something like "That is just a theory" to discount someone's explanation and this makes the idea of theory in everyday language appear to be something that is not very useful.

Scholars have a very different idea about what theories are, but this is not to say that all scholars agree on a single definition. To the contrary, there are many definitions of theory used in scholarship (see Tables 1.1 and 1.2). But when we look across all these definitions, we can see three similarities that indicate where scholars generally agree. First, theories are concerned with *providing explanations* of a field's phenomenon of interest. Thus they are more than simple descriptions. For example, Littlejohn (1999) argues that the essence of theories is explanation. "Explanation is more than merely naming and defining variables; it identifies regularities in the relationships among those variables. Explanations account for an event by referring to what is going on within the event or between it and some other event. In simplest terms, explanation answers the question, Why?" He continues, "An explanation designates some logical force among variables that makes particular outcomes 'necessary'" (Littlejohn, 1999, p. 23). "Although a simple taxonomy, or organized list of concepts, may be considered a theory, most scholars would say that this is only a step toward a scholarly theory, which must include some explanatory mechanism or set of propositions that explain how the concepts are related to one another" (p. 957).

While the phenomenon reveals itself through individual elements that are observable to humans, the phenomenon is not any one of these elements or even an assemblage of the elements; the phenomenon is more—it is the pattern of the elements that is not just the *What* of the phenomenon but also the *How* and the *Why*. Theories then are designed initially to capture the essence of the *What* but

Table 1.1. Conceptions of Theory

Babbie (1998, p. 51):
* A systematic set of interrelated statements intended to explain some aspect of social life

Hoover (1984, p. 38):
* A set of interrelated propositions that suggest why events occur in the manner that they do

Infante, Rancer, and Womack (1990, p. 37):
* A set of interrelated propositions that suggest why events occur in the manner that they do

Littlejohn (2009, p. 957):
* Human constructions designed to capture what theorists believe the order of the subject matter to be.
* A unified, or coherent, body of propositions that provide a philosophically consistent picture of a subject. The propositions should be generalizable, that is, they should deal with broad patterns in aggregates. They must reduce complex experience into a manageable set of concepts and propositions.

Littlejohn (1999, p. 23):
* The essence of theories is explanation, which is more than merely naming and defining variables.
  – Explanation is concerned with regularities in the relationships among variables.
  – Explanations account for an event by referring to what is going on within the event or between it and some other event.
  – Explanation answers the question: Why?
  – An explanation designates some logical force among variables that makes particular outcomes necessary

McQuail (2005, p. 5):
* A general proposition, itself based on observation and logical argument, that states the relationships among elements within the observed phenomena

---

then must also address the *How* and *Why*. This is what is meant by theories moving beyond description and into explanation.

Second, theories are abstracts of some phenomenon, that is, they capture the essence of the phenomenon in a few words relative to the complexity of the phenomenon itself. Thus parsimony is important. Theoreticians capture the essence by focusing attention on particular ideas (called concepts) and the relationships (called propositions) among those concepts. Littlejohn (2009) says, "A theory is never intended to reflect the complexity of all experience, but to distill this into a system of knowledge claims explained by a small number of properties. . . . They must reduce complex experience into a manageable set of concepts and propositions" (p. 957).

Table 1.2. Conceptions of the Purpose of Theory

Hempel (1952, p. 1):
1. To describe particular phenomena in the world of our experience
2. To establish general principles in order to predict and explain experiences

Infante et al. (1993, pp. 45–50):
1. To organize experience
2. To extend knowledge
3. To stimulate and guide further research
4. To predict new things

Littlejohn (1999):
1. To organize and summarize knowledge
2. To map the phenomenon by focusing attention on particular concepts and relationships
3. To clarify what is observed in order to understand and interpret things
4. To provide guidelines about what to observe and how to observe
5. To predict
6. To provide an open forum for debate and discussion (heuristic function)
7. To share information and insights (communicative function)
8. To control (normative function)
9. To challenge existing culture (generative function)

McQuail (2005, p. 5):
1. To make sense of observed reality
2. To guide the collection and evaluation of evidence

Reynolds (1971):
1. To generate useful scientific knowledge that is abstract (independence of time and space), intersubjective (agreement about meaning among relevant scientists), and empirically supported (can be compared to empirical findings)

And third, theories are tools for guidance. That is, they should guide scholars toward increasing their understanding of the phenomenon. This means that a theory is a wedge that breaks open the phenomenon in a way that allows scholars to enter and experience it in a meaningful way. As a guide to understanding, the theory guides scholars to insights that resonate with them and lead them to think "Aha that makes sense." As guides, theories also direct scholars in the creation and analysis of evidence. They stimulate and direct future research (Infante, Rancer, &Womack, 1993) by focusing scholars on what to observe and how to interpret meaning from those observations (Littlejohn, 1999).

Differences. Theories also exhibit differences that have led scholars to put them in different categories (see Table 1.3). However, this classification task is a difficult one because it requires scholars to weight the importance of those differences

Table 1.3. Types of Theories

Reynolds (1971):

1. Set of laws—the conception of scientific knowledge as a set of well-supported empirical generalizations or laws
2. Axiomatic—an interrelated set of definitions, axioms, and propositions that are derived from axioms
3. Causal process—a set of descriptions or causal processes

McQuail (2005):

1. Social scientific—offers general statements about the nature and processes of a phenomenon that guide the systematic and objective observation of the phenomenon so that those statements can be put to the test and validated or rejected by similar methods
2. Cultural—advances arguments that either differentiate cultural artifacts or challenge some practices
3. Normative—presents arguments that prescribe how society should be structured or how people should behave
4. Operational—argues for the application of certain practical ideas to solve problems in society
5. Everyday theory—commonsense principles that everyday people use to guide their behavior and thinking

---

and when scholars use different weightings or vary in what they consider differences, their categorization schemes vary. Thus the classification of theories has been called "one of the most daunting tasks" because "it defies clear classification" (Littlejohn, 1999, p. 12).

One example of a theory classification scheme was offered by McQuail (2005) who organized mass media theories into five categories: social scientific, cultural, normative, operational, and everyday type theories. McQuail's social scientific category includes theories that present general statements about the nature and processes of a phenomenon in order to guide the systematic and objective observation of the phenomenon so that those statements can be put to the test and validated or rejected by similar methods. The cultural category includes theories that advance arguments that either differentiate cultural artifacts or challenge some practices. The normative category includes theories that present arguments that prescribe how society *should* be structured or how people *should* behave. The operational category includes theories that argue for the application of certain practical ideas to solve problems in society. And the everyday category includes theories that are commonsense principles that people generally use to guide their behavior and thinking.

Another way to organize theories by type was suggested by Reynolds (1971) who arranged theories according to the nature of their propositions into three categories of set of laws, axiomatic, and causal processes. His set of laws category includes theories where the conception of scientific knowledge is a set of well-supported empirical generalizations or laws. The axiomatic category includes theories that present an interrelated set of definitions, axioms, and propositions that are derived from axioms. And the causal process category includes theories that present a set of descriptions or causal processes.

Types of Theories: Advocacy and Scientific

Within the field of communication, a useful way to categorize theories is to make a distinction between advocacy theories and scientific theories. An advocacy theory presents a thesis position then assembles evidence in a compelling argument to support that thesis. The thesis can be an ideology (such as Marxism or feminism) or a perspective (such as psychoanalysis). In contrast to advocacy theories, scientific theories present a set of explanatory propositions that are speculations about the phenomenon that require testing to determine their value. Scientific theories are less concerned with winning an argument than with refining their explanations so that they better fit the patterns within the phenomenon itself as revealed through empirical testing. (For more on this distinction, see Potter, 1996.)

While all theories present claims that purport to explain something about a phenomenon, advocacy theories differ from scientific theories in three major ways—the purpose of the theory, the use of evidence to support the theory, and the criteria for quality in judging a theory.

Contrasting by purpose. The purpose of advocacy theories is to present a particular thesis as an explanation of the phenomenon then convince readers of the value of that explanation. Thus the purpose is to win an argument over other scholars who argue for other theories. Knowledge is generated by arguments based on illustrating that certain perspectives—or ideologies—can produce novel insights that are interesting and useful. These scholars argue that their perspective on the phenomenon works well to reveal a different way of thinking about a phenomenon that readers have likely been taking for granted or have a faulty and/or limited understanding of because of the limitations imposed by the status quo perspectives they have been using in the past. Scholars select evidence to support their claims and fashion their arguments in a way to maximize the persuasiveness of their arguments.

In contrast, the purpose of scientific theories is to test explanations rather than to select one explanation then argue for its value. Scientific theories require researchers to gather evidence not for the purpose of *supporting* their claims (although they often hope that the evidence will do so) but instead to *test* their claims. When the gathered evidence fails to support their expectations (hypotheses), researchers must continue testing that claim by either (a) running another test to determine if the preponderance of evidence gathered in many different tests tends to add support to their claim, or (b) alter their claim to bring it into line with the results of the nonsupporting empirical evidence then run additional tests to determine if the altered claim achieves a greater degree of support. Thus a key purpose of scientific scholarship is to be progressive, that is, scientists believe that each test provides scholars with insights about how to improve either by altering speculations or by designing subsequent tests with fewer flaws.

Contrasting by treatment of evidence. Scholars who use advocacy theories look for evidence to support their position so as to maximize the strength of their argument. When they encounter evidence that weakens or refutes their position, they either ignore it or else critically analyze it to try to uncover some aspect of it that they can argue is faulty in some way.

In contrast, scholars who use scientific theories begin with tentative expectations in the form of hypotheses that they operationalize from a general claim in a theory. They then design an empirical test to generate fresh findings. If those findings support their hypotheses, then researchers conclude there is support for the theoretical explanations from which the hypotheses were operationalized. But if those empirical findings fail to support their hypotheses, then researchers conclude that the theoretical explanations have been falsified. Thus they are not trying to win an argument but to increase knowledge about the phenomenon by trying to conduct a test of the theory's claims in an unbiased a manner as possible. That is, researchers try to keep an open mind and allow the findings of their empirical studies to emerge even if those findings run counter to their initial expectations. So when the results of empirical tests fail to support a claim made by a theory, those results are still acknowledged, but those results that do not support the theory are expected to reshape the claims made by the theory so that through this long-term process of accommodating patterns of support and falsification, the set of claims made by the theory become more precise and useful explanations of the phenomenon.

Contrasting by criteria for judging quality. The value of advocacy scholarship lies in how well the user of the theory constructs a supporting argument. For example, prosecuting attorneys have a theory of a case that the accused committed the crime, so they comb through the evidence to select the strongest bits that support their argument for guilt. Prosecutors then assemble those observations (by witnesses, crime scene investigators, pathologists, etc.) into a coherent argument that supports their theory of the case. Defense attorneys sort through the same body of evidence but they are looking for elements to support a different theory—that is, that their client is not guilty. Defense attorneys then assemble the bits that support their theory into the strongest argument they can make. Juries then are empaneled to make judgments about which side has presented the higher quality case.

Some humanistic scholars conduct textual analyses where a theory (e.g., Marxist theory, feminist theory, psychoanalytic theory) guides them about how to interpret the text to arrive at particular claims that explain that text. Then they observe particular elements in those texts and select only those that best support their claims.

In contrast, scientific theories establish their quality through meeting a sequence of three criteria. First, theories need to stimulate tests of their claims. Second, the more the results of those empirical tests support the claims in the theory, the stronger the explanatory value of that theory. And third, the more that theories can accommodate the growing patterns of empirical results, the better the theories grow in precision and validity.

In summary, there are many definitions of theory but fundamentally, they all share certain characteristics. Those definitions all regard theories as focusing attention on some phenomenon of interest, providing a system of explanation of that phenomenon in a parsimonious way, and delivering guidance to scholars that helps them understand the phenomenon, collect evidence, and interpret the meaning of that evidence. There are also many different kinds of theories with the most essential distinction being between advocacy theories and scientific theories. Because most of the work in the field of media effects has been of a scientific nature, we narrow our focus onto scientific theories.

Components of Scientific Theories

There are five components to scientific theories. They are: concepts, propositions, axioms, calculus, and model. The first two of these are the most salient, that is, scholars who write about a particular theory typically focus on that theory's concepts and propositions.

1. Concepts. Concepts are the building blocks of theories (Babbie, 1998; Littlejohn, 2009; Shoemaker, Tankard, & Lasorsa, 2004). "A concept is a category or class of objects, events, situations, or processes designated by a term. A concept encompasses a group of things that share one or more attributes" (Littlejohn, 2009, p. 957).

Some concepts are primitive while others are derived. Primitive concepts are those terms that are treated as though everyone knows the definition. These are words that people use in their everyday lives and have no trouble assuming that others know their meaning (e.g., person, car, breakfast, weather). Some are easy to define (e.g., individual, woman, tree, eye). Other terms are derived; these must be defined because not everyone would know what they mean (e.g., equifinality, cybernetics, face behaviors) or because the meaning is different from how most people would normally define them (e.g., cultivation, framing, dissonance, priming, accommodation).

A special type of derived concept is the construct. There are three types of constructs. First is the ideal type (e.g., utopia, infinity, eternity), which are things that must be imagined rather than observed. Second, there are hypotheticals (e.g., attitudes, beliefs, values), which can never be observed directly so scholars hypothesize that they exist and must therefore define what they are and how we can attribute evidence for their existence. For example, aggression is a hypothetical construct that can be defined as a drive to perform harmful behaviors. Given this definition, we cannot observe a drive directly but we could argue that evidence for aggression includes things like children hitting a doll or yelling at a playmate. Third, there are constructions (e.g., socioeconomic status [SES] or intelligence). These are an amalgamation of ideas constructed in a particular way by scholars. For example, one scholar might use a construction of SES as people's household income plus their income level while another scholar might use a construction of SES as people's individual hourly wage times hours worked per year minus personal expenses plus years of college completed.

Reynolds (1971) points out that "To refer to any set of abstract concepts used to describe a phenomenon as a theory is an inappropriate use of the word if only a set of concepts is presented" (p 11). He says that a scientific theory also needs statements showing how the concepts interrelate as an explanation of that phenomenon.

2. Propositions. Propositions are relational statements that make claims about how two or more concepts are associated with one another either by covariance or causally (Babbie, 1998; Reynolds, 1971).

Propositions vary in generality, that is, the scope of their claims. When a proposition claims a relationship between two concepts, it is typically very general. However, as theoreticians add qualifiers or contingent conditions to their propositions, those statements are reduced in generality. For example, the claim that viewing violent media messages is associated with subsequent aggressive behavior is very general because as expressed, it applies to all violent messages, all people, at all times, and in all situations. If this claim were modified to say "viewing violent media messages is associated with subsequent aggressive behavior if the violence is portrayed as being perpetrated by characters who are attractive, justified in their actions, and rewarded" then the proposition is narrower in scope because it excludes certain types of portrayals. Propositions in scientific theories are more valuable when they are more general because they have greater scope; however, if the patterns of testing such a proposition show that it does not hold at such a general level, then the proposition loses its value until it is refined to account for the qualifying conditions.

3. Axioms. Axioms are the fundamental assumptions theoreticians make in order to support their theories. Babbie (1998) says that theories have a foundation in an axiomatic groundwork, which are fundamental assertions assumed to be true. Thus axioms are statements of theoreticians' beliefs upon which they construct their explanations.

Some of these assumptions can be tested to see if they hold while other assumptions cannot. For example, values are assumptions that cannot be tested and therefore cannot be confirmed or discredited, so they must be accepted. Some people believe there is a god who created the entire universe in one week and who is everywhere observing the behavior of everyone and making judgments about each individual's suitability to be accepted into a heaven after physical death. People who hold this belief accept it on faith rather than from proof. There is no adequate way within the human experience that people can acquire proof of the validity of this belief.

Scholars hold deep philosophical beliefs, such as ontology and epistemology. Ontology refers to beliefs about the existence of things, while epistemology refers to beliefs about how humans can make sense of their experiences. For example, some scholars hold an epistemological belief that humans are fundamentally limited in their perceptions so they will never be able to experience entities external to them accurately. In contrast, other scholars hold an epistemological belief that humans can distance themselves from phenomenon (including social phenomena) enough so that their observations are an objective viewing of that phenomenon.

Some axioms can be tested. When they are found to hold, the theory has a stronger foundation. However, when they are found to be faulty, the theoreticians are under pressure to alter or replace that axiom. A common example of this is the nature of definitions of key concepts. When theoreticians invent a new concept, they provide an initial definition that they believe at the time to be the best way to define the concept. However, this definition is likely to be found faulty over time as research accumulates. For example, there are theories that use the concept of gender but define it as biological sex, and this illustrates an assumption by a theoretician that all females are the same, that all males are the same, and that there are significant differences between the two groups. While this distinction holds relatively well in biology, it does not hold as well in the social sciences. Biologists have evidence of distinct differences between males and females with sex organs, hormone production, and ability to reproduce. However, within the social sciences, evidence continually shows that many females exhibit male category behaviors and that many males exhibit female category behaviors. For example, many people assume that males are more aggressive than females so that violent video games are only played by males. But research has shown that many players of violent video games are female and that many females are more aggressive than many males.

Slife and Williams (1995) point out that all theories are based on a foundation of assumptions "and these assumptions are most often not explicit." They continue "assumptions always lead to implications," which are "the consequences of an idea or theory—the conceptual costs, calculated in terms of other ideas that logically flow from it, that we are logically obligated to accept" (p. 17). They say that "any theory explains some things, but leaves many things still to be explained. These unexplained things and the implications of the theories are important, yet most often, implicit, and theorists do not usually deal with them. Only if we become aware of these implicit ideas as problems to be dealt with can we deal with them" (pp. 17–18).

4. Calculus. Scientific theories can never be tested directly because of the general nature of the concepts and propositions. The concepts need to be translated into measures, and the propositions need to be translated into hypotheses. This translation process is called operationalization. The rules of operationalization are the calculus of the theory. The calculus is a set of transforming rules by which one class of ideas (theoretical concepts) can be transformed into another class (testable variables).

The calculus is not typically addressed explicitly by theoreticians. Usually the calculus is revealed through the patterns of design decisions made by the theoreticians when they conduct empirical studies to test the claims they have made in their theories.

5. Model. The terms "model" and "theory" are sometimes used as if they were interchangeable, but this is faulty. Slife and Williams (1995) point out why there is a major distinction by saying that models display an organization of concepts—a sequence or structure that helps scholars think about components or a sequence. Models are typically graphical in display, with boxes for concepts and arrows indicating how the ideas in the boxes are related to one another. If the model is supported with definitions for the concepts and a narrative explaining how the concepts are related, then the model is part of a theory. That is, a model is not itself a theory, because it does not include enough components to qualify as a theory.

A model can take the form of flow charts, graphics, pictures, icons, or mathematical equations. Models do not add any new information to the theory beyond the propositions; instead, models deliver their value as a graphical display of the system of explanation that is captured in narrative form by the propositions.

Life Cycle of Scientific Theories

The development of scientific theories follows a life cycle pattern of creation, growth, and decline.

1. Creation. When scholars create theories, they rely on a combination of speculation and evidence. Sometimes the creation relies more on speculation and other times it relies more on evidence.

The evidence-focused method has been referred to as grounded theory, which follows the classic inductive method of science. Scholars collect observations, look for patterns across individual observations, then argue that those patterns are likely to apply to larger aggregates beyond the sample of observations from which those patterns were inferred. This process is explained in detail by Glasser and Strauss (1967) in a book entitled *The Discovery of Grounded Theory* in which they provided a rationale and method for moving beyond simply describing data generated in empirical studies to making general statements about the phenomena being examined. The authors show how patterns are discovered then provisionally verified through systematic data collection and analysis of data pertaining to that phenomenon. Therefore, data collection, analysis, and theory stand in reciprocal relationship with each other. Using the process of grounded theory, a scholar does not begin with a theory then collect evidence to support its claims. Rather, a scholar begins with an interest in examining a part of a phenomenon, then makes observations so that patterns are allowed to emerge unhampered by a priori expectations (Strauss & Corbin, 1990).

In contrast to the inductive method, which begins with observations, some scholars begin with speculation. These scholars create a set of claims as a tentative explanation for some part of the phenomenon they want to examine, then they design research studies to test their claims (Shoemaker et al., 2004). Such theories typically start as implicit understandings about the way things work, that is, they grow out of folklore, traditional wisdom, and common sense (Severin & Tankard, 2000). These theories start out as claims that are often simple aphorisms or maxims. But speculation is not enough to explain some part of a phenomenon to scientists; they need to test their claims to see if they can be supported with empirical evidence.

2. *Growth.* Whether a theory originates as a tentative set of speculations to explain a problem or arises from a perception of a pattern in a collection of data, the theory needs to develop if it is to become a useful system of explanation. This development typically follows one of three methods, as Kuhn (1970) has argued in his *The Structure of Scientific Revolutions*. First, theories can grow by extension, that is, theories add more concepts and propositions over time in order to explain more of a phenomenon. Second, theories can grow by intention, that is, theories develop a deeper and more precise understanding of the original concepts and propositions. Third, they develop through a radical reformulation such as a revolution in thinking, that is, old assumptions are rejected and new assumptions require scholars to accept a big change in concepts and propositions.

Regardless of the pattern of development, theories increase in value when they grow in terms of precision, utility, and/or explanatory power.

a. Growth in precision. Increases in precision refer to improvements in the conceptual clarity of the definitions of concepts and in the articulation of propositions. When fields are new, theoreticians' claims are fuzzy rather than precise, because the claims are based on guesses about the nature of a phenomenon, its components, how those components should be conceptualized, and how those components work together in a system of explanation. Over time, as a literature of tests grows, the contours of support and nonsupport begin to become clearer. The precision in the growth of a theory is keyed to the theoretician's ability to perceive patterns in the empirical literature and to make alterations to their claims so that the faulty areas in their system of explanation are replaced. When theoreticians use these patterns of findings to alter their definitions of concepts and reconfigure their set of propositions, their theories grow in precision. As Hempel (1952) writes, "In the initial stages of scientific inquiry, descriptions as well as generalizations are stated in the vocabulary of everyday language. The growth of a scientific discipline, however, always beings with it the development of a system of specialized, more or less abstract, concepts and of a corresponding technical terminology" (Hempel, 1952, p. 1). Hempel continues: "It is, therefore, of paramount importance for science to develop a system of concepts" which is suited for the formulation of general explanatory and predictive principles" (p. 20). He says the "vocabulary of everyday discourse, which science has to use at least initially" (p. 20), loses its value over time as scholars' understanding of the phenomenon grows and requires a greater degree of precision.

The precision of a theory also increases when theoreticians make their propositions more operative. Propositions become more operative as theoreticians increase the clarity expressing the relationship among concepts. For example, consider the proposition: "A is related to B." This expresses a relationship between two concepts but does not clarify what that relationship is. The proposition "A is related to B in a positive linear fashion" is more operative than the first proposition because it specifies a relationship with more precision. And the proposition "A is related to B in a positive linear fashion with young children but with adults the relationship is linear and negative" displays an even greater degree of precision because it specifies an age contingency.

b. Growth in utility. Utility is keyed to the degree to which theoreticians accommodate patterns that emerge through empirical testing. Oftentimes, the results of empirical tests will not support the claims made in propositions. When this occurs, their theories lose utility if theoreticians ignore the discordant findings; in contrast, when theoreticians make alterations to their propositions to accommodate the newly found patterns, then the theories increase in utility.

Utility is related to precision in research. Research studies are more useful when the designers of empirical tests have made design decisions that take maximum advantages of strong elements in the literature and avoid the weaknesses and flaws. Weaknesses are those design options that do not work as well as other options (for more detail on this, see Potter, 2018). For example, if there are multiple ways to measure a concept, designers of a research study exhibit higher precision when they demonstrate that the measure they are using is more valid than the alternatives. Flaws are design decisions that do not serve the purpose of the study or that contradict other design decisions. For example, designers who want to make claims about the prevalence of something in the general population might generate a nonrepresentative sample; this is a flaw because a nonrepresentative sample cannot be used to identify patterns that can be generalized from the sample to the population of interest.

c. Growth in explanatory power. Explanatory power refers to the degree to which the claims made in the theory have generated empirical findings that support those claims. Early tests of a claim often result in equivocal support. When this happens, theoreticians can ignore these patterns and it is likely that additional tests will also find equivocal support. Alternatively, theoreticians can analyze the patterns of equivocal support and find a way to alter their claims to make them more precise. Typically, a pattern of equivocal support for a claim indicates the need to consider contingencies, that is, the claim might hold for only one type of person, place, time, or message. When theoreticians then alter their general claims to recognize contingencies, the pattern of support can increase. Remember the example above "A is related to B." Let's say that the empirical tests of this claim show a pattern where some tests show that there is no relationship, some tests show that the relationship is positive, and some tests show that the relationship is negative. If the theoreticians are able to see a pattern in the findings that can be traced to age, for example, then they can alter their general proposition to account for the influence of age and subsequent tests will avoid weak (r = .00) findings where the results from children and adults are aggregated into a nonmeaningful average and instead show that the relationship is positive among children and at the same time negative among adults.

3. Decline. Scientific theories go into decline when theoreticians fail to alter their systems of explanation in response to emerging patterns in the empirical literature, criticisms of the theory, and changes in the phenomenon being explained. Let's examine each of these three in some detail.

Rarely will an empirical test provide unqualified support for the general claims made by a theory. More typically empirical tests will result in relatively weak or equivocal support for general claims. In this common situation, theoreticians have two options. One option is for theoreticians to alter their propositions to make them better reflect the patterns of findings from empirical testing. A second option is for theoreticians to defend their claims and blame weaknesses in the empirical tests for the pattern of weak support for the general claims in their theory. The second option is typically used by theoreticians but this option limits the growth of the theory. Blalock (1984) warns that it is often difficult to tell if a failed test is really a good test of the theory because there are so many factors that are in play, and that many theories are untestable as they are currently formulated.

Theories also need to respond to criticisms. This does not mean that theoreticians need to make all the changes that critics suggest; instead it means that theoreticians need to acknowledge the criticism and use it as a forum for dialog. By engaging in dialog, theoreticians can learn more about what is really bothering the critics and alter the theory's claims when the theoreticians feel those changes will strengthen the theory or not make the changes they feel will weaken the theory. But either way, theoreticians who fail to engage with the criticism create an artificially low ceiling on the growth of their system of explanation.

Finally, some phenomena change over time. If a theory that purports to explain that phenomenon does not change, then it loses its ability to explain that phenomenon. This is especially the case with a phenomenon that is as dynamic as media and their effects.

Conclusion

The purpose of scholarly fields is to generate knowledge about that field's phenomenon of interest then to share that knowledge. The most valuable tool in fulfilling this purpose is a good theory. Theories differ from one another in many ways; when we focus attention on how theories differ in purpose, treatment of evidence, and criteria for quality, it is useful to organize theories into two general categories of advocacy theories and scientific theories. This book focuses attention on scientific theories, not because I am arguing that scientific theories are better than advocacy theories; instead, the book focuses on scientific theories because the media effects literature is dominated by scientifically based scholarship.

Scientific theories begin as systems of explanation constructed from a combination of speculation and patterns from the empirical literature. Over time as the theory's claims are tested, those claims can increase in value when they increase their precision and explanatory power. Or those claims can decline in value if they fail to attract research interest in testing them or when tests fail to support the theory's claims and the theoreticians ignore the need to alter the claims.

To the extent that theories grow in precision and validity over time, useful knowledge grows. But when theories fail to increase the precision of their concepts and propositions, when they fail to eliminate axioms that are found to be faulty, and when they fail to alter their systems of explanation to account for patterns in empirical testing, they lose their potential utility. And a scholarly field that is guided by theories with low precision and weak validity will struggle to provide a progressively useful system of explanation about the field's focal phenomenon. Blalock (1984) writes, "One of the basic premises of scientific research is that one proceeds by eliminating or modifying those theories that fail to make correct predictions" (p. 138). He argues that when a field does not eliminate inadequate theories, the field becomes cluttered with alternatives and "once the alternative theories become sufficiently numerous, it also becomes so difficult to attempt syntheses—or even summaries—that no one makes the effort. Each theory is studied superficially" (p. 140).

References

Babbie, E. (1998). *The practice of social research* (8th ed.). Belmont, CA: Wadsworth.

Blalock, H. M., Jr. (1984). *Basic dilemmas in the social sciences.* Beverly Hills, CA: Sage.

Glasser, B., & Strauss, A. (1967). *The discovery of grounded theory.* Chicago, IL: Aldine.

Hempel, C. G. (1952). *Fundamentals of concept formation in empirical science.* Chicago, IL: University of Chicago Press.

Hoover, K. R. (1984). *The elements of social scientific thinking* (3rd ed.). New York, NY: St. Martin's Press.

Infante, D. A., Rancer, A. S., & Womack, D. F. (1990). *Building communication theory.* Prospect Heights, IL: Waveland Press.

Infante, D. A., Rancer, A. S., & Womack, D. F. (1993). *Building communication theory* (2nd ed.). Prospect Heights, IL: Waveland Press.

Kuhn, T. S. (1970). *The structure of scientific revolutions* (2nd ed.). Chicago, IL: University of Chicago Press.

Littlejohn, S. W. (1999). *Theories of human communication* (6th ed.). Belmont, CA: Wadsworth.

Littlejohn, S. W. (2009). Theory. In S. W. Littlejohn & K. A. Foss (Eds.), *Encyclopedia of communication theory* (pp. 957–958). Los Angeles, CA: Sage.

McQuail, D. (2005). *McQuail's mass communication theory* (5th ed.). Thousand Oaks, CA: Sage.

Potter, W. J. (1996). *An analysis of thinking and research about qualitative methods*. Hillsdale, NJ: Lawrence Erlbaum Associates.

Potter, W. J. (2018). An analysis of patterns of design decisions in recent media effects research. *Review of Communication Research, 6*, 1–29. doi: 10.12840/issn.2255-4165.2018.06.01.014

Reynolds, P. D. (1971). *A primer in theory construction*. Indianapolis, IN: Bobbs-Merrill.

Severin, W. J., & Tankard, J. W. (2000). *Uses of mass media. Communication theories: Origins, methods, and uses in the mass media* (5th ed.). White Plains, NY: Longman.

Shoemaker, P. J., Tankard, J. W., Jr., & Lasorsa, D. L. (2004). *How to build social science theories*. Thousand Oaks, CA: Sage.

Slife, B. D., & Williams, R. N. (1995). *What's behind the research? Discovering hidden assumptions in the behavioral sciences*. Thousand Oaks, CA: Sage.

Strauss, A., & Corbin, J. (1990). *Basics of qualitative research: Grounded theory procedures and techniques*. Newbury Park, CA: Sage.

CHAPTER TWO

The Field of Media Effects

Like all scholarly fields, media effects research began in an exploratory phase where scholars had to start with speculations about their focal phenomenon, created concepts, tried out definitions for those concepts, and made guesses about which concepts were most important and how those concepts were related to each other. To accomplish these tasks, media effects scholars borrowed ideas and methods from the more established contiguous fields, especially from psychology, sociology, and political science. Researchers began testing their initial speculations about what media effects were and how they occurred. As the empirical literature grew, patterns of findings began to emerge that showed some of those early speculations were more useful than others.

Then in the later third of the last century, the field began to transition out of its initial exploratory phase and into a more explanatory phase as a number of scholars created systems of explanation that were built from the emerging patterns in the growing literature. The most notable of these systems of explanation were cultivation theory (Gerbner, 1969), agenda setting theory (McCombs & Shaw, 1972), framing (Goffman, 1974), uses and gratifications (Blumler & Katz, 1974), social learning theory (Bandura, 1977), and third person (Davison, 1983).

In this chapter, I will show how the field of media effects has struggled with its evolution out of an exploratory phase and into an explanatory one. This will provide the necessary background for answering questions about how far the field has evolved so far, the factors that have enhanced that evolution, and the factors that have held the field back from making more progress in that evolution.

Evolution

The 20th century was a period of great technological development that produced industries that have come to be known as the mass media. Researchers began studying the effects of the media, particularly newspapers, film, and radio, almost a century ago (Pearce, 2009). By the mid-1900s, a large number of scholars were attracted to media effects as television became a dominant medium, with almost all households having a television receiver. Television reached virtually complete household penetration shortly after midcentury, and scholars began conducting a great deal of research about the effects of such a powerful medium. Then in the last few decades of the 20th century, newer technologies caught the attention of vast audiences as major content providers turned these newer channels of information distribution into mass media. As the number of media outlets grew with the dissemination of cable TV, computers, the internet, and portable devices even more, scholars were attracted to the study of media effects. The first two decades of the 21st century have shown the media undergoing enormous changes in terms of their business practices, their conceptions of audiences, and the content they produce.

The scholarly field of media effects has also been undergoing an evolution from exploration to explanation in order to keep up with its focal phenomenon. In this section, I will compare and contrast the two phases along four analytical dimensions: motivation for research studies, the design of research studies, the perspectives on building knowledge, and the nature of findings.

Exploratory Phase

Like with all scholarly fields, media effects studies started out in an exploratory phase. The exploratory phase of research is characterized by wide-ranging debates where the purpose has been to ask as many questions as possible and to try as many approaches, methods, and designs as possible to see what generates the most useful answers to which questions, such as: What are the intended and unintended effects of media on audiences? Which media, types of messages, and message elements are especially influential in bringing about which effects? And are there certain types of audience members who are especially influenced by the media?

1. Motivation for research studies. In the exploratory phase, researchers are driven by curiosity about a topic so they pose a question. For example, during the 1950s, researchers were curious about why television had spread so fast in the culture and why people were spending more time with it, so they posed questions such as: Why do people like TV so much? Why do people spend more time with TV than with other media? In the 1960s there was a lot of cultural unrest with the protest of the Vietnam War and with the assassination of leaders such as President Kennedy, his brother, and Martin Luther King. Researchers were curious about the power of TV to influence people so they posed questions such as: Does watching violence on TV lead people to behave more aggressively?, Are particular age groups more vulnerable to TV's influence?, and Why is there so much violence on TV?

All questions about the media were useful because scholars were trying to figure out what media effects there were and how they came about. No approach, method, or assumption was considered out of bounds; all were tried for their usefulness in addressing all kinds of questions. Researchers were guided by intuition, creativity, and the bits and pieces of knowledge about the media that were scattered across other scholarly fields. This brainstorming activity was necessary to "feel our way in the dark" and find out where the boundaries and contours of the phenomenon were.

2. Design of research studies. To help in this exploratory process of examining the new phenomenon of the mass media, scholars imported ideas and methods from other fields. This is understandable because other fields—particularly the more established social sciences and humanities—had theoretical and methodological traditions that they had been using as tools to examine the mass media within the context of their own scholarship. Media scholars found it very helpful to use these tools and continued to import these ideas heavily even into the late 20th century (Reeves & Borgman, 1983; Rice, Borgman, & Reeves, 1988).

3. Perspective on building knowledge. In the exploratory phase, researchers rely on the inductive method, that is, they collect data, then look for patterns in those data. When they find a pattern—such as a statistically significant treatment difference across means or a relatively strong degree of association among variables—they report their findings as a tentative answer to their research question.

Using this inductive approach, scholars could ignore no question because they could not be sure which question would tap into a rich mine of insight. The posing of any question was valuable because so little was known about the mass media. The results of just about any research study had the potential to contribute something useful to knowledge.

4. Nature of findings. In the exploratory phase of research, findings are highly tentative for two reasons. First, the use of the inductive method to build knowledge is a process that begins with researchers making observations, then speculating about patterns across those observations that can reveal something about a focal phenomenon. These initial guesses about patterns require testing so they can be confirmed through replication. When additional testing continually supports the initial guesses about patterns, those patterns gradually gain status over time as trusted findings. More typically however, those initial guesses will require refinement over time as continual testing reveals that those initial guesses were too broad, too superficial, or faulty in some way. Thus the findings produced initially in a new line of research are much more tentative than the findings produced after many rounds of testing.

A second reason why findings produced in the exploratory phase of research are tentative is that research designs are typically weaker in the exploratory phase. When researchers conduct a programmatic line of research, they learn more not just about the phenomenon they are studying, but also about how to design their studies to avoid practices that are found to be faulty or weak.

Thus the research designed to generate answers to questions in the exploratory phase of a scholarly field is limited to producing suggestive answers to questions rather than definitive answers. While some of those suggestive answers may be found to be highly accurate explanations about parts of the field's focal phenomenon, most of them start out as very rough approximations that if continually tested and refined will grow into more valid explanations.

Explanation Phase

In evolving from an exploratory phase to an explanatory phase, a scholarly field demonstrates a shift in values that shows up in practices about motivation of research studies, how they are designed, their perspective on building knowledge, and what constitutes useful findings.

1. Motivation for research studies. In contrast to exploratory research with its question-motivation, explanatory research is motivated by a desire to test general claims. These claims can be informal, such as researchers' speculations about media effects, or they can be formal, such as propositions in theories.

Explanatory researchers are more motivated by extending the depth of a scholarly field rather than by extending its breadth. This means that researchers become less interested exploring what new effects can be discovered or exploring what new factors might be influencing those effects, because the field has evolved to a point where a great many effects and factors of influence have already been well documented. Instead they are motived more by a desire to determine which of those effects are the most important and which factors are most influential.

Once a field has generated a good deal of suggested findings across the span of the phenomenon, the challenge shifts to sorting through those suggestive findings and testing which are robust enough to be general claims and which are sensitive to contingencies. This requires more programmatic research to get below surface findings and unpack the complexity of the phenomenon. Thus the research is less concerned with questions about which effects might be taking place and much more concerned about which effects are the most powerful, the most prevalent, and the most widespread.

2. Design of research studies. In the explanatory phase, researchers rely on a more deductive approach where they start with general principles to guide their design of new tests through a process of operationalization. That is, they take general statements and translate those ideas into specific measures. The challenge is to make operational design decisions that are improvements over past research so that the findings they generate will be more useful. Designers of research studies reject the exploratory value of "anything goes" and instead are sensitive to the essential need that research be progressive, that is, researchers need to learn from the mistakes exhibited in the literature and exhibit improvements in all areas of their designs. Thus scholars with an explanatory perspective present a much more critical analysis of the literature where they identify faulty design decisions in previous studies and demonstrate that their designs use more valid measures, more useful samples, and more appropriate statistical procedures. Thus as the strength of their designs increases so too does the value of their findings.

3. Perspective on building knowledge. When moving the focus of the field from producing individual studies to generating knowledge, scholars pay more attention to issues of validity and calibration. Thus reviews of the literature move away from listing studies descriptively and more toward critically analyzing the literature. Critical analysis is about organizing the review by issues; not just by findings but also by study design features. Critical analysis is also about evaluating the findings of studies based on the strength of their designs and analyses. This leads to the rejection of some findings and the calibration of other findings so that equivocal statements of findings are resolved. The primary scholarly work in the explanatory phase is identifying the most important findings in the existing literature and organizing them in a way to extend their power of capturing the essence of our phenomenon. In this calibration process, researchers begin with an analysis of existing definitions for key terms, so they can weed out the less useful definitions and further explicate the more useful ones. Researchers make a critical assessment of existing theories, so they can focus on deducing stronger tests from their key propositions, use the results of those empirical tests to pare away faulty predictions, and extend the theory's predictive power by synthesizing additional propositions.

And researchers regard methods as tools that are useful only insofar as they can access various parts of our phenomenon of interest.

When designing their studies, researchers focus much more on developing knowledge than on using methods. In exploratory research, scholars are trained on methods so they design studies where they can use their methods; in contrast, explanatory-focused scholars design studies in a way to maximize the contribution of their eventual findings, so they search for methods that will allow them to build the strongest design to generate that type of finding.

Perhaps the most important characteristic of the explanatory phase is the focus on the big picture, that is, the nature of the media as the field's phenomenon of interest. Thus, scholars focus on contributing to systems of explanation rather than generating another set of findings. Empirical studies are essential. But when scholars design their individual studies and get down to the micro-details of their one topic, their decisions are better when they keep in mind how their study fits into the map of the overall phenomenon. When researchers think carefully about how to position their eventual findings as they design their studies, they will be better able to highlight the value of their contribution to the overall progression of knowledge. Without such positioning in the design, the findings easily can get lost in the clutter of a fragmented literature. This is why programmatic research is so important; each new study is clearly positioned along a developing path. Theories guide scholars more efficiently along paths of programmatic research. This is also why critical reviews of the literature are so important; they provide a map of a particular topic area. And at the most macro-level, this is why a general framework is so important; it can provide the global map of the full phenomenon.

With explanatory research, there is a shift away from contributing one-shot studies and toward building on the work of other scholars. This requires a focus on convergence of sharing definitions, assumptions, and procedures. An effect of convergence is the bringing together of scholars into a more unified field. The more we share a common understanding of the nature of our phenomenon and how best to go about constructing explanations for it, the more we will share a sense of community and hence achieve a higher scholarly profile. Kuhn (1970) provided a definition of a scientific community that can be applied usefully to any scholarly community: "Bound together by common elements of their education and apprenticeship, they see themselves and are seen by others as . . . responsible for the pursuit of a set of shared goals, including the training of their successors. Such communities are characterized by the relative fullness of communication within the group and by the relative unanimity of the group's judgment in professional matters" (p. 296). Community requires convergence.

4. Nature of findings. In the explanatory phase, research studies are designed so that the findings are more definitive than suggestive. Thus the findings make their contribution less in expanding the breadth of knowledge and more in elaborating knowledge by developing greater depth in their explanations.

Current State of the Field

Large Fragmented Literature

Now in the early 21st century, the published research literature that examines some aspect of the mass media has grown to a very large size and covered a great many topics. A decade ago, the size of this literature was estimated to already be over 6,000 published studies (Potter & Riddle, 2006). Clearly the phenomenon of media effects has been of great interest to many researchers.

Although it is a positive indicator of health of the scholarly field that so many scholars have generated such a large literature, critics have pointed out that the value of this literature has been limited by its fragmented nature (Berger, 1991; Hardt, 1992; Jensen & Rosengren, 1990; McQuail, 1989; Pietila, 1994; Power, Kubey, & Kiousis, 2002). This literature continues to be plagued by little synthesis across studies, little programmatic research, many theories but with a small proportion of the literature that is theory-driven research, and little translation of ideas and methods from other fields where they were originally developed for other purposes.

1. Limited programmatic research. In *Milestones in Mass Communication Research*, Lowry and DeFleur (1988) argued that the "study of mass communication has been particularly unsystematic." They elaborated this point by saying that scholars "almost never coordinated their efforts or built upon the results of previous research" and that many of the questions guiding the research "were not theoretically significant" (p. 3). This condition persists today. Scholars who publish many studies typically will do a study or two on one topic and then move on to another topic, publish a few studies on that topic, and then move on to another topic. This pattern can be characterized as a "honeybee" approach to research, where scholars are busy bees whose attention is attracted by so many interesting topics (flowers in bloom). They flit from one topic to another as they make their way across the field of so many attractive kinds of flowers. The positive aspect of this "honeybee" nature of the research is that many topics get explored. Also, the travels of the bees have an effect of cross-pollinating topics with ideas and methods from other topics.

However, there is a limitation to this honeybee approach. While cross-pollination of ideas has some value, the development of a scholarly field requires a sustained effort of constructing knowledge. To shift the metaphor, think of hundreds of craftsmen interested in creating a new town in an open field. If those workers take a honeybee approach, then each craftsman does a piece of work at one place then moves on to another place and on and on. There is no overall design of streets, neighborhoods, electrical systems, etc. Over time, there are more and more pieces of construction but without an overall design, those pieces contribute more to a condition of congestion and chaos than to a condition of producing the systems required for a livable city.

To the extent that scholars spend time trying out lots of different topics, the field is prevented from building much elevation—that is, there are few places where scholars conduct programmatic research that is essential to elaborating knowledge on a topic.

Definitional variation. A major indicator of fragmentation is that many of the key terms are used with varying meaning across scholars. For example, the term *media violence* exhibits considerable variation in definitions, especially when we look at how this term has been defined by content analysts (see Potter, 1999). Some of these definitions included verbal acts, while most did not; some include accidents, while others are limited to intentional acts; some required action to be explicitly depicted on the screen, while others allowed action to be implied.

Another example of definitional confounding is with the term *flow*. Raymond Williams (1974) used *flow* to refer to how people experience a sequence of messages in a medium, such as television. He explained that television programs do not exist as discrete entities in the minds of viewers. Rather, a kind of flow across texts is the central experience of the medium (p. 95)—a fact that accounts for much of television's critical significance. This is when the audience member continues an exposure while having one message replace another and where a message is interrupted by other messages. Thus, to Williams, *flow* is an endless random juxtaposition of different texts. Newcomb and Hirsch (1984) picked up on this idea but referred to the elements as "viewing strips." In contrast, Csikszentmihalyi (1988) used the term *flow* to refer to a psychological state of being swept away by a task where the person loses a sense of time and place in the pursuit of a highly engrossing goal. Other scholars have referred to the same idea but use a different term, such as *transportation* (Bilandzic & Busselle, 2008; Green & Brock, 2000). Definitional variation is not limited to the few examples I have presented; it is common throughout the field of media effects. When a field is in its exploratory phase, definitional proliferation is valuable because it highlights a range of meaning. But over time, scholars in a field need to look for patterns where certain meanings are more valuable than others; where multiple meanings are found to be valuable, there then needs to be a relabeling so that the different meanings are uniquely identified. When a field has many niche scholars each with their own specialized meaning for a particular term, then communication across niches is limited. To the extent that a field avoids the scholarly tasks of comparing and contrasting meanings, evaluating meanings for utility, and relabeling, it is very difficult to group findings together into meaningful patterns of knowledge. The definitional confounding substantially increases the costs to readers and serves to slow down the sharing of meaning. The field's diversity turns into confusion and this limits the ability of scholars to form a true community.

Low Elevation

A second problem with the slow evolution of this scholarly field from an exploratory phase to an explanatory phase is its low elevation of knowledge. What do I mean by "low elevation" of knowledge? Think of the findings of each empirical study as forming a base of a pyramid. Scholars who review the literature on a particular topic make statements about patterns across the relevant findings on that topic, and these statements move us up a level on the pyramid because these statements are more general than the description of results from any one research study. When scholars look for patterns across several topic areas, they move knowledge up another step in generality. The more steps upward a field exhibits, the more elevation there is in its knowledge—movement away from listing individual particulars and toward constructing nested layers of general patterns. Because the purpose of scholarly fields is to generate knowledge—not just empirical findings— the health of a scholarly field can be seen in how much elevation it has achieved.

Recall from the previous chapter that scholarly fields employ a hermeneutic process where the findings of individual studies are used to construct a big picture of the field's focal phenomenon. Think of this big picture articulation as being the tip of the pyramid. Thus the more layers of synthesizing results a field has produced, the more general are those statements that explain the phenomenon and the more clear the big picture becomes. Fields that place a high premium on quality reviews of the literature generate more evaluation of findings, more integration of patterns, and more calibration of what is most important—all of which serves to increase the elevation of knowledge in the field. With the field of media effects, it appears that the scholarly energy is focused much more on conducting individual empirical studies than in undertaking the tasks required to build elevation.

Limited synthesis. There are few published efforts at synthesizing parts of this very large literature. By *synthesis,* I mean that when a literature is reviewed, it is not just described or summarized but that a scholar conducts a critical analysis of that literature and provides fresh insights about patterns of findings. Thus synthesis is a multistep process that entails breaking a literature down into component issues (such as design issues or findings contingent on factors of participants or media messages), evaluating the credibility of findings along each analytical dimension, filtering out findings that fail to meet the standard used in the evaluation, calibrating the importance of the filtered-in findings, identifying patterns across the most important and valid findings, then using those perceived patterns as a springboard for presenting fresh insights into the nature of the phenomenon examined by the literature.

The literature examined in a synthesis can be relatively small, such as a handful of studies relevant to the design of a particular study like what authors do when presenting a review of the literature in an article of an empirical study. Or the reviewed literature can be relatively large, such as when scholars write a chapter on a broad topic for an edited volume. When a field has skilled syntheses at all levels, there is a greater chance that the faulty findings are weeded out and that the focus is put on the most important findings that can be trusted to create explanations of the phenomenon that can move the scholarly field forward.

In the media effects field, almost all of the work published in even the top-rated scholarly journals are descriptive reports of empirical studies. In their content analysis of the mass media effects literature, Potter and Riddle (2006) analyzed 936 articles that were concerned with media effects published in 16 scholarly journals. Only 47 articles (5.0 %) were not quantitative analyses of data gathered in an empirical study, and most of these (n = 36) were stand-alone narrative reviews, while the remaining 11 published articles were meta-analyses. I want to point out two things this content analysis revealed. First, it appears that new empirical work is much more valued than secondary work that uses the findings of empirical studies to analyze, evaluate, and calibrate those findings in order to create claims for general patterns that would elevate the knowledge in the field. And second, while narrative reviews and meta-analyses contribute to the development of scholarly fields, their contribution is limited when they are uncritical, that is, they accept all published work on a topic as equally valid and useful. When reviewers of the literature are descriptive and not critical, they disregard the scholarly task of filtering and thus the studies with the weakest designs and/or findings are given equal weight with the studies with the strongest designs and/or findings.

When synthesis work is valued much less than exploratory empirical work, almost all the scholarly effort is expended on growing the base of the pyramid. This results in an ever larger fragmented literature where the findings of individual studies are left alone in isolation rather than integrated into knowledge patterns. When there is little interest in perceiving patterns across the best studies while discounting the findings from weaker studies, a field achieves little elevation. And when a field has little elevation of knowledge, researchers labor in a field with scattered findings, thus making it very difficult to choose the most important areas to work on and to access the full set of best thinking when conducting a literature review.

Limited translation. There is little translation of ideas into media effects research from other fields. While importing ideas into a field can be a good thing—by expanding the pool of ideas to consider and tools to try—it can also be a problem if those ideas are not adapted well to the specific needs of the importing field. Media scholars are more likely to import ideas from other social sciences rather than cite other media scholars in communication. To illustrate this point, Reeves and Borgman (1983) studied nine core communication journals. They reported that communication scholars are dependent on journals outside of communication, with communication journal articles exhibiting five cites of other journals for each cite they receive. In a subsequent bibliometric analysis and network analysis of citations in 20 communication journals from 1977 to 1985, Rice and colleagues (1988) found that for all communication journals, the average impact ratio was .43, which was the lowest impact ratio among 10 social science fields. A ratio of 1.0 means that the articles published in a journal received an average of one citation per year subsequent to its publication. So an impact ratio of .4 means that the articles a journal published this year will receive an average of one citation every 2.5 years. This indicates that compared with other social sciences, communication scholars are much less likely to cite the work of other scholars publishing in their journals. This pattern gives greater weight to the conclusion that the degree of programmatic research is lower in communication than in other fields.

This is *not* an argument that we need to invent all our own ideas, especially when contiguous fields offer so many great ideas that have usefulness for mass media scholars. However, I *am* arguing that when we import an idea, we typically need to transform it in some way to fit the purpose of explaining some aspect of the mass media, and this usually requires some translation. These translations serve to tailor the constructs for our own purposes. Over time, we need to cite more of our translations in proportion to the untranslated constructs from other fields. Also, over time, we will find that we have special needs for mapping that are different from other fields, and therefore there are no constructs we can import. In these cases, we need to develop our own constructs. But doing this requires greater attention to our own special mapping arcs, but in order to do this, we need more programmatic research to develop greater sensitivity to our own special challenges.

In summary, it appears that the field of media effects research is fragmented for several reasons. There is an ever-expanding literature, but because so little of it is programmatic or theory driven, there is great difficulty in synthesizing the major findings across studies. C. R. Berger (1998), writing about the field of communication research in general, said, "The traditionally high level of fragmentation manifested by the field seems to be increasing as the field expands. Although specialization is almost an inevitable consequence of growth, the fact that there is no particular theoretical paradigm or touchstone theory around which communication researchers might organize their efforts is a least one source of concern" (p. 101).

Role of Theory in Media Effects Scholarship

Theories can be very useful tools in generating and communicating knowledge. When a theory is introduced into a literature, it offers the potential to efficiently guide research on a particular topic if it presents a clear set of ideas and offers a system of explanation that shows how those ideas are related to one another. If the claims in the theory are tested repeatedly in programmatic research, then knowledge builds systematically. The theory matures when theoreticians use the emerging patterns from the empirical tests of their claims to refine their systems of explanation. And the scholarly field matures as the knowledge structure about the field's focal phenomenon is elaborated. Thus the more that theories mature, the more valuable a scholarly field becomes.

What is the pattern in the use of theories to guide designers of research studies in the field of media effects? In this section we first look at those patterns then we look for explanations for why those patterns exist.

Many Theories

There are a large number of theories in the media effects literature. While no one has yet attempted to identify all the different theories mentioned in the published media effects literature, I found over 150 in a content analysis of media effects articles published in a sampling of eight communication journals published from 2003 to 2008 (Potter, 2009). When compiling this list, I used a broad conception of theory that included any scholarly attempt to organize, predict, or explain some aspect of the media effects phenomenon. Given the limited sampling of journals and years, this finding of 150 theories is likely to be an underreporting of the total number of theories in the full literature of media effects. Even so, the 150 identified theories (see Table 2.1) reveal a great variety of explanation. While a few of these theories are widely known, others are relatively unknown either because they are new or have yet to be discovered by many scholars. Some are formal systems

Table 2.1. Partial List of Media Effects

Advertising	Elite Pluralism
Affluent Society	Empathy Activation
Agenda Building	Encoding–Decoding
Agenda Setting	Excitation Transfer
Aggression	Exemplification
Associative Network Building	Expectancy Value
Attitude Construct Creation	Fraction of Selection
Audience as Commodification	Framing
Audience Construction by Media	Gatekeeping
Audience Flow	Global Village
Audience Polarization	Gratification Seeking
Automatic Activation	Gravitation
Availability-Valence Altering	Hegemony
Buffering	Heuristic Processing
Capacity Limits	Hidden Persuaders
Catharsis	Homogenization
Channel Repertoire Reinforcement	Imitation
Character Affiliation	Indirect Effects
Civic Engagement	Information Flow
Coalition Building	Information Seeking
Cognitive Dissonance	Integrated Response
Cognitive Response	Interpretation by Social Class
Conservative/Moralist Decision Making	Interpretive Resistance
Consumer Culture Creation and Reinforcement	Knowledge Gap
Cue Activation	Least Objectionable Programming
Cultivation	Levels of Processing
Cultural Imperialism	Limited Capacity Information Processing
Culture of Narcissism	Marketplace Alteration
Decision Making	Mass Audience
Diffusion of Innovations	Media Access
Direct Effects	Media Culture
Disinhibition	Media as Culture Industries
Disposition Altering	Media Enjoyment
Distribution of Knowledge	Media Enjoyment as Attitude
Double Action Gatekeeping	Media Entertainment
Double Jeopardy	Media Flow
Drench	Media System Dependency

(Continued)

Table 2.1. *Continued*

Elaboration Likelihood	Medium as Message
Message Construction	Psychological Conditioning
Mood Management	Rally Effect
Motivated Attention and Motivated Processing	Reasoned Action
Neo-associationistic Thinking	Reception
Neo-mass Audience	Resource Dependency
Network Political Priming	Revealed Preferences
News Content	Ritual Reinforcement
News Diffusion	Selective Exposure
News Factory	Selective Gatekeeping
News Frame Creation	Selective Perception
News Selection	Semiotic Interpretations
News Worker Socialization	Social Cognitions
One-Dimensional Man	Social Construction of Meaning
Parasocial Interaction	Social Construction of Media Technologies
Perception of Hostile Media	Social Identity
Persuasion	Social Norms
Play	Sociology of News
Pluralistic Ignorance	Spiral of Silence
Political Signification	Synapse Priming
Political Socialization	Technological Determinism
Polysemic Interpretations	Television Trivialization of Public Life
Power Elite	Third Person Effect
Priming	Transactional Effects
Principled Reasoning	Transmission of Information
Profit-Driven Logic of Safety	Transportation of Audiences
Program Choice	Two-Step Flow
Proteus effect	Uses and Dependency
Pseudo-events Blur Reality	Uses and Gratifications
Psychodynamics	Video Malaise

of explanations that have generated many tests of their claims, while others have been generated from an inductive process in a single study. While most focus their explanations on a small piece of the overall media effects phenomenon, a few are broader and would qualify as middle-range theories (Merton, 1967). Some have been constructed by social scientists working in media studies or related fields (such as psychology, sociology, political science, economics, anthropology, business, and education), while others have been created by humanistic scholars working in fields (such as film studies, comparative literature, linguistics, feminist studies, ethnic studies, and art). Some of these explanations display the term *theory* in their titles, while others are referred to as models, hypotheses, or effects. Regardless of their origin or their title, each of these listed in Table 2.1 provides an articulation of a relationship among concepts as a way to explain something about the phenomenon of media effects.

Small Proportion of Research Is Theory Guided

Even though the field of media effects research has many theories available to guide the construction of empirical tests, a sizable proportion of our literature continues to ignore not only these identified theories but all theories. For example, in an analysis of published literature on mass communication from 1965 to 1989 in eight competitive peer-reviewed journals, Potter, Cooper, and Dupagne (1993) found that only 8.1 % of 1,326 articles were guided by a theory and provided a test of that theory; another 19.5 % were tests of hypotheses, but these hypotheses were not derived from a theory. A similar pattern was found in an analysis of studies published in *Journalism & Mass Communication Quarterly*, when Riffe and Freitag (1997) reported that only 27.6 % of the studies used an explicit theoretical framework, and there was no change in this percentage over the 25-year period they examined from 1971 to 1995. Similar findings were reported by Kamhawi and Weaver (2003) who examined all articles published in 10 communication journals from 1980 to 1999 and found that only 30.5 % specifically mentioned a theory. Trumbo (2004) in an updating of the Potter et al. (1993) content analysis reported finding that 18 % of 2,649 studies he examined from 1990 to 2000 were guided by a theory, and that an additional 24 % mentioned a theory but did not use it to create either an hypothesis or a research question to guide their studies. Potter and Riddle (2007) analyzed media effects articles published in 16 journals from 1993 to 2005 and found that 35 % of coded articles featured a theory prominently.

The pattern of findings across all these content analysis shows a slow but discernable growth in the proportion of media effects empirical studies using theory, although it is difficult to make clear comparisons across those studies due to different definitions of theory. However, the general trend appears to be an increase in theory-driven research from 34 % until 1990, then 42 % from 1990 to 2000, if we use a broad definition of theory.

We need to be careful that we do not equate the mentioning of a theory with using a theory to guide a research study. When we look for articles that begin with a mention of an existing media effects theory then use that theory's conceptualizations as a basis for deducing hypotheses to test a claim in the theory, we can see that there still appears to be an increase in the use of theory but with lower proportions—from 8.1 % (Potter et al., 1993) to 18 % (Trumbo, 2004) to 28.0 % (Potter, 2018).

While the increase in the proportions of the media effects research that is guided by theory is a positive trend, it is still alarming that such a high proportion of our current research literature is still ignoring theories. Media scholars have repeatedly argued for the importance of theory in developing the field of media effects (Kamhawi & Weaver, 2003; McQuail, 2005; Nabi & Oliver, 2009; Potter, 2009). When major scholars in the field of mass communication were surveyed several decades ago, 63 % of respondents thought that the theoretical development should be a lot better (So & Chan, 1991). And interpreting the results of their content analysis, Kamhawi and Weaver (2003) argued that "theoretical development is probably the main consideration in evaluating the disciplinary status of the field. As our field grows in scope and complexity, the pressure for theoretical integration increases" (p. 20).

Journal reviewers have also been found to be critical of the lack of use of theory. An analysis of reviewer comments for 120 manuscripts submitted to the *Journal of Communication* found that one of the most important concerns of those reviewers was a lack of theoretical integration (Neuman, Davidson, Joo, Park, & Williams, 2008, p. 220). But yet, about three quarters of the media effects research published in top scholarly journals is *not* motivated by a theory and about half of the published research studies appear to ignore theories altogether.

Why This Pattern?

With so many theories available to guide researchers in the design of their studies, why do so many designers of studies ignore all this potential guidance? Theories can deliver a great deal of efficiency to researchers by giving them access to concepts with a higher degree of explication, which helps researchers design studies with greater efficiency and precision. Good theories provide researchers with a history of measurement and data gathering procedures showing a progression of increasing validity, and they provide researchers with a much stronger context for interpreting their findings in a more conceptual and useful manner. With all these advantages that theories have to offer researchers, why do so many study designers continue to ignore theory guidance?

One possible answer is that the existing theories are not very helpful. That is, while theories have the potential to offer researchers many advantages, the existing theories fall short of delivering on that potential. There are two ways to test this, although they are both indirect ways. One way is to look at patterns of design decisions in theory-driven research compared to nontheory exploratory research. A second way is to examine the heuristic ability of theories.

If theories offer guidance to designers of empirical studies, then those studies should be more likely to avoid methodological weaknesses. For example, one methodological weakness in the media effects literature is the use of attribute variables as surrogates for active influences. Researchers who design a study to test if a media effect is contingent on gender socialization patterns might ask their participants to simply respond whether they are a male or a female, which is a biological attribute but easy to measure. If these researchers instead were testing this claim made by an existing theory, then the theory is likely to provide them with a history of previous tests that would show that this operationalization was faulty and alert designers to use a specific test of gender socialization that has been validated. Therefore, if theories are useful in providing guidance to designers of empirical studies, then those studies should show a pattern of avoiding methodological weaknesses compared to a pattern of studies that are exploratory.

To test this explanation, I examined articles of media effects published in six leading communication journals from 2010 to 2015 (Potter, 2018). I recorded whether the study was theory guided, patterns of design decisions, and strength of findings as indicated by proportion of variance explained. Of the total of 211 articles analyzed, 166 (78.7 %) mentioned at least one media effects theory. This figure is quite a bit higher than figures reported in previous content analyses. However, mentioning a theory is not the same as using a theory to guide the design of a study. Again using 211 studies as a base, about half of the coded articles mentioned at least one theory but did not use any of those theories to generate hypotheses; instead these studies either developed their own hypotheses (33.6 %) and tested them or developed their own model (16.6 %) and tested that new model. Only 59 (28.0 %) were theory driven, that is, the authors referenced an existing theory, deduced hypotheses from that theory, and conducted their study to test those hypotheses (Table 2.2).

I expected that the theory-driven studies as a group would exhibit lower percentages of methodological weaknesses compared to the nontheory-driven studies. Furthermore, I expected that the theory-driven studies would exhibit findings that explained a higher proportion of variance compared to the nontheory-driven group of studies. This is not what I found. The general patterns found in my sample are shown in Table 2.3. Notice that the authors of 43.6 % of studies in the sample reported using an easy-to-measure attribute as a surrogate for an active influence and that this percentage was higher in the group of studies that were not theory driven compared to studies that were theory driven, which is what I expected, but those differences were not large enough to be statistically significant. Out of the nine examined methodological

Table 2.2. Methodological Patterns

Widespread design problems

87.3 % measured the effect variable at only one point in time

> Problem: Almost all media effects studies assume change, that is, media influence alters something in respondents. But in surveys, cross-sectional data are not adequate to suggest change. And in experiments, postexposure data alone are not adequate to suggest change, even when those single-point measures from individuals are averaged to form group means.

81.6 % used nonrepresentative samples

> Problem: The patterns from nonrepresentative samples cannot be generalized and there is no basis for the use of inferential statistics.

64.8 % measured mundane behaviors with self-reports

> Problem: Self-report data, especially about mundane behaviors and behavioral intentions, have repeatedly been found to have very low validity.

56.7 % reported inferential statistics without providing a basis to warrant their use.

> Problem: Inferential statistics require representative samples in order to make p-values meaningful. In experiments, random assignment of participants to conditions is required in order to make p-values meaningful.

54.0 % made no attempt to establish a case for validity of measures

> Problem: The default seems to be that all measures are valid.

43.6 % reported using attribute variables as surrogates for active influences

> Problem: Surface characteristics of individuals (such as sex and age) are not valid indicators of active factors (such as gender socialization, development cognitively, emotionally, morally)

Problems with design of experiments

86.3 % of experiments reported no balance check on the assignment of Ss to treatments

> Problem: It is faulty to assume that treatment groups result in a balance of participants on the traits and key characteristics that are sensitive to the influence being tested. Even with random assignment of participants to treatment conditions, the probability of matching is infinitesimal.

72.6 % of experiments reported no manipulation check of their treatments

> Problem: The assumption that all participants in the same assigned condition experience the same treatment is faulty.

45.3 % of experiments indicated no random assignment of their participants to treatments

> Problem: Without random assignment of participants to experimental conditions, researchers have no basis for using inferential statistics, yet researchers still use these statistical procedures.

Table 2.3. Uniformity of Patterns Across Theory Usage

Data Gathering	All (%)	No Theory (%)	Theory Deduced Hs (%)	Tested Model (%)	
Sample Represent	19.4	20.5	28.0	16.6	$X^2 = 0.07$ df = 2 $p = .701$
Attribute Surrogate	43.6	48.7	37.3	37.1	$X^2 = 2.80$ df = 2 $p = .247$
Behavior Self-Report	64.8	65.5	62.7	65.7	$X^2 = 0.15$ df = 2 $p = .927$
Validity Support	46.0	39.3	57.6	48.6	$X^2 = 5.41$ df = 2 $p = .067$
Change Scores	12.7	11.8	16.9	8.6	$X^2 = 1.57$ df = 2 $p = .456$
Experiment Method	45.0	41.9	49.2	48.6	$X^2 = 4.14$ df = 4 $p = .387$
Random Assignment	55.3	51.0	64.3	52.9	$X^2 = 1.32$ df = 2 $p = .518$
Balance Check	13.8	14.3	10.7	17.6	$X^2 = 0.44$ df = 2 $p = .801$
Manipulation Check	27.7	24.5	28.6	35.3	$X^2 = 0.75$ df = 2 $p = .686$
Median Variance Expl	13.8	14.5	9.8	18.2	$F = 2.604$ df = 2 $p = .078$

features, eight of them showed the theory-driven studies avoiding these methodological shortcomings slightly more often than the nontheory-driven studies, but these differences are too slight to be statistically significant. Also, surprisingly, the nontheory-driven studies exhibited a pattern of explaining more variance (median =14.5 %) compared to theory-driven studies (9.8 %).

These findings provide a bit of support for the argument that theory-driven studies are more likely to have stronger designs in the sense they are more likely to avoid practices that we have come to realize are faulty in the general social science literature. However, the differences I found between theory-driven and nontheory-driven studies are often tiny. For example, 65.5 % of nontheory-driven studies used self-report measures of mundane behaviors compared to "only" 62.7 % of theory-driven studies. The bigger picture and more important finding here is that the media effects literature continues to be built on studies where designers

In his analysis of 20 years of journalism research, Wilbur Schramm (1957) reflected on how far the field of media studies had come since 1935 by looking at the pressing questions of the time. He cited the work of Malcolm Willey who took stock of research on journalism in 1936 and listed what the most important unanswered questions were about journalism in the United States: How many newspapers are there in the United States? How are these geographically distributed? How are the numbers changing, if at all? How many communities are there in the United States in which newspapers are published? Is the number increasing or decreasing? How many newspapers are published in each community? By 1957, journalism researchers had provided clear answers to all these questions and more. Schramm then laid out a series of questions for 1957 and among them were: What is the effect of violence in the mass media? Do media affect juvenile delinquency? How do the media influence public opinion? How can the media be used in teaching situations? How can textbooks be best used as a teaching aid?

Now 60 years later, we have made some varying progress on these questions but we have yet to provide clear answers. Of course, Schramm's set of 1957 questions were more challenging than Willey's set of 1936 questions. But we have also had far more time and far more resources, yet we have only equivocal answers at best. Why?

frequently select weaker design options over stronger ones, even though given the size of the empirical literature of media effects, scholars should be well aware of these weaknesses.

Conclusion

The scholarly field of media effects has grown in many ways since its beginnings almost a century ago. Like all scholarly fields, it has faced many challenges as it has sought to generate and share knowledge about media effects. Arguably, the most important tool in engaging these tasks well is theory. While scholars have created a large number of theories over the years, it appears that only a handful of these theories are generally well known among scholars and have generated relatively large literatures of tests of their claims.

In the next section of this book, I will develop a strategy to analyze what can be regarded as the most important theories of media effects. Then I will systematically use this strategy to critically analyze each of those core theories.

References

Bandura, A. (1977). *Social learning theory*. Englewood Cliffs, NJ: Prentice-Hall.

Berger, C. R. (1991). Communication theories and other curios. *Communication Monographs, 58*, 101–113.

Berger, C. R. (1998). Processing quantitative data about risk and threat in news reports. *Journal of Communication, 48*(3), 87–106.

Bilandzic, H., & Busselle, R. W. (2008). Transportation and transportability in the cultivation of genreconsistent attitudes and estimates. *Journal of Communication, 58*, 508–529.

Blumler, J. G., & Katz, E. (1974). *The uses of mass communications: Current perspectives on gratifications research*. Beverly Hills, CA: Sage.

Csikszentmihalyi, M. (1988). The flow experience and its significance for human psychology. In M. Csikszentmihalyi & I. S. Csikszentmihalyi (Eds.), *Optimal experience: Psychological studies in flow in consciousness* (pp. 15–35). New York, NY: Cambridge University Press.

Davison, W. P. (1983). The third-person effect in communication. *Public Opinion Quarterly, 47*(1), 1–15. doi:10.1086/268763

Gerbner, G. (1969). Toward 'cultural indicators:' The analysis of mass mediated public message systems. *AV Communication Review, 17*(2), 137–148.

Goffman, E. (1974). *Frame analysis: An essay on the organization of experience*. New York, NY: Harper & Row.

Green, M. C., & Brock, T. C. (2000). The role of transportation in the persuasiveness of public narratives. *Journal of Personality and Social Psychology, 79*, 701–721.

Hardt, H. (1992). *Critical communication studies: Communication, history and theory in America*. New York, NY: Routledge.

Jensen, K. B., & Rosengren, K. E. (1990). Five traditions in search of the audience. *European Journal of Communication, 5*, 207–238.

Kamhawi, R., & Weaver, D. (2003). Mass communication research trends from 1980 to 1999. *Journalism & Mass Communication Quarterly, 80*(1), 7–27.

Kuhn, T. (1970). *The essential tension: Selected studies in scientific tradition and change*. Chicago, IL: University of Chicago Press.

Lowry, S. A., & DeFleur, M. L. (1988). *Milestones in mass communication research*. New York, NY: Longman.

McCombs, M. E., & Shaw, D. L. (1972). The agenda-setting function of mass media. *Public Opinion Quarterly, 36*(2), 176. doi:10.1086/267990. ISSN 0033-362X

McQuail, D. (1989). Communication research: Past, present and future. In M. Ferguson (Ed.), *Public communication: The new imperatives* (pp. 135–151). London: Sage.

McQuail, D. (2005). *McQuail's mass communication theory* (5th ed.). London: Sage.

Merton, R. K. (1967). *On theoretical sociology*. New York, NY: Free Press.

Nabi, R. L., & Oliver, M. B. (Eds.). (2009). *Media processes and effects*. Los Angeles, CA: Sage.

Neuman, W. R., Davidson, R., Joo, S.-H., Park, Y. J., & Williams, A. E. (2008). The seven deadly sins of communication research. *Journal of Communication, 58*, 220–237.

Newcomb, H., & Hirsch, P. M. (1984). Television as a cultural forum: Implications for research. In W. Rowland & B. Watkins (Eds.), *Interpreting television* (pp. 58–73). Beverly Hills, CA: Sage.

Pearce, K. J. (2009). Media and mass communication theories. In S. W. Littlejohn & K. A. Foss (Eds.), *Encyclopedia of communication theory* (pp. 623–627). Los Angeles, CA: Sage.

Pietila, V. (1994). Perspectives on our past: Charting the histories of mass communication studies. *Critical Studies in Mass Communication, 11*, 346–361.

Potter, W. J. (1999). *On media violence.* Thousand Oaks, CA: Sage.

Potter, W. J. (2009). *Arguing for a general framework for mass media scholarship.* Thousand Oaks, CA: Sage.

Potter, W. J. (2018). An analysis of patterns of design decisions in recent media effects research. *Review of Communication Research, 6*, 1–29, doi:10.12840/issn.2255-4165.2018.06.01.014

Potter, W. J., Cooper, R., & Dupagne, M. (1993). The three paradigms of mass media research in mainstream journals. *Communication Theory, 3*, 317–335.

Potter, W. J., & Riddle, K. (2006, November). *A content analysis of the mass media effects literature.* Paper presented at the annual convention of the National Communication Association, San Antonio, TX.

Potter, W. J., & Riddle, K. (2007). Profile of mass media effects research in scholarly journals. *Journalism & Mass of Communication Quarterly, 84*, 90–104.

Power, P., Kubey, R., & Kiousis, S. (2002). Audience activity and passivity. In W. B. Gudyknst (Ed.), *Communication yearbook* (Vol. 26, pp. 116–159). Mahwah, NJ: Erlbaum.

Reeves, B., & Borgman, C. L. (1983). A bibliometric evaluation of core journals in communication research. *Human Communication Research, 10*, 119–136.

Rice, R. E., Borgman, C. L., & Reeves, B. (1988). Citation networks of communication journals, 1997–1985: Cliques and positions, citations made and citations received. *Human Communication Research, 15*, 256–283.

Riffe, D., & Freitag, A. (1997). A content analysis of content analyses: Twenty-five years of *Journalism Quarterly. Journalism & Mass Communication Quarterly, 74*, 873–882.

Schramm, W. (1957). Twenty years of journalism research. *Public Opinion Quarterly, 21*, 91–107.

So, C., & Chan, J. (1991, August). *Evaluating and conceptualizing the field of mass communication: A survey of the core scholars.* Paper presented at the annual meeting of the AEJMC, Boston.

Trumbo, C. W. (2004). Research methods in mass communication research: A census of eight journals 1990 to 2000. *Journalism & Mass Communication Quarterly, 80*(2), 417–436.

Williams, R. (1974). *Television: Technology and cultural form.* New York, NY: Schocken.

Analysis of Core Theories

CHAPTER THREE

The Analysis Strategy

This chapter lays out the analysis strategy used in the next six chapters. We begin with presenting 14 analytical dimensions that are used to examine media effects theories. These 14 analytical dimensions are arranged in four groupings: (1) Original conceptualization of the theory, (2) Components of the theory, (3) Empirical testing of the claims made by the theory, and (4) Theory development over time. See Table 3.1 for a summary of these analytical dimensions. The final section in this chapter explains how the analytical dimensions will be used.

Original Conceptualization of the Theory

The first task in this analysis strategy is to determine the nature of each of the six theories when they were first introduced. This step entails examining each theory along five analytical dimensions: (1) Conceptual foundation, (2) Authors' introduction of the theory, (3) Conceptualization of the idea of media, (4) Conceptualization of the idea of media effect, and (5) Conceptualization of the idea of media influence.

Conceptual Foundation

This analytical dimension refers to the way the creators of a theory analyzed the existing scholarly literatures to position their theory as building on particular ideas

Table 3.1. Summary of Analytical Dimensions

---

1. Conceptual Foundation

When the author(s) introduced their theory, how did they provide a foundation for it?
   * To what extent did they rely on a critical analysis of scholarly literatures?
   * To what extent did they rely on patterns in the empirical literatures?

2. Theory Introduction

What reason did authors provide for introducing this particular system of explanation?
   * Did they point out gaps or problems in the media effects literature?
   * Did they show how their system of explanation could fill in the gaps and ameliorate the problems?

3. Conceptualization of Media

How did the authors define media and set the boundaries of what media meant in their theory?
   * Type of definition for media (ostensive, formal, etc.)
   * Constraints by channel, vehicle, genre, or message

4. Conceptualization of media effect

How did the authors define and set the perimeter of their particular effect?
   * Constraints by target (individual, groups, macro, or several?)
   * Constraints by time (immediate, long term, or both?)
   * Constraints by type (cognitive, attitudinal, belief, affect, physiology, behavior?)
   * Constraints by valence (positive, negative, or both?)
   * Constraints by intentionality (intentional, unintentional, or both?)

5. Conceptualization of Media Influence

How did the authors link media influence with the effect(s)?
   * Effect is primarily acquiring something new
   * Effect is primarily triggering or activating something in the target
   * Effect is primarily altering something existing in the target
   * Effect is primarily reinforcing something existing in the target

6. Key Concepts

What were the most important concepts in the theory when it was introduced?
   * How was each concept defined?

7. Core Propositions

What was the core set of explanatory statements when the theory was introduced?
   * How was the process of influence articulated?
   * How complex was the structure of the process of influence (contingent factors and intervening factors)?
   * How complex was the relationship (nonlinear, asymmetrical, thresholds, etc.)?

(Continued)

Table 3.1. *Continued*

---

8. Foundational Assumptions

What were the expressed and unexpressed assumptions underlying the authors' system of explanation?

* What was the conceptualization of "audience?" (mechanistic, interpretive)
* What were the methodological assumptions? (sampling, measurement, etc.)

9. Stimulating Scholarly Attention

To what extent has the theory stimulated scholarship?

* Empirical tests
* Conceptual publications, such as reviews and critiques

10. Major Lines of Research

What are the significant lines of programmatic research that have been conducted to test the claims of the theory?

11. Empirical Validity

To what extent has the empirical literature found support for theory's claims?

* Degree of support for claims made by propositions
* Degree of support for conceptualizations, such as definitions of concepts
* Degree of support for assumptions made by the theory

12. Conceptual Development

What changes have theoreticians made to the theory of a conceptual nature?

* Altering definitions of existing concepts
* Adding new concepts
* Altering propositions
* Adding new propositions
* Altering axioms

13. Methodological Development

What changes in methodological guidance have theoreticians made over time?

* Sampling
* Measurement
* Data analysis

14. Current Challenges

What are the major challenges to the theory at this time?

* As stimulated by patterns of findings from empirical research
* As stimulated by changes in the focal phenomenon

---

and thus extending the progression of explaining media effects in some way. That is, we identify how theory creators established a conceptual foundation for their system of explanation by acknowledging that particular ideas from scholarly literatures influenced them in the creation of their theory.

Authors' Introduction of the Theory

When authors introduce a theory into a scholarly literature, they have an obligation to justify how their theory can extend knowledge about the phenomenon that their theory is designed to explain. That is, theoreticians need to show how their system of explanation builds from solid ideas already in the literature and progresses to fill a gap or to overcome some faulty elements exhibited in an existing theory or theories. Therefore, the introduction of a theory requires a critical analysis of the scholarly literature in order to highlight foundational ideas as well as to identify gaps and to reveal faulty elements in existing explanations.

Conceptualization of Media

This analytical dimension refers to how theoreticians define the media. This dimension is important because it generates information that can be used in determining the scope of the theoreticians' system of explanation. Are the theoreticians regarding media effects in a narrow reductionistic way, such as limiting their theory to only one technological channel, one genre of content, or one particular message? Or are the theoreticians attempting to explain all media?

This analytical dimension is also important because it generates information that can be used to make judgments about precision. Analyses along this dimension will reveal how deeply the theoreticians have thought about the ideas that are most important to their theory and how carefully they have been in transmitting meaning to readers about how they conceptualize the media. Sometimes theoreticians will provide a formal definition of media, but more typically they will define the media ostensively by naming channels, vehicles, genres, or particular messages. While ostensive definitions at first appear clear because they name concrete elements, ostensive definitions are fuzzy from a scholarly perspective because they fail to provide classification rules. To illustrate, when theoreticians talk about media effects in terms of television's influence, readers cannot know if the theoreticians mean the large screen sitting in a person's home or also include moving images on computer screens and mobile devices; programming offered at fixed times or video on demand; or programming from broadcasters, cable providers, or amateurs. In scholarly settings, formal definitions are superior to ostensive definitions because they present classification rules that reduce ambiguity of meaning.

Conceptualization of Media Effect

The most important concept in a media effects theory is the presumed effect. There are many possible effects as a broad definition will indicate (Potter, 2011):

> Media influenced effects are those things that occur as a result—either in part or in whole—from media influence. They can occur immediately during exposure to a media message or they can take a long time to occur over the course of many exposures. They can last for a few seconds or an entire lifetime. They can show up clearly as a change but they can also reinforce existing patterns, in which case the effect appears as no change. They can affect individual people, or all people in the form of the public. They can also affect institutions and society.

Notice that this definition lays out four dimensions for an analysis: targets, time, change or reinforcement, and type of effect. All four of these dimensions will be used in analyzing media effects theories.

Targets. Who or what is conceptualized as experiencing the effect? Is it individuals? If so, is it all individuals or only certain types? Or is it some kind of aggregate of people (such as groups or the public), or is it an aggregate that transcends people (such as institutions, society, culture)?

Time. Does the theory regard the media-influenced effect as occurring during an exposure to a particular message or as taking a longer time to manifest itself? Also, is the effect short lived or does it last a long time?

Change or reinforcement. Most theories attempt to explain some sort of change, which is conceptualized as a difference of something in targets after an exposure compared to before the exposure. Some theories explain media influence as reinforcement of some preexisting condition in targets.

In order to avoid the trap of equating nonchange with reinforcement, consider that media effects have three properties—intensity, direction, and weight. For example, think of a typical measure of attitudes using a Likert scale. If a person has attitude X and this attitude is found to be unchanged (same intensity and direction) over time despite the person being exposed repeatedly to media messages, this is often interpreted to be a reinforcement-type effect, because there is an implied change in the weightiness of the attitude. While the attitude itself does not change intensity or direction over time, it becomes more weighty—through reinforcement it becomes harder to change. With attitudes, the direction refers to whether a person has a positive or negative attitude about something; the intensity refers to how strong the attitude is; and the weight refers to how fixed the attitude is.

In order to distinguish a reinforcement effect from a prediction of nonchange, reinforcement is defined as an effect where the direction and intensity remain unchanged while the weight increases. If all three properties remain the same, then this is evidence for nonchange.

Type of effect. There are six possible types of effects on individuals (Potter, 2011). These six differ in terms of the part of the person affected or the character of the experience of the effect within an individual. These six are cognition, belief, attitude, affect, physiology, and behavior. All individual-level media effects studies examine how the media exert an influence on one or more of these six types. For examples, see Table 3.2.

Table 3.2. Media Effects Template: Individual Unit Effects

Type of Effect	Media Influence Functions			
	Acquiring	Triggering	Altering	Reinforcing
Cognition	Memorize Message Element	Recall Information	Change Memory Structure	Strengthen Skills Construction of a Pattern Reinforce Connections
Belief	Accept a Belief	Recall Belief	Change Belief	Strengthen Generalization Construction of a Belief
Attitude	Accept Attitude	Recall Attitude	Change Attitude	Strengthen Evaluation Construction of a New Attitude Reinforce Attitudes
Affect	Learn Emo Information	Recall Emo	Change Emo Sensitivity	Strengthen Emo Connection
Physiology	Mood Change	Reinforce Mood	Automatic Response	Reinforce Reactions
Behavior	Learn Behaviors	Recall of Behavior	Behavioral Change Imitation of Behavior	Reinforce Habits Performance of Novel Behavior

A cognitive media effect occurs when media exposure influences a person's mental processes or the product of those mental processes. The most easy to document cognitive effect is the acquisition of factual information from media messages, such as from books, newspapers, television news stories, and informational websites. The human mind can absorb information from media messages through the process of memorization. However, the human mind can do far more than memorize; it can transform information into knowledge. This transformation of information can take the form of inferring patterns across media messages. The human mind can also group media messages in different ways to create new meanings. It can generalize beyond media messages to generate principles about real life. The media have been found to trigger all of these mental activities, so this category of cognitive effects on individuals is very large.

Beliefs have been defined as cognitions about the probability that an object or event is associated with a given attribute (Fishbein & Ajzen, 1975). Simply stated, a belief is faith that something is real or is true. The media continually create and shape our beliefs by showing us more of the world than we are able to see directly for ourselves. None of us have ever met George Washington, but we all believe he existed and was one of the founders of the United States as a country, because we have read about him in history books and websites and seen films about him. Each of us holds beliefs about the existence of a great many things we have never seen directly in our real lives; many of these beliefs have come from media messages.

Attitudes are judgments about something. For example, people see a character in a film and make judgments about that character's attractiveness, hero status, likeability, etc. When the media also present stories about people, events, issues, and products in the real world, these stories often trigger the need for us to make our own judgments about controversial issues, political candidates, advertised products, etc.

Affect refers to the feelings that people experience. This includes emotions and moods. The media can trigger emotions, especially fear, lust, and laughter. The media also provide people with lots of opportunities to manage their moods, such that when we are feeling stressed with all the problems in our real lives, we can chill by listening to music, forget our problems by watching videos, or lose ourselves in the experience of playing games on the Internet.

A physiological effect is an automatic bodily response. The body response can be either purely automatic (such as pupil dilation, blood pressure, galvanic skin response) or quasi-automatic (heart rate, sexual responses). For example, when people watch an action/adventure movie, their heart rate and blood pressure typically increase. Their muscles tense and their palms sweat as they experience a fight-or-flight reaction that has been hard-wired into the brains of all humans.

Threats trigger attention, and the body prepares itself to fight a predator or to flee. This automatic fight-or-flight effect has enabled the human race to survive for thousands of years.

Behaviors are typically defined as the overt actions of an individual (Albarracin, Zanna, Johnson, & Kumkale, 2005). Media effects researchers have conducted a lot of studies where they observe people's media exposure behaviors to see which media they use and how they use those media. Researchers also expose people to particular media messages, then observe their subsequent behaviors for things like acting aggressively, buying advertised products, and debating political issues.

It is important to make a clear distinction among these six types in order to achieve a high level of precision in the analysis. In the empirical literature of media effects, there are many examples of terms being used as synonyms in some instances and not in others, which leads to confusion. In this book, the above six categories are presented as being distinct from one another. Terms like opinions are largely avoided, but when used refer to attitudes. The term "perception" is not a synonym for attitudes or beliefs but instead means a description by humans of what comes in through the five human senses. And behavior requires actual action, not a self-report of past actions, which are either cognitions (memories of vivid occurrences) or beliefs (claims for past behavioral patterns or intentions for possible actions people may take in the future).

Valence. This refers to whether the media effect is considered good or bad, which suggests several questions. Does the theory focus only on negative effects or does it also include positive effects? Who gets to decide what is positive and what is negative?

Intentionality. Does the theory focus only on intentional effects or does it include unintentional ones? Does it treat intentionality from the perspective of the sender (media industries) or the receivers (audiences)?

Conceptualization of Media Influence

How do the media exert their influence? There are four possible functions of influence that media can exert: triggering, acquiring, altering, and reinforcing (see Potter, 2009, 2011 for detail on the development of these four categories). These four are functions in the sense that they refer to distinct actions that influence and shape the character of an effect differently across the timing, type, valence, and intentionality of the media effect.

Triggering function. The triggering function is an immediate-type effect. While a person is exposed to the media, certain things in a message can immediately stimulate something in the individual. The triggering function is applicable for all six categories of effects. A media message could activate the recall of previously learned information, the activation of an existing attitude or belief, an emotion, a physiological reaction, or a previously learned behavioral sequence. For example, people who watch horror movies have all kinds of emotions, physiological patterns, and behaviors triggered during the exposure.

The media can also trigger a process that sets a person off on a sequence involving many steps. For example, when people read some news coverage about a political candidate that they have never heard about before, they have no existing attitude about that candidate. During exposure to this news coverage, people can take the information from the news story and compare it to their standard for political candidates and create an attitude. This is different than simple acquisition, because the person is not memorizing someone else's attitude presented in the media but is instead going through a construction process in the creation of his/her own attitude; in this case the media message element of a new piece of information triggered in the person the construction of a new attitude.

The media can also trigger a reconstruction process. A media message might present information that does not conform to a person's existing knowledge structure, so the person must do something to incorporate the new information into his/her existing knowledge structure. For example, let's say that Mark has a very favorable attitude about a particular breakfast cereal but then is exposed to a media message that presents facts about the breakfast cereal using contaminated ingredients. This new information is likely to trigger a reevaluation of his previously positive attitude.

Acquiring function. The acquiring function includes those effects where people pay attention to certain elements in media messages and remember those elements. Every media message is composed of elements, such as facts, images, sounds, the depiction of a sequence of events. During exposures to these messages, individuals acquire and retain some of these elements. During a media exposure a person could pay attention to certain elements in a message and keep those elements in his/her memory. This is an immediate effect because the element is committed to memory during the exposure to the message. This memory might last a few seconds or many years, but it is not how long the memory lasts that determines whether the effect is an immediate one or not—it is when the effect first occurs.

The acquiring function is applicable to all types of effects except for physiology where media messages have no power to *create* a physiological element in an individual. People can also acquire beliefs, attitudes, affective information, and behavioral sequences in the same manner through the use of the skill of memorization. With all of these types of effects, the media are creating something in a person's mind that was not there before the exposure. It is possible to argue that all of these effects are essentially cognitive, because they all require the use of the cognitive skill of memorization and the retention of information in the individual's memory. And that is a valid point. However, while the processes and the skills used may be the same across categories, the nature of what is retained is very different. Thus the function remains the same (acquiring), but the effect itself is different and requires different categories of cognition, belief, attitude, and behavior.

Altering function. During an exposure, the media can alter something that is already present in the individual. The altering function works with all types of effects. Media messages can alter a person's knowledge structures with the addition of new facts. A belief can be altered when the media present a fact revealing that an individual's existing belief was faulty. The media can alter individuals' standards for use in constructing attitudes. Individuals who continually expose themselves to arousing elements in stories of horror and violence will have their natural fight–flight response worn down. By shifting content, the media can alter a person's mood. And when individuals continually play interactive games, this practice serves to improve their hand–eye coordination and reduce reaction times to stimuli.

The alteration can show up immediately (i.e., during an exposure or immediately after the exposure to the media message) or it can take a long time to show up. The alteration can be temporary (i.e., disappear after a few seconds) or it can last a long time. Most of the research on long-term media effects is based on assumptions of long-term media influence as a gradual shaping process. This is a kind of a drip-drip-drip process of message after message slowly altering our knowledge structures. Greenberg (1988) reminds us that there are also "drench" influences. He says that not all media messages have the same impact and that not all characters in media stories are equally influential on our beliefs and attitudes. Some portrayals stand out because they "are deviant, are intense, and thus are more important viewing experiences" (p. 98).

Reinforcing function. Through repeated exposures, the media gradually and continually add greater weight to something already existing in a person, thus making that something more permanent and harder to change. The reinforcement function is applicable to all six types of effects. When the media continually present the same people in the news over and over, individuals' knowledge structures about those people become more rigid and less likely to be open to change later. When the media present the same beliefs and attitudes, individuals' comfort levels with those beliefs and attitudes become so strong that they are not able to change those beliefs or attitudes. When the media present the same kinds of messages every week or every day, individuals' behavioral patterns of exposure become more fixed and harder to change.

Original Components

The essential components of any theory are its key concepts, core propositions, and foundational assumptions. Thus we use an analytical dimension on each of these three when examining the content of the media effects theories when they were introduced.

Key Concepts

All media effects theories feature at least two key concepts. One of these is the effect and the other is the media influence. The effect concept is easy to identify because typically a theory derives its name from it (e.g., agenda setting, cultivation, third person). The media influence can be broad (all media exposures) or very specific (e.g., pop-up ads on informational websites). The simplest form of a media effects theory is to use these two concepts in one proposition and express the relationship between these two as simple and direct.

When we look beyond these two essential concepts (the effect and the influencer), we can identify other concepts that can be categorized as being either contingent or intervening. Some theories make claims that their primary relationship (media leading to some effect) is contingent in some way, such as applying only to a certain kind of person or situation. Some theories also feature additional concepts as intervening factors between the media and the effect. An intervening concept identifies a condition that makes the primary relationship (media leading to some effect) indirect such that the intervening concept changes the simple direct relationship by amplifying it, reducing it, blocking it, or reversing it.

Core Propositions

The core propositions convey the essence of the theory's system of explanation. Each proposition expresses a relationship between two or more concepts. The set of propositions is the system of explanation.

Foundational Assumptions

Foundational assumptions are the beliefs held by a theory's creators that underlie the system of explanation. These beliefs are typically assumed rather than articulated, which makes them often difficult to identify. Typically the assumptions that theoreticians make are taken for granted by both the theoreticians and other scholars. Thus scholars feel no need to address them in their work because they believe that all their readers hold the same assumptions.

Some foundational assumptions are deep-seated beliefs that can be metaphysical such as ontological beliefs (i.e., assumptions about the nature of the phenomenon itself) or epistemological beliefs (i.e., assumptions about human capacity to perceive phenomena and to make sense of them). These assumptions are typically about change and determinism.

Assumptions about change. There are three prevalent views on change in science: unilinear, recursive progression, and dialectical. Unilinear change is a belief that things evolve from a lessor state to a more highly developed one. This is seen in Darwin's theory of evolution. This perspective was held by Comte, Spencer, Durkheim, Wundt, and Piaget. For example, Comte felt that the progress of civilization resulted from the instinctive tendency of the human race to perfect itself.

Recursive progression views change as occurring in repeating cycles. For example, deciduous trees go through seasonal cycles where they sprout leaves in the spring and shed their leaves every autumn. They repeat this cycle year after year. For example, Max Weber revealed a belief about a recursive progression to society in his sociological theory when he claimed that society oscillates with social changes as a consequence of historical periods of growth and decline. The underlying feeling is a developmental one, but a development that is achieved by rotating through cycles not by a straight, linear progression.

Dialectical change arises from the conflict produced by opposing forces where those forces are acting in different directions. If one of those forces wins out, then change occurs only in the direction that the winning force produces. But when the two forces continue in opposition, the change is an oscillation between the two directions in order to accommodate both.

Assumptions about determinism. Hypotheses can be posed with an underlying assumption of determinism, meaning A determines B or A always leads to or causes B. In contrast, an hypothesis can reflect a probabilistic expectation (i.e., B will follow A most of the time or almost always, or with 60 % probability, and so on). In social sciences, hypotheses almost always are expressed simply in statements that appear to state a deterministic relationship; however, these statements are typically tested with probabilistic statistical analyses.

Other assumptions are developed by theoreticians through experience in designing many research studies. Typically researchers will learn to relax or ignore many of the rules learned in methods classes. They do this by taking shortcuts in sampling, measurement, data analysis, and interpretations, because they learn how to become efficient, that is, to make the designs strong enough to get their studies published.

While scholars will never be able to eliminate all assumptions, they can reduce the number of faulty assumptions by first recognizing what they are then trying to determine if they warrant continued belief. In his book *Basic Dilemmas in the*

Social Sciences, Blalock (1984) says "the more information that is missing, the more untested assumptions we have to make in order to compensate." He continues, "whenever one is in doubt about an assumption, the temptation is to hide it from view possibly by using vague language or simply playing it down by embedding it in a number of innocuous assumptions or a technical discussion that most readers are unlikely to follow" (p. 135). But this strategy only serves to hide the weaknesses temporarily rather than fix them.

Empirical Testing

By publishing a theory to make it public, theoreticians invite scholars to test their claims. Some of these claims are pure speculations by the theoreticians, while other claims were carefully crafted from syntheses of existing literatures. In either case, the claims must be tested if they are to be regarded as scientific. Scientists test claims by devising empirical tests to see if the claims hold when they make their observations. We will use three analytical dimensions to look at the track record of research testing the claims of each theory—stimulating scholarly attention, major lines of research, and empirical validity.

Stimulating Scholarly Attention

Measures of scholarly attention to a theory—or its heuristic value—include how often the theory is cited, how many empirical tests it has generated, how prominently it is featured in reviews of the media effects literatures, and even how much critical attention it has stimulated. Thus a theory that has generated many empirical tests—even if all those tests fail to support its claims—exhibits high heuristic value. Also, a theory that has generated a great deal of negative criticism and no empirical tests would also demonstrate relatively high heuristic value. These examples illustrate that while heuristic value is an important criterion for evaluating theories, it should not be the only criterion to use when making an overall assessment of a theory's value.

Major Lines of Research

When a theory has stimulated a good deal of empirical testing, this body of research can be organized into lines of research. It is important to identify lines of research that test a theory in order to see patterns about what is being tested and what is being ignored.

Empirical Validity

Empirical validity refers to the extent to which the results of empirical tests have supported the claims made by the theory. Theories with larger empirical literatures displaying findings that support their claims are more valuable than theories with smaller amounts of support. Also, theories that generate tests showing strong support for its claims are more valuable than theories that generate tests showing only weak support.

Theories that have been around for decades and that have generated many empirical tests of its claims typically have a literature that includes studies that have failed to support one or more claims in the theory. If the nonsupport is small in proportion to the support, then the theory on balance is more useful. However, if the proportion of nonsupport is relatively high, the theory could still be regarded as useful if the theoreticians show a track record of altering the theory to adjust their claims in response to the nonsupportive findings, which brings us to the next set of analytical dimensions.

Theory Development

It is important to track a theory over time to determine whether the theoreticians have made alterations to their claims. As researchers conduct empirical studies to test the claims made by a theory, they produce a literature that typically shows the need to make alterations to claims in propositions. The empirical literature also typically generates indications that definitions of concepts may be faulty and/or that particular methods are less useful than other methods. These indications suggest the need for theoreticians to make alterations to their theories. In this section, we use three analytical dimensions to determine the extent to which the literatures on these core theories have indicated the need for theoretical alterations as well as the theoreticians' track records in responding to those needs. These three dimensions are: conceptual development, methodological development, and current challenges.

It is also important to track *how* a theory develops by examining three types of patterns. One pattern entails examining the empirical research to determine how much support there is for the theory's propositions as well as documenting results of tests that falsify parts of the theory. A second pattern requires examining what critics find of value in the theory and where they think the theory should be altered in some way. A third pattern involves examining how well the theoreticians have demonstrated awareness of changes in their focal phenomenon. In tracking all three of these, the key characteristic to observe is its openness, that is, to what degree have the theoreticians exhibited a willingness to alter their original conceptualizations in order to increase the precision and utility of their theories? Do the theoreticians recognize that their explanations are tentative, contextual, and qualified?

Conceptual Development

This analytical dimension focuses attention on whether the theoreticians have made refinements to their initial theory in response to patterns of findings in empirical testing, in response to critics, and/or in response to changes in the phenomenon they are attempting to explain.

Theoreticians tend to present relatively simple propositions because they are the most general. However, over time as propositions are tested, they are typically found to be less general, that is, the claims made in a general proposition are not found to hold for all types of people, all types of media messages, at all times, and in all settings, so theoreticians are likely to introduce contingent concepts to delimit their systems of explanation. Also, over time as propositions are tested, they are typically found to be less simple, that is, the claims made in a general proposition can be enhanced with the incorporation of additional concepts that work together to increase the explanatory value of the theory.

Frequently the findings of research studies will fail to find support for a theory's claim. Typically, scholars will tolerate these as anomalies, attributing them to problems with how particular researchers have operationalized the ideas in the theory in order to conduct empirical testing. However, as the research literature grows, some claims made by the theory may continually be found to fail to achieve empirical support. If the theoreticians refuse to acknowledge a growing pattern of nonsupport, then they are exhibiting a closed approach to their theory. In contrast, theoreticians who continue to alter their theories to bring them in line with the research literature exhibit a higher degree of openness.

Criticism of a theory can be processed by theoreticians in two ways. One way is where theoreticians are defensive and argue that critics do not understand their theory. A second way is for theoreticians to learn about what bothers scholars about their system of explanation and to attempt to overcome the problems identified in the criticism. The way theoreticians respond indicates their scholarly openness.

Methodological Development

Once a theory has stimulated a good deal of empirical testing, methodological patterns develop. Some theoreticians limit their concern to conceptual features while others provide researchers with methodological guidance as they increase the precision of their calculus. This analytical dimension directs attention to how well the theoreticians have made alterations to their calculus by cautioning researchers to avoid weaker design decisions.

Current Challenges

The final analytical dimension focuses on the challenges that are currently facing the theory. As theories age, the theoreticians are presented with a sequence of challenges, and if theoreticians can keep up with meeting those challenges, their theories maintain their vitality and usefulness. But if theoreticians continually resist changing their theories without good reason, those theories lose their ability to explain media effects.

When a field's focal phenomenon changes, a theory's system of explanation can quickly lose its value. This is especially the case with a dynamic phenomenon such as the media effects where content has been constantly evolving; the needs and patterns of audiences have been fragmenting into more specialized niches; and especially because the delivery systems of media messages have changed so much with digitization, mobility, and interactivity. With technological innovations, the idea of channel (e.g., television, film, newspaper) as a medium has eroded. Also, the now mobile nature of media reception means that messages are constantly shaping every aspect of our lives. And perhaps most importantly, the interactive capabilities offered by digital media have fundamentally changed the nature of media content and audience experience. These major changes in the field's focal phenomenon have put a great deal of pressure on theoreticians to make significant alterations to their systems of explanation to keep pace with the changes in the phenomenon.

Applying the Analysis Procedure

Now that the analytical dimensions have been laid out above, we need to deal with two issues before conducting the actual analysis. First, we need to determine the sample of theories to be analyzed. Second, we need to determine who is a theoretician.

The Sample of Media Effects Theories

Many media effects theories appear in the literature. One content analysis found 144 different theories in the media effects literature (Potter & Riddle, 2007) and another reported finding over 600 (Bryant & Miron, 2004. But even though many theories have been found to be mentioned in the literature, few of these theories have been mentioned often. For example, Kamhawi and Weaver (2003) examined all articles published in 10 communication journals from 1980 to 1999 and found that only three theories were mentioned in as many as 10 % of those articles. Another content analysis was conducted by Bryant and Miron (2004) who analyzed 1,806 media research articles published in three journals (*Journalism & Mass Communication Quarterly, Journal of Communication,* and *Journal of Broadcasting & Electronic Media*) from 1956 to 2000 and found references to "604 different theories, general scientific paradigms and schools of thought" (p. 664) but only 26 of those theories were mentioned in 10 or more articles. A third content analysis of the use of theories in media effects research was conducted by Potter and Riddle (2007) who analyzed media effects articles published in 16 journals from 1993 to 2005 and found mentions of 144 theories, but that only 12 of these theories were mentioned in 5 or more studies in the sample of 936 published research articles. The remaining 132 theories were spread out over 168 articles.

These many theories reveal a great variety of explanation. Some are formal systems of explanations that have generated many hypothetic-deductive tests, while others have arisen through an inductive process reported by a single study. While most focus their explanations on a small piece of the overall mass media phenomenon, a few are broader and would qualify as middle-range theories (Merton, 1968). And although a few of these theories are widely known, others are relatively unknown either because they are new or have yet to be discovered by many scholars.

In undertaking the task of analyzing media effects theories, we favor depth over breadth. Therefore we focus attention on a relatively small subset of theories that are considered the most major and most visible, then conduct a detailed, in-depth analysis of each. The process of selecting the set of major media effects theories used three filters. First, it had to be regarded as a theory given the following definition: any systematic explanation based on ideas (concepts and constructions) that seek to organize, predict, or explain some aspect of a phenomenon. This ruled out things like schools of thought and paradigms, which are foundational to theories but typically too abstract to offer researchers much guidance in designing empirical studies. A second criterion for selection is that a theory had to identify some effect—either in individuals or larger aggregates—that the theoreticians claimed to be influenced at least in part by media. And third, it had to be shown to be a core media effects theory in at least two of the three content analyses (Bryant

& Miron, 2007; Kamhawi & Weaver, 2003; Potter & Riddle, 2007). There were six theories that were found to meet all three criteria. These are Agenda Setting, Cultivation, Framing, Social Learning, Third Person, and Uses and Gratifications.

Determining the Theoreticians

Each of these six theories was introduced into the scholarly literature by a publication—either a book or an article in a scholarly journal. The authors of those publications are identified as the original theoreticians. Some of these theoreticians continued to publish articles and books on their theory, but others did not. This leads to the question: Who should be regarded as the theoreticians over the course of the theory's development?

The six theories in this analysis can be organized into four patterns with regard to who controls the theory as a theoretician. The first pattern includes theories where there has been one primary theoretician from introduction to the current time. This is the case with Albert Bandura and social learning theory, where almost all of Bandura's theoretical work has been single authored by him. This is also the case with Maxwell McCombs and agenda setting theory. Agenda setting was introduced by McCombs and a coauthor—Donald Shaw, but over time McCombs has consistently been an author of all theory pieces about agenda setting although some of those articles and book chapters have had coauthors.

A second pattern is exhibited with cultivation theory, which was introduced by George Gerbner. However, Gerbner put together a team of researchers to test his claims and he continued to publish empirical articles as well as reviews and theory pieces with these team members as coauthors over the next several decades. Since

Table 3.3. Core Theories of Media Effects

Date Introduced	Name of Theory	Primary Theoretician(s)	Size of Literature	
			Sch Estimate	GoogleSch
1969	Cultivation	Gerbner	500+ (2010)	1,540,000
1972	Agenda Setting	McCombs and Shaw	425+ (2009)	2,070,000
1974	Framing	Goffman		1,110,000
1974	Uses and Gratifications	Blumler and Katz		73,900
1977	Social Cognitive Learning	Bandura		3,350,000
1983	Third Person	Davison	60 (2008)	3,910,000

Gerbner's death in 2006, some members of his team have continued to publish reviews of cultivation theory, especially Michael Morgan, Nancy Signorielli, and James Shanahan.

A third pattern is exhibited by framing theory and third person theory, which were both created by scholars who have since moved on to other topics and have not published their own empirical studies or even a review of the literature for decades. And a fourth pattern is exhibited by uses and gratifications theory, which was introduced by multiple scholars each of whom published a few subsequent articles but each of whom largely abandoned the theory to other scholars.

To reveal who was regarded as the theoretician on each of the six theories, see Table 3.3. This table lays out the publications that were used as the basis for this analysis. And to make sense of what kinds of publications were used as a basis for this analysis, see Tables 3.4 and 3.5.

Table 3.4. Types of Theory-Relevant Publications

I. Theory Introduction
    A. Synthesis-Focused Introduction
        * Theoreticians conduct a critical analysis of past theories and conceptualizations that results in a clear articulation of a shortcoming
        * Theoreticians show how they build from the ideas they regard as strong from the various literatures then assemble those strong ideas into a single system of explanation
        * Where there are gaps in their system (no identified strong ideas from their critical analysis of the literatures), theoreticians use reasoning to fill the gaps
    B. Empirical Pattern-Focused Introduction
        * Theoreticians cite a series of their own research studies that present intriguing findings and introduce their theory as a way of explaining those findings
        * Theoreticians conduct a critical analysis of the existing empirical literature on a topic and cite some intriguing findings that motivated them to provide their own system of explanation
        * The value of this approach is keyed to theoreticians' scholarly ability to critically evaluate the literature and synthesize
    C. Speculation-Focused Introduction
        * Theory presented as pure speculation; very little grounding in past conceptualizations
        * Focus is on a perceived shortcoming in the scholarly field and the theoreticians argue that their system of explanation is one they thought up to address that shortcoming
        * This approach is rationalism and relies on ethos and logos to be effective

(Continued)

Table 3.4. *Continued*

II. Empirical Publication
    A. Tentative Support
       * Empirical tests resulting in support for the claims made by the theory
    B. Tentative Falsification
       * Empirical tests that fail to find support for the claims made by the theory
       * Authors of a test focus on tentativeness; acknowledge limitations of their test
    C. Strong Falsification
       * Empirical tests that fail to find support for the claims made by the theory
       * Authors cite a pattern of nonsupport in the previous literature of similar tests
       * Authors present their work as a critical test; acknowledge that the nonsupport is more a function of faulty propositions in the theory than faulty operationalizations used in the test
    D. Testing for Extension(s) to the Theory
       * Researchers design a study that brings in another concept not yet in the theory, then operationalizes that concept as a variable that is tested along with other variables to see if the newly introduced variable increases the theory's predictive or explanatory ability
       * Researchers design a study that alters the definition of a key concept in the theory and tests its value compared to the old way of defining
    E. Critical Test
       * Researchers operationalize a test of the theory along with tests of other theories to provide a direct comparison that reveals which theory generates the strongest predictions

III. Review of the Literature
    A. Critical Review
       * By authors other than the theoreticians
           Conceptual problems
           Methodological problems
           Recommendations for improvement
       * By the theoreticians
           Arguing in defense of theory
           Take a stance of attempting to provide greater clarification
           Willingness to make alterations to their theory
           Conceptual alterations
           Methodological alterations

(Continued)

Table 3.4. *Continued*

B. Synthesis Review
    Focus on sorting through literature and highlighting most important findings
C. Descriptive Review
    This type of review lists findings from empirical research in a structured manner.
    The structure of the review is typically by media (channel, vehicles, types of
    message topic) or by type of effect (cognitive, attitude, belief, affect, physiology,
    behavior, etc.)

Table 3.5. Theory-Focused Publications

Cultivation Theory

Theory Introduction

Gerbner, G. (1966). On defining communication: Still another view. *Journal of
Communication, 16*(2), 99–103.

Gerbner, G. (1967). An institutional approach to mass communications research. In
L. Thayer (Ed.), *Communication theory and research: Proceedings of the first international
symposium* (pp. 429–445). Springfield, IL: Charles C. Thomas Publisher.

Gerbner, G. (1969a). Toward 'cultural indicators': The analysis of mass mediated public
message systems. In G. Gerbner, O. Holsti, K. Krippendorff, W. J. Paisley, & P. J.
Stone (Eds.), *The analysis of communication content: Developments in scientific theories and
computer techniques* (pp. 123–132). New York, NY: John Wiley & Sons.

Gerbner, G. (1969b). Toward 'cultural indicators': The analysis of mass mediated public
message systems. *AV Communication Review, 17*(2), 137–148.

Alterations/Elaborations in Theory

Gerbner, G., Gross, L., Morgan, M., & Signorielli, N. (1980). The mainstreaming
of America: Violence profile no. 11. *Journal of Communication, 30*(3), 10–29.
doi:10.1111/j.1460-2466.1980.tb01987.x.

Theoretician Reviews

Gerbner, G. (1972). Violence and television drama: Trends and symbolic functions. In
G. A. Comstock & E. Rubinstein (Eds.), *Television and social behavior, Vol. 1. Content
and control* (pp. 28–187). Washington, DC: U.S. Government Printing Office.

Gerbner, G. A. (1973). Cultural indicators: The third voice. In G. Gerbner, L. P. Gross,
& W. H. Melody (Eds.), *Communication technology and social policy* (pp. 555–573).
New York, NY: John Wiley & Sons.

Gerbner, G. (1990). Epilogue: Advancing on the path of righteousness (maybe). In
N. Signorielli & M. Morgan (Eds.), *Cultivation analysis: New directions in media effects
research* (pp. 249–262). Newbury Park, CA: Sage.

(Continued)

Table 3.5. *Continued*

Gerbner, G. (1999). What do we know? In J. Shanahan & M. Morgan (Eds.), *Television and its viewers: Cultivation theory and research* (pp. ix–xiii). Cambridge, UK: Cambridge University Press.

Gerbner, G., Gross, L., Morgan, M., & Signorielli, N. (1986). Living with television: The dynamics of the cultivation process. In J. Bryant & D. Zillmann (Eds.), *Perspectives on media effects* (pp. 17–40). Hillsdale, NJ: Erlbaum.

Morgan, M. (2009). Cultivation analysis and media effects. In R. L. Nabi & M. O. Oliver (Eds.), *The Sage handbook of media processes and effects* (pp. 69–82). Los Angeles, CA: Sage.

Morgan, M. (2012). *George Gerbner: A critical introduction to media and communication theory.* New York, NY: Peter Lang.

Morgan, M., & Shanahan, J. (2010). The state of cultivation. *Journal of Broadcasting & Electronic Media, 54,* 337–355.

Morgan, M., Shanahan, J., & Signorielli, N. (2009). Growing up with television: Cultivation processes. In J. Bryant & M. B. Oliver (Eds.), *Media effects: Advances in theory and research* (3rd ed., pp. 34–49). New York, NY: Routledge.

Morgan, M., & Signorielli, N. (1990). Cultivation analysis: Conceptualization and methodology. In N. Signorielli & M. Morgan (Eds.), *Cultivation analysis: New directions in media effects research* (pp. 13–34). Newbury Park, CA: Sage.

Shanahan, J., & Morgan, M. (1999). *Television and its viewers: Cultivation theory and research.* Cambridge, UK: Cambridge University Press.

Agenda Setting Theory

Introduction of Agenda Setting Theory

McCombs, M. E., & Shaw, D. L. (1972). The agenda-setting function of mass media. *Public Opinion Quarterly 36*(2), 176. doi:10.1086/267990. ISSN 0033-362X.

Theoreticians Reviews and Alterations

McCombs, M. (2004). Setting the agenda: The mass media and public opinion (Repr. ed., p. 198). Cambridge: Blackwell Pub.

McCombs, M. (2005). A look at agenda-setting: Past, present and future. *Journalism Studies, 6*(4), 543–557. doi:10.1080/14616700500250438.

McCombs, M., & Bell, T. (1996). The agenda-setting role of mass communication: An integrated approach to communication theory and research (pp. 93–110). Mahwah, NJ: Erlbaum.

McCombs, M., & Reynolds, A. (2002). News influence on our pictures of the world. In J. Bryant & D. Zillmann (Eds.), *Media effects: Advances in theory and research* (3rd ed., pp. 1–18). Mahwah, NJ: Erlbaum.

McCombs, M., & Reynolds, A. (2009). How the news shapes our civic agenda. In J. Bryant & M. B. Oliver (Eds.), Media effects: Advances in theory and research (3rd ed., pp. 1–16). New York, NY: Routledge.

(Continued)

Table 3.5. *Continued*

McCombs, M., Shaw, D. L., & Weaver, D. H. (1997). Communication and democracy: Exploring the intellectual frontiers in agenda-setting theory. Mahwah, NJ: Erlbaum.

McCombs, M. E., & Shaw, D. L. (1993). The evolution of agenda-setting research: Twenty-five years in the marketplace of ideas. *Journal of Communication, 43*(2), 58–67. doi:10.1111/j.1460-2466.1993.tb01262.x.

McCombs, M. E., Shaw, D. L., & Weaver, D. H. (2014). New directions in agenda-setting theory and research. Mass Communication & Society, 17(6), 781–802. doi:10.10 80/15205436.2014.964871.

Other Reviews

Iyengar, S., & Kinder, D. (1987). *News that matters: Television and American opinion.* Chicago, IL: University of Chicago Press.

Rogers, E., & Dearing, J. (1988). Agenda-setting research: Where has it been, where is it going? In J. A. Anderson (Ed.), *Communication Yearbook 11* (pp. 555–594). Newbury Park, CA: Sage.

Rogers, E. M., Dearing, J. W., & Bregman, D. (1993). The anatomy of agenda-setting research. *Journal of Communication, 43*(2), 68–84. doi:10.1111/j.1460-2466.1993.tb01263.x.

Wanta, W., & Ghanem, S. (2007). Effects of agenda-setting. In R. W. Preiss, B. M. Gayle, N. Burrell, M. Allen, & J. Bryant (Eds.), *Mass media effects research: Advances through meta-analysis* (pp. 37–51). Mahwah, NJ: Erlbaum.

Weiss, D. (2009). Agenda-setting theory. In S. W. Littlejohn & K. A. Foss (Eds.), *Encyclopedia of communication theory* (pp. 31–33). Los Angeles, CA: Sage.

Willnat, L. (1997). Agenda setting and priming: Conceptual links and differences. In M. McCombs, D. L. Shaw, & D. Weaver (Eds.), *Communication and democracy: Exploring the intellectual frontiers in agenda-setting theory* (pp. 51–66). Mahwah, NJ: Erlbaum.

Framing Theory

Origin

Bateson, G. (1972). *Steps to an ecology of mind.* New York, NY: Ballantine Books.

Goffman, E. (1974). *Frame analysis: An essay on the organization of experience.* New York, NY: Harper & Row.

Reviews

Chong, D., & Druckman, J. N. (2007). Framing theory. *Annual Review of Political Science, 10,* 103–126. doi:10.1146/annurev.polisci.10.072805.103054.

Scheufele, D. A. (1999). Framing as a theory of media effects. *Journal of Communication,* 49(1), 103–122.

Scheufele, D. A. (2000). Agenda-setting, priming, and framing revisited: Another look at cognitive effects of political communication. *Mass Communication & Society, 3*(2&3), 297–316. doi:10.1207/S15327825MCS0323_07.

(Continued)

Table 3.5. *Continued*

Scheufele, D. A., & Iyengar, S. (forthcoming). The state of framing research: A call for new directions. In K. Kenski & K. H. Jamieson (Eds.), *The Oxford Handbook of political communication theories*. New York, NY: Oxford University Press.

Tewksbury, D., & Scheufele, D. A. (2009). News framing theory and research. In J. Bryant & M. B. Oliver (Eds.), *Media effects: Advances in theory and research* (pp. 17–33). New York, NY: Routledge.

Volkmer, I. (2009). Framing theory. In S. W. Littlejohn & K. A. Foss (Eds.), *Encyclopedia of communication theory* (pp. 407–408). Los Angeles, CA: Sage.

Uses and Gratifications Theory

Origin

Blumler, J. G., & Katz, E. (1974). *The uses of mass communications: Current perspectives on gratifications research*. Beverly Hills, CA: Sage.

Katz, E., Blumler, J. G., & Gurevitch, M. (1974a). Utilization of mass communication by the individual. In J. G. Blumler & E. Katz (Eds.), *The uses of mass communications: Current perspectives on gratifications research* (pp. 19–32). Beverly Hills, CA: Sage.

Katz, E., Blumler, J., & Gurevitch, M. (1974b). Uses of mass communication by the individual. In W. P. Davison & F. T. C. Yu (Eds.), *Mass communication research: Major issues and future directions* (pp. 11–35). New York, NY: Praeger.

Katz, E., Haas, H., & Gurevitch, M. (1973). On the use of the mass media for important things. *American Sociological Review, 38*(2), 164–181.

Theoretician Reviews & Elaborations

Katz, E. (1987). Communication research since Lazarsfeld. *Public Opinion Quarterly, 51*, 525–545.

Levy, M., & Windahl, S. (1985). The concept of audience activity. In K. E. Rosengren, L. A. Wenner, & P. Palmgreen (Eds.), Media gratifications research: Current perspectives (pp. 109–122). Beverly Hills, CA: Sage.

Palmgreen, P. (1984). Uses and gratification: A theoretical perspective. In R. N. Bostrom (Ed.), *Communication yearbook* (Vol. 8, pp. 20–55). Beverly Hills, CA: Sage.

Palmgreen, P., Wenner, L. A., & Rosengren, K. E. (1985). Uses and gratifications research: The past ten years. In K. E. Rosengren, L. A. Wenner, & P. Palmgreen (Eds.), *Media gratifications research: Current perspectives* (pp. 11–37). Beverly Hills, CA: Sage.

Rubin, A. M. (1986). Uses, gratifications, and media effects research. In J. Bryant & D. Zillmann (Eds.), *Perspectives on media effects* (pp. 281–301). Hillsdale, NJ: Erlbaum.

Rubin, A. M. (2009a). Uses and gratifications: An evolving perspective of media effects. In R. L. Nabi & M. B. Oliver (Eds.), *The Sage handbook of media processes and effects* (pp. 147–159). Los Angeles, CA: Sage.

Rubin, A. M. (2009b). Uses-and-gratification perspective on media effects. In J. Bryant & M. B. Oliver (Eds.), *Media effects: Advances in theory and research.* (pp. 165–184). New York, NY: Routledge.

(Continued)

Table 3.5. *Continued*

Other Reviews

Littlejohn, S. (1999). *Theories of human communication* (6th ed.). Albuquerque, NM: Wadsworth.

McQuail, D. (1984). With benefits to hindsight: Reflections on uses and gratifications research. In *Critical Studies in Mass Communication, 1*, 177–193.

McQuail, D. (2005). *McQuail's mass communication theory* (5th ed.). Thousand Oaks, CA: Sage.

Social Cognitive Theory

Origin

Bandura, A. (1963). *Social learning and personality development.* New York, NY: Holt, Rinehart, and Winston.

Bandura, A. (1977). *Social learning theory.* Englewood Cliffs, NJ: Prentice-Hall.

Theoretician Review/Elaborations

Bandura, A. (1986). *Social foundations of thought and action: A social cognitive theory.* Englewood Cliffs, NJ: Prentice-Hall.

Bandura, A. (1997). *Self-efficacy: The exercise of control.* New York, NY: Freeman.

Bandura, A. (2001). Social cognitive theory of mass communication. *Media Psychology, 3,* 265–299.

Bandura, A. (2002). Social cognitive theory of mass communication. In J. Bryant & D. Zillmann (Eds.), *Media effects: Advances in theory and research* (2nd ed., pp. 121–153). Mahwah, NJ: Erlbaum.

Bandura, A. (2009). Social cognitive theory of mass communication. In J. Bryant & M. B. Oliver (Eds.), *Media effects: Advances in theory and research* (3rd ed., pp. 94–124). New York, NY: Routledge.

Other

Pajares, F., Prestin, A., Chen, J., & Nabi, R. L. (2009). Social cognitive theory and media effects. In R. L. Nabi & M. B. Oliver (Eds.), *Media processes and effects* (pp. 283–297). Los Angeles, CA: Sage.

Third Person Effect Theory

Origin

Davison, W. P. (1983). The third-person effect in communication. *Public Opinion Quarterly, 47*(1), 1–15. doi:10.1086/268763.

Reviews

Lasorsa, D. L. (1992). How media affect policymakers: The third-person effect. In J. D. Kennamer (Ed.), Public opinion, the press and public policy (pp. 163–175). New York, NY: Praeger.

(Continued)

Table 3.5. *Continued*

Paul, B., Salwen, M. B., & Dupagne, M. (2000). The third-person effect: A meta-analysis of the perceptual hypothesis. Mass Communication & Society, 3(1), 57–85. doi:10.1207/s15327825mcs0301_04

Perloff, R. M. (1999). The third-person effect: A critical review and synthesis. Media Psychology, 1(4), 353–378. doi:10.1207/s1532785xmep0104_4.

Perloff, R. M. (2009). Mass media, social perception, and the third-person effect. In J. Bryant & M. B. Oliver (Eds.), *https://books.google.com/books?id=2BeOAgAAQBAJ&pg=PA252* (3rd ed., pp. 252–268). New York, NY: Routledge. ISBN 9781135591106.

Sun, Y., Pan, Z., & Shen, L. (2008). Understanding the third-person perception: Evidence from a meta-analysis. Journal of Communication, 58(2), 280–300. doi:10.1111/j.1460-2466.2008.00385.x.

Summary

The 14 analytical dimensions presented in this chapter are used to structure the analysis of each of the six core theories of media effects in the following six chapters. The information laid out in those six chapters then forms the basis for the evaluation task, which is the focus of the third major part of this book.

References

Albarracin, D., Zanna, M. P., Johnson, B. T., & Kumkale, G. T. (2005). Attitudes: Introduction and scope. In D. Albarracin, B. T. Johnson, & M. P. Zanna (Eds.), *The handbook of attitudes* (pp. 3–19). Mahwah, NJ: Erlbaum.

Blalock, H. M., Jr. (1984). *Basic dilemmas in the social sciences*. Beverly Hills, CA: Sage.

Bryant, J., & Miron, D. (2004). Theory and research in mass communication. *Journal of Communication, 54*(4), 662–704.

Fishbein, M., & Ajzen, I. (1975). *Belief, attitude, intention, and behavior: An introduction to theory and research*. Reading, MA: Addison-Wesley.

Greenberg, B. S. (1988). Some uncommon television images and the drench hypothesis. In S. Oskamp (Ed.), *Television as a social issue* (pp. 88–102). Newbury Park, CA: Sage.

Kamhawi, R., & Weaver, D. (2003). Mass communication research trends from 1980 to 1999. *Journalism & Mass Communication Quarterly, 80*(1), 7–27.

Merton, R. K. (1968). *Social theory and social structure*. New York, NY: Free Press.

Potter, W. J. (2009). *Arguing for a general framework for mass media scholarship*. Thousand Oaks, CA: Sage.

Potter, W. J. (2011). Conceptualizing mass media effect. *Journal of Communication, 61*, 896–915.

Potter, W. J., & Riddle, K. (2007). A content analysis of the media effects literature. *Journalism & Mass of Communication Quarterly, 84*, 90–104.

CHAPTER FOUR

Cultivation Theory

Cultivation theory is a macro-level system of explanation about mass media effects that was introduced by George Gerbner in the late 1960s, who then assembled a research team to help him conduct a series of empirical tests of his system of explanation over the next several decades. By the 1970s other media scholars were attracted to the idea of cultivation and within four decades, the cultivation literature grew to well over 500 published studies (Morgan & Shanahan, 2010), making it one of the most visible and tested theories of media effects.

Original Conceptualization of Cultivation Theory

Introduction of the Theory

George Gerbner introduced cultivation theory into the scholarly literature with a relatively short essay that he published in three different outlets with minor alterations across the three (1967, 1969a, 1969b). He said that his intention was to create a system of explanation of media effects that was different from what he considered the dominant form of mass media research at the time, which he characterized as a literature of experiments that were designed to test whether particular message elements exhibited a direct, immediate effect on participants.

As an alternative to this type of research, Gerbner presented cultivation as a macro-systems approach that focused on long-term effects on large aggregates (like the public) and institutions (like mass media organizations). Gerbner explained, "I use the term [cultivation] to indicate that my primary concern in this discussion is not with information, education, persuasion, etc., or with any kind of direct communication 'effects'" (p. 139). Instead, he said his theory was more concerned with the knowledge and beliefs that were gradually cultivated in a population that was constantly being exposed to media messages in their everyday lives.

Key to cultivation theory is its focus on public information with an "awareness that a certain item of knowledge is publicly held (i.e., not only known to many, but *commonly known that it is known to many*) makes collective thought and action possible. Such knowledge gives individuals their awareness of collective strength (or weakness), and a feeling of social identification or alienation" (pp. 139–140). Thus Gerbner was not interested in explaining the immediate effect of any particular message on individuals; instead he was interested in whether there were beliefs that were widespread in the population and if so, whether those beliefs could be attributed to particular meanings that were widespread across all media messages.

Conceptual Foundation

Given Gerbner's conceptualization of cultivation as a macro-theory about how meaning is manufactured and its effect on large aggregates, it appears that he drew ideas from at least five well-established scholarly literatures. These five literatures are: the European cultural approach, the American sociological approach, public opinion research, the measurement of meaning, and models of media influence. However, this attribution is only my inference, because Gerbner never credited any of those scholars associated with those literatures in either his introductory essays or in any of his subsequent work. His three introductory essays include a total of only 11 references, 9 of which are to his own work. The closest he came to giving credit to any of the thinkers who provided him with the ideas that were foundational to cultivation theory was when he said, "Philosophers, historians, anthropologists, and others have, of course, addressed themselves to such problems before" (1969b, p. 139) but he never explained what those ideas were nor how they influenced his own thinking.

European cultural approach. Gerbner's approach to media effects evokes the ideas of the Frankfurt School (e.g., Marcuse, Gramsci, Adorno) which was a group of European scholars who applied the ideas of Karl Marx to social and cultural contexts rather than political and economic ones. For example, Marcuse (1964) developed the idea of the influence of media on manipulating the public so it would conform to the needs of the power elites. Gerbner was building on this idea when he wrote "Our theoretical point of departure, then is that changes in the mass production and rapid distribution of messages across previous barriers of time, space and social grouping bring about systematic variations in public message content whose full significance rests in the cultivation of collective consciousness about elements of existence" (Gerbner, 1969b, p. 138). Gerbner (1967) defines culture as "that system of messages which cultivates the images of a society. The dominant communication agencies produce the message systems which cultivate dominant image patterns. They cultivate the broadest common notions of what is, what is important and what is right. They structure the public agenda of existence, priorities and values" (1967, p. 434).

It appears that Gerbner also drew from the ideas of the Italian Marxist philosopher Antonio Gramsci (1948) who developed a theory of cultural domination that explained that cultural elites exercise power over the public by controlling the flow of ideas, which Gramsci called "cultural hegemony." Thus the ruling class establishes and exerts its cultural dominance by imposing its *Weltanschauung* (worldview) in a way that makes the worldview appear as natural and inevitable to the public. Gramsci argued that the public is trained not to question this worldview, so this worldview becomes accepted as the status quo. And as long as the public accepts this worldview, which is communicated to the public through a continual flow of media messages, the elites remain comfortably in power.

A student of Gerbner and part of his research team, Michael Morgan (2012) explains, "Gerbner also collaborated with Theodor Adorno on his classic 1954 article 'How to Look at Television,' which explored the psychodynamics of television drama and taught him to look for the hidden messages and cultural assumptions in stories" (p. 6). However, Gerbner never credited Adorno—or any member of the European cultural approach—in any of his writings about cultivation.

American sociological approach. It appears that Gerbner also drew heavily from the ideas of the American sociological approach as an explanation of acculturation in a society and how public opinion is formed and shaped. At the time Gerbner introduced his idea of cultivation, a variety of general sociological theories had offered explanations about how society is structured and how large aggregates of people are influenced by opinion leaders and institutions (including the mass media) to interpret the meaning of their world and learn norms and social information (Bell, 1961; Berger & Luckmann, 1967; Bramson, 1961; Kornhauser, 1959; Mills, 1951, 1956). For example, C. Wright Mills (1951, 1956), a sociologist, developed a theory that placed the mass media as a central factor in creating and shaping the public's view of the world. Also in their *The Social Construction of Reality*, Berger and Luckmann (1967) argued that social reality is created by individuals and institutions and that the mass media are an important agency in selecting a particular view of reality and disseminating that view widely.

Public opinion. Gerbner's focus on the public rather than on individuals also borrows directly from the ideas of Walter Lippmann (1922) who in his classic book *Public Opinion* argued that the media put pictures in the heads of the public. Gerbner writes, "The truly revolutionary significance of modern mass communication is its 'public-making' ability. That is the ability to form historically new bases for collective thought and action quickly, continuously and pervasively across precious boundaries of time, space, and culture" (1969b, p. 140).

Measurement of meaning. The idea that messages conveyed meaning was not new with Gerbner. In fact there was a long-standing debate about whether meaning was in the messages or in the interpretations provided by receivers. Charles Osgood and Percy Tannenbaum did groundbreaking work on this topic and published the classic *The Measurement of Meaning* in 1957 (Osgood, Suci, & Tannenbaum, 1957). Despite the fact that Gerbner collaborated with both Osgood and Tannenbaum early in his career (Morgan, 2012), he did not acknowledge any of their work as a foundation for his cultivation theory.

Also, Gerbner argued that "the common symbolic environment that gives public meaning and sense of direction to human activity" (1969b, p. 138), which is uncredited to any theory, not even the work of George Herbert Mead (1934) who created a very influential theory about how people interpret symbols to create their meaning. Shanahan and Morgan (1999) explain: "Communication to Gerbner is 'interaction through messages,' a distinctly human (and humanizing) process which both creates and is driven by the symbolic environment which constitutes culture. The symbolic environment reveals social and institutional dynamics, and because it expresses social patterns it also cultivates them. This, then is the original meaning of 'cultivation'—the process within which interaction through messages shapes and sustains the terms on which the messages are premised" (p. 12).

Models of media influence. In 1957, Westley and MacLean published a model to guide theory development about the mass media in which they argued that the media exert both a direct and an indirect influence on the public and on society and that these influences are constant and ongoing over time. Furthermore, much of what Gerbner was recommending had already been stated by Jay Blumer (1964) in his proposed outline of research that should be undertaken to conduct better research into the effects of television in Britain. Blumer laid out the debates that had been taking place regarding the influence of television on the public then made a series of recommendations that emphasized the importance of conducting better analyses of media content, that is, to go beyond simple counting of surface characteristics and instead "establish what values protagonists pursue most often, in what situations of value conflict they are placed, and how those conflicts are resolved" (Blumer, 1964, p. 228). He also called for the study of long-term effects by which he meant longitudinal research with multiple points of data gathering.

Conceptualization of Media

In Gerbner's original conception, cultivation theory was concerned with the influence of all mass media, because he believed that there were certain meanings that were widespread throughout all media and all kinds of content. This is a key characteristic that set cultivation apart from other theories as well as the tradition of media effects research up to that time. While he acknowledged that there were differences across different kinds of messages and different media, he regarded those differences as superficial and minor. He argued that the most important meanings were the deep ones that were widespread across all media and across all types of content.

When Gerbner formed his research team and began testing this claim of widespread meaning, he limited his focus to the single medium of television reasoning that this was a good place to start testing because television was the dominant storytelling of the time (Gerbner, 1969a, 1969b). Also he focused only on analyzing the content of entertainment programming and children's Saturday morning programming provided by the three dominant commercial networks at the time (ABC, CBS, NBC). These limitations were presented as operational choices rather than reflections that the theory itself was concerned only with one medium or a subset of programming.

Conceptualization of Media Effect

Gerbner's original conceptualization of effect was broad-scale public thinking and action. He argued that the media have the ability to shape "collective thought and action quickly, continuously, and pervasively across previous boundaries of time, space, and culture" (1969, p. 140). Thus his theory ignored immediate effects and placed its complete focus on long-term effects. Also, he was interested in the large aggregate of the public, not any one type of individual. And the type of effect was knowledge, behavior, and especially beliefs.

Conceptualization of Media Influence

In his introduction of cultivation theory, Gerbner presented the influence of the media as being traceable to the messages they produced. That is, he claimed that the mass media were an institution that had developed certain practices, which led them to shape their messages in particular ways. Those messages—regardless of the type of message or the channel used to transmit them—all shared a common meaning that reflected those institutional practices. It was this common meaning then that exerted influence on the entire public.

Original Components

When Gerbner (1967, 1969a, 1969b) introduced his theory, it had three inter-related components arranged in a system (see Table 4.1). The first component focused on the media as institutions; a second component focused on media messages and their meanings; and the third component focused on the public and how it was influenced by the constant flow of media messages everyday over long periods of time. Thus, Gerbner did not limit his theory to only effects but was also concerned with media institutions and messages in addition to those effects. However, he argued that the effect could not be explained without first under-standing the widespread meanings embedded in all media messages, which in turn could not be explained without first understanding the institutional practices that were responsible for embedding the meanings uniformly in all media messages. So his theory called for an institutional analysis of media businesses to determine what their practices were and how those practices shaped meaning throughout all the messages they produced. And he called for a message system analysis of all media content to identify what those widespread meanings were.

Table 4.1. The Three Components of Cultivation Theory

I. **Institutional Component**
   * The "mass production and rapid distribution of messages create new symbolic environments that reflect the structure and functions of the institutions that transmit them" (Gerbner, 1970, p. 69).
II. **Message Component**
   * There are certain meanings that are conveyed in all media messages regardless of medium or genre.
III. **Effects Component**
   * The more that individuals are exposed to the media, the more they will exhibit cultivated beliefs.
   * A belief can be regarded as being cultivated by the media when it reflects the widespread meaning through all media messages instead of actual patterns in the real world.

Key Concepts

The original theory was focused on three key concepts: symbolic environments, widespread meaning, and cultivated beliefs (see Table 4.2).

Within the institutional component, Gerbner argued that the "mass production and rapid distribution of messages create new symbolic environments that reflect the structure and functions of the institutions that transmit them" (Gerbner, 1970, p. 69). In his original writings, Gerbner offered some questions to help readers think about what the symbolic environments were but he never offered details himself by providing answers to those questions. For example, he suggested that one characteristic of influence in creating such symbolic environments was the media's commercial nature but he never developed this idea in enough detail to specify how the media's commercial nature shaped the content they produced.

Within the message component, Gerbner claimed that there were certain mass-produced meanings that were widespread throughout the entire mass media environment. He directed researchers to use scientific content analyses to identify what these widespread meanings were, but he never provided any guidance about how to translate counts of frequency of various content features into received meaning. Instead when he began publishing his team's annual content of television, he simply reported how often certain characteristics (such as violent acts, male characters) appeared in television shows.

Within the effects component, Gerbner contended that the widespread meanings presented across all media cultivated public beliefs. Gerbner claimed that mass-produced messages form "a common culture through which communities cultivate shared and public notions about facts, values, and contingencies of human existence" (Gerbner, 1969b, p. 123).

Core Propositions

The original theory presented three core propositions. One of these was that the way the media as institutions were structured and how they functioned led to the creation and maintenance of symbolic environments that reflected the values of the media institutions. Second, the symbolic environments within the media institutions shaped the production of messages that exhibited certain meanings that were widespread across all messages they produced. And third, people became cultivated to certain beliefs as a result of everyday exposure to media messages.

When Gerbner and his team began publishing their tests of cultivation theory, the focus was placed most strongly on the third of these components—looking for evidence of cultivation effects on the population. He translated this theoretical proposition into the testable hypothesis: People who continually experience higher

Table 4.2. Key Elements of Cultivation Theory

I. Key Concepts

Symbolic environments—the mass media organizations are primarily businesses that form an institution and like other institutions they have developed practices that make it possible for them to fulfill their institutional purposes. Regardless of whether a media organization is big or small, a private company or a public entity, or produces message for one medium rather than another, they all share an environment that depends on symbolic activities to produce their messages.

Widespread meanings—there are deeply embedded meanings in all media messages that are widespread across all types of messages and transmitted by all types of media channels.

Cultivation—the process of the media acculturating the general population; the process by which everyone learns the same lessons about society.

II. Core Propositions

The mass media organizations share institutional practices that shape the way they manufacture their messages, such that all the produced messages have deep structure meanings.

The "mass production and rapid distribution of messages create new symbolic environments that reflect the structure and functions of the institutions that transmit them" (Gerbner, 1970, p. 69).

The messages that the media manufacture all share the same meanings at a deep, fundamental level and these meanings can be explained by the organizations' institutional practices.

When people are constantly exposed to media messages in their everyday lives, they come to perceive those deeply embedded meanings and accept them.

The more that individuals are exposed to the media, the more they will exhibit cultivated beliefs.

III. Foundational Assumptions

All media organizations are institutions with a relatively uniform symbolic environment. If there are differences across media companies, those differences are relatively unimportant.

The above assumption is required in order to accept the second assumption that all media companies produce messages with widespread meanings, that is, those meanings show up in all kinds of messages across all media.

Media influence is a relatively automatic process that is uniform across all kinds of people, that is, it does not matter what your gender is or your age, your intelligence, your socioeconomic status, educational level or other personal characteristic or ability; all that matters is how much media you are typically exposed to everyday.

People are able to perceive the deeply embedded meanings across all media messages.

People are passive. They are not active processes of meaning; instead, they simply accept the meanings they perceive to be presented in the messages.

A belief can be regarded as being cultivated by the media when it reflects the widespread meaning through all media messages instead of actual patterns in the real world.

---

levels of exposure to media messages are more likely to exhibit cultivated beliefs compared to people who continually experience lower levels of exposure to media messages.

Foundational Assumptions

Cultivation theory as introduced by Gerbner requires the acceptance of three fundamental assumptions. First, the theory was built on the assumption that all media organizations are institutions with a relatively uniform symbolic environment. If there are differences across media companies, those differences are relatively unimportant. This assumption is required in order to accept the second assumption that all media companies produce messages with widespread meanings, that is, those meanings show up in all kinds of messages across all media. The third assumption is that the media effect is the cultivation of these widespread meanings into public beliefs in a relatively automatic process that is uniform across all kinds of people, that is, it does not matter what your gender is or your age, your intelligence, your socioeconomic status, educational level, or other personal characteristics or ability; all that matters is how much media you are typically exposed to everyday. Also, people are regarded being both perceptive and passive in their encounters with the media messages, that is, everyone is able to perceive the embedded meanings accurately and they simply accept those meanings.

Notice that these three assumptions suggest a process in which the first assumption needs to be tested first, because if it does not hold, then it makes no sense to move onto research and testing the second or third assumptions. But this was not a process that Gerbner and his team followed; instead they started with the third assumption and never tested either the first or the second assumptions.

Empirical Testing

Calculus

To guide researchers in their tests of his three major claims presented in his system of explanation, Gerbner outlined three types of analysis: institutional analysis, message system analysis, and cultivation analysis. With institutional analysis, Gerbner directed researchers to look for "changes in the mass production and rapid distribution of messages across previous barriers of time, space, and social grouping" to determine how those changes "bring about systematic variations in public message content" (Gerbner, 1969b, p. 124).

With message system analysis, Gerbner recommended that the search for these widespread meanings should be undertaken in a scientific manner. "What distinguishes the analysis of public mass-mediated message systems as a social scientific enterprise from other types of observation commentary, or criticism is the attempt to deal comprehensively, systematically, and generally rather than specifically and selectively or ad hoc with problems of collective cultural life" (1969a, p. 141). He also cautioned that content analysts should look for patterns of meaning across the total media landscape and therefore make no distinction between information versus entertainment, fact versus fiction, high culture versus low culture, good versus bad, images versus words, or levels of artistic excellence. Thus the purpose of message system analysis was to identify meanings that (a) could be attributed to institutional practices of mass production of messages and (b) were found to be disseminated widely across the entire media landscape.

Cultivation analysis, Gerbner (1973) argued, "begins with the insights of the study of institutions and the message systems they produce, and goes on to investigate the contributions that these systems and their symbolic functions make to the cultivation of assumptions about life and the world" (p. 567). Because the mass-produced messages form the culture, Gerbner believed that their influence on the public should be exhibited over the long term by reinforcement as well as change. "The dynamics of continuities, rather than only of change, need to be considered in the examination of mass-produced message systems and their symbolic functions. Such examination is necessarily longitudinal and comparative in its analysis of the processes and consequences of institutionalized public acculturation" (p. 569).

Gerbner and his team created a set of operational practices that they repeated in all their tests of cultivation over more than 25 years. Also, when other media scholars began conducting their own tests of cultivation, they typically followed this set of operational practices. These operational practices exhibit seven characteristics. The first two of these characteristics refer to the patterns of practices within the message system analysis literature. These are the practices of limiting their sampling frame to TV messages and the equating of frequency with meaning. In their initial message system analysis studies, Gerbner and his research team designed a series of content analyses that narrowed the focus down from all mass media to the single medium of television. To justify this reduction, they argued that "commercial television, unlike other media, presents an organically composed total world of interrelated stories (both drama and news) produced to the same set of market specifications." They further limited the scope of their content analysis by examining only the programs presented on primetime and children's weekend morning programming provided by the three dominant commercial television networks at the time, reasoning that these programs had the largest viewership and if there were particular meanings widespread across the entire media landscape, those meanings should be in evidence in their sample. They further limited their focus by examining only entertainment programming but provided no reasoning to support this decision (e.g., Gerbner et al., 1977). While they gradually expanded their content analyses from looking at the topic of violence to looking also at other topics such as gender roles, marriage and family, aging, race/ethnicity, occupational status, affluence, the environment, politics, and mental illness (Morgan & Shanahan, 2010), they consistently stayed with the same sampling frame of mainstream television entertainment.

The second pattern of operational practices in message system analysis was the using of frequency counts as a surrogate for meaning. For example, when they found a high frequency of occurrence of violent acts from their yearly content analyses, they concluded that the television world was mean and violent (e.g., Gerbner et al., 1977).

When operationalizing cultivation analysis, the cultivation team made a series of design decisions that reveal five key features: use of national probability samples, cross-sectional surveys, assumption of stable TV viewing, focus on beliefs as a cultivation indicator, and categorical analyses of the relationship between TV exposure and cultivation indicators. The cultivation team typically used data gathered by a commercial polling firm that each year conducted a national telephone survey of households randomly sampled so that it represented the adult population of the United States. The survey design was cross-sectional where respondents were measured once, rather than longitudinally where the same respondents would have been measured year after year to determine if there were changes in respondents' TV exposure, their cultivated beliefs, or the relationship between the two.

Television exposure was measured by asking respondents how many hours of television they watched on an average day last week. This reveals their assumption of habitual viewing, that is, that people watch TV habitually and that their exposure patterns varied little from day to day, week to week, or year to year. They routinely divided these continuous distributions of hours viewed into three categories: light viewing, moderate viewing, and heavy viewing.

Cultivation indicators were measured by presenting respondents with two choices of beliefs (one reflecting the television world and the other reflecting the real world) and asking them which of the two they believed to be more accurate. "For example, one cultivation question asks: 'During any given week, what are your chances of being involved in some kind of violence? About one in ten? About one in a hundred?'" (Gerbner, Gross, Jackson-Beeck, Jeffries-Fox, & Signorielli, 1978, p. 195). While one of these answers is closer to the television world figure and the other is closer to the real-world figure, neither answer is accurate. The providing of inaccurate answers was an operational decision that was motivated by their belief that the accurate answers were too extreme and would therefore look like trick questions (Shanahan & Morgan, 1999, pp. 53–54).

When computing the relationship between television exposure and cultivation indicators, they used two procedures to look for evidence of cultivation effect. One procedure was to compute the degree of relationship between viewing level and selection of an answer on the cultivation indicator (TV answer vs. real-world answer). Thus the larger the coefficient, the stronger the evidence for heavy viewers picking the TV world answer compared to the lighter viewers picking that answer. The other procedure was to calculate what they call a cultivation differential, which was the difference between the percentage of respondents in the heavy viewing group who selected the TV world answer compared to the percentage of respondents in the light viewing group who selected the TV world answer. Thus when the cultivation differential was positive, it indicated that a larger percentage of the heavy users compared to the light users had selected the TV world answer.

Stimulating Scholarly Attention

By the late 1970s, the cultivation system of explanation started attracting the attention of media effects scholars who essentially used the cultivation team's operational practices and ran their own tests of the theory (e.g., Christiansen, 1979; Fox & Philliber, 1978). From the 1970s until today, the cultivation system of explanation has been attracting the attention of media effects scholars, many of whom have published studies that they label as cultivation. "As of 2010, over 500 studies directly relevant to cultivation have been published—and more than 125 since 2000" (Morgan & Shanahan, 2010, p. 337). Also, several content analyses of the published literature in communication have identified cultivation as one of the most visible media effects theories (Bryant & Miron, 2004; Potter & Riddle, 2007).

Almost all of the published tests of cultivation theory generally follow a standard model based on the calculus laid out by Gerbner and his team. These studies use a survey method to generate data on three kinds of variables: media exposure, cultivation indicators, and control variables. Respondents are asked how many hours of media (almost always television) they have been exposed to in a typical week (or last week). Respondents are asked about their beliefs about things (e.g., the world is mean and violent) on an intensity scale or they are asked to estimate the occurrence of things (e.g., percentage of crimes that are violent, their chances of being a victim of a crime) by providing a number (or selecting from several multiple choice answers). Control variables are typically demographics (e.g., biological sex, educational level).

Extensions. As the number of tests of cultivation theory grew, there were examples of researchers who tested some extensions to the established operational practices, particularly with cultivation indicator measures. These studies appeared to accept Gerbner's original conceptual definition for a cultural indicator then sought to test alternative measures in order to fill in the gaps across the range of meaning laid out by that conceptual definition. One example of this is the development of cultivation indicator measures on additional topics. For example, these researchers added to the variety of cultural indicators by testing people's beliefs about mental illness (Diefenbach & West, 2007), beliefs about substance abuse (Minnebo & Eggermont, 2007), acceptance of homosexuality (Calzo & Ward, 2009), and beliefs about the environment (Holbert, Kwak, & Shah, 2003), to name a few of these extensions of topics.

Another line of research that expanded the operationalizations of cultivation indicators examined different types of measures of effects beyond beliefs, such as knowledge, attitudes, behaviors, and emotions. For example, Hawkins and Pingree (1980) tested different types of cultivation indicators to see if knowledge (where respondents were asked to provide estimates of the prevalence of occurrences such as crime) was related to beliefs. Hawkins and Pingree (1980) and others (Gerbner, Gross, Morgan, & Signorielli, 1986; Potter, 1991) found that the different types of measures were not related to each other very strongly. In reviewing this research, Shanahan and Morgan (1999) argued that when testing for cultivation indicators within the topic of violence, researchers should consider at least three types of measures—knowledge (perceptions of the amount of violence in society), beliefs (about one's likelihood of being victimized by violence), and emotion (fear of being victimized). Furthermore, they speculated that there are perhaps even more than three types of measures that would serve as valid operationalizations of cultivation indicator as originally conceptualized by Gerbner.

There has also been a pattern of some media effects scholars who essentially accept cultivation theory but who design tests to determine if another variable or two could increase cultivation's predictive power over and above that of using only TV viewing as the exposure variable. These tests have added variables such as perceived reality (Busselle, Ryabalova, & Wilson, 2004; Potter, 1986), transportation (Bilandzic & Busselle, 2008), and distance (Bilandzic, 2006; Hetsroni, Elpariach, Kapuza, & Tsfoni, 2007; Van den Bulck, 2003). Also, other researchers have tried to increase the explanatory power of cultivation by incorporating constructs and propositions from other theories, such as knowledge gap theory (Niederdeppe, Fowler, Goldstein, & Pribble, 2010), theory of reasoned action (Beullens, Roe,

& Van den Bulck, 2011; Nabi & Sullivan, 2001), spiral of silence (Shanahan, Scheufele, Yang, & Hizi, 2004), elaboration likelihood model (Schroeder, 2005; Williams, 2006), and mental models (Roskos-Ewoldsen, Davies, & Roskos-Ewoldsen, 2004).

Filling gaps. When we divide the cultivation literature into tests of claims for Gerbner's three components, we can see that the literature exhibits a concentration in cultivation analysis while institutional analysis has been ignored. As for institutional analysis, there is no evidence that Gerbner or his team published any research to test their claim that "the mass production and rapid distribution of messages create new symbolic environments that reflect the structure and functions of the institutions that transmit them" (Gerbner, 1970, p. 69).

While reviewers of the cultivation literature (Morgan, 2009; Morgan & Shanahan, 2010; Morgan et al., 2009; Shanahan & Morgan, 1999) continually acknowledge the importance of institutional analysis in the cultivation system of explanation, they rarely cite any research in this area, although there is a fairly well-developed literature on this very topic (for reviews of this literature, see Grossberg, Wartella, & Whitney, 1998; McQuail, 2005).

Empirical Validity

The pattern of findings from studies labeled as tests of the cultivation system of explanation shows that support for Gerbner's claims is null (institutional analysis), partial (message system analysis), and weak (cultivation analysis). Support for the existence of widespread meanings across the television landscape is partial, because almost all of the message system analysis research is concentrated on looking for patterns within the narrow sampling frame of TV entertainment programming, which has been further reduced to focus on mainstream channels and limited dayparts. Although there are message system analyses of news and informational programming (e.g., Lee & Niederdeppe, 2011; Romer, Jamieson, & Aday, 2003), the findings from these studies have not been integrated with findings from other types of programming in a complete enough fashion to support the claim that there are widespread meanings throughout the media.

As for cultivation analysis, the evidence that supports cultivation theory's explanation of television's influence on public beliefs has been persistently weak. This was pointed out by early critics of the theory (Hirsch, 1980; Hughes, 1980), and despite the huge growth in the literature since that time, the low ceiling of predictive power has not been raised. A meta-analysis of 5,799 separate findings derived from 97 studies/samples of tests of cultivation analysis reports that the average correlation across all those findings is .10 and that the average partial correlation is .09 (Shanahan & Morgan, 1999). This means television exposure predicts only about 1 % of the variation in cultivation indicators.

The empirical support of cultivation appears especially weak when we compare it to the level of support generated by other media effects theories. For example, agenda-setting theory is arguably the one media effects theory closest to cultivation in terms of its examination of patterns of meaning in media messages and the influence of those message patterns on large aggregates of people in the course of their everyday lives. Unlike cultivation theory, agenda-setting theory has been shown to have a relatively strong predictive power (r =.53) in a meta-analysis of its empirical literature (Wanta & Ghanem, 2007).

The strength of findings in the cultivation analysis literature also appears relatively weak when we compare them to the strength of findings determined by meta-analyses of other media effects such as the third-person effect (r = .500; Paul, Salwen, & Dupagne, 2000); inoculation effect (r =.430; Banas & Rains, 2010); hostile media effect (r =.296; Hansen & Hyunjung, 2011); effect of listening to popular music on mood and attitudes (r =.210; Timmerman et al., 2008); influence of sexually explicit materials on physiological and psychological reactions (r =.212 to .248; Allen et al., 2007); and engagement with media entertainment on knowledge, attitudes, and behaviors (r =.270; Tukachinsky & Tokunaga, 2013).

As for the topic of the effects of violence, which has been the most popular cultural indicator, cultivation analysis has been much weaker at predicting effects than have other systems of explanation. For example, Paik and Comstock (1994) conducted a meta-analysis of 217 studies examining the effect of exposure to television violence on antisocial behavior and report that the average effect size is r =.31. Also, Anderson et al. (2010) conducted a meta-analysis on 130 research reports that presented over 380 effect size estimates based on over 130,000 participants and found an average effect size of r = .217 on experiments testing the effect of playing violent video games on aggressive behavior. They also found an average effect size of r = .183 from cross-sectional surveys.

When researchers conduct tests to compare the explanatory power of cultivation with another media effects theory, they typically find cultivation to be the weaker explanation. For example, Diefenbach and West (2007) compared cultivation with the third-person effect and found the third-person effect to be a stronger explanation. Gross and Aday (2003) found that local news exposure accounted for an agenda-setting effect but did not cultivate fear of being a victim of crime. Martins and Harrison (2012) found that social identity theory was a stronger predictor of preadolescents' global self-esteem than was cultivation theory.

In summary, the empirical validity for the cultivation effect is weak. The literature that claims to test the cultivation effect contains studies that have not met the minimum requirements for such tests, particularly ignoring the essential foundation of a message system analysis. Also, the tests fail to show that everyone is effected by media exposure, nor that more than a small percentage of heavier viewers are more likely to exhibit cultivated beliefs compared to viewers at lower levels of exposure.

Theory Development

Conceptual Criticisms

There have been three primary conceptual criticisms of cultivation theory. These are the inadequate conceptualizations of meaning as well as the process of influence and the failure to reduce the scope of the theory when research shows lack of support for certain parts of the theory.

Meaning. The most essential concept in cultivation theory is meaning. In introducing cultivation theory, Gerbner argued that meanings (not just messages) were manufactured by media organizations; that these meanings were the product of the symbolic environments of all those media organizations; that these meanings were widespread across all kinds of messages regardless of channels of transmission; and that it was the widespread existence of these meanings that was the agent of cultivation, that is, these media-manufactured meanings were what shaped the beliefs of all people in the culture. However, Gerbner did not specify what these meanings were in his introduction of the theory; instead he left this task to researchers to identify those meanings and suggested that they use the social scientific method of content analysis to identify these meanings. His own research team continually used this method to identify meanings in media messages and published their yearly analysis over the next several decades.

Beyond his introduction of cultivation theory, Gerbner never elaborated his conception of meaning; however, his conceptualization of meaning can be inferred from examining his operational practices. When scholars have made such inferences, they typically criticize Gerbner's conceptualization for two problems (Hughes, 1980; Newcomb, 1978; Potter, 1993, 2014).

One of these criticisms of Gerbner's conception of meaning is that he seems to conceptualize meaning as arising from simple repetition of certain symbols rather than as arising from the contextual patterns of those symbols. This problem can be clearly illustrated with the way he uses the findings of his content analyses of violence on TV. From what we can see in how Gerbner and his team treated meaning in violence, they simply counted occurrences, then reasoned that people who were exposed to more occurrences of violence should be cultivated to believe that the world is a mean and violent place. But we know from the way violence is typically portrayed in the media, especially on television shows, that the bad guys are always caught and punished, either through death or incarceration. So it is likely that many people use the context of widespread punishment to infer a meaning that the world is safe and ordered because police are highly successful in solving crimes and removing violent offenders from society.

A second criticism of the way Gerbner seems to conceptualize meaning is that for him, meaning appears to be something that resides exclusively in the messages and that all people accept the same meaning as presented. Gerbner does not allow for people to be interpretive beings who can negotiate their own meanings for any of the messages to which they are exposed.

Process of influence. A second area of conceptual criticism is the lack of explanation about the process of influence. Early criticism focused on the need to include other variables in the system of explanation, at least as control variables (Hirsch, 1980; Hughes, 1980). These critics pointed out that when demographics were used as control variables, the strength of the cultivation relationship changed and this change indicates that public beliefs are traceable to a person's age, gender, and socioeconomic status as much as, if not more than, the amount of television viewing.

In a larger sense, this criticism about the theory's lack of attention to the process of influence is really a call for more explanation about the shape of the relationship between amount of media exposure and cultivated beliefs (Potter, 1993). Because cultivation is a long-term effect, we need to see the theory address the issues of thresholds, shapes of increases, and ceilings. That is, perhaps there is a threshold below which no cultivation is observed or a ceiling of time where the cultivation effect tops out.

Failure to reduce scope. As the tests of cultivation theory grew in number, it became clear that many of Gerbner's original claims were receiving no support, but Gerbner made no alterations to his claims in order to bring them in line with what researchers were finding. This failure to demonstrate openness stimulated criticism in two areas.

One of these areas was that Gerbner failed to reduce the scope of his claim that the media were cultivating everyone. Originally Gerbner had argued the media have the ability to shape "collective thought and action quickly, continuously, and pervasively across previous boundaries of time, space, and culture" (1969, p. 140). This is a very broad claim that included everyone. But tests of this claim repeatedly show that there are large numbers of people who show no evidence of cultivation. Much of the cultivation research, including that produced by Gerbner's own team, has shown the cultivation effect is not widespread, but that it shows up in only a small percentage of the population. When examining the extent of evidence for cultivation in typical cultivation analysis studies, sizable percentages of respondents—even in the heavy viewing groups—do not choose the TV world cultivation indicator. For example, Hetsroni and Tukachinsky (2006) found that only 13 % to 28 % of their respondents showed evidence of a cultivation effect depending on the topic.

Gerbner was aware of these persistently weak relationships and defended his system of explanation by saying that cultivation's effect was cumulative over time, which brings us to the second major problem. Gerbner's defense was shown to have been faulty, because there was no evidence that cultivation's influence was cumulative. To the contrary, the evidence suggested that the cultivation effect was *not* cumulative. In their meta-analysis, Shanahan and Morgan (1999) report that cultivation differentials are lower for older respondents than for younger ones. And longitudinal tests have either found no support (Morgan, 1982) or equivocal support (Morgan, 1987) for a cumulative influence. Although the findings of these two longitudinal studies challenge the validity of the cultivation explanation of media effects, cultivation researchers have let those findings stand unaltered for almost three decades by not conducting additional longitudinal studies while they continue to claim that the influence is cumulative.

Conceptual Alterations by Theoreticians

Gerbner never responded to criticism about widespread meanings. However, he did start using control variables in his designs but he never provided a rationale for the inclusion of particular controls, so this alteration appears to be more of an operational change that was not incorporated into the theory itself.

The one conceptual change that Gerbner did make to the theory was the introduction of two new constructs—mainstreaming and resonance. Gerbner, Gross, Morgan, and Signorielli (1980) explained "the 'mainstream' can be thought of as a relative commonality of outlooks that television tends to cultivate. By 'mainstreaming' we mean the sharing of that commonality among heavy viewers in those demographic groups whose light users hold divergent views" (p. 15). Mainstreaming is the blending process by which heavy TV viewers from disparate groups develop a common outlook on the world through constant exposure to the same images and labels on TV. Heavy television viewing may override individual differences and perspectives, creating more of an American (and increasingly global) "melting pot" of social, cultural, and political ideologies.

Resonance is characterized as a "double dose" of meaning that comes from both real-world experience and TV messages. To test for a resonance effect, researchers look for "a feature of the television world (that) has special salience for a group" (Gerbner et al., 1980, p. 23). For example, people who live in dangerous high-crime neighborhoods and watch a lot of television get a double dose of exposure to crime. Therefore, these people should exhibit a higher than average degree of cultivation—a resonance effect—from the television exposure because those TV exposures resonate with their real-world environment.

Conceptual Alterations by Researchers

There is a growing number of studies where scholars have rejected at least one of Gerbner's most fundamental claims and replaced them with their own claims. Thus these studies have moved outside the boundaries of cultivation theory as established by Gerbner, particularly in two ways. One of these boundary-crossing trends has been a move away from a macro-focus into a micro-focus and the second has been a move away from regarding the locus of meaning in the media messages toward regarding the locus of meaning in receivers.

Movement into micro. One of the core characteristics of cultivation theory is its macro-level focus. While Gerbner did not reject the value of micro-level research, he declared that it was outside the boundaries of his theory. In all his publications, he maintained this boundary, saying, "the comparison of responses of those who claim to prefer or view this and that type of programming (one particular genre), instead of measures of total viewing, is likely to yield confusing, contradictory, and misleading results" (Gerbner, 1990, p. 257). And in 2002, he wrote, "We do not minimize the importance of specific programs, selective attention and perception, specifically targeted communications, individual and group differences, and research on individual attitude and behavior change. But giving primary attention to those aspects and terms of traditional media effects research risks losing sight of what is most distinctive and significant about television as the common storyteller of our age" (Gerbner, Gross, Morgan, Signorielli, & Shanahan, 2002, p. 44).

Despite this clear boundary for cultivation analysis, many researchers have moved away from using total TV viewing as a predictor of cultivation indicators and moved toward testing more micro-measures of exposure. For example, some researchers argued that evidence for a belief in a mean and violent world should be more attributable to exposure to violent programming more than to total TV exposure, and their empirical tests generally confirmed this expectation as genre-level exposures (crime drama and news) were found to be stronger predictors of cultivation than total TV viewing exposure (Grabe & Drew, 2007; Hawkins & Pingree, 1980; Potter, 1988). Other researchers testing additional cultivation indicator topics also found that when they used more specific-level television exposure measures, they were able to predict respondents' beliefs better. These studies have tested exposure to make-over programs (Kubic & Chory, 2007; Nabi, 2009), romantic shows (Segrin & Nabi, 2002), medical dramas (Chory-Assad & Tamborini, 2003; Van den Bulck, 2002), and local news programming (Romer et al., 2003). Also, some studies claimed to test a cultivation effect from exposure to a single TV series such as Grey's Anatomy (Quick, 2009) or from playing one particular video game (Williams, 2006).

Reviewers of the cultivation literature seem to be conflicted about whether to include these studies as being cultivation or not (Morgan & Shanahan, 2010; Morgan, Shanahan, & Signorielli, 2014; Shanahan & Morgan, 1999). For example, Morgan and Shanahan (2010) raised the question about when "genre-specific effects should be called 'cultivation'" (p. 340) and answered the question with a caution that "such work can fragment the systemic aspects of the overall viewing experience, and observed relationships may reflect selective exposure more than cultivation" (p. 341). But they then went ahead and reported this literature anyway, labeling it "Genre-Specific Cultivation." And more recently they still claimed "The notion that media genre is a critical component in assessing the phenomenon of cultivation goes against one of the basic tenets or assumptions of cultivation" (Morgan et al., 2014, p. 491).

Another indicator of this shift from macro to micro is the growing number of studies that take a short-term focus on effects, such as studies that use an experiment to present participants carefully constructed message elements and collect outcome data immediately after exposure to those controlled treatments (e.g., Bilandzic & Busselle, 2008; Williams, 2006). Although Gerbner objected to experiments as providing adequate tests of cultivation, reviewers of this literature exhibit acceptance of findings of experiments along with findings from surveys as evidence of cultivation (Morgan & Shanahan, 2010; Morgan, Shanahan, & Signorielli, 2009; Morgan et al., 2014; Romer, Jamieson, Bleakley, & Jamieson, 2014; Shanahan & Morgan, 1999). For example, Morgan and Shanahan (2010) said, "Cultivation clearly construes messages as systems, which are by definition as macro as one can get. Some other approaches tend to reduce messages to components, especially if they can be easily manipulated in laboratory settings. Both of these conceptions survived quite nicely side-by-side through the decades. In an era of mass communication, macro level conceptions may seem to have the most explanatory power. In an era of mediated interpersonal communication and fragmented audiences, such macro level conceptions may seem less relevant" (p. 351).

Initially, the key characteristics of Gerbner's theory were that it focused attention at the macro-level of broad-scale institutional practices, widespread meaning, and long-term acculturation. It was naturalistic, that is, it did not manipulate exposures or messages but instead acknowledged individuals' typical patterns of media exposure in their everyday lives. And it took a systems approach by emphasizing the importance of tracing how the media's institutional practices shaped meanings in the mass production of messages that were then widely disseminated and thereby shaped public knowledge and beliefs over the long term.

Shift of meaning locus from messages to receivers. A second kind of boundary-crossing research has been a shift in the locus of meaning. In introducing cultivation, Gerbner placed the locus of meaning exclusively in the media messages and regarded research that examined how receivers interpreted meaning as being out of bounds for cultivation theory. He argued that he was not concerned with how "different individual and group selections and interpretations of messages take place." He continued, "Whether I accept its 'meaning' or not, like it or not, or agree or disagree is another problem. First I must attend to and grasp what it is about" (1969b, p. 125). Thus while Gerbner recognized that there were individual differences in interpretations of messages, cultivation was not concerned about those variations in interpretations; instead, cultivation focused on the dominant meanings that the media presented to the public. Thus, Gerbner regarded message system analysis as an essential antecedent to cultivation analysis; a clear understanding of the dominant meanings in media messages was an essential first step in the process of constructing cultivation indicator items. Gerbner argued, "Survey questioning used in cultivation analysis should reflect the over-arching content configurations embedded in television's message systems" and should not look for differences in individual interpretations across people (Gerbner, 1990, p. 257).

There is a growing literature labeled as cultivation that rejects Gerbner's perspective on meaning and instead regards the locus of meaning as residing in receivers (e.g., Bilandzic & Busselle, 2008; Busselle, 2003; Martins & Harrison, 2012; Nabi, 2009). Thus these researchers employ a reasoning process that moves away from what Gerbner laid out in his theory, which requires the conduct of message system analysis first to identify widespread meanings, then using these meanings to guide the construction of cultivation indicators. In contrast, this new line of "cultivation" research first constructs a variety of cultivation indicators, then tests which indicators are most strongly related to heavy TV viewing (usually of a genre rather than all TV viewing) then presents the stronger relationships as evidence for a cultivation effect of viewing TV. Furthermore, reviews of the cultivation literature (Morgan & Shanahan, 2010; Morgan et al., 2009, 2014) now acknowledge these studies as tests of cultivation without working through the implications of this type of research for cultivation theory.

Another indicator of this shift in locus of meaning within the "cultivation" literature is the growing number of studies that take a cognitive approach in examining how people go about remembering media messages and use those memories to construct their responses to cultivation indicator items (e.g., Shrum, 2004). In reviewing this literature Shanahan and Morgan (1999) cautioned, "we believe that to become sidetracked by the peculiarities of how individuals receive, process, interpret, remember, and act on messages can distract attention from the more central questions of cultivation research" (p. 172). However, they devoted an entire chapter to reviewing that particular literature.

There appears to be a trend toward this boundary-crossing research. To illustrate, a search of the Communication Abstracts database of scholarly publications from 2010 to 2014 using keywords of cultivation theory and its synonyms reveals 37 articles reporting empirical tests. Five of those are content analyses, and the remaining 32 are effects studies. Of these 32, a total of 13 do not provide tests of any of Gerbner's claims; instead they mention cultivation theory as a possible benefactor of their findings without linking those findings to a specific claim made in that theory. The remaining 19 publications position themselves as tests of cultivation theory in their introductions, review of literatures, and rationales. Of these 19, only 8 present a foundation for their cultivation indicators in a message system analysis (either where the authors provided the results of their own message system analysis or cited relevant findings from a content analysis), while the other 11 reason backward from respondents' selection of their answers on a cultivation indicator as being the meaning presented in the media. Also, of the 19 tests of cultivation, only 5 used a macro-measure of TV exposure, with the remaining 14 using only micro-level exposure measures (e.g., exposure to genres or particular TV programs). Thus of the 32 published articles referencing cultivation published in that 5-year period, only 3 stayed within the boundaries of cultivation theory by using both a macro-measure of exposure and a meaning analysis as a foundation for the cultivation indicators. Thus there is a growing number of published studies labeling themselves as cultivation research that reject one or more of the most central ideas in Gerbner's theory. This clearly indicates that many media effects researchers have a different conception of cultivation than that presented by Gerbner.

Methodological Criticisms

Critics have been harshest on cultivation theory for methodological features, especially in five areas (Hughes, 1980; Newcomb, 1978; Potter, 1993). These are the measurement of exposure, cultural indicators, meaning, time, and the use of statistical analysis.

Measurement of exposure. Television exposure was measured by asking respondents how many hours of television they watched on an average day last week. This reveals evidence for the assumption of habitual viewing, that is, that people watch TV habitually and that their exposure patterns vary little from day to day, week to week, and year to year. But the problem with this measurement is that it asks people to report on mundane habitual behaviors, and self-reports on these types of behaviors have not been found to exhibit much validity.

Although Gerbner had conceptualized exposure in a macro-long-term manner, he never factored into any of his analyses how many years his participants had been exposed to the media. When other researchers have factored in years of exposure in addition to how many hours of TV people watched last week, they found no evidence of a cumulative effect.

Measurement of cultural indicators. One of these areas of methodological criticism focuses on the way cultivation indicators are measured. Recall from above that cultivation indicators were typically measured by presenting respondents with two choices of beliefs (one reflecting the television world and the other reflecting the real world) and asking them which of the two they believed to be more accurate. "For example, one cultivation question asks: 'During any given week, what are your chances of being involved in some kind of violence? About one in ten? About one in a hundred?'" (Gerbner et al., 1978, p. 195). While one of these answers is closer to the television world figure and the other is closer to the real-world figure, neither answer is accurate. The providing of inaccurate answers was an operational decision that was motivated by their belief that the accurate answers were too extreme and would therefore look like trick questions (Shanahan & Morgan, 1999, pp. 53–54).

Measurement of meaning. A third methodological criticism was that Gerbner never provided guidance about how to measure the widespread meanings other than to tell researchers to use content analyses to count the occurrence of manifest elements (e.g., the presence of guns, blood, female characters). This led to cartoons with its stylized violence as being continually found to be the most violent area of television, while shows with fewer acts of violence depicted with a great deal of blood, gore, and suffering were regarded as much less violent than cartoons. The use of this "bean counting" type of approach to content analysis was criticized as failing to capture the meaning in the portrayals. These critics called for the consideration of contextual characteristics (i.e., humor, fantasy, the consequences of actions) when trying to assess meaning of media messages.

Measurement of time. Another criticism of cultivation theory has been its treatment of time (Potter, 1993). When Gerbner introduced his theory as a macro-system of explanation about media influence, it appeared that time was an important factor in acculturation, that is, the more exposure people had to media-generated meanings, the more likely they would be acculturated to incorporate those meanings as personal beliefs. But when Gerbner and his team designed their research studies, they exhibited a serious flaw in their operationalization of time. They conducted surveys that measured how many hours their respondents were exposed to TV on an average week, but they did not measure how many years of exposure their participants had. For example, heavy viewers of television were typically considered those people who watched television at least three hours per day or 21 hours per week. A person's age did not matter. Thus an 18-year-old who watched TV 3 hours per day was considered a heavy viewer while a person who was 65 who watched 2 hours per day was not. Thus the 18-year-old person was expected to show more evidence of being cultivated after her approximately 17,500 hours of viewing (16 years × 3 hours per day) compared to the 65-year-old person who had experienced about 46,000 hours of viewing (63 years × 2 hours per day).

Use of statistical analysis. A fifth methodological criticism focused on the simplistic nature of the analyses, which looked for correlations between exposure levels and cultivation indicators categorically. For example, the media exposure measure was typically truncated into levels (light, medium, and heavy). This meant that all people who said they watched TV on average at least 3 hours per day were all regarded as heavy viewers even though some of these people watched 21 hours per week (exactly 3 hours a day) while others might have watched 70 hours per week.

Current Challenges

It appears that scholars in the field of media effects have developed three conceptions of cultivation theory over time (Potter, 2014). One conception is that cultivation is a mass media theory that was introduced by Gerbner and maintained by him throughout the course of his life. A second conception arises from the pattern of operational practices used by researchers who have published what they presented as tests of various parts of Gerbner's system of explanation. And a third conception is exhibited by researchers who operate within a general socialization perspective and who largely ignore the conceptualizations of Gerbner as they explore a variety of ways that media exert their influence on individuals. This raises two important questions about the future of cultivation theory. One of these questions is: Who gets to say what alterations are made to cultivation theory? Gerbner is no longer alive and while the members of his team are still publishing reviews of the cultivation literature, none of them has seemed to take Gerbner's place as the controlling theoretician on cultivation; instead, they continue to publish descriptive reviews of the growing body of literature that purportedly tests the theory (Morgan, 2009, 2012; Morgan & Shanahan, 2010; Morgan et al., 2009) without making any alterations to the original theory even when the findings from the research do not support the theory's claims.

However, there are dozens of other scholars who have each published more than one test of cultivation and appear to be extending the theory, which leads us to the second question: How much can the original ideas of cultivation be altered before we must regard the newly evolving configuration as something substantially different to a degree that it makes no sense to continue referring to it as cultivation theory?

Regardless of who steps up to take over for Gerbner as the scholarly force behind cultivation, the theory is facing some serious challenges that have been neglected for decades and now have reached a critical point mainly because of recent changes in the phenomenon of media. The most serious of these challenges is demonstrating that there are widespread meanings throughout the media. This is a central tenet of cultivation theory, and if this assertion cannot be accepted then it makes no sense to claim that the amount of exposure to the media explains the degree to which individuals have acquired their beliefs through cultivation. However, not only has this claim never received sufficient support from empirical testing, Gerbner and his team never demonstrated a willingness to test it. While there are many studies that have examined content in mainstream commercial television, there are a few studies that have looked at other kinds of television content such as news, informational programming, and especially advertising. This omission is especially glaring given Gerbner's argument that television has such a strong commercial interest so that we should expect those commercial values to show up strongest and most consistently in the great amount of advertising messages they present. Despite this lack of an adequate research basis, Gerbner et al. (2002) continued to make claims that television's "drama, commercials, news, and other programs bring a relatively coherent system of images and messages into every home" (p. 44). And this claim is still being made today that multinational media conglomerates "dominate the cultural symbolic environment with stable and consistent messages about life and society . . . despite the emergence of so many specialized new channels and so many different types of programs that are often targeted to smaller and smaller audiences" (Morgan et al., 2014, p. 481).

A second challenge to the viability of cultivation theory is the need to synthesize the findings across studies in the existing message system analysis literature. Although there are a number of reviews of this literature (Morgan, 2009; Morgan & Shanahan, 2010; Morgan et al., 2009, 2014; Romer et al., 2014; Shanahan & Morgan, 1999), these reviews are largely descriptive inventories of a growing list of topics, rather than a careful sorting through the findings to identify the meanings that have been found to have limited scope (and where those limits are) and the meanings that have been found consistently across all types of messages and throughout all media. This lack of synthesis work is especially troubling because Gerbner himself argued for the importance of synthesizing findings across content analyses when he criticized the literature of media content analysis at the time he introduced cultivation as being "piecemeal, sporadic, uncoordinated, and rarely comparable over time and across cultures" (1973, p. 557). Now more than four decades later, there is a much larger literature documenting patterns of content in the media; however, this literature is still fragmented because it continues to lack the synthesis needed to coordinate findings across genres, dayparts, channels, media, and cultures. Without such a synthesis, there is no basis to make a claim that meanings are widespread across media. While it is not a problem for a theory to present such a claim as an invitation for researchers to test it, it does become a problem when decades of research fail to fill in the gaps to an extent that we can believe that this claim has been adequately tested and found to have consistent support to establish its credibility.

It has now become difficult to identify what cultivation theory is because the conceptualization presented by Gerbner in his introduction publications differs in many important ways from the conceptualization that arises from his long-term program of research he designed to test his claims. In his introductions he consistently presents cultivation theory as a macro-effect that continuously alters the thinking and behavior of the entire population due to institutional practices of media businesses that then shape the content they produce. There are certain meanings embedded in media messages that are widespread across them all regardless of medium or genre and its the constant repetition of these same meanings that alter the way people think and behave. In contrast, his long-term program of research focuses on beliefs, not cognitive processes in thinking and not behavior. Also, his research is less concerned with testing the claim of cultivation being pervasive and more concerned with differences in beliefs at different levels of media exposure.

Conclusions

Cultivation theory has been popular among media effects researchers ever since it was introduced in the late 1960s. However, over time most of the research that claims to test cultivation shows substantial rejections of some of the key ideas that Gerbner used as foundations for cultivation. While the theory itself has changed very little since it was introduced, the research that purports to test the theory has changed quite a bit. Now tests of cultivation theory are really explorations into whether the media play a role as a more general process of socializing people. There is almost no interest in examining whether there are widespread meanings across all media or even within one medium. Nor has there been any interest in examining how the media function as an institution or how the media shape messages.

Compared to what was introduced as cultivation theory in the late 1960s, the current form of the theory has lost much of its original scope as researchers and subsequent cultivation theoreticians have ignored the institutional and message parts of the theory while focusing solely on the cultivation indicator part, and that part has lost its general claim and is now examined primarily within small sets of content types. Also, the large literature of empirical tests have failed to show more than a very weak relationship between amount of exposure and cultivated beliefs. Given the lack of openness of the theory to test its main claims adequately, its resistance to elaborate its system of explanation over time, and the changes in the phenomenon it tries to explain, it appears that it has lost its relevance.

Key Sources

Theory Introduction

Gerbner, G. (1967). An institutional approach to mass communications research. In L. Thayer (Ed.), *Communication theory and research: Proceedings of the first international symposium* (pp. 429–445). Springfield, IL: Charles C. Thomas Publisher.

Gerbner, G. (1969a). Toward 'cultural indicators': The analysis of mass mediated public message systems. In G. Gerbner, O. Holsti, K. Krippendorff, W. J. Paisley, & P. J. Stone (Eds.), *The analysis of communication content: Developments in scientific theories and computer techniques* (pp. 123–132). New York, NY: John Wiley & Sons.

Gerbner, G. (1969b). Toward 'cultural indicators': The analysis of mass mediated public message systems. *AV Communication Review, 17*(2), 137–148.

Foundational literature

Bell, D. (1961). *The end of ideology.* New York, NY: Collier Books.

Berger, P., & Luckmann, T. (1967). *The social construction of reality.* Garden City, NJ: Anchor.

Blumer, J. G. (1964). British television – the outlines of a research strategy. *The British Journal of Sociology, 15*(3), 223–233.

Bramson, L. (1961). *The political context of sociology.* Princeton, NJ: Princeton University Press.

Gramsci, A. (1948). *Selections from the prison notebooks.* New York, NY: International Publishers.

Kornhauser, W. (1959). *The politics of mass society*. New York, NY: Free Press.

Lippmann, W. (1922). *Public opinion*. London: Transaction.

Marcuse, H. (1964). *One-dimensional man*. London: Routledge.

Mead, G. H. (1934). *Mind, self and society*. Chicago: University of Chicago Press.

Merton, R. K. (1957). *Social theory and social structure*. Glencoe, IL: Free Press.

Mills, C. W. (1951). *White collar*. New York, NY: Oxford University Press.

Mills, C. W. (1956). *The power elite*. New York, NY: Oxford University Press.

Osgood, C. E., Suci, G. J., & Tannenbaum, P. H. (1957). *The measurement of meaning*. Urbana, IL: University of Illinois Press.

Westley, B., & MacLean, M. (1957). A conceptual model for mass communication research. *Journalism Quarterly, 34*, 31–38.

Alterations/elaborations in theory

Gerbner, G., Gross, L., Morgan, M., & Signorielli, N. (1980). The mainstreaming of America: Violence profile no. 11. *Journal of Communication, 30*(3), 10–29. doi:10.1111/j.1460-2466.1980.tb01987.x.

Criticisms

Doob, A., & Macdonald, G. (1979). Television viewing and fear of victimization: Is the relationship causal? *Journal of Personality and Social Psychology, 37*, 170–179. doi: 10.1037/0022-3514.37.2.170.

Gerbner, G., Gross, L., Morgan, M., & Signorielli, N. (1981). A curious journey into the scary world of Paul Hirsch. *Communication Research, 8*, 39–72.Hirsch, P. (1980). The "scary world" of the non viewer and other anomalies: A reanalysis of Gerbner et al.'s finding of cultivation analysis. *Communication Research, 7*, 403–456. doi:10.1177/009365028000700401.

Hirsch, P. (1981a). On not learning from one's own mistakes: A reanalysis of Gerbner et al.'s findings on cultivation analysis. Part II. *Communication Research, 8*, 3–37.

Hirsch, P. (1981b). Distinguishing good speculation from bad theory: Rejoinder to Gerbner et al. *Communication Research, 8*, 73–95.

Hughes, M. (1980). The fruits of cultivation analysis: A reexamination of some effects of television watching. *Public Opinion Quarterly, 44*, 287–302.

Newcomb, H. (1978). Assessing the violence profile of Gerbner and Gross: A humanistic critique and suggestions. *Communication Research, 5*, 264–282.

Potter, W. J. (1993). Cultivation theory and research: A conceptual critique. *Human Communication Research, 19*, 564–601.

Potter, W. J. (1994). Cultivation theory and research: A methodological critique *Journalism Monographs*. Columbia, SC: Association for Education in Journalism.

Potter, W. J. (2014). A critical analysis of cultivation theory. *Journal of Communication, 64*(6), 1015–1036.

Wober, J. M. (1978). Televised violence and paranoid perception: The view from Great Britain. *Public Opinion Quarterly, 42*, 315–321.

Zillmann, D., & Wakshlag, J. (1985). Fear of victimization and the appeal of crime drama. In D. Zillmann & J. Bryant (Eds.), *Selective exposure to communication* (pp. 141–156). Hillsdale, NJ: Erlbaum.

Reviews

Gerbner, G. (1990). Epilogue: Advancing on the path of righteousness (maybe). In N. Signorielli & M. Morgan (Eds.), *Cultivation analysis: New directions in media effects research* (pp. 249–262). Newbury Park, CA: Sage.

Gerbner, G. (1999). What do we know? In J. Shanahan & M. Morgan (Eds.), *Television and its viewers: Cultivation theory and research* (pp. ix–xiii). Cambridge: Cambridge University Press.

Gerbner, G., Gross, L., Morgan, M., & Signorielli, N. (1986). Living with television: The dynamics of the cultivation process. In J. Bryant & D. Zillmann (Eds.), *Perspectives on media effects* (pp. 17–40). Hillsdale, NJ: Erlbaum.

Gerbner, G., Gross, L., Morgan, M., & Signorielli, N. (1994). Growing up with television: The cultivation perspective. In J. Bryant & D. Zillmann (Eds.), *Media effects: Advances in theory and research* (pp. 17–48). Hillsdale, NJ: Erlbaum.

Gerbner, G., Gross, L., Morgan, M., Signorielli, N., & Shanahan, J. (2002). Growing up with television: Cultivation processes. In J. Bryant & D. Zillmann (Eds.), *Media effects: Advances in theory and research* (2nd ed., pp. 43–67). Mahwah, NJ: Erlbaum.

Morgan, M. (2009). Cultivation analysis and media effects. In R. L. Nabi & M. O. Oliver (Eds.), *The Sage handbook of media processes and effects* (pp. 69–82). Los Angeles, CA: Sage.

Morgan, M. (2012). *George Gerbner: A critical introduction to media and communication theory.* New York, NY: Peter Lang.

Morgan, M., & Shanahan, J. (2010). The state of cultivation. *Journal of Broadcasting & Electronic Media, 54*, 337–355.

Morgan, M., Shanahan, J., & Signorielli, N. (2009). Growing up with television: Cultivation processes. In J. Bryant & M. B. Oliver (Eds.), *Media effects: Advances in theory and research* (3rd ed., pp. 34–49). New York, NY: Routledge.

Morgan, M., & Signorielli, N. (1990). Cultivation analysis: Conceptualization and methodology. In N. Signorielli & M. Morgan (Eds.), *Cultivation analysis: New directions in media effects research* (pp. 13–34). Newbury Park, CA: Sage.

Shanahan, J., & Morgan, M. (1999). Television and its viewers: Cultivation theory and research. Cambridge: Cambridge University Press.

Signorielli, N., & M. Morgan (Eds.). (1990). *Cultivation analysis: New directions in media effects research.* Newbury Park, CA: Sage.

> **Current Description of Cultivation Theory**
> Morgan, M., Shanahan, J., & Signorielli, N. (2014). Cultivation theory in the twenty-first century. In R. S. Fortner & P. M. Fackler (Eds.), *The handbook of media and mass communication theory* (pp. 480–497).Walden, MA: John Wiley & Sons.

References

Allen, M., Emmers-Sommer, T. M., D'Alessio, D., Timmerman, L., Hanzal, A., Korus, J. (2007). The connection between the physiological and psychological reactions to sexually explicit materials: A literature summary using meta-analysis. *Communication Monographs, 74*(4), 541–560.

Anderson, C. A., Shibuya, A., Ihori, N., Swing, E. L., Bushman, B. J., Sakamoto, A., … Saleem, M. (2010). Violent video game effects on aggression, empathy, and prosocial behavior in Eastern and Western countries: A meta-analytic review, *Psychological Bulletin, 136*(2), 151–173.

Banas, J. A., & Rains, S. A. (2010). A meta-analysis of research on inoculation theory. *Communication Monographs, 77*(3), 281–311.

Bell, D. (1961). *The end of ideology.* New York, NY: Collier Books.

Berger, P., & Luckmann, T. (1967). *The social construction of reality.* Garden City, NJ: Anchor.

Beullens, K., Roe, K., & Van den Bulck, J. (2011). The impact of adolescents' news and action movie viewing on risky driving behavior: A longitudinal study. *Human Communication Research, 37*, 488–508. doi:10.1111/j.1468-2958.2011.01412.x

Bilandzic, H. (2006). The perception of distance in the cultivation process: A theoretical consideration of the relationship between television content, processing experience, and perceived distance. *Communication Theory, 16*, 333–355. doi:10.1111/j.1468-2885.2006.00273.x

Bilandzic, H., & Busselle, R. W. (2008). Transportation and transportability in the cultivation of genre-consistent attitudes and estimates. *Journal of Communication, 58*, 508–529. doi:10.1111/j.1460-2466.2008.00397.x

Blumer, J. G. (1964). British television – The outlines of a research strategy. *The British Journal of Sociology, 15*(3), 223–233.

Bramson, L. (1961). *The political context of sociology.* Princeton, NJ: Princeton University Press.

Bryant, J., & Miron, D. (2004). Theory and research in mass communication. *Journal of Communication, 54*, 662–704. doi:10.1111/j.1460-2466.2004.tb02650.x

Busselle, R. W. (2003). Television exposure, parents' precautionary warnings, and young adults' perceptions of crime. *Communication Research, 30*, 530–556.

Busselle, R. W., Ryabalova, A., & Wilson, B. (2004). Ruining a good story; Cultivation, perceived realism and narrative. *Communications: The European Journal of Communication Research, 29*(3), 365–378.

Calzo, J., & Ward, L. (2009). Media exposure and viewers' attitudes toward homosexuality: Evidence for mainstreaming or resonance? *Journal of Broadcasting & Electronic Media*, *53*(3), 365–378.

Chory-Assad, R. M., & Tamborini, R. (2003). Television exposure and the public's perceptions of physicians. *Journal of Broadcasting & Electronic Media*, *47*, 197–215. doi:10.1207/s15506878jobem4702_3

Christiansen, J. B. (1979). Television role models and adolescent occupational goals. *Human Communication Review*, *5*(4), 335–337.

Diefenbach, D., & West, M. (2007). Television and attitudes toward mental health issues: Cultivation analysis and third person effect. *Journal of Community Psychology*, *35*, 181–195. doi:10.1002/jcop.20142

Fox, W. S., & Philliber, W. W. (1978). Television viewing and the perception of affluence. *The Sociological Quarterly*, *19*, 103–112.

Gerbner, G. (1967). An institutional approach to mass communications research. In L. Thayer (Ed.), *Communication theory and research: Proceedings of the first international symposium* (pp. 429–445). Springfield, IL: Charles C. Thomas Publisher.

Gerbner, G. (1969a). Toward 'cultural indicators': The analysis of mass mediated public message systems. In G. Gerbner, O. Holsti, K. Krippendorff, W. J. Paisley, & P. J. Stone (Eds.), *The analysis of communication content: Developments in scientific theories and computer techniques* (pp. 123–132). New York, NY: John Wiley & Sons.

Gerbner, G. (1969b). Toward 'cultural indicators': The analysis of mass mediated public message systems. *AV Communication Review*, *17*(2), 137–148.

Gerbner, G. (1970). Cultural indicators: The case of violence in television drama. *The Annals of the American Academy of Political and Social Science*, *388*, 69–81.

Gerbner, G. (1973). Cultural indicators: The third voice. In G. Gerbner, L. P. Gross, & W. H. Melody (Eds.), *Communication technology and social policy* (pp. 555–573), New York, NY: John Wiley & Sons.

Gerbner, G. (1990). Epilogue: Advancing on the path of righteousness (maybe). In N. Signorielli & M. Morgan (Eds.), *Cultivation analysis: New directions in media effects research* (pp. 249–262). Newbury Park, CA: Sage.

Gerbner, G., Gross, L., Eleey, M. F., Jackson-Beeck, M., Jeffries-Fox, S., & Signorielli, N. (1977). TV violence profile no. 8: The highlights. *Journal of Communication*, *27*(2), 171–180. doi:10.1111/j.1460-2466.1977.tb01845.x

Gerbner, G., Gross, L., Jackson-Beeck, M., Jeffries-Fox, S., & Signorielli, N. (1978). Cultural indicators: Violence profile no. 9. *Journal of Communication*, *28*(3), 176–207. doi:10.1111/j.1460-2466.1978.tb01646.x

Gerbner, G., Gross, L., Morgan, M., & Signorielli, N. (1980). The main streaming of America: Violence profile no. 11. *Journal of Communication*, *30*(3), 10–29. doi:10.1111/j.1460-2466.1980.tb01987.x.

Gerbner, G., Gross, L., Morgan, M., & Signorielli, N. (1986). Living with television: The dynamics of the cultivation process. In J. Bryant & D. Zillmann (Eds.), *Perspectives on media effects* (pp. 17–40). Hillsdale, NJ: Erlbaum.

Gerbner, G., Gross, L., Morgan, M., Signorielli, N., & Shanahan, J. (2002). Growing up with television: Cultivation processes. In J. Bryant & D. Zillmann (Eds.), *Media effects: Advances in theory and research* (2nd ed., pp. 43–67). Mahwah, NJ: Erlbaum.

Grabe, M.E., & Drew, D. (2007). Crime cultivation: Comparisons across media genres and channels. *Journal of Broadcasting & Electronic Media, 51*, 147–171. doi:10.1080/08838150701308143

Gramsci, A. (1948). *Selections from the prison notebooks.* New York, NY: International Publishers.

Gross, K., & Aday, S. (2003). The scary world in your living room and neighborhood: Using local broadcast news, neighborhood crime rates, and personal experience to test agenda setting and cultivation. *Journal of Communication, 53*, 411–426. doi:10.1111/j.1460-2466.2003. tb02599

Grossberg, L., Wartella, E., & Whitney, D. C. (1998). *Media Making: Mass media in a popular culture.* Thousand Oaks, CA: Sage.

Hansen, G. J., & Hyunjung, K. (2011) Is the media biased against me? A meta-analysis of the hostile media effect research. *Communication Research Reports, 28*(2), 169–179. doi:10.108 0/08824096.2011.565280

Hawkins, R., & Pingree, S. (1980). Some processes in the cultivation effect. *Communication Research, 7*, 193–226. doi:10.1177/009365028000700203

Hetsroni, A., Elpariach, H., Kapuza, R., & Tsfoni, B. (2007). Geographical proximity, cultural imperialism, and the cultivation effect. *Communication Monographs, 74*(2), 181–199.

Hetsroni, A., & Tukachinsky, R. H. (2006). Television-world estimates, real-world estimates, and television viewing: A new scheme for cultivation. *Journal of Communication, 56*, 133–156. doi:10.1111/j.1460-2466.2006.00007.x

Hirsch, P. (1980). The "scary world" of the non viewer and other anomalies: A reanalysis of Gerbner et al.'s finding of cultivation analysis. *Communication Research, 7*, 403–456. doi:10.1177/009365028000700401

Holbert, R. L., Kwak, N., & Shah, D. (2003). Environmental concern, patterns of television viewing, and pro-environmental behaviors: Integrating modes of media consumption and effects. *Journal of Broadcasting & Electronic Media, 47*(2), 177–196.

Hughes, M. (1980). The fruits of cultivation analysis: A reexamination of some effects of television watching. *Public Opinion Quarterly, 44*, 287–302.

Kornhauser, W. (1959). *The politics of mass society.* New York, NY: Free Press.

Kubic, K. N., & Chory, R. M. (2007). Exposure to television makeover programs and perceptions of self. *Communication Research Reports, 24*(4), 283–291.

Lee, C. J., & Niederdeppe, J. (2011). Genre-specific cultivation effects. *Communication Research, 38*(6), 731–753.

Lippmann, W. (1922). *Public opinion.* London: Transaction.

Marcuse, H. (1964). *One-dimensional man.* London: Routledge.

Martins, N., & Harrison, K. (2012). Racial and gender differences in the relationship between children's television use and self-Esteem: A longitudinal panel study. *Communication Research, 39*(3), 338–357. doi:10.1177/0093650211401376

McQuail, D. (2005). *Mass communication theory* (5th ed.). Thousand Oaks, CA: Sage.

Mead, G. H. (1934). *Mind, self and society.* Chicago: University of Chicago Press.

Mills, C. W. (1951). *White collar.* New York, NY: Oxford University Press.

Mills, C. W. (1956). *The power elite.* New York, NY: Oxford University Press.

Minnebo, J., & Eggermont, S. (2007). Watching the young use illicit drugs: Direct experience, exposure to television and the stereotyping of adolescents' substance use. *Young, 15*(2), 129–144.

Morgan, M. (1982). Television and adolescents' sex-role stereotypes: A longitudinal study. *Journal of Personality and Social Psychology, 43,* 947–955. doi:10.1037/0022-3514.43.5.947

Morgan, M. (1987). Television, sex-role attitudes and sex-role behavior. *Journal of Early Adolescence, 7,* 269–282.

Morgan, M. (2009). Cultivation analysis and media effects. In R. L. Nabi & M. O. Oliver (Eds.), *The Sage handbook of media processes and effects* (pp. 69–82). Los Angeles, CA: Sage.

Morgan, M. (2012). *George Gerbner: A critical introduction to media and communication theory.* New York, NY: Peter Lang.

Morgan, M., & Shanahan, J. (2010). The state of cultivation. *Journal of Broadcasting & Electronic Media, 54,* 337–355.

Morgan, M., Shanahan, J., & Signorielli, N. (2009). Growing up with television: Cultivation processes. In J. Bryant & M. B. Oliver (Eds.), *Media effects: Advances in theory and research* (3rd ed., pp. 34–49). New York, NY: Routledge.

Morgan, M., Shanahan, J., & Signorielli, N. (2014). Cultivation theory in the twenty-first century. In R. S. Fortner & P. M. Fackler (Eds.), *The handbook of media and mass communication theory* (pp. 480–497). Walden, MA: John Wiley & Sons.

Nabi, R. L. (2009). Cosmetic surgery makeover programs and intentions to undergo cosmetic enhancements: A consideration of three models of media effects. *Human Communication Research, 35,* 1–27. doi:10.1111/j.1468-2958.2008.01336.x

Nabi, R. L., & Sullivan, J. L. (2001). Does television viewing relate to engagement in protective action against crime?: A cultivation analysis from a theory of reasoned action perspective. *Communication Research 28*(6), 802–825. doi:10.1177/009365001028006004

Newcomb, H. (1978). Assessing the violence profile of Gerbner and Gross: A humanistic critique and suggestions. *Communication Research, 5,* 264–282.

Niederdeppe, J., Fowler, E. F., Goldstein, K., & Pribble, J. (2010). Does local television news coverage cultivate fatalistic beliefs about cancer prevention? *Journal of Communication, 60,* 230–253. doi:10.1111/j.1460-2466.2009.01474.x

Osgood, C. E., Suci, G. J., & Tannenbaum, P. H. (1957). *The measurement of meaning.* Urbana, IL: University of Illinois Press.

Paik H., & Comstock G. (1994). The effects of television violence on antisocial behavior: A meta-analysis. *Communication Research, 21*(4), 516–546. doi:10.1177/009365094021004004

Paul, B., Salwen, M. B., & Dupagne, M. (2000). The third-person effect: A meta-analysis of the perceptual hypothesis. *Mass Communication & Society, 3*(1), 57–85. doi:10.1207/S15327825MCS0301_04

Potter, W. J. (1986). Perceived reality and the cultivation hypothesis. *Journal of Broadcasting & Electronic Media, 30,* 159–174.

Potter, W. J. (1988). Three strategies for elaborating the cultivation hypothesis. *Journalism Quarterly, 65,* 930–939.

Potter, W. J. (1991). Examining cultivation from a psychological perspective: Component sub-processes, *Communication Research, 18,* 77–102. Retrieved from http://search.proquest.com/docview/617935812?accountid=14522

Potter, W. J. (1993). Cultivation theory and research: A conceptual critique. *Human Communication Research, 19,* 564–601.

Potter, W. J. (2014). A critical analysis of cultivation theory. *Journal of Communication, 64*(6), 1015–1036.

Potter, W. J., & Riddle K. (2007). A content analysis of the media effects literature. *Journalism & Mass Communication Quarterly, 84,* 90–104. doi:10.1177/107769900708400107

Quick, B. (2009). The effects of viewing *Grey's Anatomy* on perceptions of doctors and patient satisfaction. *Journal of Broadcasting & Electronic Media, 53,* 38–55. doi:10.1080/08838150802643563

Romer, D., Jamieson, K. H., & Aday, S. (2003). Television news and the cultivation of fear of crime. *Journal of Communication, 53,* 88–104. doi:10.1111/j.1460-2466.2003.tb03007.x

Romer, D., Jamieseon, P., Bleakley, A., & Jamieson, K. H. (2014). Cultivation theory: Its history, current status, and future directions. In R. S. Fortner & P. M. Fackler (Eds.), *The handbook of media and mass communication theory* (pp. 115–136). Walden, MA: John Wiley & Sons.

Roskos-Ewoldsen, B., Davies, J., & Roskos-Ewoldsen, D. R. (2004). Implications of the mental models approach for cultivation theory. *Communication: The European Journal of Communication Research 29*(3), 345–363.

Schroeder, L. M. (2005). Cultivation and the elaboration likelihood model: A test of the learning and construction and availability heuristic models. *Communication Studies, 56*(3), 227–242. doi:10.1080/10510970500181215

Segrin, C. & Nabi, R. L. (2002). Does television viewing cultivate unrealistic expectations about marriage? *Journal of Communication, 52,* 247–263. doi:10.1111/j.1460-2466.2002.tb02543.x

Shanahan, J., & Morgan, M. (1999). Television and its viewers: Cultivation theory and research. Cambridge: Cambridge University Press.

Shanahan, J., Scheufele, D., Yang, F., & Hizi, S. (2004). Cultivation and spiral of silence effects: The case of smoking. *Mass Communication & Society, 7*(4), 413–428.

Shrum, L. J. (2004). The cognitive processes underlying cultivation effects are a function of whether the judgments are on-line or memory-based. *Communications: The European Journal of Communication Research, 29*(3), 327–344.

Timmerman, L. M., Allen, M., Jorgensen, J., Herrett-Skjellum, J., Kramer, M. R., Ryan, D. J. (2008). A review and meta-analysis examining the relationship of music content with sex, race, priming, and attitudes. *Communication Quarterly, 56*(3), 303–324.

Tukachinsky, R., & Tokunaga, R. S. (2013). The effects of engagement with entertainment. *Communication Yearbook, 37,* 287–321.

Van den Bulck, J. (2002). The impact of television fiction on public expectations of survival following inhospital cardiopulmonary resuscitation by medical professionals. *European Journal of Emergency Medicine, 9*(4), 325–329.

Van den Bulck, J. (2003). Is the mainstreaming effect of cultivation an artifact of regression to the mean? *Journal of Broadcasting & Electronic Media, 47*(2), 289–295. doi:http://dx.doi.org/10.1207/s15506878jobem4702_8

Wanta, W., & Ghanem. S. (2007) Effects of agenda setting. In R. W. Preiss, B. M. Gayle, N. Burrell, & J. Bryant (Eds.), *Mass media effects research: Advances through meta-analysis* (pp. 37–51). Mahwah, NJ: Erlbaum.

Williams, D. (2006). Virtual cultivation: Online worlds, offline perceptions. *Journal of Communication, 56,* 69–87. doi:10.1111/j.1460-2466.2006.00004.x

CHAPTER FIVE

Agenda-Setting Theory

Agenda-setting theory focuses its system of explanation on the relationship between patterns in news coverage and the public's beliefs about what is currently most important in society. The theory claims that the media agenda influences the public agenda. The media agenda is reflected by what is emphasized most in news coverage. The public agenda is reflected by what issues people think are the most important ones in society at a given time. Thus the public's agenda is shaped by the media agenda as people come to believe that the issues most emphasized in news coverage are the most important issues for them to think about.

Original Conceptualization of Agenda-Setting Theory

Introduction of the Theory

Maxwell McCombs and Donald Shaw introduced agenda-setting theory as an explanation for their findings from a research project that they called the "Chapel Hill study," which used both a survey and a content analysis of media coverage of the 1968 presidential campaign. In the survey part of their research project, McCombs and Shaw (1972) asked 100 uncommitted voters in Chapel Hill, North Carolina, a set of questions, such as "What are you most concerned about these days?" They also analyzed the contents of political news coverage presented by nine media outlets that included five newspapers (four local newspapers and *The New York Times*), two news magazines (*Time* and *Newsweek*) and two broadcast networks (NBC and CBS evening news). In their analysis of data, they compared patterns of news coverage with patterns of public opinion about what the public regarded as the major issues in the 1968 presidential campaign.

The authors said they originally designed their Chapel Hill study to test "selective exposure," which was a popular theory at the time when scholars operated from a perspective that the media had very limited and weak effects largely because people were highly selective in their exposure to media messages. The researchers reasoned that if selective exposure was a viable explanation of differences in public opinion, then there should be differences in what people believed to be the most important issues and that those differences in belief should follow party lines. That is, people who identified with a particular political party should believe what their party told them were the most important issues of the day, and this belief would be reinforced during campaigns as the party faithful selectively exposed themselves to only those messages that confirmed their existing beliefs. Because the different political parties focused on different issues, McCombs and Shaw reasoned that there should be differences in belief about what the public thought were the most important issues and that those differences should follow party lines.

McCombs and Shaw (1972), however, did not find a pattern supporting the selective exposure explanation. Instead, they found that there was a high degree of agreement about which issues were most important across all members of the public regardless of political affiliations. They also found that these widespread public beliefs about which issues were most important (the public's agenda) matched media coverage of issues (the media agenda) rather than what the political parties regarded as most important (political party agendas). Furthermore, this association between the public agenda and the media agenda—as indicated by which topics were given the most space, time, and prominence in the news media—was very strong (r = .90). They concluded their article with the argument that the media create a consensus among all members of the public concerning which issues are most important in a political campaign.

Conceptual Foundation

In explaining their unexpected finding, McCombs and Shaw (1972) drew from the ideas of Lippmann (1922), Cohen (1963), and Lang and Lang (1966). Fifty years earlier, Lippmann (1922) had published a book called *Public Opinion* in which he laid out a detailed argument about how the news media influence people. Lippmann reasoned that most people had very limited contact with the actual workings of the political system but that they still had a lot of knowledge about political affairs from news coverage. Thus the media were powerful because they connected people to the events in the world that people could not experience directly. The media put images in the minds of the public about those events. Although he did not use the term "agenda setting," Lippmann was putting forth an agenda-setting-like explanation. In his first chapter "The World Outside and the Pictures in Our Heads," Lippmann reasoned that the media provide people with windows to the vast world beyond their direct experience, and in so doing, the media create cognitive maps of that world. Furthermore, he claimed that public opinion is a response to the media-constructed world rather than to the actual world.

Building on the ideas of Lippmann, Bernard Cohen (1963) claimed that the press "may not be successful much of the time in telling people what to think, but it is stunningly successful in telling its readers what to think about." Cohen explained that the "world will look different to different people, depending on the map that is drawn for them by writers, editors, and publishers of the paper they read" (Cohen, 1963, p. 13).

Another set of foundational ideas that McCombs and Shaw used came from Lang and Lang (1966) who argued that "The mass media force attention to certain issues. They build up public images of political figures. They are constantly presenting objects suggesting what individuals in the mass should think about, know about, have feelings about" (p. 468).

In reworking the ideas of Lippmann, Cohen, and the Langs to explain their empirical findings, McCombs and Shaw claimed that the media agenda exerted a powerful one-way influence on the public agenda. Thus McCombs and Shaw were returning to a perspective on media effects as being powerful, which was an idea that had lost favor among media scholars through the 1950s and 1960s as the findings from empirical studies during those decades continually showed that media effects were fairly weak to nonexistent and that when evidence for even moderate effects occurred, it was limited to relatively small groups. This "limited effects perspective" was established primarily by Lazarsfeld, Berelson, and Gaudet (1948) in a book length analysis of the influence of the media on voters during a presidential election then reinforced by Klapper in his classic *Effects of Mass Communication* (1960). McCombs and Shaw were breaking with this limited effects perspective by claiming that the mass media—at least in the realm of news messages—were exhibiting a strong and continual influence on the public (McCombs & Reynolds, 2009).

At the same time that McCombs and Shaw were conducting their "Chapel Hill study," G. Ray Funkhouser (1973) was conducting a very similar study. Although all three scholars presented the findings of their different studies at the same academic conference, Funkhouser has not received as much credit as McCombs and Shaw for creating the agenda-setting explanation of media influence. Perhaps a reason for this was that McCombs and Shaw published their findings in an academic journal earlier than did Funkhouser and that McCombs and Shaw continued to study this phenomenon for decades after their initial publication while Funkhouser did not.

Conceptualization of Media

In their conceptualization of media, McCombs and Shaw presented a very broad conceptualization to include all media, although they typically focused on broadcast TV and daily newspapers in their examples and research. However, there is nothing in the articulation of their explanation that would rule out other media channels that transmitted news. However, they did limit their theory to one type of message—news—and ignored all other types of content.

Conceptualization of Media Effect

Initially agenda-setting theory was limited to an effect on beliefs; it was not concerned with cognitive, affective, attitudinal, physiological, or behavioral types of effects. Also, it was not concerned with how the effect occurred, only that it did occur.

Conceptualization of Media Influence

McCombs and Shaw regarded news media influence to be strong and widespread. However, that influence was conceptualized as working only one way, that is, from media agenda to the public agenda; it was not concerned initially with how the public agenda might be influencing the media agenda. But as the theory developed over time, the idea of agenda building was added, and this additional area opened up examinations into how the public—along with other factors—influenced the construction of the media agenda.

Original Components

Key Components

Originally the theory was very simple with only two constructs assembled into one proposition. The two constructs were the media agenda and the public agenda.

The media agenda was conceptualized as what the news media in general exhibited as the most important issues in a political campaign. It was operationalized as the frequency with which each issue was covered by the news media, so a content analysis of news messages was necessary to count how often each issue was mentioned. Then the issues that were covered by the media were rank ordered by the number of times they were mentioned during a given period of time. Issues with the highest rankings were considered the most salient in news coverage and therefore were designated as the media agenda.

The public agenda was a construct that focused on which issues the public believed were most important. This was operationalized in public opinion surveys where people were asked which issues concerned them the most. Those issues that the public ranked highest were considered to be the public's agenda at that time.

Core Proposition

The core proposition of agenda-setting theory was that the media agenda would be highly correlated in a positive direction with the public agenda. Underlying this association was the belief that the media agenda was a causal agent of the public agenda. This single proposition was very simple, expressing a direct, one-way, linear relationship between the media news agenda and the public's issue agenda.

Originally there were no intervening variables that would illuminate the process of influence, nor were there any contingent variables that partitioned the general public into subgroups. Thus the association between the media agenda and the public agenda was believed to be direct and general (applying to everyone).

Also, the original theory had no propositions explaining any of the underlying processes of agenda setting. That is, the original theory was not concerned with industry processes about how the news media constructed their agenda or *why* certain issues made it into the media agenda while others did not. Nor was the original theory concerned with audience processes about how individuals interpreted meaning from news messages in order to arrive at their beliefs about what was most important.

Foundational Assumptions

The authors constructed their original theory on two fundamental assumptions. First, they assumed that the media agenda influenced the public agenda in a causal, one-way direction. While their tests were correlational, their language suggested causation because the media agenda always preceded the public agenda.

A second assumption was that this media influence was powerful, that is, the media could influence a person's beliefs about the importance of issues in as little as one exposure. This assumption is revealed in their not testing for amount of exposure. That is, McCombs and Shaw never tested for how much exposure people had to the news media so they assumed that it did not matter if people had one exposure to the news media messages or many.

Empirical Testing

Stimulating Scholarly Attention

Since its introduction in 1972, the agenda-setting theory has motivated researchers to conduct hundreds of tests of its claims. It was estimated that during the first 25 years of existence, the theory stimulated more than 200 separate articles and more than a dozen books (Rogers, Dearing, & Bregman, 1993). When McCombs and Reynolds published a review of the growing literature in 2009, they claimed that there were then more than 425 empirical tests of the agenda-setting influence.

"Coming to grips with the totality of what has been written about agenda setting is an exceedingly complex task. As in many areas of mass communication research, work relevant to this topic is spread out not only over many journals within the field, but also over journals in several adjacent academic field" (Kosicki, 1993, pp. 101–102). Also, the size of the growing research literature makes it difficult to organize. Fortunately, the original theoreticians have periodically published reviews of the growing research along with the incorporation of many of these findings into the theory itself, showing that the theory has evolved considerably over the last five decades.

In 1993, McCombs and Shaw published "The evolution of agenda-setting research: Twenty-five years in the marketplace of ideas" in which they argued that up to that point, the research on agenda setting had exhibited four phases. "The opening phase was marked by the publication of McCombs and Shaw's original research in 1972" (p. 59). The second phase was composed of empirical studies that attempted to replicate their initial findings and also to "investigate the contingent conditions that enhance or limit media agenda setting, with particular emphasis on the concept of need for orientation because it provides a psychological explanation for agenda setting" (p. 59). The third phase began a few years later by extending the idea of agendas by (1) moving beyond issues and examining the characteristics of political candidates as agenda attributes and (2) broadening the examination of issues beyond political campaigns. Then in the 1980s there was a fourth phase that focused on the sources of the media agenda.

In his next major review of this growing literature, McCombs (2005) observed that agenda setting had been tested in hundreds of studies worldwide and that it had grown to a point where it needed five categories to organize it all. Calling these five categories stages of development of the theory, McCombs (2005) said they were: (1) basic agenda-setting effects, which focused on McCombs and Shaw's original design and focused on the salience of objects, which were typically issues in political campaigns; (2) attribute agenda setting, which focused on the attributes of the objects; (3) psychology of agenda-setting effects, which focused on significant individual differences in the responses to the media agenda that involve psychological variables such as need for orientation, personal relevance; (4) sources of the media agenda, which focuses on who sets the media agenda such as interactions among news organizations, journalistic norms; and (5) consequences of agenda-setting effects, which focus on how people form an opinion, priming opinions, and behaviors. He also grappled with the persistent problem of conceptualizing and measuring issue salience.

The agenda-setting literature continued to grow. In 2014, McCombs, Shaw, and Weaver published another review saying, "Beginning with a tightly focused study in Chapel Hill of media effects on the salience of issues among the public, agenda setting has evolved into a broad theory" (p. 782). They continued, "The core concepts of agenda-setting theory are an object agenda, attribute agenda, and the transfer of salience between pairs of agendas. In the now vast research literature on agenda setting, there are many different operational definitions of these core concepts" (p. 783). In their 2014 review, they needed seven categories to capture all the developments with agenda-setting theory (see Table 5.1). Let's examine these seven areas in some detail.

1. Basic agenda setting. This is the oldest line of research and follows from the original test published by McCombs and Shaw (1972). Referred to as "first-level agenda setting," this line of research continued to generate studies to test the relationship between the media agenda and the public agenda. However, instead of limiting the focus to issues during political campaigns, researchers expanded the scope of topics to examine the media agenda on the public agenda regarding the salience of issues, political figures, and other objects of attention. For example, researchers conducted tests to determine if agenda setting applied to public

Table 5.1. Seven Facets of Agenda-Setting Research and Evolution

I. First-Level Agenda Setting

The media agenda determines the public agenda in terms of salience.

* The news media build a consensus in the public about what are the most important issues of the day, that is, the news media teach people what to think about.

The agenda-setting effect is robust and widespread.

* Not limited to news coverage but also applies to entertainment and advertising.
* Not limited to geography but is found all over the world.
* Not limited to traditional media and has been found with all kinds of media including digit forms.

II. Second-Level Agenda Setting (Attributes)

The media agenda determines the public agenda in terms of attributes.

* The news media teach people *what* to think on issues they cover most.
* The attributes of the issues, political figures, and other objects of attention that the media highlight repeatedly will be regarded as the most important attributes of those issues, political figures, and other objects of attention by members of the public.

Attributes can be cognitive and/or affective

* Cognitive attributes are details of information about the issue or topic
* Affective attributes trigger emotions in audiences about the issue or topic

III. Third-Level Agenda Setting (Networks)

Examines the way the network of attributes presented by the media in their coverage of issues influences how the public perceives those issues as people develop their own networks of attributes.

IV. Factors of Influence

While the agenda-setting effect is widespread across all kinds of people, there are some factors that are more influential than others.

* The more saliently the media present particular issues, political figures, and other objects of attention, the more likely those issues, political figures, and other objects of attention will be regarded as most important by members of the public.
* The agenda-setting effect is stronger on people with a higher need for orientation. The need for orientation is exhibited through a two-step process as the individuals evaluate relevance and uncertainty. That is, when people are confronted with a topic in the media, they first evaluate whether that particular topic is relevant to them. When people perceive the relevance of a topic to be high, they then evaluate their degree of uncertainty about the topic. If they feel they have all the information they need about a topic, their uncertainty is low. But when uncertainty is high, then their need for orientation is also high.
* Other characteristics of people are not important to agenda setting, that is, the agenda-setting effect is so robust and general that the inclusion of personal characteristics as contingent variables in research designs does not increase or decrease the strength of the agenda-setting effect.

(Continued)

Table 5.1. *Continued*

V. Consequences

The consequences of exposure to the news media are not limited to learning about what is important or the attributes of important issues. Agenda-setting theory now also claims that the media agenda also influences public attitudes, opinions, and behavior.

VI. Origins of the Media Agenda

The media agenda is shaped by three primary factors: Major sources who provide the information for news stories, other news organizations, and journalism's norms and traditions.

  * Other factors can also be influential but that influence is filtered through journalistic norms and traditions.

VII. Agenda Melding

People merge the civic agendas presented by the media with their personal views and experience to create a satisfying picture of the world.

From McCombs et al. (2014).

beliefs about advertising (Ghorpade, 1986), about business practices and corporate reputation (Berger, 2001; Carroll & McCombs, 2003), about violence in society (Lowry, Ching, Nio, & Leitner, 2003), and about health (Ogata Jones, Denham, & Springston, 2006). This line of research also expanded into tests of agenda setting in other countries besides the United States. The agenda-setting effect has been found in Europe (McCombs, Llamas, Lopez-Escobar, & Rey, 1997; Peters, 1994; Princen, 2007), China (Zhang, Shao, & Bowman, 2012), and Korea (Kim & Lee, 2006; Lee, Lancendorfer, & Lee, 2005; Lim, 2011). And this line of research also expanded to test for agenda-setting influence of newer media (Roberts, Wanta, & Dzwo, 2002; Wallsten, 2007).

2. Attribute agenda setting. This line of research examines the characteristics of news stories to determine which of those characteristics are most influential. Because this line of research is concerned with more than whether highly covered issues were related to the public agenda and instead focuses on the way those issues are covered, it requires a more elaborate measurement of the public agenda.

This line of research has been labeled as "second-level agenda setting" to distinguish it from the original kinds of tests that were then labeled as "first-level agenda setting." While first-level agenda setting is concerned with the media telling people *what to think about*, second-level agenda setting is concerned with the media telling people *what to think*, that is, what positions they should take on the issues (Weiss, 2009). This line of research has also been called "attribute agenda setting" because it focuses on the attributes in the messages. Thus second-level agenda setting moves beyond simply looking at which issues are most salient and also looks at the particular attributes of those issues. For example, attributes in the presentation of an issue would include things like whether statistics were presented, the use of anecdotes, whether the issue is presented from a negative or positive point of view, the amount of factual material presented, and whether there are appeals to emotions. All of these attributes can be used to increase an issue's salience (first-level agenda setting) but they can also alter the way people think about the issue (second-level agenda setting).

The key to examining how media messages influence public beliefs is to examine which characteristics of messages are most persuasive. When an issue is presented in the media, that presentation includes many attributes of the issue of both a cognitive and an affective nature. The cognitive attributes provide information that describes various characteristics of the issue, while affective components convey information about the issue's tone (positive, negative, neutral). For example, Ghanem (1997) found that attributes with low psychological distance (i.e., the issue is presented as being familiar) were associated with the issue having greater salience on the public agenda.

Another factor that was found to affect the strength of the agenda-setting effect was the degree to which an issue was obtrusive (Rogers & Deering, 1988). Obtrusiveness refers to how many people have encountered experiences with the issue in their everyday lives. For example, the issue of gasoline prices is likely to have high obtrusiveness because most people continually buy gasoline, while the issue of European immigration is likely to have lower obtrusiveness because most people do not experience such a thing in their everyday lives. Thus when an issue is obtrusive, it is more likely to trigger the attention from the news media, which are more likely to cover that issue, and thus the more likely people will pay attention to such coverage and believe the issue is important. Moreover, even when obtrusive issues do not receive much media coverage, the public still regard them as important (Lang & Lang, 1981).

Unobtrusive issues, in contrast, are things that most people would regard as remote from their everyday experience, such as high-level wrongdoing by government officials. Thus, when people have little direct experience with an issue, the less obtrusive it is and the public opinion on that issue will be influenced much more by the media (Lang & Lang, 1981; Rogers & Deering, 1993; Zucker, 1978). Also, unobtrusive issues require more media coverage over a longer period of time in order to get onto the public agenda compared to obtrusive issues that require much less coverage to influence the public agenda.

3. Network agenda setting. Called "third-level agenda setting," this line of research focuses on "the extent to which the news media can transfer the salience of relationships among a set of elements to the public" (McCombs, Shaw, & Weaver, 2014). That is, researchers have moved beyond the limited perspective that the media only influence the salience of issues. Now agenda-setting researchers also contend that the media condition people to believe that certain elements in issues are related to one another. For example, Guo, Vu, and McCombs (2012) have shown that when journalists write their news stories, they typically present sets of attributes that serve to make the issue salient in the minds of audience members. Thus in news stories there are clusters of elements that typically appear together such that when journalists mention one attribute of an issue, audience members activate an entire cluster of remembered attributes in their minds. Guo and colleagues argued that when researchers design their studies to determine which attributes in news stories are most influential in creating the public agenda, they need to avoid regarding those attributes as being independent from one another and instead examine how those attributes are interconnected in a network-like structure in the minds of audience members.

4. Differences across individuals. Although agenda-setting studies typically find that while the public agenda in general follows the media agenda, there are individuals who do not display an agenda-setting effect. Some researchers have examined the characteristics of audience members to determine which of those characteristics are likely to predict whether an individual is likely to display an agenda-setting effect or not. The major factors that have been found to account for these differences across individuals are need for orientation and sensitivity.

Need for orientation. One concept that has been found to explain differences across audience members when it comes to whether people will accept the media agenda is "need for orientation." McCombs and colleagues have tested this concept and found that some people have a high need for orientation (in which case the media will exert a stronger agenda-setting influence) while other people have a low need for orientation. McCombs defines this concept as being a combination of the ideas of relevance and uncertainty. Relevance suggests that individuals will not seek news messages on issues that are not personally relevant to them. Uncertainty refers to individuals' beliefs about whether they already have enough information on an issue. Thus, individuals who feel that an issue is personally relevant to them and also feel that they do not have enough information on the issue will have a high need for orientation and therefore will expose themselves to more news messages on those issues, and this heightened exposure is likely to lead to an agenda-setting effect (McCombs, 2004; Weaver, 1977). However, researchers have found that the strongest agenda-setting effects were with people at a moderate need for orientation (under conditions of low interest and high uncertainty) (Perloff & Krause, 1985).

The need for orientation varies across different people so the key to understanding how people orient to the media is to examine the cognitive processes that people evoke when attending to media messages. One of these cognitive processes that people evoke is the accessibility heuristic (Price & Tewksbury, 1997) where accessibility refers to either how recently a person has been exposed to a particular issue or how often a person has been exposed to that issue (Kim et al., 2002). When an issue is accessible to them, which means it is already on the top of their minds, they do not need to expend much cognitive effort in processing the meaning of that message and are therefore likely to rely much more on what they remember from past exposures to information on that issue (Iyengar & Kinder, 1987; Scheufele & Tewksbury, 2007). When researchers ask people to tell them what society's most important problem is, people typically respond with the problem that the media have focused on most recently (Iyengar, 1991), which is a memory-based explanation for agenda setting (Scheufele, 2000). Such an explanation assumes that individuals make judgments on the issues based on information that is most easily retrievable from their memory (Iyengar, 1991). This memory-based explanation is traceable to the work of Tversky and Kahneman (1974) who showed that the formation of individuals' judgments directly correlates with "the ease in which instances or associations could be brought to mind" (p. 208). Exposures to media messages create memory traces that can be easily recalled later when people are exposed to new media messages. This explains why issues with which people are most familiar have a greater influence on how they process the meaning of newer messages.

Sensitivity. The way the media cover an issue interacts differently with different audience's preexisting sensitivities to produce changes in issue concerns. Audience members who are highly sensitive to an issue or problem will be much less affected by media coverage of that issue or problem compared to lower sensitivity individuals. For example, Erbring and colleagues (1980) have shown that people who avoid talking about political issues are more susceptible to an agenda-setting influence because they depend more heavily on media content than those who interact with other people and thereby are also influenced by the information they receive in conversations.

5. Consequences of agenda setting. Originally the theory focused on beliefs, but over time, researchers have examined other types of effect measures beyond beliefs, such as behaviors and emotions. Several researchers have found changes in behaviors attributed to agenda setting, such as getting a breast exam screening for cancer (Ghorpade, 1986; Ogata Jones et al., 2006). Also, agenda setting has been shown to have effects on emotions, such as fear of crime (Lowry et al., 2003) and feelings about political candidates (Coleman & Wu, 2010; Marcus, Neuman, & MacKuen, 2000).

6. Origins of the media agenda. Initially the agenda-setting explanation was one way (i.e., the media agenda influenced the public agenda), but over time it has recognized a more reciprocal relationship. Researchers have found that various publics exert an influence on the media agenda, so now the theory includes a two-way explanation.

Agenda setting was originally conceived as an unintended effect of news organizations on the public but has also been tested as an intended effect when people and organizations have tried to shape news coverage. Research has shown that there are groups who work hard to influence the media agenda and this line of research has often been labeled as agenda building (McCombs & Gilbert, 1986; Rogers & Dearing, 1988). These studies typically examine influences from outside the media organizations, such as from advertisers (Ghorpade, 1986) and public relations experts (Carroll & McCombs, 2003).

The theory has expanded to deal with agenda building in addition to agenda setting. While "agenda setting" refers to the effect of the media agenda on the public agenda, "agenda building" focuses on how both the media and the public agendas influence public policy (Rogers & Dearing, 1988). Berkowitz (1992) has elaborated on this distinction by introducing the terms policy agenda setting and policy agenda building. He sought to expand the original system of explanation of agenda setting to include a larger set of variables to explain how policymakers have their agenda influenced by both the media agenda and the public agenda. Some groups have been found to have a greater ease of access than other groups and are thus more likely to get their demands placed on an agenda in contrast to other groups. For example, researchers have found that policymakers generally exhibit more influence on the media agenda than do other groups of people who serve as sources of news for journalists because policymakers often have a better understanding of journalists' needs for reliable and predictable information (Berkowitz, 1992). This is especially the case with government-affiliated news sources at the local, state, and national levels (Berkowitz, 1992). This is because these news sources are more successful than other news sources in providing clear definitions of issues, and this serves to delineate the issues and problems much better so journalists tend to rely on these news sources more (Berkowitz, 1992; Hilgarten & Bosk, 1988). Which interpretations of "reality" will dominate public discourse has implications for the future of the social problem, for the interest groups and policymakers involved, and for the policy itself (Hilgarten & Bosk, 1988). To illustrate, Gusfield (1981) showed that highway deaths associated with alcohol consumption have been presented in a variety of ways. One way to present this problem is to blame cars by presenting them as lacking safety features. Another way to present this problem is to blame irresponsible drunken drivers. Yet another way to present the problem is to show poor highway design. When there are different ways of framing an issue as a problem, there are different sources of news that compete to frame the problem in a way that insures that other groups receive the blame while their own group is shown as faultless. Thus journalists must navigate this competition when determining how to tell their story.

The relationship between the media and policymakers is symbiotic where both groups have been found to share an unofficial set of ground rules. Journalists need access to official information, and policymakers need media coverage, so each party can serve the fundamental needs of the other party. Therefore, policymakers who understand the ground rules the best will be most capable of influencing the way journalists write their stories (Berkowitz, 1992).

Oftentimes the needs of journalists and policymakers are incompatible. For example, when a disaster strikes, journalists require a constant flow of information to cover the story, but policymakers might want to slow things down so they can control the story and thus avoid looking bad if the public is likely to blame them for the disaster (Berkowitz, 1992; Rogers & Dearing, 1988).

The agenda-building perspective attributes importance not only to mass media and policymakers, but also to social processes, such as the social environment. As you can see, as agenda-setting theory expands its scope, it draws in additional variables into its system of explanation. By adding agenda building to its scope, agenda setting starts to deal with the many variables that have been found to shape society and its institutions that are concerned with creating public agendas. Thus more people and entities are drawn into its scope.

The rise of the Internet has stimulated the idea of mass involvement, where every organization and every person now has the potential to influence the public agenda. Anyone can now post any opinions on any public issue on Internet bulletin boards or the Usenet newsgroup by Netizens, and these opinions all have a chance of influencing all kinds of agendas (Kim & Lee, 2006; Lee et al., 2005; Lim, 2011). Research has shown that Internet bloggers do in fact influence agendas. For example, Wallsten (2007) tracked mainstream media coverage and blog discussion of 35 issues during the 2004 presidential campaign and found that journalists began discussing the issues that most concerned bloggers.

People can now use the Internet to build agendas in a three-step process, according to Kim and Lee (2006). In the first step, a single blogger could express an opinion that ripples out to other blogs, personal homepages, and bulletin boards. This is called Internet-mediated agenda-rippling. In the second step, online news or websites pick up this movement of opinion and report on it, which leads to a dissemination of the agenda to more online publics. This is called agenda diffusion in the Internet. Finally in the third step, traditional media report the online agenda to the public so that the agenda is then disseminated to both offline and online publics. This is called Internet-mediated reversed agenda setting.

7. *Agenda melding.* Scholars have noticed something they have named "agenda melding," which focuses "on the personal agendas of individuals vis-à-vis their community and group affiliations" (Ragas & Roberts, 2009). This line of research focuses on the way people merge the civic agendas of the media with their valued reference communities and their personal views in order to create a satisfying picture of the world. Over time, groups and communities come to represent a "collected agenda of issues" (Ragas & Roberts, 2009).

In the past, people would have to learn what the values of a group were then adopt the agenda of the group if they wanted to belong to that group. Now people can form their own agendas then get on the Internet to find groups that have similar agendas with which they agree. Until recently, agenda setting was limited to general topics and it was geographically bound because travel was limited (Ragas & Roberts, 2009). But now with the proliferation of mobile devices, wi-fi, and social networking sites, people can easily find blogs and bulletin boards on every conceivable topic. Thus, the Internet makes it possible for people anywhere in the world to find others with similar agendas and collaborate with them.

Empirical Validity

Published tests of the theory typically report strong support for agenda setting. For example, after a careful review of the literature and a series of experiments that Iyengar and Kinder (1987) conducted themselves, they concluded that "our evidence decisively sustains the agenda-setting hypothesis. The verdict is clear and unequivocal: It issues from sequential experiments that last a week, from assemblage experiments that last an hour, and from time-series data that span seven years; it holds across different measures of importance, and it is confirmed for a variety of problems, from national defense to social security" (p. 33). Two decades later, Wanta and Ghanem (2007) published a meta-analysis of 90 agenda-setting studies and found a mean correlation of +.53, with almost all tests finding a correlation between .47 and .59, which indicates that the relationship between the media agenda and the public agenda is strong and remarkably consistent.

Theory Development

Since its introduction, the agenda-setting theory has undergone a great deal of conceptual development. It appears that little of this development has been generated by criticism of the theory because there has not been much published criticism relative to other media effects theories. Instead, it appears that many scholars have been attracted to the original conceptualization and tested extensions to the theory by conducting empirical studies.

Criticisms

Criticism of the agenda-setting theory over the years has been relatively mild compared to that of other theories. It has also been fairly constructive, that is, the criticisms have provided suggestions for improving various aspects of this theory, which have then been applied by those critics or other scholars.

    1. Conceptual criticism. Perhaps the strongest criticism of the theory was leveled by Iyengar and Kinder (1987) when they argued, "Although research on agenda-setting has proliferated over the last decade, so far, unfortunately, the results add up to rather little . . . Agenda-setting may be an apt metaphor, but it is no theory" (p. 3). Although these authors were using this argument as the basis for creating their own theory, it seems exaggerated because by that time agenda setting had stimulated many empirical studies and the findings of those studies consistently found rather strong support for the agenda-setting explanation. Also, Iyengar and Kinder did not explain why they felt agenda setting was not a theory, that is, they did not present their conception of what a theory was then show how agenda setting failed to meet that conception.

    Other criticisms have focused on faulty assumptions and fuzzy initial conceptualizations. As for assumptions, Fiske (1986) challenged the view of a passive audience. He argued that media influence was not automatic and powerful; instead people are interpretive beings who process meaning from messages. Another assumption regarded as faulty is that the influence from the media is one-way and causal. Kosicki (1993) observed, "Agenda setting is a distinctly causal hypothesis, suggesting that media treatment of issues causes changes in public opinion or behavior. Researchers studying agenda setting tend to discuss it as a dynamic process" but that "there are some conceptual concerns with this causal hypothesis" (p. 106).

    2. Methodological criticism. Agenda setting has been criticized for faulty operationalizations of important concepts (Edelstein, 1993; Kosicki, 1993). For example, Kosicki argued that "often conceptual and operational definitions do not match" (1993, p. 106). Edelstein (1993) pointed out that the operationalizations of "thinking about" typically did not conform to its conceptualization of "salience discrimination, which is operationalized as the importance that media and audiences accord to an event, and the causal relationship that exists between media and audience judgments about that importance" (p. 85). In essence he is claiming that the term "thinking about" refers more to cognitive processing and attention than to attitudes, opinions, and feelings, which is how it is typically measured. He argued that there is variation across the "thinking about" measures that it makes it difficult to make comparisons across studies.

Criticism has focused especially on how the public agenda has been measured. Originally it was measured as salience, but other studies have measured it as awareness, attention, or concern, which have been found to generate differing outcomes. Critics argue that these are not all valid operationalizations of the same concept of public agenda so they should not be reported as such. Also, critics have pointed out that when studies aggregate media content categories and public responses into very broad categories, it is hard to tell if the concepts are operationalized properly, and this aggregating can result in inflated correlation coefficients (Rogers & Dearing, 1988).

Perhaps the most serious methodological criticism has been that while the theory's main proposition makes a causal claim, few studies have been designed in a way to test a causal claim (Kosicki, 1993; McQuail, 1987). For example, Kosicki (1993) argued that "the most common types of studies seem to be one-time cross sections" when they needed to be longitudinal.

Conceptual Development

When we compare the above criticisms with the latest articulations of the theory (e.g., McCombs et al., 2014) we can see that all of these perceived shortcomings have been addressed by additional empirical testing and that the findings of those subsequent studies have been incorporated into the theory itself. Over the years McCombs and Shaw (1993) have displayed a good deal of willingness to alter their theory as they have incorporated new ideas from other scholars and researchers. They explain that "communication research does operate in a marketplace of ideas that is the quintessential laissez-faire market. The role of our journals is to create a market for ideas advanced by members of the field" (p. 58). They say the "hearty evolution of agenda-setting research in the marketplace of ideas over the past 25 years is itself preview to a robust future of scholarly publication, theoretical integration, and conceptual innovation. There is no question that the literature will grow as scholars continue to expand agenda setting into new domains" and that "major new research venues and new insights will be called into existence" (McCombs & Shaw, 1993, p. 65). This shows that they regard themselves more as stimulators and guiders of the research rather than controllers of a theory. In supporting these changes, Kosicki (1993) pointed out that agenda setting "[h]as proven to be remarkably flexible, having expanded well beyond its initial boundaries of matching aggregate media agendas with aggregate public opinion data" (p. 117).

The most salient pattern in this evolution is the moving beyond the original explanation, which is now referred to as first-level agenda setting, to a second and now a third type of agenda setting. Also the theory now includes explanations about agenda building as well as how individuals process meaning from media messages to arrive at not just their beliefs about which issues are important but also about how to think about those issues themselves.

Current Challenges

Agenda-setting theory is currently struggling with three major challenges. First, with the widespread use of the Internet, the idea of a media agenda is questionable. Second, with the fragmentation of the public into many different specialized interest groups, the idea of a public agenda is also questionable. Third is an ongoing debate about the role of framing.

Viability of the Concept of Media Agenda

The growing use of the Internet, especially the use of social networks to get one's news, has generated a divergence of opinions about the viability of the idea of a media agenda. Some scholars have claimed the agenda-setting process is just as strong from Internet sources as it has been with traditional print (Roberts et al., 2002). However, other scholars have claimed that the use of the Internet has reduced the power of traditional to create an agenda-setting effect (Meraz, 2011; Wallsten, 2007). This weakening can be explained by a distinction between what has been referred to as "vertical media" and "horizontal media." Critics argue that traditional media such as newspapers and broadcast television are less relevant now because of their vertical nature, that is, traditional media are organized with a flow of authority, power, and influence coming from the top and flowing down to the public. In contrast, the Internet is a horizontal medium where everyone can become a source of information and influence; power is not concentrated in the hands of a small elite. Because individuals are likely to have different agendas that they can easily share on the Internet, there are now likely to be many media agendas at any given point in time.

Viability of the Concept of Public Agenda

A dominant trend in our culture over the last few decades has been the fragmentation of previously large audiences into much smaller niche audiences, where each audience has its own special needs. Mass media have shifted away from attempting to attract large general audiences; now media attempt to create vehicles designed to serve the needs of small niche audiences, and this tends to add to the fragmentation of the culture. Today, there is a serious question about what it means to talk about a "public" as if it were a large community of people all of whom share the same beliefs and attitudes.

When people search the Internet for news, they typically seek out the types of information that is of most interest to them. And because the Internet provides such a wide variety of information and news providers, every individual can find a provider that fits their particular needs. Given these conditions, it is highly questionable that there still exists something that can be referred to as a "public agenda" that is shared by a substantial proportion of the population.

Now that agenda-setting theory has also included the idea of agenda melding, it appears that the theory itself has been shifting away from its original purpose of documenting widespread public agendas. Recall that the idea of agenda melding focuses attention "on the personal agendas of individuals vis-à-vis their community and group affiliations" (Ragas & Roberts, 2009) and how these personal agendas work with more general agendas to create an amalgam in each individual. Individuals then seek out others who share their perceptions of what is important. Using the Internet, individuals can now easily find other people who share their values and do not need to depend on traditional news providers to tell them what is important (Ragas & Roberts, 2009). Today people can create their own agendas then find others who will reinforce their sense of what is important. Thus it is more likely that there are many agendas being exhibited simultaneously in any population.

Role of Framing

There is a continuing debate about the relationship of framing theory to agenda-setting theory. Some scholars argue that framing is a part of agenda-setting theory while other scholars argue that the two are distinct in many ways.

As research on second-level agenda setting became more prominent, scholars began noticing a considerable overlap with framing theory, which triggered a debate about whether framing was an idea to be subsumed under agenda-setting theory or whether framing was unique enough to be considered a separate theory (McCombs, 2004). Let's examine both sides of this controversy.

Same. McCombs and colleagues claim that the idea of framing is a natural extension to the theory (McCombs et al., 2014). They argue that the term "framing" refers to the process of organizing, defining, and structuring a story, so framing provides an explanation for how news stories are presented and how that presentation influences whether the issue in a story shapes the public agenda. Framing refers to the way news stories are presented, that is, the way particular story elements are presented first and highlighted leads audiences to process those messages in a certain way and follow a particular line of interpretation (Entman, 1993; Scheufele, 1999). The media's selective use of certain frames affects the way the audience thinks about the issue.

The premise that framing is about selecting "a restricted number of thematically related attributes" for media representation can be understood as the process of transferring the salience of issue attributes (i.e., second-level agenda setting) (McCombs, Shaw, & Weaver, 1997, p. 106). Thus they are arguing in essence that framing falls under the umbrella of agenda setting.

Scholars most closely associated with the theory (e.g., McCombs, Shaw, Weaver) argue that framing is an essential part of agenda setting. According to Weaver, framing and second-level agenda setting share three similarities but only one difference. As for the similarities, both are more concerned with how issues are depicted in the media than with which issues are prominently reported. Second, both focus on what are regarded as the most salient aspects presented in the descriptions of issues presented in the news. And third, both are concerned with *ways* of thinking rather than the *objects* of thinking. As for the difference, Weaver acknowledged that framing allows for a broader range of cognitive processes, such as moral evaluations, causal reasoning, appeals to principle, and recommendations for treatment of problems, whereas second-level agenda setting focuses almost exclusively on the salience of attributes of an object.

Different. Some scholars argue that agenda setting and framing are very different. For example, Scheufele and Tewksbury (2007) claim that framing and agenda setting are distinct in three ways. First, they differ in their theoretical boundaries. Second, they operate via distinct cognitive processes. These scholars argue that framing is distinct from agenda setting because framing is based on the idea of applicability, which is conceptually different from the idea of accessibility that is the foundation for agenda setting. To illustrate this difference, we need to look at the way Goffman (1974) introduced framing theory when he argued that individuals actively classify and interpret their life experiences to make sense of the world around them. These classifications and interpretations then become the individual's preexisting and long-standing schema. Scheufele (2000) explains that framing influences how the audience thinks about issues, not by making certain aspects more salient than others (i.e., accessibility), but by invoking interpretive cues that correspond to the individuals' preexisting schema (i.e., applicability). Also, framing is more likely to take place when these interpretive cues correspond with or activate individuals' preexisting cognitive schema (Kim et al., 2002). Applicability, in this regard, refers to finding the connection between the message in the media and the framework individuals employ to interpret the issue (Scheufele & Tewksbury, 2007). Kim and his colleagues (2002) highlight this distinction between the applicability and accessibility by arguing that framing posits that individuals each have their own interpretation of an issue, regardless of the salience of an issue. Thus a person's schema, which is their set of interpretations and beliefs, is more influential in determining the public agenda than is how saliently an issue is covered by the media. In contrast, agenda setting posits that only salient issues in the media will become accessible in people's minds when they evaluate or make judgments on the issue. While this debate continues (Scheufele, 2000), it should be acknowledged that there is overlap between the two theories in terms of their use of cognitive processes that people employ when constructing meaning from media messages.

Third, the two theories predict different outcomes, because they posit different processes of influence. For example, in framing theory, people are believed to activate a frame based on how important they believe that frame to be. In agenda-setting theory, people think an issue is salient through a process of accessibility, that is, people select a mental schema that is the easiest to access. That is, the way framing effects transpires is different from the way second-level agenda setting is supposed to take place (i.e., accessibility).

Scheufele and Tewksbury (2007) argue that, because accessibility and applicability vary in their functions of media effects, "the distinction between accessibility and applicability effects has obvious benefits for understanding and predicting the effects of dynamic information environments."

Given the nature of the current debate, both sides of the argument present valid points. Perhaps with additional research, the empirical evidence will amass on one side and the debate will thus be resolved.

Conclusions

As a theory of media effects, agenda setting has grown enormously since its introduction in 1972. It has attracted many researchers who have run hundreds of tests of its claims. That growing body of research has not only supported the original claims of the theory but has also served to greatly expand the scope and precision of the theory. Now the theory has not only a first level but also a second and third level of agenda setting. It has also expanded its scope to explain how the media agenda is constructed and how individuals process the media agenda to experience consequences beyond beliefs to also include emotions and behaviors.

This growth in scope, precision, heuristic value, and empirical validity has been guided by the original theoreticians and their close colleagues who have remained active in developing the theory by responding to criticism as well as incorporating a vast array of empirical findings into a theory that has continually grown in its explanatory power over the years of its existence.

Key Sources

Foundational Scholarship

Berelson, B. R., Lazarsfeld, P. F., & McPhee, W. N. (1954). *Voting*. Chicago, IL: University of Chicago Press.

Cohen, B. C. (1963). *The press and foreign policy*. Princeton, NJ: Princeton University Press. ISBN 978-0-87772-346-2.

Lang, K., & Lang, G. E. (1959 original; 1966). The mass media and voting. In E. Burdic & A. J. Brodbeck (Eds.), *American voting behavior* (pp. 217–235). New York, NY: Free Press.

Lazarsfeld, P. F., Berelson, B., & Gaudet, H. (1948). *The people's choice*. New York, NY: Columbia University Press.

Lippmann, W. (1922). *Public opinion*. New York, NY: Macmillan.

McCombs, M., & Gilbert, S. (1986). News influence on our pictures of the world. In J. Bryant & D. Zillmann (Eds.), *Perspectives on media effects* (pp. 1–15). Hillsdale, NJ: Erlbaum.

Trenaman, J., & McQuail, D. (1961). *Television and the political image*. London: Methuen and Co.

Introduction of Agenda Setting Theory

McCombs, M. E., & Shaw, D. L. (1972). The agenda-setting function of mass media. *Public Opinion Quarterly, 36*(2), 176. doi:10.1086/267990. ISSN 0033-362X.

Alterations/Elaborations in Theory

McCombs, M. E., & Shaw, D. L. (1993). The evolution of agenda-setting research: Twenty-five years in the marketplace of ideas. *Journal of Communication, 43*(2), 58–67. doi:10.1111/j.1460-2466.1993.tb01262.x.

McCombs, M. E., Shaw, D. L., & Weaver, D. H. (2014). New directions in agenda-setting theory and research. Mass Communication & Society, 17(6), 781–802. doi:10.1080/1 5205436.2014.964871.

Reviews

Iyengar, S., & Kinder, D. (1987). *News that matters: Television and American opinion.* Chicago, IL: University of Chicago Press.

McCombs, M. (2004). Setting the agenda: The mass media and public opinion (p. 198, Repr. ed.). Cambridge: Blackwell Pub.

McCombs, M. (2005). A look at agenda-setting: Past, present and future. *Journalism Studies, 6*(4), 543–557. doi:10.1080/14616700500250438.

McCombs, M., & Bell, T. (1996). The agenda-setting role of mass communication: An integrated approach to communication theory and research (pp. 93–110). Mahwah, NJ: Erlbaum

McCombs, M., & Reynolds, A. (2002). News influence on our pictures of the world. In J. Bryant & D. Zillmann (Eds.), *Media effects: Advances in theory and research* (3rd ed., pp. 1–18). Mahwah, NJ: Erlbaum.

McCombs, M., & Reynolds, A. (2009). How the news shapes our civic agenda. In J. Bryant & M. B. Oliver (Eds.), *Media effects: Advances in theory and research* (3rd ed., pp. 1–16). New York, NY: Routledge.

McCombs, M., Shaw, D. L., & Weaver, D. H. (1997). Communication and democracy: Exploring the intellectual frontiers in agenda-setting theory. Mahwah, NJ: Erlbaum.

Rogers, E., & Dearing, J. (1988). Agenda-setting research: Where has it been, where is it going? In J. A. Anderson (Ed.), *Communication yearbook 11* (pp. 555–594). Newbury Park, CA: Sage.

Rogers, E. M., Dearing, J. W., & Bregman, D. (1993). The anatomy of agenda-setting research. *Journal of Communication, 43*(2), 68–84. doi:10.1111/j.1460-2466.1993.tb01263.x.

Wanta, W., & Ghanem, S. (2007). Effects of agenda-setting. In R. W. Preiss, B. M. Gayle, N. Burrell, M. Allen, & J. Bryant (Eds.), *Mass media effects research: Advances through meta-analysis* (pp. 37–51). Mahwah, NJ: Erlbaum.

Weiss, D. (2009). Agenda-setting theory. In S. W. Littlejohn & K. A. Foss (Eds.), *Encyclopedia of communication theory* (pp. 31–33). Los Angeles, CA: Sage.

Willnat, L. (1997). Agenda setting and priming: Conceptual links and differences. In M. McCombs, D. L. Shaw, & D. Weaver (Eds.), *Communication and democracy: Exploring the intellectual frontiers in agenda-setting theory* (pp. 51–66). Mahwah, NJ: Erlbaum.

Criticisms

Edelstein, A. S. (1993). Thinking about the criterion variable in agenda-setting research. *Journal of Communication, 43*(2), 85–99.

Gozenbach, W. J., & McGavin, L. (1997). A brief history of time: A methodological analysis of agenda setting. In M. McCombs, D. L. Shaw, & D. Weaver (Eds.), *Communication and democracy: Exploring the intellectual frontiers in agenda-setting theory* (pp. 115–136). Mahwah, NJ: Erlbaum.

Kosicki, G. M. (1993). Problems and opportunities in agenda-setting research. *Journal of Communication, 43*(2), 100–127.

Scheufele, D. A., & Tewksbury, D. (2007). Framing, agenda setting, and priming: The evolution of three media effects models. *Journal of Communication, 57*, 9–20.

Current Form of Theory

McCombs, M. E. (2014). Setting the agenda: The mass media and public opinion. Cambridge: UK Polity Press.

References

Berger B. (2001). Private issues and public policy: Locating the corporate agenda in agenda-setting theory. *Journal of Public Relations Research, 13*(2), 91–126.

Berkowitz, D (1992). Who sets the media agenda? The ability of policymakers to determine news decisions. In J. D. Kennamer (Ed.), *Public opinion, the press, and public policy* (pp. 81–102). Westport, CT: Praeger.

Carroll, C. E., & McCombs, M. (2003). Agenda-setting effects of business news on the public's images and opinions about major corporations. *Corporate Reputation Review 6*(1), 36–46.

Cohen, B. C. (1963). *The press and foreign policy*. Princeton, NJ: Princeton University Press. ISBN 978-0-87772-346-2.

Coleman, R., & Wu, H. D. (2010). Proposing emotion as a dimension of affective agenda setting: Separating affect into two components and comparing their second-level effects. *Journalism & Mass Communication Quarterly, 87*, 315–327. doi:10.1177/107769901008700206

Edelstein, A. S. (1993). Thinking about the criterion variable in agenda-setting research. *Journal of Communication, 43*(2), 85–99.

Entman, R. M. (1993). Framing: Toward clarification of a fractured paradigm. *Journal of Communication, 43*(4), 51–58. doi:10.1111/j.1460-2466.1993.tb01304.x.

Erbring, L., Goldenberg, E. N., & Miller, A. H. (1980). Front-page news and real-world cues: A new look at agenda-setting by the media. *American Journal of Political Science, 24*, 16–49. doi:10.2307/2110923

Fiske, J. (1986). Television: Polysemy and popularity. *Critical Studies in Media Communication, 3*(4), 391–408.

Funkhouser, G. (1973). The issues of the sixties: An exploratory study in the dynamics of public opinion. *Public Opinion Quarterly, 37*(1), 62–75. doi:10.1086/268060

Ghorpade, S. (1986). Agenda setting: A test of advertising's neglected function. *Journal of Advertising Research 26*(4), 23–27.

Goffman, E. (1974). *Frame analysis: An essay on the organization of experience.* New York, NY: Harper & Row.

Guo, L. V., Hong, T., & McCombs, M. (2012). An expanded perspective on agenda-setting effects: Exploring the third level of agenda setting [Una extensión de la perspectiva de los efectos de la Agenda Setting . Explorando el tercer nivel de la Agenda setting]. *Revista de Comunicación 11,* 51–68.

Gusfield, J. R. (1981). *The culture of public problems.* Chicago, IL: University of Chicago Press.

Hilgarten, S., & Bosk, C. L. (1988). The rise and fall of social problems: A public arenas model. *American Journal of Sociology, 94,* 53–78. doi:10.1086/228951

Iyengar, S. (1991). *Is anyone responsible? How television frames political issues.* Chicago, IL: University of Chicago Press.

Iyengar, S., & Kinder, D. (1987). *News that matters: Television and American opinion.* Chicago, IL: University of Chicago Press.

Kim, S., Scheufele, D. A., & Shanahan, J. (2002). Think about it this way: Attribute agenda-setting function of the press and the public's evaluation of a local issue. *Journalism & Mass Communication Quarterly, 79,* 7–25.

Kim, S. T., & Lee, Y. H. (2006). New functions of Internet mediated agenda-setting: Agenda-rippling and reversed agenda-setting. *Korean Journal of Journalism & Communication Studies, 50*(3), 175–205.

Klapper, J. T. (1960). *The effects of mass communication.* Glencoe, IL: Free Press.

Kosicki, G. M. (1993). Problems and opportunities in agenda-setting research. *Journal of Communication, 43*(2), 100–127.

Lang, K., & Lang, G. E. (1959 original; 1966). The mass media and voting. In E. Burdic & A. J. Brodbeck (Eds.), *American voting behavior* (pp. 217–235). New York, NY: Free Press.

Lang, G. E., & Lang, K. (1981). Watergate: An exploration of the agenda-building process. In G. C. Wilhout & H. de Bock (Eds.), *Mass Communication Review Yearbook* (pp. 447–468). Beverly Hills, CA: Sage.

Lazarsfeld, P. F., Berelson, B., & Gaudet, H. (1948). *The people's choice.* New York, NY: Columbia University Press.

Lee, B., Lancendorfer, K. M., & Lee, K. J. (2005). Agenda-setting and the internet: The intermedia influence of internet bulletin boards on newspaper coverage of the 2000 general election in South Korea. *Asian Journal of Communication, 15*(1), 57–71. doi:10.1080/0129298042000329793

Lim, J. (2011). First-level and second-level intermedia agenda-setting among major news websites. *Asian Journal of Communication, 21*(2), 167–185. doi:10.1080/01292986.2010.539300

Lippmann, W. (1922). *Public opinion.* New York, NY: Macmillan.

Lowry, D. T., Ching, T., Nio, J., & Leitner, D. W. (2003). Setting the public fear agenda: A longitudinal analysis of network TV crime reporting, public perceptions of crime, and FBI crime statistics. *Journal of Communication, 53*(1), 61–73.

Marcus, G. E., Neuman, W. R., & MacKuen, M. (2000). *Affective Intelligence and political judgment*. Chicago, IL: University of Chicago Press. ISBN 978-0-226-50469-8.

McCombs, M. (2004). *Setting the agenda: The mass media and public opinion* (p. 198, Repr. ed.). Cambridge: Blackwell Pub.

McCombs, M. (2005). A look at agenda-setting: Past, present and future. *Journalism Studies, 6*(4), 543–557. doi:10.1080/14616700500250438.

McCombs, M., & Gilbert, S. (1986). News influence on our pictures of the world. In J. Bryant & D. Zillmann (Eds.), *Perspectives on media effects* (pp. 1–15). Hillsdale, NJ: Erlbaum.

McCombs, M., Llamas, J. P., Lopez-Escobar, E., & Rey, F. (1997). Candidate images in Spanish elections: Second-level agenda setting effects. *Journalism & Mass Communication Quarterly, 74*(4), 703–717. doi:10.1177/107769909707400404

McCombs, M., & Reynolds, A. (2009). How the news shapes our civic agenda. In J. Bryant & M. B. Oliver (Eds.), *Media effects: Advances in theory and research* (3rd ed., pp. 1–16). New York, NY: Routledge.

McCombs, M. E., & Shaw, D. L. (1972). The agenda-setting function of mass media. *Public Opinion Quarterly, 36*(2), 176. doi:10.1086/267990. ISSN 0033-362X

McCombs, M. E., & Shaw, D. L. (1993). The evolution of agenda-setting research: Twenty-five years in the marketplace of ideas. *Journal of Communication, 43*(2), 58–67. doi:10.1111/j.1460-2466.1993.tb01262.x

McCombs, M., Shaw, D. L., & Weaver, D. H. (1997). *Communication and democracy: Exploring the intellectual frontiers in agenda-setting theory*. Mahwah, NJ: Erlbaum.

McCombs, M. E., Shaw, D. L., & Weaver, D. H. (2014). New directions in agenda-setting theory and research. *Mass Communication & Society, 17*(6), 781–802. doi:10.1080/152054 36.2014.964871

McQuail, D. (1987). *Mass communication theory: An introduction*. London: Sage.

Meraz, S. (2011). The fight for 'how to think': Traditional media, social networks, and issue interpretation. *Journalism, 12*(1): 107–127. doi:10.1177/1464884910385193

Ogata Jones, K., Denham, B. E., & Springston, J. K. (2006). Effects of mass and interpersonal communication on breast cancer screening: Advancing agenda-setting theory in health contexts. *Journal of Applied Communication Research, 34*, 94–113. doi:10.1080/00909880500420242. ISSN 0090-9882

Perloff, R. M. (1985). *Mass media and political thought : An information-processing approach* (1. print. ed.). Beverly Hills: Sage. ISBN 0-8039-2516-6

Peters, B. G. (1994). Agenda-setting in the European community. *Journal of European public policy, 1*(1), 9–26. doi:10.1080/13501769408406945

Price, V., & Tewksbury, D. (1997). New values and public opinion: A theoretical account of media priming and framing. In G. A. Barnett & F. J. Boster (Eds.), *Progress in communication sciences: Advances in persuasion* (Vol. 13, pp. 173–212). Greenwich, CT: Ablex.

Price, V., Tewksbury, D., & Powers, E. (1997). Switching trains of thought: The impact of news frames on readers' cognitive responses, *Communication Research, 24*(5), 481–506.

Princen, S. (2007). Agenda-setting in the European Union: A theoretical exploration and agenda for research. *Journal of European Public Policy, 14*(1), 21–38. doi:10.1080/13501760601071539

Ragas, M., & Roberts, M. (2009). Agenda setting and agenda melding in an age of horizontal and vertical media: A new theoretical lens for virtual brand communities. *Journalism & Mass Communication Quarterly, 86*(1), 45–64. doi:10.1177/107769900908600104

Roberts, M., Wanta, W., & Dustin Dzwo, Tzong-Horng (2002). Agenda setting and issue salience online. *Communication Research, 29*(4), 452–465. doi:10.1177/0093650202029004004

Rogers, E., & Dearing, J. (1988). Agenda-setting research: Where has it been, where is it going? In J. A. Anderson (Ed.), *Communication yearbook 11* (pp. 555–594). Newbury Park, CA: Sage.

Rogers, E. M., Dearing, J. W., & Bregman, D. (1993). The anatomy of agenda-setting research. *Journal of Communication, 43*(2), 68–84. doi:10.1111/j.1460-2466.1993.tb01263.x

Scheufele, D. A. (1999). Framing as a theory of media effects. *Journal of Communication,* 49(1), 103–22

Scheufele, D. A. (2000). Agenda-setting, priming, and framing revisited: Another look at cognitive effects of political communication. *Mass Communication & Society, 3*(2&3), 297–316. doi:10.1207/S15327825MCS0323_07

Scheufele, D. A., & Tewksbury, D. (2007). Framing, agenda setting, and priming: The evolution of three media effects models. *Journal of Communication, 57,* 9–20.

Tversky, A., & Kahneman, D. (1974). Judgment under uncertainty: Heuristics and biases. *Science, 185,* 1124–1131.

Tversky, A., & Kahneman, D. (1981). The framing of decisions and the psychology of choice. *Science, 211*(4481): 453–458. doi:10.1126/science.7455683. PMID 7455683

Wallsten, K. (2007). Agenda setting and the blogosphere: An analysis of the relationship between mainstream media and political blogs. *Review of Policy Research, 24*(6), 567–587. doi:10.1111/j.1541-1338.2007.00300.x

Wanta, W., & Ghanem, S. (2007). Effects of agenda-setting. In R. W. Preiss, B. M. Gayle, N. Burrell, M. Allen, & J. Bryant (Eds.), *Mass media effects research: Advances through meta-analysis* (pp. 37–51). Mahwah, NJ: Erlbaum.

Weaver, D. (1977). Political issues and voter need for orientation. In D. L. Shaw & M. E. McCombs (Eds.), *The emergence of American public issues* (pp. 107–120). St. Paul, MN: West

Weiss, D. (2009). Agenda-setting theory. In S. W. Littlejohn & K. A. Foss (Eds.), *Encyclopedia of communication theory* (pp. 31–33). Los Angeles, CA: Sage.

Zhang, G., Shao, G., & Bowman, N. D. (2012). What is most important for my country is not most important for me: Agenda-setting effects in China. *Communication Research, 39*(5), 662–678. doi:10.1177/0093650211420996

Zucker, H. (1978). The variable nature of news media influence. *Communication Yearbook, 2,* 225–246.

CHAPTER SIX

Framing Theory

Within the field of media effects, framing theory provides an explanation about how the design of media messages along with a person's cognitive structures guides audiences through the process of interpreting the meaning of media messages. Although framing theory was developed outside the field of media effects, it has demonstrated great value to media effects researchers by providing a useful explanation about how people encounter any symbol system and process meaning from those encounters.

Original Conceptualization of Framing Theory

Conceptual Foundation

What we regard as framing theory arose in the 1970s with a confluence of two streams of ideas that had been around for a long time. One of these streams flowed from the thinking about rhetoric several millennia ago. It emphasized the idea that the way messages are constructed—or framed—matters. Rhetorical theories have long presented ideas about how orators should structure their messages in order to achieve the effects they want. These rhetorical ideas were translated into the realm of social science in 1959 when the sociologist Erving Goffman published *The Presentation of Self in Everyday Life*. Using imagery from theater, Goffman wrote about how people attempt to guide the impression that others might make of them by controlling their appearance and how they act.

The other stream of influence arose throughout the 1900s as social sciences moved into a cognitive perspective by studying the mental practices of humans. One of the first of these writings was from the journalist Walter Lippmann (1922) who published *Public Opinion* in which he argued that the public perceived the world through stereotypes that serve as pictures in our heads. These ideas were further developed as social scientists studied how humans process meaning from messages (Kahneman & Tversky, 1979, 1984; Sherif, 1967).

Introduction of Framing Theory

Framing theory as we know it today was introduced when scholars put the two foundational sets of ideas together in the early 1970s, but there is some disagreement about which scholar should get credit for being the first to do this. Some scholars (Shah, Kwak, Schmierbach, & Zubric, 2004) claim that framing theory was introduced by the anthropologist Gregory Bateson in his 1972 book *Steps to an Ecology of Mind*. Other scholars (Volkmer, 2009) claim that framing theory was introduced by the sociologist Erving Goffman in his 1974 book entitled *Frame Analysis: An Essay on the Organization of Experience*, which was an extension of Goffman's 1959 book, *The Presentation of Self in Everyday Life*. In the later book, Goffman used a phenomenological approach to argue that people construct meaning of the world based on their life experiences, beliefs, and knowledge.

Conceptualization of Media

As a media effects theory, framing's conceptualization of the media is very broad. The theory explains that all media, vehicles, and messages exhibit "frames in communication." It is not possible for a media message to be frameless. For example, journalists cannot produce a frameless news story. While journalists' intentions may be to present facts in a straightforward manner, their news stories are always constructions within a frame. The frame of a news story constrains and shapes the meaning of the covered event for the audience by the way details are selected and presented in the story. The frame provides context in the way it delineates problems, implies causes, suggests remedies, and indicates the need for moral judgments.

Conceptualization of Media Effect

The theory also conceptualizes the media effect very broadly. Everyone experiences framing effects constantly; no one is outside the explanation that people all use internal cognitive templates to guide their understanding of all their experiences, including all experiences from exposure to media messages. The media effect can be cognitive, attitudinal, affective, belief, or behavioral. It can be immediate or long term. It can be positive or negative. And it can be intentional or unintentional. There are times when creators of messages (e.g., advertisers and media consultants in political campaigns) consciously select message elements and meticulously arrange those elements in a way to elicit particular meanings in the minds of their audiences. But even when message producers are not trying to elicit the triggering of planned meanings from media messages, framing effects still occur.

Conceptualization of Media Influence

The media influence is conceptualized primarily as triggering, but the theory also allows for the functions of altering and reinforcing. The theory claims that the various elements in any media message trigger audiences to attribute meaning by evoking people's schema. The schema themselves are altered and reinforced through subsequent usage as people are exposed to the continual stream of media messages daily over the course of their lives.

Original Components

Key Concepts

Framing theory focuses attention on two key concepts—frames in communication and frames in thought. Let's examine these two constructs in some detail.

Frames in communication. Frames in communication refer to the way messages are constructed. For example, when journalists construct a news story, they must select what elements to put into the story and which of those included elements to feature most prominently. These decisions constitute the framing of the story. "To frame is to select some aspects of a perceived reality and make them more salient in a communicating text, in such a way as to promote a particular problem definition, causal interpretation, moral evaluation, and/or treatment recommendation for the item described" (Entman, 1993, p. 52). The frame is the news angle or the context for the story (Tuchman, 1978).

Entman (1993) argues that frames in communication serve four functions. They "define problems, determine what a causal agent is doing with what costs and benefits, usually measured in terms of common cultural values; diagnose causes by examining the forces creating the problem; make moral judgments by evaluating causal agents and their effects; and suggest remedies by offering and justifying treatments for the problems and predict their likely effects. A single sentence may perform more than one of these four framing functions, although many sentences in a text may perform none of them" (p. 52). Entman continues, "The text contains frames, which are manifested by the presence or absence of certain keywords, stock phrases, stereotyped images, sources of information, and sentences that provide thematically reinforcing clusters of facts or judgments" (p. 52).

Frames in thought. Frames in thought are sets of memories, interpretations, and explanations of reality that exist in people's minds. These frames influence how we interpret, process, and communicate meaning. Called schema by cognitive scientists, frames in thought are learned and altered through people's experiences.

People continually use their frames in thought on a day-to-day basis, even though they are typically unaware that they are using them because the process is so automatic. People use these schemas to filter the flood of media messages automatically, thus screening out all messages that do not match a person's criteria for attention. Criteria can be personal standards of what the person considers interesting, important, or arousing. Messages that display elements that meet a person's criteria are screened in and trigger the person's attention. Then once a message is screened in, the person uses the schema to guide the interpretation of its meaning. Thus schemas are essential to the filtering of messages and to the guiding of interpretation of meaning.

The advantage for people in using these frames in thought is efficiency. Frames in thought are heuristics or mental shortcuts that make it possible for people to process media messages very quickly with almost no cognitive effort. Human beings are by nature "cognitive misers," meaning they prefer to do as little thinking as possible (Fiske & Taylor, 1991), so they rely on their schema to provide them with a quick and easy way to process information. However, frames in thought also come with a risk of experiencing one of their disadvantages. Because people do not expend much mental effort when automatically using these frames, they sometimes apply the wrong frame or extract a faulty meaning. This condition of automaticity among receivers of messages gives the senders of these messages a good deal of power when they know how to frame their messages in a way to evoke particular schema in the minds of their receivers. Skilled message designers can manipulate audiences into accepting beliefs that are faulty or not in the audience's best interests (Entman, 1993).

Goffman further claimed that people have a "primary framework," which is a fundamental set of beliefs that people take for granted and use as a default in typical situations. A primary framework consists of many elements that can be grouped into two sets: natural and social. Natural elements treat events as stand-alone occurrences; they regard the event literally and do not make inferences about any influences that might have caused the events. In contrast, social elements regard events as socially driven occurrences that are strongly influenced by the needs and actions of other individuals and institutions.

Core Propositions

The central proposition in framing theory is that people use their frames in thought to filter messages then to process meaning from those media messages that they choose to pay attention to. Thus these frames in thought guide selection of messages by filtering out messages that do not conform to the existing frames in thought. Then when a message has been filtered in, people (1) are influenced most by the frames in communication (i.e., elements that are salient in the message) and (2) use frames in thought as guides to process the elements in those messages to interpret their meaning.

Framing theory claims that people have many frames in their memories and that with any given message, there are several frames that could guide the processing of messages. Which frames do people use most often? The theory answers this question with the concepts of accessibility and availability. When a frame is accessible or available (i.e., at the top of a person's mind at a given time so that it is easy to use), it is regarded as being "strong" enough to be judged relevant or applicable to the subject at hand.

It is important to note here that the strength of a frame is determined by how accessible and how available it is, not how accurate it is. Strong frames are not the same thing as morally or intellectually superior arguments. A frame is considered strong not because it is superior but because it has high appeal for audiences. Thus frames can be strong even though they contain exaggerations and even outright lies as those frames have high audience appeal. Sometimes strong frames are composed of highly partisan symbols and ideas linked strongly to an ideology rather than on direct information about the substance of a message. Thus when people use strong frames—as they typically do—they can end up making faulty interpretations of the meaning in the messages.

Foundational Assumptions

Framing theory regards meaning as residing both in the message and in the mind of receivers. Producers of media messages create meaning by the way they structure the message and make certain elements most salient while ignoring other elements. The message's frame directs audience attention toward certain ideas, images, and sounds. Then audience members interpret the meaning of messages by using mental schema. These schemas are formed in the mind of each person from an accumulation of experiences from both media messages and real-world interactions.

Empirical Testing

Researchers have used a range of methods to test the effects of framing. Chong and Druckman (2007) observe that "scholars have demonstrated framing effects with experiments, surveys, and case studies across a range of issues" (p. 109). This range of methods is not surprising given the range of scholars who have been attracted to framing theory enough to conduct tests of its claims.

Stimulating Scholarly Attention Across Fields

As described in the introduction, the many ideas of framing theory have arisen from rhetoric and a variety of social sciences, particularly sociology, political science, psychology, and economics. Those ideas are still found useful across the social sciences as all kinds of scholars have conducted research on framing.

In sociology, framing theory has been used as a guide for examining the influence of "social norms and values, organizational pressures and constraints, pressures of interest groups, journalistic routines, and ideological or political orientations of journalists" (Scheufele, 2000). Framing theory has also stimulated sociologists to examine how people "process complex information in their everyday lives by reducing social perception to judgments about causal attribution" (Tewksbury & Scheufele, 2009, p. 18). A classic example of how a sociologist used framing theory was how Todd Gitlin (1980) used the theory to demonstrate that during the 1960s, the news media trivialized the student New Left movement.

Scholars in political science are typically interested in how frames in communication are constructed about political issues and candidates in elections and how these news frames influence public opinion. Candidates running for political office will typically use rhetorical devices to encourage their audiences to arrive at particular interpretations that favor the candidate. For example, a candidate delivers a speech that presents a problem in a way that one and only one solution is viable; audiences who listen to the speech are led to believe that the candidate has a clear vision about which problems are important and which solutions will work best. Thus political parties are in the business of framing issues in a particular manner so that the solutions they favor are presented as the only logical conclusions that audiences can draw.

In psychology, researchers focus on how individuals create their frames in thought (often called schema) from their experiences with media messages. Psychological scholars have also conducted a good deal of research to determine how individuals use those frames in cognitive processing as they interpret the meaning of messages in subsequent exposures.

Economists are concerned with how people make decisions about resources, and framing theory has been used to show that messages can mislead people. That is, when people are presented with a choice in a message, their choice is influenced by the way the choice is framed in that message.

Notable Lines of Research

The theory has stimulated a great deal of research. This research can be organized into four general categories: frame building, frame usage, framing effects, and how people use frames to process meaning.

1. Frame building. The theory has generated many studies designed to increase understanding about the types of frames found in media messages as well as the influences that account for how those frames get constructed.

Types of Frames. Researchers have come up with several ways of categorizing types of frames. One distinction is between episodic and thematic frames. Iyengar (1991) explains an episodic news frame "takes the form of a case study or event-oriented report and depicts public issues in terms of concrete instances," while a thematic news frame "places public issues in some more general abstract context ... directed at general outcomes or conditions." Iyengar (1991) carefully analyzed six years of television news stories to determine the frames used to present the issue of poverty and found that news stories concerning poverty were twice as likely to be presented with an episodic frame compared to a thematic frame. This pattern reveals that news viewers are presented with stories about poverty that are much likely to be anecdotal (showing the problem of a particular individual) rather than informing viewers about the broad patterns of poverty in society and the economy. Does this make a difference in how viewers attribute meaning to the problem with poverty? The answer is yes. Experiments have found that when people watch episodic news coverage of poverty, they are more than twice as likely as those who watched thematic news coverage of poverty to attribute responsibility of poverty to the poor themselves rather than society. Given the predominance of episodic framing of poverty, Iyengar argued that television news shifts responsibility of poverty from the government and society to the poor themselves. Iyengar then moved beyond the issue of poverty to look at other political issues and concluded that this pattern held, that is, when the news media cover an issue in an episodic manner, this type of coverage diverts audiences away from thinking about the issue as a problem with institutions such as politics or society and more of a problem with individuals making bad decisions. Thus when news coverage is dominated by episodic framing of complex social issues people become less likely to support government efforts to address those issues and instead simply blame the victims of social ills.

A more detailed way to organize the research literature on framing has been offered by Fairhurst and Sarr (1996) who argue that researchers have tested the influence of seven different kinds of frames. These seven are: metaphor (to frame an abstract idea by comparing it to something concrete); stories (to present an idea in a narrative to make it more vivid and understandable); tradition (using rituals to illustrate cultural beliefs in a way that shows the significance in the mundane); slogan-jargon-catchphrase (to frame an idea with a catchy phrase to make it more memorable and relatable); artifact (using objects with an intrinsic symbolic value, such as a symbol that holds more meaning than the object to which it refers); contrast (to describe an idea in terms of what it is not); and spin (to present a concept in such a way as to convey a value judgment that serves to create an inherent bias by definition).

Influences. Researchers have examined the influences on how frames get constructed in media messages, especially testing Goffman's (1974) initial conceptualization of internal and external influences. As for influences *inside* a news room, Goffman listed five aspects of news work that likely influence how journalists frame a certain issue. These are: (1) societal norms and values; (2) organizational pressures and constraints from within the world of journalism; (3) external pressures from interest groups and other policymakers from outside the world of journalism; (4) professional routines that journalists are expected to practice; and (5) ideological or political orientations of the journalists. As for those influences that come from *outside* the news room, Goffman claimed that frame building comes from elites, including interest groups, government bureaucracies, and other political or corporate actors. Empirical studies show that the influences from elites seem to be strongest for issues in which journalists and various players in the policy arena can find shared narratives.

2. Frame usage. Another line of research has focused on how people access frames in their minds and use them to interpret the meaning of media messages. This line of research has contributed to the development of several theoretical constructs including salience, availability, accessibility, and applicability.

Salience. Salience refers to how vividly a message element appears to audiences. Entman defined salience as "making a piece of information more noticeable, meaningful, or memorable to audiences" (p. 53). For example, when journalists are tasked with covering an event, they must determine what is to be presented as most important in their story. They could focus on the event itself and its timeliness. They could focus on the current occurrence in the context of what has happened before and thus emphasize a trend. They could focus on a particular person involved in order to personalize or humanize the event. Or they could focus on reactions to the event by people who were influenced by it even when they were not part of the event itself. The choice the journalist makes about what is most important is then featured most prominently in the story and it becomes the frame of the story because of its salience.

Availability. At times, people will make a conscious decision about which frames in thought to use. In such a situation, people will think about what frames are available and choose one to use as their frame in thought. However, this will require some effort so they need to be motivated to expend the required effort, and this motivation requires one of two conditions to be met. First, individuals can become more motivated to engage in conscious evaluation when those individuals are exposed to opposing points of view. Second, when people are sufficiently motivated, they will consider competing points of view that either come to mind spontaneously or are suggested by a particular frame (Stapel et al., 1998). Thus, either personal motivation or alternative points of view will stimulate individuals to decide how to interpret the meaning of a message when there are conflicting considerations (Druckman, 2001).

Accessibility. Accessibility refers to frames that are used most often by a person or at least the frames that have been used most often recently. Thus, the accessibility of a frame increases to the extent it is used. Frames that are used most often are most accessible.

Wyer and Srull (1984) explain that the employment of accessibility involves a three-step process. In the first step, individuals remember related pieces of information by placing them into "referent bins," which are like containers for information in their long-term memory. Second, people organize those "referent bins" by placing at the top of their mind those bins that they have used most recently along with those that they typically use most frequently. Thus the top of the mind bins are the most accessible. Then third, people tend to retrieve the most accessible pieces of information when they are faced with the task of interpreting the meaning of a message.

Sometimes people are aware of what is accessible but most times they are not (Higgins, 1996). Other times, the most accessible information will not be sufficient for interpreting meaning, so the individual will consciously evaluate the applicability of the accessible information and if it is not judged as applicable, the individual will see out additional information from mental bins. In sorting through the additional information, the individual will be guided by the need for applicability (Eagly & Chaiken, 1993).

Applicability. When people are exposed to a novel news frame, they need to work a bit harder to interpret its meaning. They need to search through their schema to find the one that is the most applicable to the task of interpreting the news story using that frame. People who have a well-developed set of schema on a particular topic will be more likely to find an applicable schema to help them interpret a news story on that topic that uses a novel frame. However, those people who have few schema or schema with little detail will be forced to select a poor schema to help them interpret the message.

3. *Framing effects.* There are three ways that researchers have measured the effect of frames in media messages (Chong & Druckman, 2007). One way is to follow a persuasion model and design an experiment with multiple treatment groups. Each treatment group is exposed to the same story but the framing is different for each treatment group. Then researchers look for which treatment results in the greatest persuasion effect. For example, Nelson, Clawson, and Oxley (1997) designed an experiment where they exposed participants to a news story that presented the Ku Klux Klan's plan to hold a rally. The researchers divided their participants into two conditions. In one condition, participants were asked to read a news story that framed the issue in terms of public safety concerns, and in the other condition participants read the same news story that framed the issue in terms of free speech considerations. The researchers found a strong persuasive effect traceable to how the story was framed. The participants who were exposed to the public safety condition considered public safety as being most applicable for deciding whether the Klan should be allowed to hold a rally; these participants expressed a lower tolerance of the Klan's right to hold a rally. In contrast, participants who were exposed to the free speech condition considered the idea of free speech as being most applicable for deciding whether the Klan should be allowed to hold a rally; these participants expressed greater tolerance of the Klan's right to hold a rally.

Almost all of the research that tests the effects of framing is designed to manipulate the frames, that is, the way information is presented, then measure effects to see whether those effects can be attributed to framing. To illustrate, Entman (1993) asked research participants to imagine an outbreak of a particularly bad disease, then to consider two programs that were being proposed as alternatives to combat the disease. One group of participants was told that in a group of 600 people, program A will save 200 people, while Program B has 1/3 probability that 600 people will be saved, and a 2/3 probability that no people will be saved. When confronted with this choice, 72 % of participants preferred program A. A second group of participants was told that in a group of 600 people, program C would result in 400 people dying, while program D would offer a 1/3 probability that nobody will die, and a 2/3 probability that 600 people will die. In this decision frame, 78 % preferred program D. Notice that programs A and C are identical, as are programs B and D. When the programs were presented in terms of lives saved, most participants preferred the secure program of A. However, when the programs were presented in terms of expected deaths, most participants chose the gamble D. The key finding of this study, as well as the findings from many other similar research studies, is that the way a problem is framed can significantly influence how people regard the problem and how they select from among possible solutions to the problem.

   4. Process of influence. How do frames exert their process of influence? Research conducted to answer this question has taken two interesting paths: testing for intervening variables and neuroimaging.

   Intervening variables. Intervening variables have been found to be important in explaining the process of influence. Chong and Druckman (2007) point out that many researchers have found intervening variables that are part of the process of influence leading to framing effects (e.g., Barker, 2005; Brewer, 2001; Druckman, 2001; Shen & Edwards, 2005). For example, Brewer (2001) found that people who have strong opinions about a topic are less likely to be influenced by how messages are framed. He conducted a framing experiment on the topic of gay rights and found that people who had strong values about gay rights were less amenable to frames that contradicted those values. However, people who did not have strong preexisting opinions were found to exhibit a framing effect.

   Studies of another intervening variable—knowledge—have produced conflicting results. Some framing studies have found stronger framing effects on less knowledgeable individuals (e.g., Kinder & Sanders, 1990), whereas other studies have found the opposite (Nelson et al., 1997; Slothuus, 2008). Druckman and Nelson (2003) argued that the conflicting results can be attributed to a failure to control for prior attitudes. They claim that knowledge is an important confound, so failure to control for the amount of knowledge that people have on a topic is a serious research design flaw because people with high knowledge on a topic also tend to possess entrenched beliefs, and it is the entrenched beliefs rather than the high knowledge that reduced susceptibility to a framing effect.

   Another intervening variable that has been examined is the perceived applicability or strength of a frame. Druckman (2001) found that when frames are delivered by credible sources, they are more likely to shift opinions. Also researchers have found that when frames invoke long-standing cultural values, they are more likely to evoke the use of strong frames (Chong & Druckman, 2007; Gamson & Modigliani, 1987).

Chong and Druckman (2007) argue that framing effects depend on a combination of factors. These factors include individual motivations, the strength of the frame, how often the frame is repeated, and the environment in which people experience the frames.

Neuroimaging. Neuroscientists have linked the framing effect to neural activity in the human brain. De Martino and colleagues point out that the brain area known as the amygdala as well as the the orbital and medial prefrontal cortex (OMPFC) both influence the role of emotion on decisions. These researchers conducted a study where they gave their participants a financial decision-making task while using an fMRI (functional magnetic resonance imaging) to monitor their brain activity. They found that there was greater activity in the OMPFC of those research subjects less susceptible to the framing effect (De Martino, Kumaran, Seymour, & Dolan, 2006). This research clearly shows that elements in the framing of a message can activate different parts of the human brain and this creates different paths of cognitive processing when interpreting messages.

Empirical Validity

Framing theory has generated a good deal of empirical support. This can be seen by reading the results of individual research studies or narrative reviews of the literature.

Unfortunately there are no meta-analyses of a framing effect in general, but there is one meta-analysis of parts of the framing literature. Piñon and Gambara (2005) published a meta-analysis of 51 independent primary studies that presented 151 estimations of the effect size with nearly 13,500 subjects. They found that the effect of certain types of frames, as indicated by a d index, was 0.437 for risky frames, 0.260 for attribute frames, and 0.444 for goal frames.

Theory Development

Criticisms

1. Conceptual criticisms. One of the most serious and persistent criticisms of framing theory is that it has been defined in many different ways and this has created a good deal of confusion about what it really is (Chong & Druckman, 2007; Tewksbury & Scheufele, 2009). For example, Tewksbury and Scheufele (2009) argued that framing in communication literature has been characterized by "conceptual obliqueness and operational inconsistency" (p. 17). They explained that "part of this vagueness at different levels stems from the fact that framing researchers have often approached the theory very inductively and examined framing as a phenomenon without careful explication of the theoretical premises and their operational implications" (p. 17).

Within the literature of framing theory, there are some concepts where scholars apply different labels to the same thing. For example, frames in thought are often referred to as schemata, categories, scripts, and stereotypes, to name just a few synonyms. This definitional slippage has led at least one scholar to be highly critical of the theory. For example, Entman (1993) called framing "a scattered conceptualization" and "a fractured paradigm" that "is often defined casually, with much left to an assumed tacit understanding of the reader." In an effort to provide more conceptual clarity, Entman suggested that frames "select some aspects of a perceived reality and make them more salient in a communicating text, in such a way as to promote a particular problem definition, causal interpretation, moral evaluation, and/or treatment recommendation for the item described."

2. Methodological criticisms. Critics have focused on three problems with tests of framing theory. First, Tewksbury and Scheufele (2009) argue that the inductive nature of the research has resulted in many micro-findings that are not tied into a search for identifying "master frames," which are the widespread ones that are potentially applicable across all issues because they deal with more enduring cultural themes.

Second, critics have argued that researchers have failed to pay enough attention to framing as a multilevel problem. Tewksbury and Scheufele (2009) argue that "not only has the label of 'framing' been used to describe phenomena that are clearly not framing, but we have also yet to clearly delineate which effects in everyday news coverage of issues are due to informational content differences and which ones are a function of differences in the mode of presentation or other framing devices" (p. 29).

Third, media effects research often experiences something of a disjuncture between the hypothesized nature of some effect and the limitations of the methods chosen to study it. Tewksbury and Scheufele (2009) complain that researchers want to look at the long-term shaping nature of the media flow of messages on people's frames but their research rarely is longitudinal. Chong and Druckman (2007) also criticized framing research for not being more longitudinal by saying, "Most studies of framing effects consist of a single session for each subject, with effects tested shortly after exposure to communications. Future studies should examine the impact of framing across longer durations of time, with individuals being exposed to streams of competing information intended to parallel the give and take of political campaigns. This would allow us to examine how varying rates of learning and forgetting influence the magnitude of framing effects, and to identify conditions under which individuals might become inoculated against attempts to manipulate their preferences" (p. 118).

Conceptual Alterations

Over time, researchers have suggested that new ideas be added to the theory and some of the findings from framing research that have been incorporated into the theory itself. These additions include: frame alignment, frame bridging, frame amplification, frame extensions, and frame transformation.

Frame alignment. Frame alignment refers to a situation where the frame in a news story (frame in communication) lines up with a person's schema (frame in thought) and/or a more general belief system held by the public. When all three of these align, the influence of the news story is stronger. Snow and Benford (1988) regard frame alignment as an essential strategy for social mobilization. They explain that when particular frames become congruent and complementary, then frame alignment occurs and that this alignment produces frame resonance, which makes the framing effect more powerful.

Frame bridging. Frame bridging links clusters of people who share similar beliefs but who have otherwise not had any means to share their beliefs with a broader group of people. Frame bridging works by engaging the "linkage of two or more ideologically congruent but structurally unconnected frames regarding a particular issue or problem" (Snow et al., 1986, p. 467).

Frame amplification. Frame amplification refers to "the clarification and invigoration of an interpretive frame that bears on a particular issue, problem, or set of events" (Snow et al., 1986, p. 469). In order for frame amplification to occur, a person must have a preexisting set of values and beliefs; the frame then invigorates those existing values or beliefs.

Frame extensions. Frame extensions refers to how a social movement will widen the frame of its messages in order to appeal to a larger number of people. The frame is widened by attempting to encompass the "views, interests, or sentiments of targeted groups" (Snow et al., 1986, p. 472).

Frame transformation. Frame transformation refers to how social movements will substantially alter the framing of their messages in order to keep up with changing times or to eliminate faulty thinking in its past. Frame transformation becomes necessary when the old ways of framing messages "may not resonate with, and on occasion may even appear antithetical to, conventional lifestyles or rituals and extant interpretive frames" (Snow et al., 1986, p. 473). When this happens, the social movement will become irrelevant unless it can attract new followers by espousing new values and new meanings.

Two types of frame transformation exist. One of these is called domain-specific transformation. This can occur when a social movement attempts to alter the status of groups of people. The second of these is called global interpretive frame transformation. This can occur when a social movement wants to make a large change in its nature, so it engages in a significant change of worldviews, a total conversion of thought, or an uprooting of everything familiar. An example of this on the macro-level would be a radical change in government, such as a movement from communism to market capitalism. An example of this on an individual level would be a major religious conversion.

Current Challenges

There seem to be two challenges currently facing framing theory. One of these is to increase the precision in the use of key ideas. The second is for the theory to establish its uniqueness.

Increase Precision in Definitions

As seen in the criticism section above, there are many examples of a term being used with many different meanings. Also, there are examples of a single idea being referred to with many different names. This problem is understandable given how framing has grown in many different fields. But the continual confusion makes it difficult for knowledge to be synthesized across those fields when meanings are fluctuating.

Establishing Uniqueness

Framing theory grew out of well-recognized research traditions (especially rhetoric and cognitive psychology) that have continued to be productive. The theory has grown in prominence alongside other similar theories, especially agenda setting and persuasion. While it is good that framing theory is linked to other theories and research traditions, it faces a challenge of continually highlighting its uniqueness so that scholars do not regard it as being subsumed under another theory.

Framing and agenda setting. Framing is in many ways tied very closely to agenda setting theory (Volkmer, 2009). Agenda setting started out as a system of explanation about how media can attract people to specific topics. Over time, agenda setting theory has grown to include explanations about how that process works, which is what framing theory has always focused its attention on. Supporters of framing theory take this explanation a step further by specifying how message characteristics exert their influence on audiences. For example, with news stories, agenda setting theory is more focused on whether the public is influenced by the salience of certain issues, whereas framing theory is more concerned with how news gatekeepers organize and present the ideas, events, and topics they cover.

There is currently a debate over whether framing theory is independent from agenda setting theory, as was mentioned in the previous chapter. McCombs and other agenda setting scholars argue that framing should be incorporated into their agenda setting theory. They point out that agenda setting has developed into an umbrella that subsumes the ideas of framing into an overarching model of media effects that links media production, content, and audience effects (McCombs, Llamas, Lopez-Escobar, & Rey, 1997). Specifically, they show that what they developed as second level of agenda setting incorporates all the ideas currently in framing theory.

In contrast, Scheufele (2000) claims that, unlike agenda setting, framing does not rely primarily on accessibility so that it is inappropriate to combine framing with agenda setting. Scheufele's claim is supported by some empirical evidence (Nelson et al., 1997) that demonstrated that applicability (as predicted by framing), rather than salience (as predicted by agenda setting), is a better explanation for how people interpret the meaning of messages. Nelson et al. demonstrated that accessibility accounted for only a minor proportion of the variance in framing effects, while applicability accounted for a much larger proportion of variance. They explain, "frames influence opinions by stressing specific values, facts, and other considerations, endowing them with greater apparent relevance to the issue than they might appear to have under an alternative frame."

Framing and persuasion. Some scholars regard framing as part of persuasion but others argue that there is an important difference (Chong & Druckman, 2007; Nelson & Oxley, 1999). For example, Nelson and Oxley (1999) point out that persuasion is measured as a difference in attitude, while framing is measured by a difference in the weight of a person's attitude. To illustrate this distinction consider media coverage of a controversy over whether a local government should approve a proposed housing project. Framing takes place if a media message causes economic considerations to become more important relative to environmental considerations. In contrast, persuasion occurs if the message alters one's evaluation of the issue so that a person changes her mind from support to opposition.

Conclusions

Framing theory is a fairly broad theory. It applies to all kinds of messages in all media channels, and its effect is not limited by type, valence, or intentionality. Its effect was originally regarded as triggering, which is an immediate effect but over time framing has been viewed as having both long-term and immediate effects.

It has been criticized for lack of precision due to varying conceptualizations about what framing is. This problem persists largely because the theory has no single scholar controlling it so the ideas of multiple scholars continue to circulate.

It has stimulated a good deal of scholarly attention not just within media studies but in other scholarly fields as well. Researchers have generated a relatively large literature of tests, although it is difficult to find a review that estimates the size of that literature. And those tests generally support the claims made by the theory.

Key Sources

Background

Boulding, K. E. (1956). *The image: Knowledge in life and society*. Ann Arbor, MI: University of Michigan Press.

Goffman, E. (1959). *The presentation of self in everyday life*. Garden City, NY: Doubleday Anchor Books.

Origin

Bateson, G. (1972). *Steps to an ecology of mind*. New York, NY: Ballantine Books.

Goffman, E. (1974). *Frame analysis: An essay on the organization of experience*. New York, NY: Harper & Row.

Reviews

Chong, D., & Druckman, J. N. (2007). Framing theory. *Annual Review of Political Science, 10*, 103–126. doi:10.1146/annurev.polisci.10.072805.103054.

Druckman, J. N. (2001). The implications of framing effects for citizen competence. *Political Behavior, 23*(3), 225–256. doi:10.1023/A:1015006907312.

Entman, R. M. (1993). Framing: Toward clarification of a fractured paradigm. *Journal of Communication, 43*(4), 51–58. doi:10.1111/j.1460-2466.1993.tb01304.x.

Fairhurst, G. T., & Sarr, R. A. (1996). *The art of framing: Managing the language of leadership*. San Francisco, CA: Jossey-Bass.

Kahneman, D., & Tversky, A. (1984). Choices, values, and frames. *American Psychologist, 39*(4), 341–350. doi:10.1037/0003-066X.39.4.341.

Nelson, T. E., Oxley, Z. M., & Clawson, R. A. (1997). Toward a psychology of framing effects. Political Behavior, 19(3): 221–246. doi:10.1023/A:1024834831093.

Scheufele, D. A. (1999). Framing as a theory of media effects. Journal of Communication, 49(1), 103–122.

Scheufele, D. A. (2000). Agenda-setting, priming, and framing revisited: Another look at cognitive effects of political communication. Mass Communication & Society, 3(2&3), 297–316. doi:10.1207/S15327825MCS0323_07.

Scheufele, D. A., & Iyengar, S. (2014. The state of framing research: A call for new directions. In K. Kenski & K. H. Jamieson (Eds.), The Oxford handbook of political communication theories. New York, NY: Oxford University Press. doi:10.1093/oxfordhb/9780199793471.013.47

Tewksbury, D., & Scheufele, D. A. (2009). News framing theory and research. In J. Bryant & M. B. Oliver (Eds.), Media effects: Advances in theory and research (pp. 17–33). New York, NY: Routledge.

Tversky, A., & Kahneman, D. (1981). The framing of decisions and the psychology of choice. Science, 211(4481), 453–458. doi:10.1126/science.7455683. PMID 7455683.

Volkmer, I. (2009). Framing theory. In S. W. Littlejohn & K. A. Foss (Eds.), Encyclopedia of communication theory (pp. 407–408). Los Angeles, CA: Sage.

Criticisms

Chong, D., & Druckman, J. N. (2007). Framing theory. Annual Review of Political Science, 10, 103–126. doi:10.1146/annurev.polisci.10.072805.103054.

Entman, R. M. (1993). Framing: Toward clarification of a fractured paradigm. Journal of Communication, 43(4), 51–58. doi:10.1111/j.1460-2466.1993.tb01304.x.

Tewksbury, D., & Scheufele, D. A. (2009). News framing theory and research. In J. Bryant & M. B. Oliver (Eds.), Media effects: Advances in theory and research (pp. 17–33). New York, NY: Routledge.

References

Barker, D. (2005). Values, frames, and persuasion in presidential nomination campaigns. Political Behavior, 27, 375–394.

Brewer, P. R. (2001). Value words and lizard brains: Do citizens deliberate about appeals to their core values? Political Psychology, 22, 45–64.

Chong, D., & Druckman, J. N. (2007). Framing theory. Annual Review of Political Science, 10, 103–126.

De Martino, B., Kumaran, D., Seymour, B., & Dolan, R. J. (2006). Frames, biases, and rational decision-making in the human brain. Science, 313(5787), 684–687. doi:10.1126/science.1128356. PMC 2631940. PMID 16888142.

Druckman, J. N. (2001). The implications of framing effects for citizen competence. *Political Behavior, 23*(3), 225–256. doi:10.1023/A:1015006907312

Druckman, J. N., & Nelson, K. R. (2003). Framing and deliberation: How citizens' conversations limit elite influence. *American Journal of Political Science, 47*, 729–745.

Eagley, A. H., & Chaiken, S. (1993). Attitude structure and function. In D. Gilbert, S. T. Fiske, & G. Lindsey (Eds.), *Handbook of social psychology* (Vol. 2, pp. 269–322). Boston, MA: McGraw-Hill.

Entman, R. M. (1993). Framing: Toward clarification of a fractured paradigm. *Journal of Communication, 43*(4), 51–58. doi:10.1111/j.1460-2466.1993.tb01304.x

Fairhurst, G. T., & Sarr, R. A. (1996). *The art of framing: Managing the language of leadership*. San Francisco, CA: Jossey-Bass.

Fiske, S. T., & Taylor, S. E. (1991). *Social cognition* (2nd ed.). New York, NY: McGraw-Hill.

Gamson, W. A., & Modigliani, A. (1987) The changing culture of affirmative action. *Research in Political Sociology, 3*, 137–177.

Gitlin, T. (1980). *The whole world is watching: Mass media in the making and unmaking of the New Left*. Berkeley, CA: University of California Press.

Goffman, E. (1974). *Frame analysis: An essay on the organization of experience*. New York, NY: Harper & Row.

Higgins, E. T. (1996). Knowledge activation: Accessibility, applicability, and salience. In E. T. Higgins & A. W. Kruglanski (Eds.), *Social psychology: Handbook of basic principles* (pp. 133–168). New York, NY: Guilford.

Iyengar, S. (1991). *Is anyone responsible? How television frames political issues*. Chicago, IL: University of Chicago Press.

Kahneman, D., & Tversky, A. (1979). Prospect theory: An analysis of decision under risk. *Econometrica, 47*, 263–291.

Kahneman, D., & Tversky, A. (1984). Choices, values, and frames. *American Psychologist, 39*(4), 341–350. doi:10.1037/0003-066X.39.4.341

Kinder, D. R., & Sanders, L. M. (1990). Mimicking political debate with survey questions. *Social Cognition, 8*, 73–103.

Lippmann, W. (1922). *Public opinion*. London: Transaction.

McCombs, M. E., Llamas, J. P., Lopez-Escobar, E., & Rey, F. (1997). Candidate images in Spanish elections: Second-level agenda-setting effects. *Journalism & Mass Communication Quarterly, 74*, 703–717.

Nelson, T. E., Clawson, R. A., & Oxley, Z. M. (1997). Media framing of a civil liberties conflict and its effect on tolerance. *American Political Science Review 91*(3), 567–583. doi:10.2307/2952075

Nelson, T. E., & Oxley, Z. M. (1999). Issue framing effects on belief importance and opinion. *The Journal of Politics, 61*, 1040–1067.

Nelson, T. E., Oxley, Z. M., & Clawson, R. A. (1997). Toward a psychology of framing effects. *Political Behavior, 19*(3): 221–246. doi:10.1023/A:1024834831093

Pinon, A., & Gambara, H. (2005). A meta-analytic review of framing effect: Risky, attribute and goal framing. *Psicothema, 17*(2), 325–331.

Scheufele, D. A. (2000). Agenda-setting, priming, and framing revisited: Another look at cognitive effects of political communication. *Mass Communication & Society, 3*(2&3), 297–316. doi:10.1207/S15327825MCS0323_07

Shah, D. V., Kwak, N., Schmierbach, M., & Zubric, J. (2004). The interplay of news frames on cognitive complexity. *Human Communication Research, 30*, 102–120.

Shen, F., & Edwards, H. H. (2005). Economic individualism, humanitarianism, and welfare reform: A value-based account of framing effects. *Journal of Communication, 55*, 795–809.

Sherif, M. (1967). *Social interaction: Processes and products.* Chicago: Aldine.

Slothus, R. (2008). More than weighting cognitive importance: A dual-process model of issue framing effects. *Political Psychology, 29*, 1–28.

Snow, D. A., & Benford, R. D. (1988). Ideology, frame resonance, and participant mobilization. *International Social Movement Research, 1*, 197–217.

Snow, D. A., Rochford, E. B., Worden, S. K., & Benford, R. D. (1986). Frame alignment processes, micromobilization, and movement participation. *American Sociological Review, 51*(4), 464–481. doi:10.2307/2095581

Tuchman, G. (1978). *Making news: A study in the construction of reality.* New York: Free Press.

Volkmer, I. (2009). Framing theory. In S. W. Littlejohn & K. A. Foss (Eds.), *Encyclopedia of communication theory* (pp. 407–408). Los Angeles, CA: Sage.

Wyer, Jr., R. S., & Srull, T. K. (1984). Category Accessibility: Some theoretic and empirical issues concerning the processing of social stimulus information. In E.T. Higgins, N. A. Kuiper, & M. P Zanna (Eds.), *Social Cognition.* Hillsdale, NJ: The Ontario Symposium.

CHAPTER SEVEN

Uses and Gratifications Theory

Uses and gratifications theory provides a system of explanation about why people expose themselves to the media in general as well as to particular media, their vehicles, and their messages. The central idea in this explanation is that people seek gratifications from their exposures so they continuously select those media options that have the strongest expectations for gratification. Thus, this explanation of media usage assumes that audience members are aware of their needs and that they are rational in using strategies to satisfy their needs.

Original Conceptualization of the Theory

Conceptual Foundation

In the early half of the 20th century, media scholarship was focused on effects as most theoreticians and researchers sought to explain how the mass media affected individuals and aggregates. However, some scholars (e.g., Berelson, 1949; Herzog, 1944; Lazarsfeld & Stanton, 1944, 1949; Warner & Henry, 1948) took the position that they were less concerned with media effects than with what people were doing with the media and why. These scholars argued that people are active in seeking out particular media and messages so that there must be some expectation of satisfaction to explain their exposure behavior.

The exploration of gratifications that motivate people to be attracted to certain media is almost as old as empirical mass communication research itself (McQuail, 1983) and it appears to have grown out of three social sciences approaches: functionalism, economics, and psychology.

Functionalism. The functional approach was influential in media studies from the 1920s to the 1940s (Blumler & Katz, 1974). This approach motivated some researchers to identify the functions that media were serving in people's lives. In these studies, researchers discovered a list of functions served either by some specific content or by the medium itself (Katz, Blumler, & Gurevitch, 1974b). For example, radio soap operas were found to satisfy their listeners' needs for advice, support, and emotional release (Herzog, 1944; Warner & Henry, 1948). Also, newspapers were found to be more than deliverers of information; they also satisfied audience needs for security by the way they helped structure readers' daily routines and provide them with topics of conversation that could be shared with others (Berelson, 1949).

Some scholars tried to organize the functions of using media into typologies. For example, Lasswell (1948) introduced a four-functional interpretation of the media on a macro-sociological level to organize all the needs that media were satisfying. Laswell's four functions were surveillance, correlation, entertainment, and cultural transmission for both society and individuals. Others created slightly different typologies (McQuail, Blumler, & Brown, 1972; Wright, 1960).

Economic approach. Wilbur Schramm (1954) argued that people make their selection of media exposures by comparing their expectation of a reward with effort required. He presented what he called the fraction of selection, which is a formula for determining which form of mass media an individual would select. The formula helped to decide the amount of gratification an individual would expect to gain from the medium compared to how much effort she/he had to make to achieve gratification.

Psychological approach. Some scholars used a psychological approach by looking for cognitive constructs—such as needs and motives—to explain media exposures. For example, Abraham Maslow suggested that needs were structured like a pyramid with the largest, most fundamental needs at the base. From the bottom-up, Maslow's pyramid is composed of levels for Biological/Physical, Security/Safety, Social/Belonging, Ego/Self-Respect, and Self-Actualization needs at the top.

Blumler and McQuail (1969) studied the 1964 election in the United Kingdom by examining people's motives for watching political programs on television. By categorizing the audience's motives for viewing a certain program, they aimed to classify viewers according to their needs in order to understand potential mass media effects. Several years later, Katz, Gurevitch, and Haas joined Blumler and McQuail in their investigations of how audiences selected media content for exposure. The studies by Katz and his colleagues laid a theoretical foundation of building the uses and gratifications approach. Since then, the research on this topic has been strengthened and extended. The current status of uses and gratifications theory is still based on Katz's first analysis, particularly as new media forms have emerged in such an electronic information age when people have more options of media use.

Introduction of the Theory

Jay Blumler and Elihu Katz are generally credited with introducing uses and gratifications as a theory in their 1974 publication of a book entitled *The Uses of Mass Communications: Current Perspectives on Gratifications Research*. They argued that media audiences were active and that it was important to study how people made their media selections and not be limited to studying only how the media affected people. In short, they were more concerned about what people did with the media instead of what the media did to people. Their book is composed of 15 chapters where 14 of those chapters were authored by media scholars who had conducted empirical research examining audience needs and motivations. In the other chapter, Katz, Blumler, and Gurevitch (1974a) reviewed the literature conducted under that approach and presented a synthesis of ideas that became known as uses and gratifications theory.

The theory was presented as an alternative to traditional theories at the time that treated people substantially as mechanisms. In contrast, uses and gratifications theory took a more humanistic approach recognizing that each individual had many reasons for using media and that those reasons differed across individuals. Furthermore the theory emphasized that people have free will to decide how they will use the media and how it will affect them. Blumler and Katz (1974) pointed out each media message has the potential to satisfy several different needs, so it was not surprising to find that different people can be attracted to the same media message for different reasons. They went so far as to argue that there are as many reasons for using the media as there are media users (Blumler & Katz, 1974).

Blumler and Katz (1974) said they had three objectives in developing uses and gratifications theory. First, they wanted to explain how individuals use mass communication to gratify their needs. Their theory sought to answer the question: What do people do with the media? Second, they wanted to discover underlying motives for individuals' media use. And third, they wanted to identify the positive and the negative consequences of individual media use.

Some scholars characterize the introduction of the theory in the early 1970s as groundbreaking and revolutionary because it shifted attention away from looking at what the media do to people and onto looking at what people do with the media. This approach differs from other theoretical perspectives in that it regards audiences as active media users as opposed to passive receivers of information. But other scholars argued that media research has always been concerned with examining why people expose themselves to the media and why they select particular vehicles and messages. Palmgreen, Wenner, and Rosengren (1985) observed that "media gratifications research was neither new nor revolutionary when posed in Blumler and Katz's landmark volume *The Uses of Mass Communications* in 1974" (p. 11). Instead it simply captured "the concerns of many mass communication researchers who felt the need for a shift to a vision of the mass communication process that more clearly embraced the concept of an active audience" (p. 11). McQuail (2005) adds that "The idea that media use depends on the perceived satisfactions, needs, wishes or motives of the prospective audience member is almost as old as media research itself" (p. 423).

Conceptualization of Media

The theory is broad with regard to media. It does not rule out any medium nor does it privilege any single medium over others (Rubin, 2009a).

Conceptualization of Media Effect

Despite the often heard claim that uses and gratification theory shifts attention away from effects and onto the audience, there are two effects predicted by the theory. One of those effects is media exposure, which is a behavioral effect that can either be immediate or long term but is typically immediate. The other effect is gratification, which is an emotional effect experienced during and immediately after the exposure.

Conceptualization of Media Influence

Because uses and gratifications theory regards audience members as active, the effects of the media are not viewed as particularly powerful, because the theory claims that people can control the effects to a large extent. The reasoning behind this claims is that because the power of selection lies with the person, people are more powerful than the media.

Furthermore, uses and gratifications theory recognizes that audience members are individuals, each with a different history with the media, different needs, and different motives. If we try to ignore these differences and look for patterns in aggregates, then the findings of research display weak predictions. But this does not mean the theory is weak, only that people who are individually powerful because of their differences look weak when those differences are not accounted for and therefore cancel each other out when the analysis is conducted at an aggregate level.

Rosengren (1974) argued that the key idea of uses and gratifications was that individual differences among audience members intervene between the media and any effects. This means that media effects are explained not just by the media content but also by audience characteristics, such as their motivations and involvement with the content.

Original Components

Key Concepts

There are two primary concepts as the title of the theory indicates—uses and gratifications. "Uses" has been conceptualized as selection. People have an overwhelming number of media messages available to them at any given time; they cannot use all media, so they must make selections.

The concept of "gratifications" was introduced into the media literature by Herzog (1944), and since that time, every scholar who writes about uses and gratifications theory grapples with this idea. Sometimes gratifications are conceptualized as functions, sometimes as needs that are satisfied, and sometimes as goals that have been achieved (see Table 7.1).

Core Propositions

When we strip uses and gratifications theory down to its core essence, we see there is one central proposition: Gratifications sought (GS) explains gratifications obtained (GO). Katz et al. (1974a) elaborated this simple connection between GS and GO by laying out a more elaborate explanation in what they articulated as the seven components of the theory they were introducing. These seven components were: "(1) the social and psychological origins of (2) needs, which generate (3) expectations of (4) the mass media or other sources which lead to (5) differential patterns of media exposure (or engagement in other activities), resulting in

Table 7.1. Organizing Conceptualizations of Gratifications

Gratifications as Functions

Lasswell (1948)

> Surveillance of the environment
> Correlation of parts of that environment
> Transmission of our heritage
> Entertainment (added by Wright, 1960)

Gratifications as Needs

McQuail et al. (1972)

> Diversion (escape from routine or problems)
> Personal relationships (companionship and social utility)
> Personal identity (self-reference, reality exploration, value reinforcement)
> Surveillance (forms of information seeking)

Katz, Haas, and Gurevitch (1973)—35 needs organized in 5 groupings

> (1) Cognitive needs, including acquiring information, knowledge, and understanding
> (2) Affective needs, including emotion, pleasure, feelings
> (3) Personal integrative needs, including credibility, stability, status
> (4) Social integrative needs, including interacting with family and friends
> (5) Tension release needs, including escape and diversion

1. *Cognitive needs:* People use media for acquiring information, but each person has different needs for information, so they will seek out different media messages.

2. *Affective needs*: People use the media to satisfy all kinds of affective needs such as seeking emotional reactions and altering their mood states.

3. *Personal integrative needs*: This is the self-esteem need. People use media to reassure their status, gain credibility and stabilize their everyday lives. People seek out media messages in order to assure themselves that they have status in society and to improve their status by using high status people in the media as role models.

4. *Social integrative needs*: People use the media to enhance the way they socialize with family, friends and relations. People are using the media as a way to socialize with people online instead of engaging in real life social gatherings.

5. *Tension-free needs*: People sometimes use the media as a means of escaping from their real lives in order to reduce tension and stress. Watching television, listening to radio, and surfing the Internet can distract people from worrying about what is happening in their real lives.

Gratifications as goals

McQuail (1983, p. 73)

1. Seeking information (finding out about relevant events and conditions in immediate surroundings, society, and the world; seeking advice on practical matters or opinion and decision choices; satisfying curiosity and general interest; learning; self-education; and gaining a sense of security through knowledge).

(Continued)

Table 7.1. *Continued*

---

2. Personal identity (finding reinforcement for personal values; finding models of behavior; identifying with valued others (in the media); and gaining insight into oneself).
3. Integration and social interaction (gaining insight into the circumstances of others; social empathy; identifying with others and gaining a sense of belonging; finding a basis for conversation and social interaction; having a substitute for real-life companionship; helping to carry out social roles; and enabling one to connect with family, friends, and society).
4. Entertainment (escaping, or being diverted, from problems; relaxing; getting intrinsic cultural or aesthetic enjoyment; filling time; emotional release; and sexual arousal).

---

(6) need gratifications, and (7) other consequences, perhaps mostly unintended ones" (p. 20). Thus, this statement suggests five propositions as follows:

1. Social and psychological traits and states explain a person's needs.
2. A person's needs generate expectations of gratifications.
3. A person's expectations for gratifications explain their media exposure patterns (as well as engagement in other activities).
4. Exposure to media messages (as well as other experiences) can trigger gratifications.
5. Exposure to media messages (as well as other experiences) can trigger other consequences.

Early on, scholars recognized that the idea of motivation underlay all of these five prepositions and they sought to elaborate on motivation. For example, Blumler (1979) elaborated the concept of motivation and made three claims. First, Blumler claimed that a cognitive-type motivation will facilitate information gain. Second, diversion and escape motivations will favor audience acceptance of perceptions of social situations in line with portrayals frequently found in entertainment materials. Third, personal identity motivations will promote reinforcement effects (pp. 31–32). Also, Rubin (2009a) argued that motivation is a key concept because it influences the selective and active manner in which people participate in media communication and the possible outcomes of those encounters.

Foundational Assumptions

Many scholars have tried to capture the set of assumptions upon which this theory is built (see Table 7.2). It appears that the core of these many assumptions is that

Table 7.2. Perceptions of Assumptions Underlying Uses and Gratifications Theory

Katz, Blumler, and Gurevitch

1. The audience is active.
2. In the mass communication process, much initiative in linking gratification and media choice lies with the audience member.
3. The media compete with other sources of satisfaction.
4. Methodologically speaking, many of the goals of mass media use can be derived from data supplied by individual audience members themselves.
5. Value judgments about the cultural significance of mass communication should be suspended while audience orientations are explored on their own terms.

Palmgreen et al. (1985, p. 14)

1. The audience is active.
2. Much media use can be conceived as goal directed.
3. Media compete with other sources of need satisfaction.
4. Substantial audience initiative links needs to media choice.
5. Media consumption can fulfill a wide range of gratifications.
6. Media content alone cannot be used to predict patterns of gratifications accurately, because needs change over time and vary across people.
7. Media characteristics structure the degree to which needs may be gratified at different times.
8. Gratifications obtained can have their origins in media content exposure in and of itself, and/or the social situation in which exposure takes place.

McQuail (2005)

1. Media and content choices are generally rational and directed toward certain specific goals and satisfactions (thus the audience is active and audience formation can be logically explained).
2. Audience members are conscious of the media-related needs which arise in personal (individuals) and social (shared) circumstances and can voice these in terms of motivations.
3. Broadly speaking, personal utility is a more significant determinant of audience formation than aesthetic or cultural factors.
4. All or most of the relevant factors for audience formation (motives, perceived or obtained satisfactions, media choices, background variables) can, in principle, be measured (p. 424).

audience members actively seek out the mass media to satisfy individual needs. This central assumption suggests a cluster of supporting assumptions. For example, when Katz, Blumler, and Gurevitch introduced the theory, they said it was built on five assumptions, as follows: (1) Communication behavior is goal-directed, purposive, and motivated; (2) People initiate the selection and use of communication vehicles; (3) A host of social and psychological factors guide, filter, or mediate communication behavior; (4) The media compete with other forms of communication in the gratification of needs or wants; and (5) People are typically more influential than the media in the effects process (Rubin, 2002).

Thus the theory clearly views people as active users of the media. Levy and Windahl (1985) provide a good description of what it means to be an "active consumer" of media by explaining that "audience activity" postulates a voluntaristic and selective orientation by audiences toward the communication process. In brief, it suggests that media use is motivated by needs and goals that are defined by audience members themselves, and that active participation in the communication process may facilitate, limit, or otherwise influence the gratifications and effects associated with exposure. It appears that this assumption has received support in the empirical literature because there is a tradition of researchers asking people to express their motivations and their gratifications. However, there is a nagging feeling that people may not be aware of all their needs, drives, and motivations, that is, there may be many of these that are unconscious, thus people may not be aware of them. By emphasizing conscious choice and free will, the theory ignored the possibility that media exert an unconscious influence over our lives and how we view the world. The idea that we simply use the media to satisfy a given need does not seem to fully recognize the power of the media in today's society.

Empirical Testing

Stimulating Scholarly Attention

The uses and gratification theory has stimulated a great deal of scholarly attention. Uses and gratifications is one of the most widely used theoretical underpinnings of communication research. As such, handbooks and yearbooks typically include chapters that summarize and reappraise the theory.

About ten years after the introduction of the theory, various scholars began publishing reviews of the growing literature (Palmgreen, 1984; Palmgreen et al., 1985) and assessed the growth of the perspective over the decade. While much has been added to the body of uses and gratifications knowledge, these chapters remain useful for identifying the important concepts and questions that undergird the perspective. Rubin (1986, 2009a, 2009b) is perhaps the most prolific of the uses and gratifications researchers. He regularly contributes chapters to handbooks that serve as model analyses of uses and gratifications. His work updates not only the significant findings but also identifies significant areas of current and future research.

Empirical Literature

Palmgreen et al. (1985) see two phases of development of the theory. The first phase focused on determining what gratifications audiences sought and organizing those gratifications into inventories or taxonomies. Blumler and Katz (1974) characterized this first phase research as providing "insightful description of audience subgroup orientations to selected media content forms" (p. 13). A good deal of the early research testing the theory used a functionalist approach and focused on formulating typologies (Rubin, 2009a) that extended and revised earlier typologies of motivations (Lasswell, 1948; McQuail et al., 1972; Wright, 1960). These typologies have guided researchers to test all sorts of motivations and functions that elaborate and extend those typologies.

The second phase was called operationalization. By this they meant that the focus shifted to explaining why audience members experienced gratifications and this involved identifying social and psychological variables that differentiated people and thereby explained why some people found gratifications from a particular exposure while others did not. Some of the more often researched variables include: mood management, affective disposition, excitation transfer, sensation seeking, modes of reception, intrinsic motivation, gender socialization of emotions, parasocial relationships, vicarious experiences, downward social comparison, and eudaimonic motivation.

Mood management. This is the most prominently cited emotional gratification of media use. People prefer to maintain a state of intermediate arousal; this is a pleasant medium. When in a bad mood, bored, or overaroused, people will seek media as regulation for or distraction from their mood (Zillmann, 1988, 2000). Users are gratified by using media to adjust their mood to whatever is currently happening. For instance, once already provoked by an aggressor and promised a chance to retaliate, males were found to prefer bad news over good news in that emotionally charged moment (Knobloch, 2003).

Affective disposition. Affective disposition theory states that people enjoy "rooting for" characters depicted as good and moral. Users experience gratification when good things happen to characters with "good" morals and also when bad things happen to "evil" or "bad" characters (Raney, 2003).

Modes of reception. Emotional involvement has been found to be associated with other modes of reception, particularly with diegetic involvement (getting absorbed in the fictional world), socio-involvement (identifying with characters), and ego-involvement (relating the film to one's own life) (Bartsch & Viehoff, 2010).

Gender socialization of emotions. This use is gratified by the idea that women enjoy feeling other-directed sadness (empathy, sympathy, and pity) because our culture values and validates women's feeling of these (Oliver, 1993); similarly, teen-age couples like to watch scary movies so the male feels protective and the female feels vulnerable (Mundorf & Mundorf, 2003).

Parasocial relationships. Consumers of entertainment media sometimes use media messages to gratify a need for social connection by becoming very attached to characters they see in entertainment media, such as characters in a TV show or newscasters (Horton & Wohl, 1956; Rubin & Perse, 1987).

Vicarious experiences. Many people obtain gratifications from entertainment media by living through the characters portrayed and imagining themselves in their lives by adopting the characters' perspectives (Green & Brock, 2000).

Downward social comparison. This gratification holds that we enjoy taking in media that portray people similar or worse off than ourselves (Knobloch & Zillmann, 2003; Mares & Cantor, 1992).

Eudaimonic motivation. Media consumers also turn to entertainment media to search for deeper meanings, insights, purpose for life, finding beauty, raising morale, experiencing strong emotions, and understanding how others think and feel (Oliver & Bartsch, 2010; Oliver & Raney, 2011).

In summary, research has shown that people use entertainment media—espe-cially movies, television, and music—to seek out a wide range of emotional grat-ifications, and that these gratifications are not mutually exclusive but can overlap with each other (Bartsch & Viehoff, 2010).

Empirical Support

Although the theory has generated many empirical tests, the empirical literature does not show much support for the theory's claims. McQuail (1984) reviewed this literature and concluded that there is little evidence of successful prediction or casual explanation of media choice and use. When McQuail (2005) updated his review two decades later, his conclusions did not change and he continued to argue that the theory failed to provide much successful prediction or causal explanation of media choice and use. He acknowledged that the reasons for poor prediction may have been due to difficulties of measurement of motives and partly the fact that much media use is actually very circumstantial and weakly moti-vated. He argued that the connection between attitude to the media and media use behavior is actually quite weak and the direction of the relationship is often uncertain. "Typologies of 'motives' often fail to match patterns of actual selection or use, and it is hard to find a logical, consistent and sequential relation between the three factors of liking/preference, actual choosing, and subsequent evaluation" (p. 426).

Theory Development

Conceptual Criticism

The uses and gratifications theory has attracted much criticism over the years. The criticism has focused on a lack of theoretical clarity, lack of support for the assumption of an active audience, and for not being scientific.

Clarity. Many critics have argued that the theory exhibits a lack of conceptual clarity (Blumler, 1979; McQuail, 1984; Rubin, 2009b; Ruggiero, 2000; Sundar & Limperos, 2013). For example, Rubin (2009b) pointed out that there is a lack of consistency in the way researchers defined key concepts. Other critics (Blumler, 1979; McQuail, 1984) argued that some of the theory's terminology needs to be further defined, particularly to make clearer distinctions between motives, satisfactions, and gratifications. Some scholars use these terms as synonyms, while others sometimes make distinctions.

Active audience. The assumption that the audience is active has been questioned (Kubey & Csikszentmihalyi, 1991; Rubin, 2009b; Severin & Tankard, 1997). For example, Rubin (2009b) says that criticism of uses and gratifications focused on the treatment of the audience as being too active or rational in its behavior. Research into audience behaviors and decision making continually shows that most media usage is relatively passive and exhibits little concentration, that is, people typically do not make conscious decisions about their media use and instead are governed by habits (Kubey & Csikszentmihalyi, 1991). Also, the theory does not take into consideration the fact that individuals may not have considered all available choices in media consumption. This has led critics to point out that the theory goes too far in claiming that people are free to choose the media and the interpretations they desire (Severin & Tankard, 1997).

A belief in an active audience suggests that each individual might have different motives, different perceptions of gratifications, and different media habits. If this is the case, then the theory has a problem making general statements. There is an individual–aggregate trade-off. The theory also highlights individual differences, that is, different people have different needs, thus allowing for individual interpretations so that a dozen people can seek out the same media message but with different expectations for how that message will provide them with gratifications. Because the theory appears to be a social science type explanation, it has an obligation to identify patterns in aggregates—the larger the aggregate the better the theory because it is able to generalize its explanations.

Not scientific. Social scientists have had a hard time figuring out what the value of the theory is, that is, both sociologists and psychologists do not regard the theory as fitting in with their way of thinking. Sociologists criticize the theory for being too reductionistic and too much focused on behaviorism (McQuail, 2005). Ruggiero (2000) argued that the theory was tested with "behaviorist and individualist in its methodological tendencies" that ignored the social context of media use. Ruggiero (2000) argued that some media use may have nothing to do with the pursuit of gratification—it may be forced upon us by social pressures.

In contrast, psychologists question the value of the theory because it resists the development of general findings. If each individual's actions and effects on those actions depend solely on the situation and if each individual has unique uses to which the media attempts to meet their gratifications, then explanations for media use vary substantially across individuals, thus making it impossible to create general propositions to explain aggregate behaviors.

Methodological Criticism

The theory has also been criticized for its methodological weaknesses. These criticisms are that the theory is too exploratory and that it exhibits many flaws in measurement.

Too exploratory. Blumler (1979) characterized the early exploratory studies into uses and gratifications as "feeding a number of audience orientations into the computer at the gratifications end and seeing what emerges at the effects end" (pp. 15–16). Palmgreen et al. (1985) said: "Unfortunately, this still constitutes a reasonably accurate description of some uses and effects studies. While gratifications are often shown to enhance or mitigate effects, the theoretical nature of the relationship is sometimes neglected or treated only ex post facto" (p. 31).

Faulty measurement. Early research required participants to identify gratifications associated with specific channels of communication, raising the possibility that they would conflate gratifications and channels. Lometti, Reeves, and Bybee (1977) argued that this could "substantially overestimate" the number of gratifications, and that attempts to address it using in-depth interviews were problematic (Lometti et al., 1977, p. 323).

Perhaps the most serious criticism of the theory is that it relies so heavily on people self-reporting their media use, which is a mundane behavior of which they have questionable recall (Rubin, 2009b). For example, Katz (1987) pointed out that it has always been extremely difficult for humans to keep accurate counts of mundane behaviors in everyday life, and yet researchers who test uses and gratifications theory have relied heavily on self-reports. This renders the data about media usage highly suspect, which prevents the findings of this research to display adequate validity (Elliot, 1974; Katz, Blumler, & Gurevitch, 1973-74). Research has found that having an intention to do something only predicts engaging in the desired behavior about 33 % of the time (Cooke & Sheeran, 2004).

Alterations to the Theory

Uses and gratifications theory has evolved since its first formal presentation in 1974. This evolution can be seen especially in changes to the idea of active audience, developing categories of gratifications, and explaining media exposure.

Active audience. Responses to valid criticisms led scholars to modify the theory's assumption that audience members were always active media users, that is, audience members are aware of and can state their own motives and gratifications for using different media. Levy and Windahl (1985) observed that the thinking about audiences evolved away from putting audience members into categories based on gratifications and instead to consider audience activity as a variable construct, with audiences exhibiting varying *kinds* and *degrees* of activity.

Categorizing gratifications. The growth of uses and gratifications was keyed to researchers looking for all kinds of gratifications. Other scholars tried to organize all this research by coming up with categories and taxonomies. Table 7.1 shows how these taxonomies have changed over time.

Explaining media exposure. This line of inquiry takes more of a psychological approach as it focuses on how audience factors such as basic needs, social situations, and the individual's background (e.g., experience, interests, and education) affect people's ideas about what they want from media and which media best meet their needs (Rubin, 2009a, 2009b).

In 1984 Philip Palmgreen blended some ideas from Karl Rosengren with Martin Fishbein's expectancy-value formula to present its first explanatory proposition. This formula specifies that the GS by a media user is the sum of his or her beliefs about what media can provide weighted by one's evaluations of those beliefs. Palmgreen and Rayburn (1985) built on this formula by arguing that people compared GS with GO by comparing their expectation of a reward with the effort required to achieve that reward. Because media exposure is a process repeated over the course of a person's life, each person has a lot of experience with GO from past exposures and this helps in forming expectations for each decision in the present.

Current Challenges

It appears that uses and gratification theory is facing three major challenges. First, it continues to struggle with clarity. Second, it still relies on the assumption that the audience is active. Third, there continues to be a tautology of explanation.

Clarity

Palmgreen et al. (1985) have argued that although uses and gratifications has been criticized for being atheoretical, this criticism "has dissolved in the face of theoretical advances made along several fronts in the last decade by uses and gratifications researchers. While these advances have been uneven and often lacking in coordination, the result has been the emergence of a rather complex theoretical structure" (p. 16). While the theory has developed a more elaborate structure of propositions and constructs, there is still a good deal of conceptual confusion about the meaning and boundaries of concepts. For example, scholars still struggle with distinctions among the terms motivations, needs, and gratifications.

Active Audience

There continues to be a problem with the assumption of an active audience. Over the years, researchers have acknowledged that audiences are not always active in searching out media content and applying logical reasoning in their selections. However, the theory has not developed an explanation for when audience members are active and when they instead default to automatic processing of the flow of media availability.

Some scholars have argued that the rise of new media has created a situation where this problem is less serious. There is a suggestion that uses and gratifications as theory may be in the process of gaining new life as a result of new communication technology, which requires an assumption of an active audience (Sundar & Limperos, 2013). They reason that it was easy to question the agency of media consumers who had three television networks from which to choose, it's much harder to argue that a consumer who now has 100 cable channels and Internet-streaming video is not making his/her own decisions.

This reasoning, however, appears to be faulty. Just because people have more media choices does not mean they make more conscious and more reasoned decisions about their exposures. To the contrary, it is likely that people now are overwhelmed by exposure choices, which leads them to a default mode of relying much more on automatic routines that can be applied with little effort and no conscious awareness. When people are faced with a thousand choices of which video to watch, this requires more of a decision than if they have only three choices. However, this does not mean that they spend the time required to carefully consider each of their thousand options before making a choice; to the contrary, it is more likely that they default to automatic routines.

Tautology of Explanation

The "elephant in the room" challenge for uses and gratifications theory has always been a lack of operational distinction between measures of gratifications and measures of media usage. While the theory often makes a clear distinction, there is a serious question about whether this distinction gets translated adequately into measures.

To illustrate this point, think of the experience that research participants face when they are asked about how much time they spend with various media, then they are asked to rate their satisfaction with those exposures. When people say they spend a great deal of time week after week with a particular medium, they are not likely to say that they derive little or no satisfaction from those exposures, because that would require them to admit to making poor decisions repeatedly and wasting their own time. Instead, it is likely that people will try to display consistency in their answer patterns, for all sorts of psychological reasons that have nothing to do specifically with media exposure or gratifications. This sets up a closed system where a particular response on one measure (media usage) demands a certain type of response on another measure (GO). The explanatory pattern from these data exhibits a tautology as follows:

Question:	What is your favorite TV show?
Answer:	X
Question:	Do you watch X a lot?
Answer:	Yes.
Question:	When you decide to watch X, do you expect to experience enjoyment when you watch X?
Answer:	Yes
Question:	When you watch X, do you experience enjoyment?
Answer:	Yes

As you can see from the above sequence, respondents are asked questions in a way that leads them to display consistency or risk appearing stupid or crazy. And this pattern of questioning is a likely explanation why data generated from this method result in showing high correlations between media exposure, gratifications expected, and self-reported GO.

Conclusions

Uses and gratifications theory provides an explanation about why people use the media to obtain particular gratifications. As a media effects theory, it focuses on behavioral effects of media exposure patterns as well as beliefs about the gratifications people expect to obtain through those exposures. The central idea in this explanation is that people seek gratifications from their exposures so they continuously select those media options that have the strongest expectations for gratification.

The theory has stimulated a great deal of empirical testing as well as criticism. It has evolved over time mainly in the way it has elaborated gratifications and used them in more precise ways to explain media exposure. However, it still faces the challenge of convincing scholars that the audience is indeed active and that its system of explanation is not a tautology.

Key Sources

Background

Herzog, H. (1944). What do we really know about daytime serial listeners? In P. F. Lazarsfeld (Ed.), *Radio research 1942-3* (pp. 2–23). London: Sage.

Katz, E. (1959). Mass communication research and the study of culture. *Studies in Public Communication, 2*, 1–6.

Lazarsfeld, P. F., & Stanton, F. (1944). *Radio research 1942-3*. New York, NY: Duell, Sloan and Pearce.

Lazarsfeld, P. F., & Stanton, F. (1949). *Communication research 1948-9*. New York, NY: Harper and Row.

Origin

Blumler J. G., & Katz, E. (1974). *The uses of mass communications: Current perspectives on gratifications research.* Beverly Hills, CA: Sage.

Katz, E., Blumler, J. G., & Gurevitch, M. (1973-74). Uses and gratifications research. *The Public Opinion Quarterly 4th ser., 37*, 509–523.

Katz, E., Blumler, J. G., & Gurevitch, M. (1974a). Utilization of mass communication by the individual. In J. G. Blumler & E. Katz (Eds.), *The uses of mass communications: Current perspectives on gratifications research* (pp. 19–32). Beverly Hills, CA: Sage.

Katz, E., Blumler, J., & Gurevitch, M. (1974b). Uses of mass communication by the individual. In W. P. Davison & F. T. C. Yu (Eds.), *Mass communication research: Major issues and future directions* (pp. 11–35). New York, NY: Praeger.

Katz, E., Haas, H., & Gurevitch, M. (1973). On the use of the mass media for important things. *American Sociological Review, 38*(2), 164–181.

McGuire, W. J. (1974). Psychological motives and communication gratification. In J. G. Blumler & E. Katz (Eds.), *The uses of mass communications* (pp. 167–196). Beverly Hills, CA: Sage Publications.

McQuail, D., Blumler, J. G., & Brown, J. (1972). The television audience: A revised perspective. In D. McQuail (Ed.), *Sociology of mass communication* (pp. 135–165). Middlesex: Penguin.

Reviews

Katz, E. (1987). Communication research since Lazarsfeld. *Public Opinion Quarterly, 51*, 525–545.

Levy, M., & Windahl, S. (1985). The concept of audience activity. In K. E. Rosengren, L. A. Wenner, & P. Palmgreen (Eds.), Media gratifications research: Current perspectives (pp. 109–122). Beverly Hills, CA: Sage.

McQuail, D. (1984). With benefits to hindsight: Reflections on uses and gratifications research. *Critical studies in mass communication theory: An introduction.* Beverly Hills, CA: Sage.

Palmgreen, P. (1984). Uses and gratification: A theoretical perspective. In R. N. Bostrom (Ed.), *Communication yearbook* (Vol. 8, pp. 20–55). Beverly Hills, CA: Sage.

Palmgreen, P., Wenner, L. A., & Rosengren, K. E. (1985). Uses and gratifications research: The past ten years. In K. E. Rosengren, L. A. Wenner, & P. Palmgreen (Eds.), Media gratifications research: Current perspectives (pp. 11–37). Beverly Hills, CA: Sage.

Rubin, A. M. (1986). Uses, gratifications, and media effects research. In J. Bryant & D. Zillmann (Eds.), *Perspectives on media effects* (pp. 281–301). Hillsdale, NJ: Erlbaum.

Rubin, A. M. (2009a). Uses and gratifications: An evolving perspective of media effects. In R. L. Nabi & M. B. Oliver (Eds.), *The Sage handbook of media processes and effects* (pp. 147–159). Los Angeles, CA: Sage.

Rubin, A. M. (2009b). Uses-and-gratification perspective on media effects. In J. Bryant & M. B. Oliver (Eds.), *Media effects: Advances in theory and research* (pp. 165–184). New York, NY: Routledge.

Ruggiero, T. (2000). Uses and gratifications theory in the 21st century. *Mass Communication & Society, 3*(1), 3–37.

Criticisms

Greenberg, B. S. (1974). Gratifications of television viewing and their correlates for British children. *The uses of mass communications: Current perspectives on gratifications research, 3*, 71–92.

Lometti, G. E., Reeves, B., & Bybee, C. R. (1977). Investigating the assumptions of uses and gratifications research. *Communication Research, 4*(3), 321–338.

Ruggiero, T. E. (2000). Uses and gratifications theory in the 21st century. *Mass Communication & Society, 3*(1), 3–37.

Severin, W. J., & Tankard, J. W. (1997). Uses of mass media. In *Communication theories: Origins, methods, and uses in the mass media.* White Plains, NY: Longman.

Sundar, S. S., & Limperos, A. M. (2013). Uses and grats 2.0: New gratifications for new media. *Journal of Broadcasting & Electronic Media, 57*(4), 504–525.

References

Bartsch, A., & Viehoff, R. (2010). The use of media entertainment and emotional gratification. *Procedia – Social and Behavioral Sciences. 5*, 2247–2255. doi:10.1016/j.sbspro.2010.07.444

Berelson, B. (1949).What 'missing the newspaper' mean. In P. F. Lazarsfeld & F. N. Stanton (Eds.), *Communication research 1948–1949* (pp. 111–129). New York, NY: Harper.

Blumler, J. G. (1979). The role of theory in uses and gratifications studies. *Communication Research, 6*(1), 9–36.

Blumler J. G., & Katz, E. (1974). *The uses of mass communications: Current perspectives on gratifications research.* Beverly Hills, CA: Sage.

Cooke, R., & Sheeran, P. (2004). Moderation of cognition-intention and cognition-behaviour relations: A meta-analysis of properties of variables from the theory of planned behaviour. *British Journal of Social Psychology, 43*(2), 159–186.

Elliott, P. (1974). Uses and gratifications research: A critique and a sociological alternative. In J. G. Blumler & E. Katz (Eds.), *The uses of mass communications: Current perspectives on gratifications research* (pp. 249–268). Beverly Hills, CA: Sage.

Green, M. C., & Brock, T. C. (2000). The role of transportation in the persuasiveness of public narratives. *Journal of Personality and Social Psychology, 79,* 701–721.

Herzog, H. (1944). What do we really know about daytime serial listeners? In P. F. Lazarsfeld (Ed.), *Radio research 1942–3* (pp. 2–23). London: Sage.

Horton, D., & Wohl, R. R. (1956). Mass communication and para-social interaction: Observations on intimacy at a distance. *Psychiatry, 19,* 215–229.

Katz, E. (1987). Communication research since Lazarsfeld. *Public Opinion Quarterly, 51,* 525–545.

Katz, E., Blumler, J. G., & Gurevitch, M. (1973–74). Uses and gratifications research. *The Public Opinion Quarterly 4th ser., 37,* 509–523.

Katz, E., Blumler, J. G., & Gurevitch, M. (1974a). Utilization of mass communication by the individual. In J. G. Blumler & E. Katz (Eds.), *The uses of mass communications: Current perspectives on gratifications research* (pp. 19–32). Beverly Hills, CA: Sage.

Katz, E., Blumler, J., & Gurevitch, M. (1974b). Uses of mass communication by the individual. In W. P. Davison & F. T. C. Yu (Eds.), *Mass communication research: Major issues and future directions* (pp. 11–35). New York, NY: Praeger.

Katz, E., Haas, H., & Gurevitch, M. (1973). On the use of the mass media for important things. *American Sociological Review, 38*(2), 164–181.

Knobloch, S. (2003). Mood adjustment via mass communication. *Journal of Communication, 53,* 233–250. doi:10.1093/joc/53.2.233

Knobloch, S., & Zillmann, D. (2003). Appeal of love themes in popular music. *Psychological Reports, 93,* 653–658. doi:10.2466/pr0.93.7.653-658

Kubey, R. W., & Csikszentmihalyi, M. (1991). *Television and the quality of life.* Hillsdale, NJ: Erlbaum.

Lasswell, H. (1948). The structure and function of communication in society. In L Bryson (Ed.), *The communication of ideas* (pp. 32–51). New York, NY: Harper.

Lazarsfeld, P. F., & Stanton, F. (1944). *Radio research 1942–3*. New York, NY: Duell, Sloan and Pearce.

Lazarsfeld, P. F., & Stanton, F. (1949). *Communication research 1948–9*. New York, NY: Harper and Row.

Levy, M., & Windahl, S. (1985). The concept of audience activity. In K. E. Rosengren, L. A. Wenner, & P. Palmgreen (Eds.), *Media gratifications research: Current perspectives* (pp. 109–122). Beverly Hills, CA: Sage.

Lometti, G. E., Reeves, B., & Bybee, C. R. (1977). Investigating the assumptions of uses and gratifications research. *Communication Research, 4*(3), 321–338.

Mares, M.-L., & Cantor, J. (1992). Elderly viewers' responses to televised portrayals of old age. *Communication Research, 19*, 459–478.

McQuail, D. (1983). *Mass communication theory: An introduction*. London: Sage.

McQuail, D. (1984). With benefits to hindsight: Reflections on uses and gratifications research. In *Critical Studies in Mass Communication Theory: An Introduction*. Beverly Hills, CA: Sage.

McQuail, D. (2005). *McQuail's mass communication theory* (5th ed.). Thousand Oaks, CA: Sage.

McQuail, D., Blumler, J. G., & Brown, J. (1972). The television audience: A revised perspective. In D. McQuail (Ed.), *Sociology of mass communication* (pp. 135–165). Middlesex: Penguin.

Mundorf, N., & Mundorf, J. (2003). Gender socialization of horror. In J. Bryant, D. Roskos-Ewoldsen, & J. Cantor. (Eds.), *Communication and Emotion. Essays in honor of Dolf Zillmann* (pp. 155–178). Mahwah, NJ: Erlbaum.

Oliver, M. B. (1993). Exploring the paradox of the enjoyment of sad films. *Human Communication Research, 19*, 315–342. doi:10.1111/j.1468-2958.1993.tb00304.x

Oliver, M.B., & Bartsch, A. (2010). Appreciation as audience response: Exploring entertainment gratifications beyond hedonism. *Human Communication Research, 26*, 53–81. doi:10.1111/j.1468-2958.2009.01368.x

Oliver, M. B., & Raney, A. A. (2011). Entertainment as pleasurable and meaningful: Identifying hedonic and eudaimonic motivations for entertainment consumption. *Journal of Communication, 61*(5), 984–1004. doi:10.1111/j.1460-2466.2011.01585.x

Palmgreen, P. (1984). Uses and gratification: A theoretical perspective. In R. N. Bostrom (Ed.), *Communication yearbook* (Vol. 8, pp. 20–55). Beverly Hills, CA: Sage.

Palmgreen, P., & Rayburn, J. D. (1985). A comparison of gratification models of media satisfaction. *Communication Monographs, 52*(4), 334–346.

Palmgreen, P., Wenner, L. A., & Rosengren, K. E. (1985). Uses and gratifications research: The past ten years. In K. E. Rosengren, L. A. Wenner, & P. Palmgreen (Eds.), *Media gratifications research: Current perspectives* (pp. 11–37). Beverly Hills, CA: Sage.

Raney, A. A. (2003). Communication and emotion. In J. Bryant, D. Roskos-Ewoldsen, & J. Cantor, (Eds.) *Essays in honor of Dolf Zillmann* (pp. 61–84). Mahwah, NJ: Erlbaum

Rosengren, K. E. (1974). Uses and gratifications: A paradigm outlined. In J. G. Blumler & E. Katz (Eds.), *The uses of mass communications: Current perspectives of gratifications research* (pp. 269–286). Beverly Hills, CA: Sage.

Rubin, A. M. (1986). Uses, gratifications, and media effects research. In J. Bryant & D. Zillmann (Eds.), *Perspectives on media effects* (pp. 281–301). Hillsdale, NJ: Erlbaum.

Rubin, A. M. (2009a). Uses and gratifications: An evolving perspective of media effects. In R. L. Nabi & M. B. Oliver (Eds.), *The Sage handbook of media processes and effects* (pp. 147–159). Los Angeles, CA: Sage.

Rubin, A. M. (2009b). Uses-and-gratification perspective on media effects. In J. Bryant & M. B. Oliver (Eds.), *Media effects: Advances in theory and research* (pp. 165–184). New York, NY: Routledge.

Rubin, A. M. (2002). The uses-and-gratifications perspective of media effects. In J. Bryant & D. Zillmann (Eds.), *Media effects: Advances in theory and research* (2nd ed., pp. 525–548). Mahwah, NJ: Erlbaum.

Rubin, A. M., & Perse, E. M. (1987). Audience activity and soap opera involvement: A uses and effects investigation. *Human Communication Research, 14,* 246–268. doi:10.1111/j.1468-2958.1987.tb00129.x

Ruggiero, T. E. (2000). Uses and gratifications theory in the 21st century. *Mass Communication & Society, 3*(1), 3–37.

Severin, W. J., & Tankard, J. W. (1997). Uses of mass media. *Communication theories: Origins, methods, and uses in the mass media.* White Plains, NY: Longman.

Sundar, S. S., & Limperos, A. M. (2013). Uses and grats 2.0: New gratifications for new media. *Journal of Broadcasting & Electronic Media, 57*(4), 504–525.

Warner, W. L., & Henry, W. E. (1948). The radio day-time serial: A symbolic analysis. *Psychological Monographs, 37*(1), 7–13, 55–64.

Wright, C. R. (1960). Functional analysis and mass communication. *Public Opinion Quarterly, 24,* 605–620.

Zillmann, D. (1988). Mood management through communication choices. *American Behavioral Scientist. 31,* 327–340. doi:10.1177/000276488031003005

Zillmann, D. (2000). Mood management in the context of selective exposure theory. In M. F. Roloff (Ed.), *Communication Yearbook. 23.* (pp. 103–123). New York, NY: Routledge.

CHAPTER EIGHT

Social Cognitive Theory

Social cognitive theory is an extensive, detailed system of explanation about how humans learn social information by observing models behaving in mediated messages as well as in real life. It was originally called "social learning theory" to set it apart from traditional learning theories that were mechanistic, behavioral approaches that limited their focus to either how organisms acquire behavioral patterns or how humans acquire factual information. The name was changed in the mid-1980s to emphasize its cognitive perspective in explaining how people process meaning from observing social behaviors then encode that meaning into memory to be used later as guides for social behaviors.

The theory presents a great many ideas gleaned from extensive reviews of the learning literature produced by psychological research over the past century. These ideas have been organized by cognitive processes (attention, retention, production, and motivation), by human capabilities (symbolizing, self-regulation, self-reflection, and vicarious experiencing), and by research considerations (antecedent determinants, consequent determinants, cognitive control, and reciprocal determinism).

Original Conceptualization of the Theory

Conceptual Foundation

As Albert Bandura was creating his system of explanation throughout his graduate training and early career as an academic, he was influenced by three research traditions. The first was the behaviorist approach to learning in the tradition of B. F. Skinner (1957, 1963) and Julian Rotter (1954). This behaviorist approach focused on classical conditioning and operant conditioning. Learning was conceptualized as the acquisition of new responses through a process of successive approximation, which required multiple trials, reinforcement for components of behavior, and gradual change. In his graduate training at the University of Iowa in the early 1950s, Bandura studied with Spence, Tolman, and Hull so he was exposed to a strong behavioral perspective on learning (Pajares, 2004). However, Bandura felt that the strict behaviorist approach to human learning was too mechanistic and that it was too limited with its focus on tedious trial-and-error learning to be able to capture the complexity of human learning.

Second, he became attracted to the ideas of Miller and Dollard who conducted a series of experimental studies of social modeling, which they described as a form of instrumental conditioning in a book entitled *Social Learning and Imitation* (1941). In this book, Miller and Dollard introduced "Social Learning and Imitation Theory" where they argued that four factors contribute to learning: drives, cues, responses, and rewards. They explained that people are more likely to imitate a behavior they observe if the model is shown being rewarded, and people will continue imitating that behavior if they are rewarded when they perform it.

Third, Bandura became interested in the influence of violent messages on viewers of television and films, especially on children. Social scientists have always been concerned with high levels of violence in the media, first in dime novels, magazine stories, and newspaper coverage, then in Hollywood films. There was continual speculation that the public's exposure to all this violence would lead to higher levels of aggression, violence, and even crime in society. This concern was heightened in the 1960s as television became the dominant media and as its programming presented a great deal of violence not just in entertainment shows but also news that was continually covering the war in Vietnam as well as assassinations of the Kennedy brothers and Martin Luther King.

Bandura brought these three traditions together as he worked out his ideas on social learning. Initially Bandura was concerned with imitative behavior, but he expanded his focus to include the learning of novel behaviors as well. Also, he came to believe that social learning often occurs even when people do not manifest the behaviors they learn. These concerns motivated Bandura to conduct a series of experiments to examine how children used social models to learn aggressive behaviors. This series of experiments, which he conducted in the early 1960s, have come to be known as the Bobo doll studies. In these experiments, Bandura showed children cartoons where characters behaved in a violent manner, then gave the children time for free play in a room with all kinds of toys including toy hammers and a Bobo doll, which is an inflatable plastic clown with a weighted base so that it tilts over when hit but bounces back for more. When Bandura observed these children during free play he saw that some imitated the violent behavior they had seen in the cartoons and some behaved aggressively in novel ways. He also found that some children did not behave aggressively, and he reasoned that those children had still learned social lessons from watching the cartoons even though they did not exhibit behaviors that would have manifested that learning. He concluded that learning can take place vicariously, that is, people can learn social lessons by watching other people and that they do not need to perform behaviors themselves and experience the consequences of their own actions. This led him to make claims about observational learning that were built less on the principles of behavioral conditioning and more on the ideas of social modeling, observational learning, and vicarious reinforcement. Extending the work of Miller and Dollard (1941), Bandura (1977) added the concepts of identification, vicarious reinforcement, and self-efficacy. Bandura showed that this observational type of learning was enhanced to the extent that observers identified with people who performed the behaviors (role models) as well as when those behaviors were rewarded or at least not punished. He also showed that the role models need not be people in real life but can also be characters in fictional stories presented through the media.

Introduction of the Theory

After 25 years of working out his ideas and testing them in an extensive series of experiments, Bandura introduced his full system of explanation in 1977 with the publication of a book entitled *Social Learning Theory*. In the book's preface he wrote "I have attempted to provide a unified theoretical framework for analyzing human thought and behavior ... Social learning theory emphasizes the prominent roles played by vicarious, symbolic, and self-regulatory processes in psychological functioning" (p. vii).

He emphasized three ideas that set his theory apart from behavioral theories. The first idea was "that human thought, affect, and behavior can be markedly influenced by observation" (p. vii). This meant that people did not have to perform a behavior to learn it; they could observe the behavior of others. Second, the theory focused on the use of symbols that enable humans "to represent events, to analyze their conscious experience, to communicate with others at any distance in time and space, to plan, to create, to imagine, and to engage in foresightful action" (p. vii). Third, he gave a central role to self-regulatory processes. "People are not simply reactors to external influence, they select, organize, and transform the stimuli that impinge upon them. Through self-generated inducements and consequences they can exercise some influence over their own behavior" (p. vii). These three ideas suggest a great many variables—many of which Bandura laid out in his book. These variables were not things he created through speculation but instead were selected through his extensive review of the learning literature. To organize all these ideas, Bandura said, "Social learning theory approaches the explanation of human behavior in terms of a continuous reciprocal interaction between cognitive, behavioral, and environmental determinants" (p. vii).

Social learning theory was essentially a synthesis of patterns of empirical findings in the psychological literature on learning. While much of that literature dealt with learning in nonhuman organisms, Bandura sought to translate these findings into a system that would be useful to explain human learning. To make such a translation, Bandura was guided by beliefs that humans are active agents in this learning process rather than automatic responders to simple stimuli. He believed that humans have free will to make choices about which messages to expose themselves to, about how to process and interpret the meanings of those messages, about how to encode those message symbols and meanings into their memories, and about whether or not to use that learning to guide their behavior.

Conceptualization of Media

While Bandura's examples and research focused on the audiovisual media of film and television, his theory's system of explanation did not exclude any of the mass media. With its emphasis on observational learning, the theory recognized the value of models across all media as well as in nonmediated situations. That is, his theory applied to all kinds of models—fictional characters, real people in news/ information programming, as well as people in real life.

Bandura's system of explanation did not privilege media effects, that is, he did not treat mediated models differently than real-world models. He did acknowledge that mass media had the power to expose people to models they could not see in their everyday lives and that the mass media had the power to expose large numbers of people to the same models simultaneously. However, he did not present a system of explanation that treated learning from mediated messages differently than the process of learning from nonmediated models.

Conceptualization of Media Effect

Bandura conceptualized the media effect as "learning," but the way he uses this term connotes something much different than traditionally used in the literature at that time, which was typically the acquisition and retention of information in some form (facts, images, sounds). Instead, Bandura treated learning less as the immediate acquisition of facts and more as a cognitive process beginning with how people perceive symbols, infer patterns, make associations across elements, and generalize to beliefs about social norms. That is, Bandura is less concerned with factual learning than with social learning. Thus when Bandura makes a claim that people learn to behave aggressively from exposures to media violence, he does not mean that people have memorized how the characters in a particular story look, act, and feel. Instead, he means that people are able to recognize certain key elements in stories, interpret the sequence of those elements in a way that constructs meaning for them, and remember their interpretation as a social lesson that can be used immediately or later to guide performance. Also, when Bandura claims that people learn emotions from watching media messages, he does not mean that people have acquired new emotions; instead he means that people have made associations between particular actions and particular emotions. It is the connection that is acquired through learning, not the emotion itself. And when Bandura claims people have learned behaviors from watching characters' behavioral sequences, he does not only mean that people have memorized a sequence of actions so that they can perform the sequence well; instead he means that people have learned the pattern of actions so that they can (1) imitate that particular behavior, (2) demonstrate that pattern in a novel way, or (3) infer a social belief that they can use to guide their behaviors in the future.

While the theory attempts to explain social behavior, which would indicate that its focal outcome variable is behavior, the theory's primary focal outcome variables are beliefs and cognitions. Because Bandura emphasized that learning can take place without the performance of behaviors, the outcome variable need not be behavior, although it can be. Instead, Bandura was more interested in cognitive processes that lead people to acquire—or construct their own—beliefs about social norms.

Conceptualization of Media Influence

The media were conceptualized as one among many factors of influence that work together in a process of what he called "reciprocal determinism." This means essentially that many factors interact in a system where they continually influence one another. There is not just one linear path that explains the flow of influence;

instead, each variable influences all others and is influenced by all others. This claim serves to make the theory amorphous, that is, there is no articulation of a path of influence as expressed in a sequence of propositions, which can be clearly tested. Rather, the theory tells researchers what to think about when designing their empirical studies, then to be open minded in exploring how all the relevant factors influence one another in each learning situation.

Original Components

The theory presents a very long list of factors that have been found to be related to the process of observational learning of social behaviors. These many factors have been identified by Bandura in his detailed review of the empirical literature on social learning. While the list of identified factors appears to be comprehensive and organized into categories, the theory does not specify which factors are most important or how they work together other than to say they all influence one another.

In his 1977 book *Social Learning Theory*, Bandura organized his ideas in six chapters: theoretical perspective, origins of behavior, antecedent determinants (of physiological and emotional responsiveness, of cognitive functions in expectancy learning, of inborn mechanisms of learning, of dysfunctional expectancy learning, and of action), consequent determinants (of external reinforcement, of vicarious reinforcement, and of self-reinforcement), cognitive control (motivation, representation of contingencies, guidance of behavior, action in covert problem solving, verification processes, and interaction of regulatory systems), and reciprocal determinism (interdependence of personal and environmental influences, reciprocal influence and the exercise of self-direction, reciprocal influence and the limits of social control).

Key Concepts

The central concept in this theory is observational learning. Bandura explains that when people observe the behaviors of others—whether in real life or in mediated messages—they engage in cognitive processes where they extract information from those observations that they use to infer social norms.

Bandura also presents a great number of other concepts that he explains are active in the process of observational learning. He organizes these into four categories of attentional processes, retentional processes, motor reproduction processes, and motivational processes. He did not regard any one of these many factors as being the most important or essential; instead he explained they all were potentially important in the process of learning and that they all influenced one another.

Core Propositions

Bandura (1977) created a great number of propositions. Table 8.1 presents the major propositions in outline form. Although this list is long, it is not exhaustive; there are many more propositions that could have appeared as subpoints in this table. Almost all of these propositions are generalizations from findings in the empirical literature, so his theory is well grounded.

While each of these propositions is testable and in fact has a history of testing that supports each individual proposition, the theory leaves readers with a question about how all these factors work together. This is where the theory shows a troubling limitation by stopping short of synthesizing all the individual propositions into an explanatory system that shows how they all work together in a more macro way. Instead, Bandura claims that each of the many variables influences the other variables and is in turn influenced by the other variables in an ongoing process he has labeled as "reciprocal determinism." This limitation makes it difficult to regard the theory as a complete system of explanation rather than as an inventory of individual relationships between pairs of variables.

There are places in his explanation where Bandura seems to articulate a process that structures many of the individual propositions. For example, Bandura explains that children who play violent video games will likely influence their peers to play as well, which then encourages them to play more often. This could lead to the children becoming desensitized to violence, which in turn will likely affect their real-life behaviors. Yes, this is one reasonable path through his variables but there seem to be many other alternative paths available given that any of these variables can—or might not—influence others. This raises a question about the value of the explanation: When there are so many possible paths available in the process of observational learning, what is the value of a theory as a system of explanation?

Also, Bandura offers little sense of calibration, that is, which factors are most influential. As for structure, he argues that some factors are antecedents, which indicates a possible claim that those identified factors are at least important—if not necessary—as conditions for a learning effect to occur, but because there are many factors in this antecedent category and because there is no calibration about their relative influence or structure to indicate any order in the exercise of their influence, scholars are left in the dark about whether or not there are dominant paths through this process of observational learning.

Table 8.1. Theory at Introduction: Structure of Propositions

I. Humans can control their thinking and behaviors by selecting, organizing, and transforming the stimuli that impinge upon them. They are not simply reactors to external influence.

   A. People imagine consequences of future actions and these representations of future outcomes are motivators of behavior.

   B. People do not learn much from repeated paired experiences unless they recognize that events are correlated.

   C. Transitory experiences leave lasting effects by being coded and stored in symbolic form for memory representation and these representations serve as guides to overt action on later occasions.

   D. Higher cognitive capacities enable people to conduct most problem solving in thought rather than in action.

      1. Symbols that represent events, cognitive operations, and relationships serve as vehicles for thought.

      2. Because a great deal of human thought is linguistically based, language development constrains thought.

   E. People continually test their thoughts through experience so they can verify which are accurate and which are faulty.

   F. The regulatory systems that organize a person's behavior do not operate independently, that is, most actions are controlled by two or more sources of influence simultaneously.

II. Most human behavior is learned observationally through a process of modeling, which has four components of attention, retention, motor reproduction, and motivation.

   A. Attentional processes determine what is selectively observed from the chaos of stimuli that confronts humans, with some of these determinants being characteristics of the model and others being characteristics of the observer.

      1. Characteristics of the model include distinctiveness, affective valence, complexity, prevalence, and functional value.

      2. Characteristics about the observer include sensory capacities, arousal level, perceptual set, and past reinforcement.

   B. Retention processes determine what is remembered from the modeling exposure; they rely on symbolic coding, cognitive organization, symbolic rehearsal, and motor rehearsal.

   C. Motor reproduction processes transform symbolic representations into appropriate actions; they include physical capabilities, availability of component responses, self-observation reproduction, and accuracy of feedback.

   D. Whether people enact the behaviors they have learned or not is determined by motivational characteristics, which focus on whether reinforcements were external, vicarious, or self.

(Continued)

Table 8.1. *Continued*

III. There are particular antecedents that enhance learning by setting up expectations about how things work in the social world.
- A. Physiological and emotional responses are triggered by events occurring closely in time.
  1. Anxiety and defensive behavior are triggered by an association with painful experiences.
  2. Aggression elicitors are developed through past experiences with aggression.
  3. Symbolic expectancy learning employs learned stereotypes as a way of anticipating what will happen with people the observe has not yet met.
  4. People can learn emotional reactions vicariously by observing others in situations they themselves have not encountered.
- B. Cognitive functions in expectancy learning
  1. People do not learn much from repeated pair experiences unless they recognize that events are connected.
  2. Affective reactions can be stimulated cognitively.
- C. Inborn mechanisms of learning are determined by physiological limitations of the sensorimotor and cortical structures people are born with.
- D. Dysfunctional expectancy learning can also occur.
  1. Coincidental association can lead to dysfunctional expectancy learning.
  2. Inappropriate generalization can lead to dysfunctional expectancy learning.
- E. Corrective learning experiences are required for people to change dysfunctional behaviors.
- F. Antecedent determinants of action vary in effectiveness by time, place, and the persons toward whom it is directed.
  1. Modeling determinants: The actions of others observed have high predictive value on the actions of the self.
  2. Extraction of contingency rules takes place when people observe multiple events and observe regularities that indicate the times and situations when certain rules apply and other times when those rules do not apply.
  3. Defective contingency learning occurs when people are unable to distinguish important connections from random or peripheral connections between behaviors and consequences.

IV. Particular reinforcement factors enhance learning.
- A. External reinforcement shapes the consequences of learning when it is repeated over time.
  1. Incentives change in the reward hierarchy as a person develops. Young children respond best to immediate physical consequence of food, stimulation, and contact but not self-actualization.
  2. Extrinsic incentives typically work best until a person has developed a learning competency in an area, then it is better to rely on intrinsic incentives.

(Continued)

Table 8.1. *Continued*

---

3. The frequency and durability of a given behavior depend on how the prevailing contingencies of reinforcement are structured.

B. Vicarious reinforcement

1. People learn through vicarious reinforcement.

2. Observed negative consequences reduce the tendency to behave in similar or related ways as the punished model.

3. The legal system of deterrence relies heavily on the inhibitory effects of exemplary punishment.

4. Rewards are generally better than punishments in motivating learning.

5. Observed consequences accruing to others provide a standard for judging whether the reinforcements one customarily receives are equitable, beneficent, or unfair.

6. Vicarious reinforcement varies in its effectiveness depending on certain factors:

   * The degree to which the model is similar to the learner.

   * Motivational function—learners are more persistent in the face of failure when they have observed models being rewarded intermittently rather than continuously.

   * Observers are easily aroused by the emotions of models.

   * The personal values of learners can be altered and shaped by the way the modeled behavior is rewarded.

   * The exemplified responsiveness of models is an integral aspect of vicarious reinforcement.

C. Self-reinforcement shows that people hold firmly to their ideological positions.

1. There are three component processes in self-regulation: performance, judgment, and self-response.

   * Performance component includes the evaluative dimensions of quality, rate, quantity, originality, authenticity, consequentialness, deviancy, and ethicalness.

   * The judgmental process involves personal standards, referential performances, valuation of activity, and performance attribution.

   * The self-response process involves self-evaluative reactions, tangible self-applied consequences, and no self-response.

2. Establishment of self-regulative functions: People learn to evaluate their behavior partly on the basis of how others have reacted to it.

3. The development of performance standards and self-reinforcement practices is generalized beyond the specific activity for which they were established.

4. Levels of self-satisfaction are determined not only by one's accomplishments but also by the standards against which the accomplishments are judged.

5. Dysfunctional self-evaluative systems: Without standards and evaluative involvement in activities, people are unmotivated, bored, and dependent upon momentary external stimulation for their satisfactions.

(Continued)

Table 8.1. *Continued*

---

      6. After individuals learn to set standards for themselves and to generate conditional self-reactions, they can influence their behavior by self-produced consequences.

      7. The maintaining of self-reinforcement systems relies on people setting negative sanctions for themselves as well as being able to predict situational determinants.

      8. Modeling is important to maintaining learning by continually observing interactions between personal and external sources of reinforcement.

      9. Self-evaluative influences do not operate unless activated.

V. Many factors work together in a process of reciprocal determinism.

VI. Reciprocal determinism

    A. Internal personal factors and behavior operate as reciprocal determinants of each other.

    B. People have free will as defined by the number of options available to them and the power to exercise them.

      1. Personal freedom increases when people develop additional competencies and thus eliminate some of the limitations on their ability to behave in certain ways.

      2. Freedom is not the opposite of determinism; instead, freedom is defined in terms of the skills at one's command and the exercise of self-influence which choice of action requires.

    C. Reciprocal influence and the limits of social control

      1. Increasing people's knowledge about modes of influence is prescribed as the best defense against external control of their behavior.

      2. Institutions set social sanctions in order to limit the control of human behavior.

From Bandura (1977).

Foundational Assumptions

There were three assumptions supporting the introduction of this theory. Two of these assumptions served to move the theory away from the mechanistic behaviorist tradition of studying learning. One of these assumptions was that humans are active agents governing their thoughts and behaviors. Second, humans can learn behaviors vicariously by simply observing those behaviors enacted by others; they do not need to perform those behaviors or practice them in a sequence of reinforcement that shapes the acquisition. Both of these initial assumptions were testable, and subsequent tests have tended to support each assumption.

A third assumption is that all the factors in the theory work together in a process of reciprocal determinism. This claim is so general it is impossible to test adequately. It would require a test of all possible pairs of variables, which can be easily done in packaged statistical programs. But the difficulty arises in the task of interpreting the findings of such a set of tests. If the strength of the relationship between all pairs of factors is equal, then it is simple to conclude that all factors are equally related to all other factors. But what if the strength of relationships varies across all those tests, which is far more likely to occur? This variation would force us to regard some relationships as stronger than others and would leave us with the question: If relationships between pairs of variables are not all equal, does this mean that all factors did not work together in an equally influential manner? Bandura offers no guidance in dealing with such a situation.

Empirical Testing

Stimulating Scholarly Attention

Since its introduction as social learning theory in 1977, it has generated a great deal of attention. A recent search of "social cognitive theory" on Google Scholar yields 8.3 million hits and when the search is narrowed down to articles it yields 2.95 million hits. Of these 14,800 were published in the 1960s; 38,100 in the 1970s; 104,000 in the 1980s; 704,000 in the 1990s; 1.5 million in the first decade of the new millennium; and 1.45 million in the next nine years. So the number of articles acknowledging the theory continues to grow.

This body of literature is composed of individual empirical studies, each providing an additional test of a relationship among a small set of variables, mostly using laboratory experiments. There are no tests of his entire system of explanation, because that would involve a great many variables. Nor are there tests of a relatively large part of his theory; instead all the tests are at a micro-level rather than at a meso-level or macro-level. Also, there are no tests of Bandura's claim that factors work together in reciprocal determination.

Empirical Validity

Reviews published by Bandura himself (2002, 2009) as well as by other scholars (Pajares, Prestin, Chen, & Nabi, 2009) generally conclude that there is considerable support for the theory (Bandura, 2002, 2009). This should not be surprising given the nature of the theory and how Bandura constructed it. When Bandura introduced the first full version of the theory in 1977, he had already spent a quarter of a century assembling findings from psychological tests of human learning. *Social Learning Theory* (1977) cited over 200 empirical tests with 28 of the citations to his own empirical work. *Social Foundations of Thought and Action: A Social*

Cognitive Theory (1986) included over 2,000 citations in its reference list with 65 references to his own empirical studies.

The body of literature does little to calibrate the strength of the influences. Perhaps this is because of Bandura's claim of reciprocal determinism. If we accept this claim, then any indicator of the strength of a relationship between any two variables must also be regarded as an indicator of the influence of all other variables and it is impossible to parse out the unique contribution of the two featured variables in the association. Also the findings from this literature do little to elaborate the structure of these factors beyond Bandura's macro categorization of factors into antecedents and consequences, that is, we do not have much understanding about which of the variables within those categories are sufficient, necessary, or substitutable. Nor do we have much of an idea about whether all associations are truly symmetric (as reciprocal determinism would suggest) or whether some are asymmetrical or a blend of the two. And if it is a blend, how are those relationships arrayed on a continuum where some are purely symmetrical at one pole, some are purely asymmetrical at the opposite pole, and the rest of the relationships vary in between?

Theory Development

Criticisms

There has been little criticism of social cognitive theory. The small amount of criticism that does exist faults the theory for not being broader. For example, some critics complain that it does not account for changes in personality and motivation due to cognitive development (Boundless, 2017). Other critics complain that it places too much emphasis on cognitive aspects and abilities and it ignores biological and hormonal influences that have been found to affect decision making (Flamand, 2009; McLeod, 2016). While people are often in control of their behavior and consciously process information during observational learning, there are many times when their minds are on automatic pilot where they are governed by influences below their awareness. Also, the chemistry of the brain and the biology of the body are important influences on thinking and behavior but these are ignored in the theory.

Perhaps the most serious criticism is that it is so broad and that it lacks a unifying principle that can be tested (Carillo, 2010). The individual parts can be tested and have been tested many times and found to hold. But there is not a way to bring all the parts together into a whole that can be tested. This is especially a problem when we consider Bandura's claim of reciprocal determinism, which says that everything influences everything else and in turn is influenced by all other factors. While this claim may be accurate, it is not very helpful with prediction or explanation. Meehl (1990) found that almost all constructs of interest to social scientists (attitudes, stereotypes, beliefs, impressions, and expectations) were related to one another, albeit weakly. He referred to this widespread pattern of low-level association throughout the social sciences as "the crud factor" to warn social scientists that it is specious to present their findings as important when they find only weak correlations. Schneider (2007) further developed this point by arguing that "the challenge for social scientists resides in their ability to conduct studies that will go beyond identifying which variables are related (as this is likely to be almost all of them)" and instead to determine "which variables are the most strongly related ... in theoretically or practically important ways" (p. 182). This illustrates the boundary of social cognitive theory's usefulness. Claiming that every variable in a theory influences and is influenced by each of the other variables is a good starting place to help scholars recognize the system-like nature of a theory. But this by itself does little to clarify the system of explanation and it does little to clarify a path of prediction. If social cognitive theory is to grow in scientific value, it needs to show that while every variable may be related to every other variable in a system, some of those variables are more primary (as thresholds and necessary conditions) and more influential than other variables.

Methodologically, the cognitive nature of the theory makes it challenging to operationalize valid measures of many of the variables. Concepts of internal states of self-efficacy, perceptions of models, and motivations require self-reporting and there are serious limitations to what humans perceive about themselves. Also people are viewed as so dynamic that it is difficult to implement the theory in its entirety. Instead, implementation is likely to focus on one or two concepts, such as self-efficacy.

Conceptual Development

Social learning theory went through a great deal of development and testing even before Bandura introduced it in 1977, and has since exhibited continual development through the mid-1980s when Bandura altered its name to social cognitive theory (Bandura, 1986). This relabeling is not an indication of a radical shift in his conceptualization but rather a major elaboration extending the ideas he laid out in 1977. *Social Learning Theory* (1977) was about 80,000 words of text. *Social Foundations of Thought and Action: A Social Cognitive Theory* (1986) was well over 300,000 words. Thus his expansion of text by almost four-fold indicates he had a lot to add to his original structure and conceptualization, and his expansion of citations ten-fold indicates his attention to patterns of research findings in the learning literature. Clearly, Bandura had added a lot of elaboration to his developing theory and he continued to do so in periodic reviews he published. Arguably, the biggest elaboration was the addition of the concept of self-efficacy—a term that was in his 1977 introduction as a relatively small idea in his treatment of antecedent determinants to observational learning. By 1986, it received its own chapter of over 40,000 words. And in 1995, he published *Self-efficacy in Changing Societies,* which was an edited book of 10 chapters written by 13 scholars in addition to Bandura himself that presented reviews of the fast-growing literature on the concept of self-efficacy and its role in social cognitive theory.

Self-efficacy simply refers to people's belief that they can successfully execute the behavior that is required to reach anticipated outcomes. Self-efficacy is a component of people's more general self-concept that includes beliefs about all sorts of things beyond the self. Bandura said (1986), "efficacy involves a generative capability in which cognitive, social, and behavioral subskills must be organized into integrated courses of action to serve innumerable purposes" (p. 391). He explained that self-efficacy influences people's thought patterns and emotional reactions during actual and anticipated transactions with their environment and determines how much "effort people will expend and how long they will persist in the face of obstacles or aversive experience" (p. 394).

It is beyond the capacity of this analysis to highlight all those elaborations but I will feature some of those extensions that were emphasized in reviews. Two decades later when he published a major review article, Bandura (2009) organized his presentation by using 16 major headings in 25 pages of text: capabilities (symbolizing, self-regulatory, self reflective, and vicarious), mechanisms governing observational learning (attentional processes, retention processes, production processes, and motivational processes), abstract modeling, acquisition and modification of affective proclivities, motivational effects, social construction of reality, social prompting function, matching methodologies with separable media effects, dual-link versus multipattern flow of influence, integrating social cognitive and social diffusion theory, modeling determinants of diffusion, adoption determinants, social networks, and flow of diffusion. Although the two structures of organization are very different, the list of individual ideas was substantially the same.

In their review of social cognitive theory, Pajares et al. (2009) said, "Given the breadth of social cognitive theory and the interconnectedness among its concepts, it can often be difficult to distill into a simple explication" (p. 284). They chose to feature four ideas that they called the four cornerstones of the theory: human agency, human capabilities, vicarious learning, and self-efficacy.

Human agency is the idea that individuals are proactively engaged in their own development and that they are able to exercise control over their thoughts, feelings, and actions (Bandura, 1986). This human agency has three modes. First there is individual agency which is evidenced when one's own influence is used to control one's own functioning. Proxy agency is when another person secures the benefits for the individual. And collective agency is when people work together to achieve common goals.

Human capabilities provide the cognitive tools that people use to influence their own destiny. Bandura presents five categories of human capabilities: symbolization, forethought, self-regulation, self-reflection, and vicarious learning.

Vicarious learning is the idea that people can learn social lessons by observing the behaviors of others and the consequences of those behaviors. This observational learning is organized into a process of four processes: attention, retention, production, and motivation.

Attention. In order to learn, observers must attend to the modeled behavior. Attention is impacted by characteristics of the observer (e.g., perceptual abilities, cognitive abilities, arousal, past performance) and characteristics of the behavior or event (e.g., relevance, novelty, affective valence, and functional value).

Retention. In order to reproduce an observed behavior, observers must be able to remember features of the behavior. Again, this process is influenced by observer characteristics (cognitive capabilities, cognitive rehearsal) and event characteristics (complexity).

Reproduction. To reproduce a behavior, the observer must organize responses in accordance with the model. Observer characteristics affecting reproduction include physical and cognitive capabilities and previous performance.

Motivation. The decision to reproduce (or refrain from reproducing) an observed behavior is dependent on the motivations and expectations of the observer, including anticipated consequences and internal standards.

Other scholars emphasize the idea of self-efficacy as the central core of the theory. Self-efficacy is the idea that individuals hold beliefs about their abilities to perform behaviors. This idea is central to social cognitive theory because Bandura argues that once a person learns a behavior through observation, the actual performance of that behavior is determined by self-efficacy, such that people will not perform those behaviors unless they believe that are capable and will be successful in those performances.

Periodically Bandura published chapter-length reviews of his theory and the empirical tests (e.g., Bandura, 2002, 2009). In each of these he would provide a brief description of his theory then highlight a different part that was undergoing elaboration at the time. For example, in his 2009 review, Bandura highlighted human capabilities (see Table 8.2) that had been suggested in his original introduction but not with much detail.

Table 8.2. Capabilities of Humans

Symbolizing Capability
1. Information comes into the human mind with the recognition of symbols, thus people do not experience the environment directly but only through symbols.
2. How people process symbols cognitively will determine what gets perceived and what gets ignored.
3. Through symbols, people give meaning, form, and continuity to their experiences.
4. People use symbols to communicate with others at any distance in time and space.

Self-Regulatory Capability
1. Self-regulation goes beyond limiting people to following external sanctions and demands and allows them to make more sophisticated decisions.
2. In evaluating their reactions, people use their internal standards.
3. Standards are learned through observation of others' and self-behavior and linking consequences to actions such that actions that are rewarded (or at least not punished) are regarded as good or useful and actions that are punished are regarded as bad or to be avoided.
4. People are motivated to reduce discrepancies. When people evaluate an observed action as bad, this produces a discrepancy between the standard and the behavior and this discrepancy motivates:
   a. Avoidance behavior
   b. Changing the standard
5. People set challenges for themselves and continually monitor their behavior to evaluate its success in progression toward meeting those challenges.
   a. Proactive control—disequalibrating discrepancies
   b. Reactive control—equilibrating discrepancies
6. When people attain a goal, they set higher goals if they have strong self-efficacy.
7. Most human behavior is directed by forethought about events and expected outcomes projected into the future.

Self-Reflective Capability
1. People continually reflect on the adequacy of their own thoughts using four modes:
   a. Enactive verification—people try out their thoughts by enacting them and determine how well they worked.
   b. Vicarious verification—people observe the behavior of others and compare that to their own thoughts.
   c. Social verification—checking the soundness of their own thoughts against the standard of what other people believe.
   d. Logical verification—people check for fallacies in their thinking by deducing conclusions from the knowledge they possess.

(Continued)

Table 8.2. *Continued*

---

2. Self-efficacy is a powerful predictor of a person's motivation to think and act. If they believe that they can develop viable plans and that those plans will work, they have high self-efficacy, and hence motivation to plan and act.

3. People consider personal self-efficacy as well as social group efficacy, that is, whether the groups they belong to are effective or not.

Vicarious Capability

1. People can learn by watching others; they do not have to try things out for themselves in order to learn.

2. The mass media have greatly expanded each person's ability to observe others.

From Bandura (2009).

Current Challenges

Unlike other theories of media effects, social learning theory has not been challenged by changes in the media environment. This is because social learning theory is broader than media and when it does deal with media, it focuses exclusively on messages and not channels. To Bandura, it does not matter whether people observe models in real life, on a large theater screen in a film, on a tiny screen on a smart phone, or in a printed book.

It appears that there are two kinds of challenges—one maintenance and one conceptual—to social cognitive theory moving forward. The maintenance challenge is to continue elaborating the details in the theory by reviewing the literature on observational learning. Bandura has been doing this for almost seven decades as that literature has grown enormously. If the theory is to maintain its value as a cutting-edge system of explanation, someone needs to transition into this task.

The conceptual challenge is to clarify the *system* of explanation. While the theory is very detailed with "building block"-type propositions there still remains a question about how all these building blocks fit together. This is not to say that the theory has little structure; to the contrary, Bandura has clearly laid out categories and continually shown which factors are in each category. What is missing is the system of explanation that can be used *a priori* to predict what individuals will learn from observing particular behaviors. The barrier to meeting this challenge is the idea of reciprocal determinism. If every factor influences every other factor and is in turn influenced by all the other factors, then there are two troubling implications. One of these implications is that the theory cannot be falsified because it cannot be adequately tested. That is, how can we parse out the influence of any one factor when its performance is determined by the performance of all other factors? It poses a problem of infinite regress.

The second of these implications is that the theory loses its scientific value as we move up from the building blocks into the larger structures of the theory. That is, there are so many factors that have to be accounted for in order to provide an explanation for any message or any outcome that every situation would likely have a different explanation. Such a system of explanation has value *a posteriori* in trying to explain why a certain outcome was manifested but it would offer little value in creating an *a priori* prediction that would be accurate.

Conclusions

The features that are most outstanding about social cognitive theory are its wide scope, high level of precision and conceptual coherence, enormous heuristic value, and strong pattern of empirical support. These qualities can be attributed to Bandura's very strong scholarship both as a careful reviewer of large literatures and as a designer of empirical tests of his ideas. He did not introduce his theory until he had spent almost 25 years developing and testing his ideas. That introduction was a book-length treatment that demonstrated a system of explanation utilizing a great many variables found important in well-established literatures. Then he spent the next four decades monitoring the growing literature of tests of his theory as well as larger literatures on learning to continually elaborate his theory.

Key Sources of Information about Social Cognitive Theory

Foundations

Bandura, A. (1963). Social learning and personality development. New York, NY: Holt, Rinehart, and Winston.

Chomsky, N. (1959). A review of B. F. Skinner's verbal behavior. Language, 35(1), 26–58. doi:10.2307/411334.

Miller, N. E., & Dollard, J. (1941). *Social learning and imitation.* New Haven, CT: Yale University Press.

Pajares, F. (2004). *Albert Bandura: Biographical sketch.* Retrieved July 27, 2017, from http://des.emory.edu/mfp/bandurabio.html

Rotter, J. (1954). Social learning and clinical psychology. Englewood Cliffs, NJ: Prentice-Hall.

Skinner, B. F. (1957). Verbal behavior. New York, NY: Appleton-Century-Crofts.

Skinner, B. F. (1963). Science and human behavior. New York, NY: Appleton.

Origin

Bandura, A. (1977). Social learning theory. Englewood Cliffs, NJ: Prentice-Hall.

Alterations/Elaborations in Theory

Bandura, A. (1986). *Social foundations of thought and action: A social cognitive theory.* Englewood Cliffs, NJ: Prentice-Hall.

Bandura, A. (1997). *Self-efficacy: The exercise of control.* New York, NY: Freeman.

Major Reviews

Bandura, A. (2002). Social cognitive theory of mass communication. In J. Bryant & D. Zillmann (Eds.), *Media effects: Advances in theory and research* (2nd ed., pp. 121–153). Mahwah, NJ: Erlbaum.

Bandura, A. (2009). Social cognitive theory of mass communication. In J. Bryant & M. B. Oliver (Eds.), *Media effects: Advances in theory and research* (3rd ed., pp. 94–124). New York, NY: Routledge.

Pajares, F., Prestin, A., Chen, J., & Nabi, R. L. (2009). Social cognitive theory and media effects. In R. L. Nabi & M. B. Oliver (Eds.), *Media processes and effects* (pp. 283–297). Los Angeles, CA: Sage.

Criticisms

Boundless. Criticisms of the Social-Cognitive Perspective on Personality. *Boundless Psychology* Boundless, Retrieved August 2, 2017, from https://www.boundless.com/psychology/textbooks/boundless-psychology-textbook/personality-16/social-cognitive-perspectives-on-personality-81/criticisms-of-the-social-cognitive-pespective-on-personality-316-12851/

Carillo, K. D. (2010). Social cognitive theory in IS research – literature review, criticism, and research agenda. In S. K. Prasad, H. M. Vin, S. Sahni, M. P. Jaiswal, B. Thipakorn (Eds.), *Information systems, technology and management. ICISTM 2010. Communications in computer and information science,* vol 54. Berlin, Heidelberg: Springer.

Flamand, L. (2009, September 10). Critique of social cognitive theory. *eHow.* Retrieved April 17, 2014, from http://www.ehow.com/about_5402265_critique-social-cognitive-theory.html

McLeod, S. A. (2016). Bandura – Social learning theory. Retrieved from www.simplypsychology.org/bandura.html

Meehl, P. E. (1990). Why summaries of research on psychological theories are often interpretable. *Psychological Reports, 66*(1), 195–244.

Schneider, S. L. (2007). Experimental and quasi-experimental designs in behavioral research: On context, crud, and convergence. In W. Outhwaite & S. P. Turner (Eds.), *The Sage handbook of social science methodology* (pp. 172–189). Los Angeles, CA: Sage.

References

Bandura, A. (1977). *Social learning theory*. Englewood Cliffs, NJ: Prentice-Hall.

Bandura, A. (1986). *Social foundations of thought and action: A social cognitive theory*. Englewood Cliffs, NJ: Prentice-Hall.

Bandura, A. (2002). Social cognitive theory of mass communication. In J. Bryant & D. Zillmann (Eds.), *Media effects: Advances in theory and research* (2nd ed., pp. 121–153). Mahwah, NJ: Erlbaum.

Bandura, A. (2009). Social cognitive theory of mass communication. In J. Bryant & M. B. Oliver (Eds.), *Media effects: Advances in theory and research* (3rd ed., pp. 94–124). New York, NY: Routledge.

Boundless. Criticisms of the Social-Cognitive Perspective on Personality. *Boundless Psychology* Boundless, Retrieved August 2, 2017, from https://www.boundless.com/psychology/textbooks/boundless-psychology-textbook/personality-16/social-cognitive-perspectives-on-personality-81/criticisms-of-the-social-cognitive-pespective-on-personality-316-12851/

Carillo K. D. (2010). Social cognitive theory in IS research – literature review, criticism, and research agenda. In S. K. Prasad, H. M. Vin, S. Sahni, M. P. Jaiswal, B. Thipakorn (Eds.), *Information systems, technology and management. ICISTM 2010. Communications in computer and information science*, vol 54. Berlin, Heidelberg: Springer.

Flamand, L. (2009, September 10). Critique of social cognitive theory. *eHow*. Retrieved April 17, 2014, from http://www.ehow.com/about_5402265_critique-social-cognitive-theory.html

McLeod, S. A. (2016). Bandura – Social learning theory. Retrieved from www.simplypsychology.org/bandura.html

Meehl, P. E. (1990). Why summaries of research on psychological theories are often interpretable. *Psychological Reports, 66*(1), 195–244.

Miller, N. E., & Dollard, J. (1941). *Social learning and imitation*. New Haven, CT: Yale University Press.

Pajares, F. (2004). *Albert Bandura: Biographical sketch*. Retrieved July 27, 2017, from http://des.emory.edu/mfp/bandurabio.html

Pajares, F., Prestin, A., Chen, J., & Nabi, R. L. (2009). Social cognitive theory and media effects. In R. L. Nabi & M. B. Oliver (Eds.), *Media processes and effects* (pp. 283–297). Los Angeles, CA: Sage.

Rotter, J. (1954). *Social learning and clinical psychology*. Englewood Cliffs, NJ: Prentice-Hall.

Schneider, S. L. (2007). Experimental and quasi-experimental designs in behavioral research: On context, crud, and convergence. In W. Outhwaite & S. P. Turner (Eds.), *The Sage handbook of social science methodology* (pp. 172–189). Los Angeles, CA: Sage.

Skinner, B. F. (1957). *Verbal behavior*. New York, NY: Appleton-Century-Crofts.

Skinner, B. F. (1963). *Science and human behavior*. New York, NY: Appleton.

CHAPTER NINE

Third-Person Theory

The Third-Person Effect (TPE) refers to a contrast in beliefs where individuals believe that other people (third persons) are more vulnerable to media influence than they are (first person). Thus the foundation of TPE is a "self-serving" perception whereby people think the media exert powerful influences but only on other people, not on themselves. This allows people to complain about the media and call for regulation of harmful content so as to control the media exposures of other people. At the same time, it excuses themselves from having to take responsibility for possible negative consequences of their own exposures as long as people tell themselves that the media have little or no influence on them personally.

When this idea was introduced into the scholarly literature in the early 1980s, it was generally regarded as an intriguing effect but not a theory. Over time as the idea attracted media effects scholars who developed explanations for why this effect continually occurs, it grew into a system of explanation about media influence that now includes work on third-person perceptions (TPPs), first-person perceptions (FPPs), and has even expanded to be called by some Presumed Media Influence (Tal-Or, Tsfati, & Gunther, 2009).

Original Conceptualization of the Theory

Conceptual Background

Shortly after World War II, sociologist W. Phillips Davison began studying how propaganda was used during the war to influence public opinion. In one study he examined an incident where the Japanese tried to discourage black American soldiers from fighting at Iwo Jima by dropping leaflets on their encampments. The leaflets tried to convince the black soldiers that they should surrender or desert. Although there was no indication that the leaflets had any effect on the soldiers, the incident preceded a substantial reshuffle among the officers and the unit was withdrawn the next day. Davison was puzzled that the commanders believed the soldiers were influenced by the leaflets even though the black soldiers were not (Davison, 1983).

Several years later while interviewing West German journalists to determine the influence of the press on foreign policy, Davison asked the journalists to estimate the influence their editorials had on readers. He found that the journalists typically said, "The editorials have little effect on people like you and me, but the ordinary reader is likely to be influenced quite a lot" (Davison, 1983). However, Davison could find no evidence to support these claims made by those journalists. Davison started going through the public opinion literature to see if he could find other instances of this pattern where people exhibited beliefs that other people (third persons) were influenced by media messages but they (first person) were not. Then in the early 1980s, Davison conducted a series of four surveys to test this pattern. In each survey he asked between 25 and 35 participants to estimate the influence of persuasive communication on themselves and others. Participants estimated self-other effects for (1) a campaign theme on gubernatorial vote choice, (2) television advertising on children, (3) the results of early presidential primaries on vote choice, and (4) campaign messages on presidential vote choice. On average they estimated (1) other New York voters were more influenced by campaign themes than they were personally, (2) other children were more influenced by television advertising than they had been personally when they were children, (3) others were more influenced by the results of early presidential primaries than they were personally, and (4) others were more influenced by campaign advertisements than they were personally. The findings from this series of informal surveys all showed support for the same pattern where respondents consistently believed that other people were more strongly affected by the media than they were personally (Davison, 1983).

Introduction of the Theory

Davison introduced the idea of TPE into the scholarly literature in an article entitled "The third-person effect in communication," which was published in *Public Opinion Quarterly* in 1983. In this article, he presented the results from his four surveys; then in a review of published studies that tested beliefs about media influence, he reinterpreted their findings to show they were in line with a TPE. He also argued that TPE was related to but distinct from other effects such as misperception of public opinion, pluralistic ignorance, and spiral of silence.

It is important to note that Davison did not refer to TPE as a theory. Instead Davison referred to this pattern as "the third-person effect" and "the third-person hypothesis," which were the names typically used by subsequent scholars (Gunther, 1995; Hoornes & Ruiter, 1996; Huh, Delorme, & Reid, 2004; McLeod, Eveland, & Nathanson, 1997; Price, Tewksbury, & Huang, 1998; Shah, Faber, & Youn, 1999; Sun, Pan, & Shen, 2008; Tiedge, Silverblatt, Havice, & Rosenfeld, 1991). However, it has also been referred to as "third-person conceptualization" (Cohen & Davis, 1991), "third-person effect model" (Gunther, 1995), and "third-person phenomenon" (Gunther & Thorson, 1992). Some scholars are careful not to refer to it as a theory. For example, in the first major review of TPE, Perloff (1999) said, "It is important to emphasize that the TPE is not a theory of public opinion, but rather a hypothesis or series of assertions about perceptions of public opinion and their effects" (p. 355) but he did not explain why he made this assertion.

While Davison's introduction of TPE in 1983 exhibits some characteristics of a theory (definitions of key concepts, a general proposition that can be tested through operationalization, and grounding in scholarly literatures), it is missing others (additional propositions that could form a set that provides a systematic explanation of some phenomenon). But this was enough to attract many scholars to this idea of TPE, and over the next few decades those scholars have elaborated many of Davison's ideas and published tests of TPE in scholarly journals. This literature now presents a system of explanation with multiple propositions that can be tested, and when they are tested have been found to be supported.

In this book, TPE is regarded as a theory because it has evolved to meet the criteria for theory as laid out in Chapter 2. It is a system of explanation that features a set of propositions and constructs; the constructs are measurable; the claims made in those propositions are testable and falsifiable by operationalizing them into hypotheses as evidenced by an already large and growing literature of empirical tests. In this chapter we will refer to it as TPE.

Conceptualization of Media

TPE's conceptualization of media is very broad. It is not limited to any one medium or vehicle. Its scope also seems to extend beyond the media, that is, nonmediated messages could also lead to the dual set of beliefs. In addition, while most of the research focuses on news and information type media messages, TPE also applies to purely persuasive type messages such as advertising and to the persuasive nature of entertainment messages.

Conceptualization of Media Effect

In his introduction of TPE, Davison (1983) clearly positioned it as a media effect where "people will tend to overestimate the influence that mass communications have on the attitudes and behavior of others. More specifically, individuals who are members of an audience that is exposed to a persuasive communication (whether or not this communication is intended to be persuasive) will expect the communication to have a greater effect on others than on themselves" (Davison, 1983, p. 3).

It is unclear where Davison placed the agency of the effect. There is no evidence that Davison or subsequent scholars regard TPE as an acquisition type effect where people are exposed to particular beliefs that they acquire as is. Instead, it appears that the media messages act more like a trigger of cognitive processes that result in formulating beliefs about oneself and others. If that is the case, then this would indicate that triggering is the type of media effect. But there is more required in order to have a TPE and that is a difference between first-person beliefs and third-person beliefs. The core essence of TPE is the difference, and it appears that the more active influence for this difference is not from the media but from cognitive processes within the individual.

Conceptualization of Media Influence

Scholars who have tested this effect seem to regard exposure to media messages as an essential antecedent to the effect, although few test for media exposure and use that as a variable to predict the effect. Instead, almost all tests of TPE focus on a variety of cognitive processes within individuals in order to explain the effect.

The conceptualization of media influence is slightly different depending on the methodologies used by researchers. Researchers who use experiments to test TPE typically examine the influence of particular message characteristics by designing different treatments that vary those characteristics, so that they can identify which characteristics in media messages are most related to TPE. Researchers who use surveys necessarily take a more general approach to influence, that is, they do not examine particular message characteristics but instead assume that the media exposures have already triggered the cognitive processes required to establish the different beliefs.

Original Components

Key Concepts

The two original concepts in TPE were third-person beliefs and first-person beliefs. These are sometimes referred to as perceptions, attitudes, and even behaviors, but they are beliefs because they fit the definition of being cognitions about the probability that an object or event is associated with a given attribute (Fishbein & Ajzen, 1975), that is, faith that something is real or is true. They are not perceptions in the sense that they are descriptions of what humans take in through the five senses; they are not evaluations that are required for attitudes; and they are not behaviors because they are typically not performed, although some surveys use self-reports of patterns of past actions or intentions of later actions, which should be considered beliefs rather than actual behaviors.

A third-person belief is a cognition that an individual holds about the persuasibility of other people, that is, the media have a strong influence on other people. In contrast, a first-person belief is a cognition an individual holds about the persuasibility of one's self. Thus the two belief concepts of TPE both focused on the idea of persuasibility, that is, the degree to which people could be (and are) influenced by exposure to media messages.

Core Propositions

The central proposition of TPE predicts a contrast between third-person beliefs and first-person beliefs, that is, there must be a difference in the two beliefs with the third-person belief indicating a higher susceptibility to media influence than a first-person belief. When individuals are exposed to a persuasive message (whether or not this communication is intended to be persuasive) in the media, they say they believe that message will have a greater effect on others than on themselves (Davison, 1983, p. 3).

Empirical Testing

The explanatory framework for the TPE has expanded considerably since the effect was first described by Davison (1983). This expansion through testing the main idea and looking for cognitive processes to explain the TPE is what has enabled the original simple idea to grow into a system of explanation.

Stimulating Scholarly Attention

TPE has attracted the attention of scholars starting with its introduction and the literature continues to grow. By 1999, TPE had already created a literature of 45 published articles (Perloff, 1999). A year later Paul, Salwen, and Dupagne (2000) conducted a meta-analysis of this literature, which was based on 32 empirical studies of TPE with 121 separate effect sizes reported. Then a few years later Sun et al. (2008) identified 60 papers and publications that tested TPE.

Patterns in the Research

Scope. A good deal of research has been conducted to test the scope of TPE. Table 9.1 shows that the TPE has been tested across a variety of messages, countries, media, and types of people as characterized by demographics. To date, researchers have yet to identify areas where TPE fails to find support.

Outcome variables. The primary outcome variable in TPE has been belief. Although some scholars have referred to the outcome variable as perceptions of others and self, those studies are really testing beliefs (mental constructions of what exists) rather than perceptions (interpretations of stimuli experienced through humans' five senses).

Over time, researchers have also made claims that they are testing TPE with behaviors. Scholars who have found support for the behavioral component have generally operationalized behavior as a willingness to censor content to stop the content from having the perceived negative persuasive impact on others (Perloff, 1999). Specifically, scholars have demonstrated that TPP predicts willingness to censor pornography (Gunther, 1995), television violence (Hoffner et al., 1999; Rojas, Shah, & Faber, 1996; Salwen & Dupagne, 1999), cigarette, beer, liquor, and gambling advertising (Shah et al., 1999), and antisocial rap music (McLeod et al., 1997). However, researchers have not found that third-person belief predicts willingness to censor news or political media content including censorship of press coverage of the O.J. Simpson trial (Salwen & Driscoll, 1997), support

Table 9.1. Empirical Patterns in Testing of TPE

Testing for Scope

Across types of messages
    General news coverage (Mutz, 1989; Perloff, 1989; Salwen & Driscoll, 1997)
        Of political campaigns (Salwen, 1998)
        Of environmental problems (Jensen & Hurley, 2005; Tewksbury et al., 2004)
        Of public opinion polls (Pan, Abisaid, Paek, Sun, & Houden, 2006; Price & Stroud, 2006)
        Of health issues (Weinstein, 1980)
    Persuasive messages
        Commercial advertising (Gunther & Thorson, 1992; Henriksen & Flora, 1999; Huh et al., 2004; Meirick, 2005; Shah et al., 1999),
        Political ads (Cohen & Davis, 1991; Meirick, 2004; Rucinski & Salmon, 1990),
        Public relations messages (Park & Salmon, 2005)
        Public Service Announcements (PSAs) (Duck & Mullin, 1995)
    Entertainment type messages
        Violence (Duck & Mullin, 1995; Hoffner et al., 1999; Rojas et al., 1996 ; Salwen & Dupagne, 1999)
        Pornography (Gunther, 1995; Lee & Tamborini, 2005; McLeod et al., 1997; Salwen & Dupagne, 1999; Scharrer, 2002)
        Rap music (McLeod et al., 1997)
Across countries
    United States (most of the above-mentioned studies)
    Germany (Peiser & Peter, 2000)
    Israel (Tsfati & Cohen, 2005)
    Australia (Duck & Mullin, 1995; Innes & Zeitz, 1988)
Across media (Antonopoulos, Veglis, Gardikiotis, Kotsakis, & Kalliris, 2015)
Across demographic groupings of age, education, and gender (Andsager & White, 2007; Henriksen & Flora, 1999; Paul et al., 2000; Tiedge et al., 1991)

for an independent commission to regulate political communication or censorship (Rucinski & Salmon, 1990), or a Holocaust-denial advertisement (Price et al., 1998).

When reviewing this literature, Perloff (1999) pointed out that these studies do not measure actual behavior; instead they measure behavioral intentions. Because we know there is very little correlation between what people say they intend to do in surveys and their actual behaviors, these outcome variables should be considered as beliefs instead of behaviors.

Explanations. A good deal of research was conducted to try to identify factors of influence that could explain why TPE occurs (see Table 9.2). These factors of influence could be arranged into three groups: factors about the media messages, factors about audience members, and processes.

In his most recent review of the TPE literature Perloff (2009) lists nine factors that have been found useful in explaining the TPE. These factors are: self-enhancement, need for control, projection, attributional biases, focus of attention, media schemas, perceived media exposure, self-categorization, and lack of access to own mental processes. The most important of these appear to be desirability of media messages, need for self-enhancement, and social distance.

Desirability of media message. Perhaps the most important contribution in the TPE empirical literature has been the finding that the desirability of a media message is a crucial factor in explaining the effect. Message desirability refers to the distinction between whether media messages are perceived as antisocial or prosocial.

This effect was first noticed by Innes and Zeitz (1988) who found that their research participants who were exposed to content with a violent message exhibited traditional TPEs but that other participants who were exposed to a public service announcement exhibited the reverse. They described this reverse effect, however, only as "something akin to a third person effect" (p. 461). Several years later, Cohen and Davis, who found that people tended to overestimate the effect of attack advertisements for disliked candidates on themselves than on others,

Table 9.2. Factors and Processes Found to Enhance TPE

Factors about People

Desire for self enhancement (Hoornes & Ruiter, 1996)

Social distance between the self and comparison groups (Cohen & Davis, 1991; Cohen et al., 1988; Davison, 1983; Duck et al., 1995; Eveland et al., 1999; Gunther, 1991; McLeod et al., 1997, 2001; Meirick, 2004, 2005; Scharrer, 2002; White, 1997)

Reference groups (Meirick, 2004)

Perceived desirability of messages (Chapin, 2000; Gunther & Mundy, 1993; Gunther & Thorson, 1992; Hoorens & Ruiter, 1996; Innes & Zeitz, 1988; White, 1997)

Factors about Media Messages

Susceptibility and severity (Shah et al., 1999)

Emotion eliciting characteristics of ads and PSAs (Gunther & Thorson, 1992)

Processes

Social comparison process (Park & Salmon, 2005)

Attributional error (Gunther, 1991, 1995; Rucinski & Salmon, 1990)

---

coined the term "reverse third-person effect" (1991, p. 687). The same year, Tiedge et al. (1991) coined the term "first-person effect" to refer to the perceived effects of media on self as being more than on others.

Most TPE studies, especially early on, dealt with messages that would be seen as "not smart to be influenced by" (Gunther & Mundy, 1993); however, it was found that the effect diminished or reversed into a first-person effect when the media message in question was prosocial or could have desirable consequences. Therefore the type of message (prosocial or antisocial) was found to be an essential explantor of TPE. With prosocial content, we should expect people to say they are strongly influenced by those messages and even more so than other people; this is known as the first-person effect.

Researchers have continually found that what was known as the TPE was strongest on beliefs about media influence of antisocial messages, especially violent and hateful messages (Andsager & White, 2007). However, when people were asked to consider the influence of media's prosocial messages, the effect was the opposite (Chapin, 2000; Gunther & Mundy, 1993; Gunther & Thorson, 1992; Hoorens & Ruiter, 1996; Innes & Zeitz, 1988; White, 1997). To illustrate, researchers found that when people were asked about media influence on antisocial topics, such as violence, irresponsible sex, and illegal drug use, respondents were likely to say that other people were much more influenced by those media portrayals than they were, which is the pattern of the TPE. However, when respondents were asked about the media influence of prosocial messages that portrayed positive traits such as altruism and generosity, those respondents were likely to say that they themselves were more influenced than other people. This later pattern has been labeled the "first-person effect."

A meta-analysis of studies of TPP found that message desirability was the most important predictor of TPP (Sun et al., 2008). TPEs are particularly pronounced when the message is perceived as undesirable—that is, when people infer that "this message may not be so good for me" or "it's not cool to admit you're influenced by this media program." In line with these predictions, people have been found to perceive content that is typically thought to be antisocial TPE to have a larger impact on others than on themselves (e.g., television violence, pornography, antisocial rap music) (Perloff, 2009). Indeed, many researchers have found evidence that undesirable messages, such as violent and hateful messages, yield a greater TPE (Andsager & White, 2007; Duck & Mullin, 1995; Gunther & Hwa, 1996; Gunther & Thorson, 1992; Hoornes & Ruiter, 1996). On the other hand, when messages are perceived as desirable, people are not so likely to exhibit a TPE. According to Perloff (2009), the first-person effect, or reversed TPE, is more common for desirable messages.

Need for self-enhancement. The patterns described above leave us with a question about why people would hold these beliefs about media influence on themselves and on other people. Perloff (1999) in his review of the early TPE literature suggested that people are motivated to preserve self-esteem even if they have to maintain unrealistically positive beliefs about themselves, that is, most people believe it is not socially desirable for them to admit they are strongly influenced by media messages, presumably because that would make them appear ignorant or weak. This explanation was supported by studies that tested the differences between desirable messages and undesirable message and found a greater TPE with undesirable messages.

According to the self-enhancement view, if the TPE is driven by a desire to preserve self-esteem, people should be willing to acknowledge effects for communications that are regarded as socially desirable, healthy, or otherwise good for the self (Hoornes & Ruiter, 1996; Tal-Or et al., 2009).

Social distance. In his introduction of TPE, Davison (1983) suggested that social distance was likely an explanation for the effect. Thus we should expect the pattern of TPE to be stronger when respondents perceive a greater distance between themselves and the others. That is, the more respondents think that a particular group of people are different from themselves, the stronger will be the TPE. "The greater the perceived social distance tween self and others, the easier it is to assume the third persons will fall prey to the effects that 'I' see through" (p. 364). The disparity of self and other is increased as perceived distance between self and comparison others is increased (Meirick, 2004, 2005).

Perloff (1999) said that "the nature of the social distance comparison between self and other depends in important ways on the identity of the hypothetical others" (p. 363). According to this notion, the magnitude of the TPE increases as the social distance between self and comparison others increases, or the hypothetical others are defined in larger, broader terms.

The social distance explanation has been tested often and typically found to hold (Cohen & Davis, 1991; Cohen, Mutz, Price, & Gunther, 1988; Duck, Hogg, & Terry, 1995; Gunther, 1991). Although social distance is not a necessary condition for the TPE to occur, increasing the social distance makes the TPE larger. In their meta-analysis, Andsager and White (2007) concluded that "Research consistently finds that others who are anchored to self as a point of reference are perceived to be less influenced by persuasive messages than are others who are not defined and, therefore, not anchored to any point of reference at all" (p. 92).

Target groups. The social distance explanation was challenged by findings that perceived exposure of a group to a message was a better predictor of perceived effects than perceived similarity to the group (Eveland, Nathanson, Detenber,

& McLeod, 1999; McLeod, Detenber, & Eveland, 2001; McLeod et al., 1997; Meirick, 2004, 2005). Thus it was reasoned that TPE was influenced to the extent that if a group is perceived as the target of a type of media content, perceived effects on them will be greater. Others have discussed this target explanation but mainly in terms of its tenability as an alternate explanation for their findings (Meirick, 2004; Scharrer, 2002). Despite the strong results of the target explanation cited above, the effect has been tested only for antisocial music lyrics. It has not been tested for messages where there would likely be less perceived variance in exposure, nor has it been tested for desirable messages. There is some evidence to suggest that the target explanation might not hold for positive messages (Meirick, 2004; Scharrer, 2002) perhaps because of incompatibility between beliefs about a group's exposure and (heretofore underexamined) beliefs about a group's predispositions toward the message's advocated behavior.

Other explanations. Researchers have also tested other explanations for TPE. Perloff (1999) notes that the majority of TPE studies attribute the psychological underpinnings of the effect to either attribution theory or biased optimism. Attribution theory predicts that actors tend to attribute their actions to situational factors, while observers tend to attribute the same actions to dispositional factors. For example, attribution theory predicts that a student who turns in a late assignment may explain to the professor that the tardiness is uncharacteristic and due to a situational factor like an unusual computer problem, while the professor might believe the tardiness was due instead to a dispositional factor like the student's laziness. In the context of the TPE, then, attribution theory explains why a person may think that he or she understands the underlying persuasive aspects of the message, while others' dispositional flaws prevent them from perceiving those same aspects (Perloff, 1999).

Biased optimism predicts that people tend to judge themselves as less likely than others to experience negative consequences and, conversely, that people tend to judge themselves as more likely than others to experience positive events. In the context of the TPE hypothesis, biased optimism explains why people judge themselves as being less likely than others to be affected by persuasion (Perloff, 1999).

Empirical Validity

Reviews of this growing literature typically conclude that there is strong and continuing support for TPE in general but that there may be particular areas where the theory is weak or lacking support. In his review of TPE, Lasorsa (1992) said that about half of the members of any sample show a TPE while the others do not. This is typically enough to show overall support for the theory. However, this finding has led researchers to look for contingent factors to try explaining why some people are susceptible while others are not. Also, researchers who have designed experiments can look for contingencies on the way the topic is presented in stimulus materials.

There have been two meta-analyses of the TPE literature and these both conclude the literature shows strong support for TPE (relative to the support of other theories and other media effects) but that there are some important contingencies. Paul et al. (2000) conducted a meta-analysis of 121 separate effect sizes reported and converted these varied statistical indicators into a common metric of an r where positive r indicated a TPE. The findings from their meta-analysis indicate the perceptual component of the TPE hypothesis received robust support ($r = .50$), especially compared to meta-analyses of other media effects theories. They also tested eight factors to see how stable the effect was: source, method, sampling, respondent, country, desirability, medium, and message. Source referred to published and unpublished studies. Method referred to surveys or experiments. Sampling referred to random and nonrandom. Respondent was either college students or noncollege people. Country was U.S. and other countries. Desirability had three values—desirable to believe, undesirable, and neither. Medium had four values (media in general, television radio, newspapers, and other). Message variable had seven values (message in general, pornography, television violence, commercial ads, politics, nonpolitical news, and other). They report finding three of these eight to be most significant: sampling, respondent, and message. Samples that were nonrandom yielded greater TPE differences than samples obtained from random samples. As for type of respondent, they found that samples composed of students yielded greater TPE differences than nonstudent samples. As for message, different types of content (e.g., general media messages, pornography, television violence, commercial advertisements, political content, nonpolitical news) have differing effects on the size of the obtained TPPs.

A few years later, Sun et al. (2008) conducted a meta-analysis of 106 studies that reported 372 effect sizes. They tested the TPE for stability using 16 test factors. Of these, seven were research characteristics (study setting, data collection method, design, study population, sampling method, measure for perceived effects, and domain of perceived effects). Four were message characteristics (desirability of message, message topic domain, persuasive intent, and functional focus). The rest were referent characteristics, such as geographical distance and sociodemographics. After finding an average effect size estimate of $d = 0.646$ ($r = .307$), the authors said, "The effect size, however, is significantly smaller than that reported in Paul et al.'s (2000) study, which, as we demonstrated, contained serious overestimation because they did not (a) apply the right effect size formula for within-subjects designs nor (b) address the statistical dependency among multiple effect sizes extracted from the same study" (p. 294).

Sun et al. (2008) also found the influence was not sensitive to five tested factors (research setting, population, between- or within-subjects design, model of data collection, or whether single- or multiple-item measures were used) but that the other 12 factors they tested were all found to be significant with message desirability being the most important. In summary, they reported "Results from a series of multilevel models show that the third-person perception is robust and not influenced by variations in research procedures. Desirability of presumed message influence, vulnerability of referent others, referent others depicted as being similar to self, and others being likely audience of the media content in question are significant moderators" (p. 280).

Theory Development

Conceptual Development

Conceptual criticism. Some reviewers of this research make a distinction between perceptions and behaviors. For example, Tal-Or et al. (2009) argue that "most research on the third-person effect to date has examined this component (perceptual) . . . Yet the reason for Davison's enthusiasm about TPPs was that he recognized the enormous ways in which these perceptions might impact the real world. However, only in recent years have scholars turned their attention to the behavioral consequences of people's biased perceptions of media coverage" (p. 104). While this at first sounds like a useful distinction—perceptions vs. behaviors—it is faulty, because the perceptions are really beliefs and when we look at what is regarded at behavioral measures in the published literature, we see that these measures are self-reports of intended behaviors or beliefs about behaviors. For example, Tewksbury, Moy, and Weis (2004) found that after the media reported on the so-called millennium buy (Y2K) that could cause havoc on computers, people said they were less likely to stockpile supplies (food, water, gasoline, cash, etc.) than other people. Research has also found that after the media make predictions of likely earthquakes, people report they are less likely to prepare their homes for such a disaster than other people. These results are highly suspect as reflecting behaviors; we have known for a long time that what people report as their behaviors and what their actual behaviors are has a weak association at best. It is more likely that these results reflect the desire of people to be consistent in their beliefs, that is, if they say they are less affected by the media then when asked about their behaviors they will say their behaviors exhibit less effect than the presumed behaviors of other people.

Conceptual alterations. Over the years, scholars have argued for other propositions to explain TPE by expanding on the original ideas from Davison. These are typically referred to as "corollaries." There are three such corollaries referred to in the literature as explanations for why the TPE occurs. These are negative influence corollary, social distance corollary, and the target corollary.

Negative influence corollary. This corollary recognizes that the TPE is sensitive to the type of content. If the type of content is antisocial (beliefs about the effects of violence, pornography, drugs, etc.), then the TPE predictions hold, that is, people believe that others are more influenced by media coverage than they are personally. However, when the content is prosocial, then the opposite is the case, that is, people generally believe that they are more likely to be influenced in a positive way compared to other people. This has sometimes been called the first-person effect, which says that sometimes people will have beliefs that media influence is stronger on them than on other people.

Gunther and Storey (2003) write about "a negative influence corollary" as a contingent factor that limits the general nature of TPE. They argued that "Although the evidence for FPP is not robust in part due to a much smaller number of effect sizes in the extant literature, it is clear that 'the negative influence corollary' (Gunther & Storey, 2003) specifies theoretical boundaries of TPP" (p. 294). However, other scholars recognize that this corollary can be incorporated into the theory if it is expanded to encompass all of the presumed media influence (Tal-Or et al., 2009).

Social distance corollary. Another cognitive process that has been associated with TPE has been called the social distance corollary where people choose to dissociate themselves from the others who may be influenced. Perloff (1999) said that "the nature of the social distance comparison between self and other depends in important ways on the identity of the hypothetical others" (p. 363) and this has "come to be called the social-distance corollary. According to this notion, the magnitude of the TPE increases as the social distance between self and comparison others increases, or the hypothetical others are defined in larger, broader terms. The greater the perceived social distance between self and others, the easier it is to assume the third persons will fall prey to the effects that 'I' see through" (p. 364). This effect has been widely cited in the research literature (Tal-Or et al., 2009) and it has been found to have strong empirical support (Paul et al., 2000).

Target corollary. The target corollary predicts that TPE will be stronger on targets who are perceived as being more involved in the issues that are being examined. There is some evidence to suggest that the target corollary might not hold for positive messages (Meirick, 2004), perhaps because of incompatibility between beliefs about a group's exposure and (heretofore underexamined) beliefs about a group's predispositions toward the message's advocated behavior. Thus was born the "target corollary"—to the extent that a group is perceived as the target of a type of media content, perceived effects on them will be greater.

Methodological Development

Most of the criticism about TPE has focused on methodological issues, especially concerning problems of validity of findings due to the way questions are asked.

Methods used. As for methods patterns, most of these studies are cross-sectional surveys although several measured at least two points in time (Price et al., 1998). Also most have used convenience samples (e.g., McLeod et al., 1997; Meirick, 2004, 2005), but a few have used national probability samples (Gunther, 1995; Huh et al., 2004; Salwen & Driscoll, 1997) or more local probability samples (Tiedge et al., 1991). Some have used personal interviews (Duck & Mullin, 1995; Innes & Zeitz, 1988; Shah et al., 1999). And a few have used experiments (Cohen & Davis, 1991; Duck & Mullin, 1995; Gunther & Thorson, 1992; Hoornes & Ruiter, 1996; Park & Salmon, 2005). Many have used undergraduate college students (Cohen & Davis, 1991; Duck & Mullin, 1995; Gunther & Thorson, 1992; Hoornes & Ruiter, 1996; McLeod et al., 1997; Meirick, 2004, 2005; Park & Salmon, 2005; Price et al., 1998).

Criticism. There has been a continuing disconnect between what Davison originally conceptualized the effect to be and how it has been tested—including tests by Davison himself. In his introduction of TPE, Davison (1983) defined the effect as "people will tend to overestimate the influence that mass communications have on the attitudes and behavior of others" (p. 3). In order to use this claim as it is worded requires the identification of a true level of influence to use as a standard upon which to determine if people are underestimating or overestimating media influence. Nowhere in the literature does a scholar tackle this task, perhaps because it is a near impossible thing to do. However, we could make a minor alteration in operationalizing tests and use as a standard the actual risk levels for various things, such as chances of being in an automobile accident due to drinking, drug use, or mobile device use. Then ask people to estimate the levels of such risks on other people. So if they estimate a risk of something covered in a media message to be 10 % and the actual level of risk to be 2 %, then this would be evidence of an overestimation. However, this kind of test exists nowhere in the TPP literature. Instead, the typical test is to ask people to estimate their own risk as well as the risk on others; if the estimate of the third person is *higher* than the estimate on self then this is taken as adequate evidence of a TPE. And if the estimate of the third person is *lower* than the estimate on self then this is taken as adequate evidence of a first-person effect. Therefore, in the empirical literature, the standards of comparison are always beliefs about media influence or risk—never actual levels of influence or risk.

A second criticism is that evidence for TPE might be a measurement artifact if it is found that the first question asked in a study serves as an anchor for respondents in answering the second question (Perloff, 1999). Many tests have been run that have altered question orders and formats; these tests have all found support for TPE (Brosius & Engel, 1996; David, Lui, & Myser, 2004; Gunther, 1995; Gunther & Hwa, 1996; Price & Tewksbury, 1996; Salwen & Driscoll, 1997; Tiedge et al., 1991). For example, Price and Tewksbury tested whether the TPE was a methodological artifact as a result of asking participants self-other questions in close proximity. Using a three-condition experiment in which they asked participants in the first condition self-only questions, participants in the second condition other-only questions, and participants in the third condition self and other questions, Price and Tewksbury's (1996) results indicate consistent estimates of self and other estimates across conditions. These results, then, indicate the effect is not the result of a methodological artifact.

Current Challenges

There seem to be two current challenges facing the theory. First, there are lingering questions about whether it qualifies as a theory. Second, it needs to increase its level of precision.

Qualify as Theory

Scholars who write about TPE sometimes refer to it only as an effect, sometimes as an hypothesis, and sometimes as a theory. When Davison (1983) first introduced the idea he called it an effect then ran several tests calling it the "third-person effect hypothesis." In his major review of TPE, Perloff (2009) refers to it as an effect, a hypothesis, and a theory by using all three terms. He calls it an effect in many places, most prominently in the title "Mass media, social perception, and the third-person effect." He also says "the third-person effect is more hypothesis than full-blown theory" (p. 254) but does not explain what is missing in order for him to consider it a theory. But then he also said that TPE is "ranked as the fifth most popular theory in 21st century mass communication research" (pp. 252–253).

It is understandable why this ambivalence existed when Davison first introduced the TPE, but over time the contributions that scholars have made to this literature have added components such that it now meets the definition of theory as derived in Chapter 2. TPE has evolved into a system of explanation that features key concepts arranged in propositions that express the relationships between two or more of those concepts. Each of those propositions is testable and they have been assembled into a set that has internal coherence as a system of explaining how the media along with other factors work together to influence the occurrence of a media effect. It also has stimulated numerous empirical tests of those propositions. For these reasons, it can—and should—be regarded as a theory.

TPE, however, is different from most of the other theories in one important respect, and this will present a considerable challenge going forward. Most of the theories analyzed in this book were introduced by a media effects scholar who continued working on it by testing it and publishing reviews of the growing empirical literature over several decades. In contrast, TPE was introduced by a sociologist who did not continue publishing tests of this theory and who did not publish reviews of the empirical literature testing his theory. However, other scholars—most notably David Perloff, Al Gunther, Michael Salwen, and Vincent Price—have each published several tests, provided probing analyses of the theory, and worked to add to its scope and explanatory power. Thus for the purposes of the analysis in this book, it has been less useful to talk about the original conceptualization of Davison, which was highly speculative and more useful to regard the theory as the set of all work that has been done over the years. But moving forward this presents a challenge about who will assume the role of guiding future development and arbitrating disagreements that might arise over how the theory should be altered and elaborated.

Whoever steps up to guide the continued development of TPE will be able to continue to mine ideas from the larger media effects literature. Over time, researchers have drawn on a variety of psychological theories to justify the TPE. Few, however, explicitly linked these theories to the TPE. Some researchers have used ego involvement (e.g., Perloff, 1989; Vallone, Ross, & Lepper, 1985), the elaboration likelihood model (e.g., White, 1997), and social categorization theory, but most have relied on attribution theory (e.g., Gunther, 1991; Hoffner et al., 1999; Rucinski & Salmon, 1990) and biased optimism (e.g., Brosius & Engel, 1996; Gunther & Mundy, 1993; Rucinski & Salmon, 1990) to explain the theoretical underpinnings of the TPE.

Precision

This theory struggled from the beginning and still struggles with precision in the defining and labeling of concepts. This can be seen in the selection of a name for the theory. When Davison (1983) introduced this theory into the scholarly literature, he used the title "The third-person effect in communication" and continually referred to it as the TPE. But he could have just as well called it the first-person effect. Better yet it should be regarded as both, but that would be too awkward.

A second area where precision is a major problem is with the conception of behavior. Reviewers of the literature make claims about the theory having two stages: perception and behavior. But the measures of behavior have tapped into beliefs (self-reports and intentions) rather than actual actions. If the theory is interested in explaining behavior, then researchers will need to design experiments that move beyond a reliance on questionable self-reports and test for actual behaviors (Tal-Or et al., 2009).

Conclusions

What started out as a report of an intriguing effect in 1983 has since grown broader in scope and as a system of explanation until it is now regarded as Presumed Media Influence (Tal-Or et al., 2009). The core idea has received considerable support over the years, and researchers have sought to think up then test explanations for why TPE occurs so consistently. We now have a growing system of explanation that has a solid core of explanation about TPE and first-person effects that has been well supported by empirical tests. In addition, the theory has been elaborated with three corollaries beyond the core and is likely to continue growing its explanatory power in the future.

Key Sources

Origin

Davison, W. P. (1983). The third-person effect in communication. Public Opinion Quarterly, 47(1), 1–15. doi:10.1086/268763.

Reviews

Lasorsa, D. L. (1992). How media affect policymakers: The third-person effect. In J. D. Kennamer (Ed.), Public opinion, the press and public policy (pp. 163–175). New York, NY: Praeger.

Paul, B., Salwen, M. B., & Dupagne, M. (2000). The third-person effect: A meta-analysis of the perceptual hypothesis. Mass Communication & Society, 3(1), 57–85. doi:10.1207/s15327825mcs0301_04

Perloff, R. M. (1999). The third-person effect: A critical review and synthesis. Media Psychology, 1(4), 353–378. doi:10.1207/s1532785xmep0104_4.

Perloff, R. M. (2009). Mass media, social perception, and the third-person effect. In J. Bryant & M. B. Oliver (Eds.), *Media effects: Advances in theory and research* (3rd ed., pp. 252–268). London: Routledge. ISBN 9781135591106.

Sun, Y., Pan, Z., & Shen, L. (2008). Understanding the third-person perception: Evidence from a meta-analysis. Journal of Communication, 58(2), 280–300. doi:10.1111/j.1460-2466.2008.00385.x.

Tal-Or, N., Tsafati, Y., & Gunther, A. C. (2009). The influence of presumed media influence: Origins and implications of the third-person perception. In R. L. Nabi & M. B. Oliver (Eds.), *Media processes and effects* (pp. 99–112). Los Angeles, CA: Sage.

Criticisms

Perloff, R. M. (1999). The third-person effect: A critical review and synthesis. Media Psychology, 1(4), 353–378. doi:10.1207/s1532785xmep0104_4.

Tal-Or, N., Tsafati, Y., & Gunther, A. C. (2009). The influence of presumed media influence: Origins and implications of the third-person perception. In R. L. Nabi & M. B. Oliver (Eds.), *Media processes and effects* (pp. 99–112). Los Angeles, CA: Sage.

References

Andsager, J. L., & White, H. A. (2007). *Self versus others: Media, messages, and the third-person effect.* Mahwah, NJ: Erlbaum. ISBN 9780805857160.

Antonopoulos, N., Veglis, A., Gardikiotis A., Kotsakis, R., & Kalliris, G. (2015). Web Third-person effect in structural aspects of the information on media websites. *Computers in Human Behavior, 44*(3), 48–58. doi:10.1016/j.chb.2014.11.022

Brosius, H-B., & Engel, D. (1996). The causes of third-person effects: Unrealistic optimism, impersonal impact, or generalized negative attitudes towards media influence? *International Journal of Public Opinion Research 7*, 142–162.

Chapin, J. R. (2000). Third-person perception and optimistic bias among urban minority at-risk youth. *Communication Research, 27*, 51–81.

Cohen, J., & Davis, R. G. (1991). Third-person effects and the differential impact in negative political advertising. *Journalism Quarterly, 68*(4), 680–688. doi:10.1177/107769909106800409

Cohen, J., Mutz, D., Price, V., & Gunther, A. C. (1988). Perceived impact of defamation. *Public Opinion Quarterly, 52*, 161–173.

David, P., Liu, K., & Myser, M. (2004). Methodological artifact or persistent bias? Testing the robustness of the thirdperson and reverse thirdperson effects for alcohol messages. *Communication Research, 31*, 206–233.

Davison, W. P. (1983). The third-person effect in communication. *Public Opinion Quarterly, 47*(1), 1–15. doi:10.1086/268763

Duck, J. M., Hogg, M. A. & Terry, D. J. (1995). Me, us and them: Political communication and the third person effect in the Australian Federation Election. *European Journal of Social Psychology, 25*, 195–215.

Duck, J. M., & Mullin, B.-A. (1995). The perceived impact of the mass media: Reconsidering the third person effect. *European Journal of Social Psychology, 25*(1), 77–93. doi:10.1002/ejsp.2420250107

Eveland, W. P., Jr., Nathanson, A. I., Detenber, B. H., & McLeod, D. M. (1999). Rethinking the social distance corollary. Perceived likelihood of exposure and the third-person perception. *Communication Research, 26*, 275–302.

Fishbein, M. & Ajzen, I. (1975). *Belief, attitude, intention, and behavior: An introduction to theory and research*. Reading, MA: Addison-Wesley.

Gunther, A. C. (1991). What we think others think: Cause and consequence in the third-person effect. *Communication Research, 18*, 355–372.

Gunther, A. C. (1995). Overrating the X-rating: The third-person perception and support for censorship of pornography. *Journal of Communication 45*(1), 27–38. doi:10.1111/j.1460-2466.1995.tb00712.x.

Gunther, A. C. & Hwa, A. P. (1996). Public perceptions of television influence and opinions about censorship in Singapore. *International Journal of Public Opinion Research, 8*(3), 248–265. doi:10.1093/ijpor/8.3.248

Gunther, A. C., & Mundy, P. (1993). Biased optimism and the third-person effect. *Journalism Quarterly, 70*, 58–67.

Gunther, A. C. & Storey, J. D. (2003). The influence of presumed influence. *Journal of Communication, 53*, 199–215.

Gunther, A. C., & Thorson, E. (1992). Perceived persuasive effects of commercials and public service announcements: The third-person effect in new domains. *Communication Research, 19*(5), 574–596. doi:10.1177/009365092019005002

Henriksen, L., & Flora, J. A. (1999). Third-person perception and children: Perceived impact of pro- and anti-smoking ads. *Communication Research, 26*, 643–665.

Hoffner, C., Buchanan, M., Anderson, J. D., Hubbs, L. A., Kamigaki, S. K., Kowalczyk, L., … Silberg, K. J. (1999). Support for censorship of television violence: The role of the third-person effect and news exposure. *Communication Research, 26*, 726–742.

Hoornes, V., & Ruiter, S. (1996). The optimal impact phenomenon: Beyond the third person effect. *European Journal of Social Psychology 26*(4), 599–610. doi:10.1002/(sici)1099-0992(199607)26:4<599::aid-ejsp773>3.0.co;2-7

Huh, J., Delorme, D., & Reid, L. N. (2004). The third-person effect and its influence on behavioral outcomes in a product advertising context: The case of direct-to-consumer prescription drug advertising. *Communication Research 31*(5): 568–599. doi:10.1177/0093650204267934

Innes, J. M., & Zeitz, H. (1988). The public's view of the impact of the mass media: A test of the "third-person" effect. *European Journal of Social Psychology 18*(5), 457–463. doi:10.1002/ejsp.2420180507

Jensen, J. D., & Hurley, R. J. (2005). Third-person effects and the environment: Social distance, social desirability, and presumed behavior. *Journal of Communication*, *55*, 242–256.

Lee, B., & Tamborini, R. (2005). Third-person effect and internet pornography: The influence of collectivism and internet self-efficacy, *Journal of Communication*, *55*, 292–310.

McLeod, D. M., Detenber, B. H., & Eveland, W. P., Jr. (2001). Behind the third-person effect: Differentiating perceptual processes for self and others. *Journal of Communication*, *51*, 678–695.

McLeod, D. M., Eveland, W. P., & Nathanson, A. I. (1997). Support for censorship of violent and misogynic rap lyrics: An analysis of the third-person effect. *Communication Research* *24*(2), 153–174. doi:10.1177/009365097024002003

Meirick, P. C. (2004). Topicrelevant reference groups and dimensions of distance: political advertising and first and thirdperson effects. *Communication Research*, *31*, 234–255.

Meirick, P. C. (2005). Rethinking the target corollary: The effects of social distance, perceived exposure, and perceived predispositions on first-person and third-person perceptions. *Communication Research* *32*(6): 822–843. doi:10.1177/0093650205281059

Mutz, D. (1989). The influence of perception of media influence. *International Journal of Public Opinion Research*, *1*, 3–24.

Pan, Z., Abisaid, J. L., Paek, H-J., Sun, Y., & Houden, D. (2006). Exploring the perceptual gap in perceived effects of media repots of opinion polls. *International Journal of Public Opinion Research*, *18*, 340–350.

Park, H. S., & Salmon, C. T. (2005). A test of the third-person effect in public relations: Application of social comparison theory. *Journalism Quarterly* *82*(1), 25–43. doi:10.1177/107769900508200103

Paul, B., Salwen, M. B., & Dupagne, M. (2000). The third-person effect: A meta-analysis of the perceptual hypothesis. *Mass Communication & Society*, *3*(1), 57–85. doi:10.1207/s15327825mcs0301_04

Peiser, W., & Peter, J. (2001). Explaining individual differences in third-person perception: A limits/possibilities perspective. *Communication Research*, *28*, 156–180.

Perloff, R. M. (1989). Ego-involvement and the third-person effect of televised news coverage. *Communication Research*, *16*, 236–262.

Perloff, R. M. (2009). Mass media, social perception, and the third-person effect. In J. Bryant & M. B. Oliver (Eds.), *Media effects: Advances in theory and research* (3rd ed., pp. 252–268). London: Routledge. ISBN 9781135591106.

Price, V., & Stroud, N. J. (2006). Public attitudes toward polls: Evidence from the 2000 U.S. presidential election. *International Journal of Public Opinion Research*, *18*, 393–421.

Price, V., & Tewksbury, D. (1996). Measuring the third-person effect of news: The impact of question order, contrast and knowledge. *International Journal of Public Opinion Research* *8*(2), 120–141. doi:10.1093/ijpor/8.2.120

Price, V., Tewksbury, D., & Huang, L-N. (1998). Third-person effects on publication of a holocaust-denial advertisement. *Journal of Communication* *48*(2), 3–26. doi:10.1111/j.1460-2466.1998.tb02745.x

Rojas, H., Shah, D. V., & Faber, R. J. (1996). For the good of others: Censorship and the third-person effect. *International Journal of Public Opinion Research 8*(2): 163–186. doi:10.1093/ijpor/8.2.163

Rucinski, D., & Salmon, C. T. (1990). The "other" as the vulnerable voter: A study of the third-person effect in the 1988 U.S. presidential campaign. *International Journal of Public Opinion Research 2*(4), 345–368. doi:10.1093/ijpor/2.4.345

Salwen, M. B. (1998). Perception of media influence and support for censorship: The third-person effect in the 1996 presidential election. *Communication Research, 25*, 259–285.

Salwen, M. B., & Dupagne, M. (1999). The third-person effect: Perceptions of the media's influence and immoral consequences. *Communication Research, 26*, 523–549.

Salwen, M. B., & Dupagne, M. (2001). Third-person perception of television violence: The role of self-perceived knowledge. *Media Psychology, 3*, 211–230.

Salwen, M. B., & Driscoll, P. D. (1997). Consequences of third-person perception in support of press restrictions in the O.J. Simpson trial. *Journal of Communication 47*(2), 60–75. doi:10.1111/j.1460-2466.1997.tb02706.x

Scharrer, E. (2002). Third-person perception and television violence: The role of out-group stereotyping in perception of susceptibility to effects. *Communication Research, 29*, 681–704.

Shah, D. V., Faber, R. J., & Youn, S. (1999). Susceptibility and severity: Perceptual dimensions underlying the third-person effect. *Communication Research 26*(2): 240–267. doi:10.1177/009365099026002006

Sun, Y., Pan, Z., & Shen, L. (2008). Understanding the third-person perception: Evidence from a meta-analysis. *Journal of Communication, 58*(2), 280–300. doi:10.1111/j.1460-2466.2008.00385.x

Tal-Or, N., Tsafati, Y., & Gunther, A. C. (2009). The influence of presumed media influence: Origins and implications of the third-person perception. In R. L. Nabi & M. B. Oliver (Eds.), *Media processes and effects* (pp. 99–112). Los Angeles, CA: Sage.

Tewksbury, D., Moy, P., & Weis, D. S. (2004) Preparations for Y2K: Revisiting the behavioral components of the third-person effect. *Journal of Communication, 54*, 138–155.

Tiedge, J. T., Silverblatt, A., Havice, M. J., & Rosenfeld, R. (1991). Discrepancy between perceived first person and perceived third-person mass media effects. *Journalism Quarterly, 68*(1/2), 141–154. doi:10.1177/107769909106800115

Tsfati, Y., & Cohen, J. (2004). Object-subject distance and the third person perception. *Media Psychology, 6*, 335–361.

Tsfati, Y., & Cohen, J. (2005). The influence of presumed media influence on democratic legitimacy: The case of Gaza settlers. *Communication Research, 32*, 794–821.

Vallone, R., Ross, L., & Lepper, M. (1985). The hostile media phenomenon: Biased perception and perceptions of media bias in coverage of the Beirut massacre. *Journal of Personality and Social Psychology, 49*, 577–585.

Weinstein, N. D. (1980). Unrealistic optimism about future life events. *Journal of Personality and Social Psychology, 39*, 806–820.

White, H. A. (1997). Considering interacting factors in the third-person effect: Argument strength and social distance. *Journalism & Mass Communication Quarterly, 74*, 557–564.

Evaluation of the Set of Core Theories

CHAPTER TEN

The Evaluation Strategy

In this chapter, I lay out the evaluative strategy that is applied in the next chapter. First, I will develop five primary and one summary evaluative dimensions to use in making assessments of the relative value of the six theories. Then second, I will describe the key features in the overall evaluation strategy.

Evaluative Dimensions

Many criteria have been suggested for the evaluation of theories (see Table 10.1). When we look across those lists and account for differences in labeling, there appear to be six criteria that can account for all those concerns expressed with different words. Those evaluative concerns are: scope, precision, heuristic value, empirical validity, openness, and overall utility. These are the evaluative dimensions that will be used in this book.

Scope

The criterion of scope poses the question: How much of the field's focal phenomenon—in this case media effects—does a theory attempt to explain? Because each of the six theories is social-scientific, scope is an important criterion. Science

Table 10.1. Conceptions of Evaluative Criteria for Theory

Littlejohn (1999) offers six criteria (pp. 36–37):

1. Theoretical scope—comprehensiveness or inclusiveness
2. Appropriateness—are the theory's epistemological, ontological, and axiological assumptions appropriate for the theoretical questions addressed and the research methods used?
3. Heuristic value—generating new ideas for research and additional theory
4. Validity—truth value:

   Utility

   Correspondence between theory and observation

   Generalizability
5. Parsimony—logical simplicity
6. Openness—tentative, contextual, and qualified

Infante, Rancer, and Womack (1993) write that there are three necessary and six desirable criteria for evaluating theories (pp. 57–65):

Necessary

1. Logically consistent—no contradictory propositions
2. Consistent with accepted facts
3. Testable

Desirable

1. Simple
2. Parsimonious
3. Consistent with related theories
4. Interpretable
5. Useful
6. Pleasing to the mind

Shoemaker, Tankard, and Lasorsa (2004) present 10 criteria for evaluating theories:

Testability

Falsifiability

Parsimony

Explanatory Power

Predictive Power

Scope

Cumulative Nature of Science

Degree of Formal Development

Heuristic Value

Aesthetics

---

attempts to provide explanations of patterns in large aggregates; there is a drive toward generality. Therefore, theories with greater scope are more valuable to the field than theories of less scope, other characteristics being equal.

The evaluation of a theory's scope—like with the other six criteria—requires a multidimensional approach, that is, there is more than one way to assess the scope of a theory. Therefore we need to look at a combination of factors in three areas of conceptualization of media, media effect, and factors of influence (see Table 10.2).

1. Conceptualization of media. Scope varies by how much of the field's focal phenomenon a theory attempts to explain. Scope suggests the following questions:

* Does the theory seek to explain all media, a set of media (e.g., print), or one particular medium (e.g., film)?
* Does the theory seek to explain effects that arise from any kind of media message or is it limited to explaining effects that arise from only a specific type of message (e.g., violence or sexual situations)?

2. Conceptualization of media effect. Does the theory seek to explain all possible types of media effects? Or is the theory limited by function, timing, target, type, valence, or intentionality? This general concern suggests more specific questions.

* Does the theory attempt to explain all four functions (acquisition, triggering, altering, reinforcing) or is it limited to a subset?
* Does the theory seek to explain media effects at all points of time or is it limited to explaining effects that occur at only one point in time (e.g., immediately after exposure to the message) or duration (lasting only several minutes)?
* Does the theory seek to explain media effects on people or aggregates? If it focuses on people, does it attempt to explain the media effect on all people or is it limited to explaining effects on a specific type of person (e.g., children or people who live in high-crime areas)?
* Does it focus on only one type of effect—cognitive, attitudinal, belief, physiological, emotional, or behavioral? Or is it more limited still by focusing on only one particular effect (e.g., behaving aggressively)?
* Does the theory seek to explain all possible media effects, regardless of whether those effects are negative or positive?
* Does the theory seek to explain only intentional effects or does it also seek to explain unintentional effects?
* Does the theory seek to explain media effects in all settings, or is it limited to explaining effects on a specific type (e.g., in classrooms, in marriage, or in public)?

Table 10.2. Summary of Evaluative Dimensions

---

1. Scope

Which of the theories' systems of explanation cover broader amounts of the phenomenon of media effects?

   A. Conceptualization of Media

   By Medium

   By Message

   B. Conceptualization of Media Effect

   By Function (acquisition, triggering, altering, reinforcing)

   By Timing

   Duration of process of influence

   Duration of manifestation of effect

   By Targets

   Level (individual, aggregates)

   Characteristics (demographics, traits)

   By Type (cognitive, attitude, belief, affect, physio, behavior)

   By Valence

   By Intentionality

   C. Factors of Influence

2. Precision

Which of the theories exhibit a greater degree of precision as evidenced by completeness in addressing all the key features in their systems of explanation as well as clarity in the expression?

   A. Foundation

   * To what extent have theoreticians critically analyzed the relevant foundational literatures in order to identify the best ideas that they can use to support their own theory and in order to identify the weaknesses and gaps in systems of explanation?

   * To what extent have theoreticians positioned their theory within relevant literatures?

   B. Key Concepts

   * To what extent have theoreticians identified the set of key concepts?

   * To what extent have theoreticians presented a detailed formal definition of each of their key concepts?

   C. System of Explanation

   * To what extent have theoreticians conveyed the core essence of their system of explanation?

   * To what extent have theoreticians conveyed the boundaries of their system of explanation?

   * To what extent have theoreticians expressed the relationships among concepts in each proposition in an operative manner?

(Continued)

Table 10.2. *Continued*

D. Guidance for Testing
  * To what extent have theoreticians laid out a calculus to guide designers of tests of theory?
E. Logical Coherence
  * To what extent does the theory demonstrate consistency across key components (definitions of concepts, system of explanation, calculus) and across time?

3. Heuristic Value

To what extent has the theory attracted the attention of scholars in the field?

A. To what extent has the theory attracted criticism from other scholars who care enough about the system of explanation to provide suggestions and arguments to try improving it?
B. To what extent has the theory attracted researchers to test its claims?

4. Empirical Validity

Which of the theories' systems of explanation has received the greatest degree of empirical support?

A. To what extent have the theory's claims been tested?
B. To what extent does the empirical literature contain valid tests of the claims made by a theory?
C. To what extent do those valid tests of a theory generate findings that support the claims made by the theory?

5. Openness

Which of the theories' systems of explanation exhibit higher degrees of openness?

A. To what extent have theoreticians engaged with critical arguments either by convincingly defending their claims or by making alterations to their theory?
B. To what extent have theoreticians demonstrated an understanding of the patterns of findings in the empirical literature testing their claims and made alterations to their system of explanations to reflect those patterns?

6. Overall Utility

Which of the theories' systems of explanation exhibit higher degrees of overall utility?

A. For media effects scholars, which theory offers the most guidance for the design of media effects studies that will make a difference?
B. For the general public, which theory has presented a system of explanation that has received the strongest support in building knowledge about media effects and the nature of risk?

---

3. Factors of influence. Does the theory focus on only one variable as an explanation for the media effect? Or does the theory highlight a list of multiple factors of influence? Or does the theory explain the effect with multiple factors working together in a system of influence?

Theories can vary in scope on each of these many characteristics. A theory's scope is greater to the extent that the theory expresses fewer limitations in its system of explanation. Thus greatest scope is exhibited when a theory provides a system of explanation for all possible functions and types of effects regardless of valence or intentionality on all types of people in all types of settings both immediately and over all periods of time. In contrast, micro theories exhibit limitations on many of these characteristics. A micro theory of media effects, for example, would focus its system of explanation on only one type of effect (e.g., acquisition of factual information), one type of target (e.g., children in the preoperational stage of cognitive development), one type of setting (e.g., parents reading stories), and one time (e.g., recall immediately after exposure).

Precision

Precision refers to the degree of completeness, clarity, and coherence that theoreticians demonstrate when describing their systems of explanation. The criterion of completeness poses the question: Are all of the major components there? Those components are foundation, key concepts, system of explanation, and calculus. The criterion of clarity focuses on how well the theoreticians communicate their meaning in each of these areas. The criterion of completeness is more primary than the criterion of clarity because if a theory has gaps, then clarity of expression in those gaps is moot. The criterion of coherence refers to how well all the parts of the theory fit together into a unified system of explanation. Thus if a concept is important, then it should have a good definition, be featured in propositions to show how it is related to other concepts, and be measured in a valid manner.

The evaluation of a theory's precision requires the examination of the major components of foundation, key concepts, system of explanation, and calculus.

Foundation. During the introduction of a theory, theoreticians need to show how they have critically analyzed relevant foundational literatures to position their new system of explanation. Precision then refers to the extent to which the theoreticians thought through the complexity of their phenomenon of interest then mined relevant literatures for their best ideas that were then used to construct a scholarly foundation for their own theory. Theoreticians also reveal gaps and weaknesses in those literatures, which are then used to motivate the need for their theory. This work provides the required foundation to position a new theory within existing literatures.

Key concepts. Precision in defining key concepts reflects the degree to which theoreticians (1) understand the various meanings of relevant concepts in their foundational literature; (2) have the ability to select (or construct) one meaning for each concept that works best in their system of explanation; then (3) communicate those meanings. Focusing now on the third of these characteristics, there are three types of definitions that theoreticians typically use to communicate their meanings. These types are primitive definitions, ostensive definitions, and formal definitions. The three types express a range from primitive being the least precise to formal being the most precise.

The use of primitive type of definitions is evidenced when theoreticians assume that all readers understand their meaning so there is no need to provide definitions. When we communicate, we treat most terms as primitive, thus assuming that others will understand what we mean by each word and combinations of words. We cannot possibly stop our flow of communication to define each word because doing so would require us to enter an infinite regress of only using previously defined terms to express the definition of each term. This is an impossible task. Instead, we must assume shared meaning. This is the case even in scholarly writing; however, with scholarly writing, authors typically deal with technical terms that have special meanings. For example, in everyday language we typically use the terms attitude, opinion, and belief as synonyms but in many social science fields these terms are typically used with different meanings from one another. So while theoreticians should not be expected to define every word they use, they should be expected to recognize which terms are likely to have different meanings across readers and then avoid assuming a sharing of meaning.

A higher level of precision is achieved when theoreticians define their terms ostensively, that is, they provide examples. While ostensive definitions are better in precision than treating terms as primitives, ostensive definitions have limitations. For example, if theoreticians claim "Our theory focuses on print media such as newspapers and magazines," do they also include webpages? When examples are provided of a concept, it is not clear if they are presented as a few selected illustrations from among many that could have been provided or if those examples provide an exhaustive list of all the components of meaning in the term being defined ostensively.

Formal definitions are those that provide classification rules so scholars can understand more precisely what the theoreticians are including and what they are excluding when they use a term. This is the most precise type of definition because it gives readers enough detail that they should be able to understand precisely what the theoreticians mean, what the theoreticians include, and what the theoreticians exclude from the meaning.

System of explanation. Precision is also reflected in how well theoreticians express the relationships among their concepts in each proposition. Propositions increase in precision when theoreticians reveal their thinking on the eight issues laid out in Table 10.3. For example, theoreticians who simply claim that concept X is related to concept Y exhibit a fairly low level of precision because they ignore the many issues that arise when making claims about relationships.

When a theory is introduced, the propositions are likely to be very general and lack many of the characteristics that would qualify them as being precise. To illustrate, consider the following example of a preposition: TV viewing is influenced by parental attitudes. This is nonoperative because it does not predict direction or intensity; it does not even make it clear which attitudes are regarded as being the influences. An example of a more operative proposition is: A person's aggressive behavior is directly proportional to the amount of televised violence to which she has been exposed. Two concepts are aggressive behavior and exposure to violence and the relationship is regarded as being positive and direct.

An indicator of how well theoreticians have developed their theories is the degree to which the relationships in their propositions are expressed with precision, that is, how well they illustrate the eight characteristics laid out in Table 10.3. For example, one typical problem is that oftentimes theoreticians will conflate covariation with causation in their expression when they want to give readers the impression of causation without putting themselves in a position to defend such a claim.

Calculus. Precision refers to the extent to which theoreticians have provided enough guidance to potential researchers so they can design empirical studies that would adequately test the claims they make in their systems of explanation.

Like with the other evaluative criteria, precision will be assessed both at the time of the theory's introduction as well as over time. When scholars introduce a theory, their ideas about concepts, propositions, and especially assumptions may not be fully formed. Therefore, it is likely that there will be problems with precision during the theory's introduction. Theoreticians who recognize these shortcomings and work to overcome them in subsequent publications generate more value for their theories than theoreticians who do not. Thus the beginning standard is established at the time the theory is created. Then over time, we can analyze theoretical writings for degree of increases in precision in each of four areas: foundations, definitions of concepts, expression of propositions, and guidance in the calculus. With foundations, we look for reviews of the literature as context for positioning the theory. With definitions of concepts, we look for major efforts at explication

Table 10.3. Precision in Expressing Relationships

1. *Type of relationship:* Do the theoreticians make clear whether relationships are coexistence, covariation, or causal?
   * Coexistence—links two or more things together; typical of definitional statements (e.g., All groups are composed of three or more persons).
   * Covariation—expresses a claim that when changes are observed in one variable there are also changes observed in a second variable (e.g., As a person's amount of exposure to violent messages from the media increases, that person's number of acts of aggression increases).
   * Causation—expresses a relationship that one variable influences another variable (e.g., Exposure to violent messages in the media triggers audiences' aggressive behavior).
2. *Intensity:* Does the theoretician express how strong the relationship is?
3. *Valence: Does the theoretician express whether the relationship is a positive or negative one?*
4. *Direction of influence:* Does the theoretician express whether the relationship is asymmetric or symmetric? If asymmetric, does the theoretician express the direction of flow of influence?
5. *Linearity:* Does the theoretician express whether the relationship is a simple linear one or that it takes a different shape such as:
   * Curvilinear
   * Threshold—there is no relationship until a threshold is passed then there is a relationship.
   * Ceiling—the relationship exists until a ceiling is reached, then the relationship disappears.
6. *Status:* Does the theoretician express whether the relationship is sufficient, necessary, or substitutable?
   * Sufficient—an identified factor (or set of factors) is all that is needed to explain the media effect fully
   * Necessary—an identified factor (or set of factors) is required as part of the explanation of a media effect but it cannot fully explain the effect
   * Substitutable—an identified factor (or set of factors) is a predictor of the effect but there are other factors that can be substituted as adequate predictors
7. *Flow of influence:* Does the theoretician express whether the influence of a factor is directly on the media effect or if it exerts an indirect influence through a path where other factors make contributions?
8. *Contingent:* Does the theoretician include clauses in the propositions in order to specify where the expressed relationship holds and where it does not?
   * Contingent on characteristics of people: The more information a person is given about a product, the less likely she is to buy it—if she has a below average IQ.
   * Contingent on type of media message: The more information a person is given about a product, the more likely she is to buy it—if the ad uses a highly credible product spokesperson.

informed by an awareness of the findings in the empirical literature as well as criticisms. With propositions, we look for increasing attention to the nature of the relationships among concepts (awareness of nonlinearity, asymmetry of pairs of concepts, as well as interactions among multiple concepts). And with the calculus, we look for increasing detail in operational guidance.

Logical coherence focuses on consistency of thinking and expression within components, across components, and over time. As for intracomponent concerns, the definition of each concept should remain consistent as the concept appears multiple times in the theory. The set of propositions should not include claims that conflict with one another.

As for across components, the definition of each concept should be consistent with the definitions in the foundation. The propositions should conform to the theory's basic assumptions about the nature of media effects and the nature of humans. And the calculus should conform to the definitions of the concepts.

Over time, the definition of each concept should be consistent across its repeated usage or if the theoreticians change the meaning, they need to provide a clear argument for why they have done that, then be consistent with the newer meaning from that point onward. There are times when a change in definition is motivated by problems with the theory that are uncovered in empirical tests; when this happens, there is little virtue in consistency when staying with original definitions only serves to erode the value of the theory.

Heuristic Value

To what extent has the theory attracted the attention of scholars in the field and stimulated them to critique the theory and test its claims? A theory with high heuristic value will generate a lot of mentions in the scholarly literature. Even better, a theory will stimulate scholars to study the theory more carefully and publish either critical reviews or empirical tests of the claims made by the theory.

Empirical Validity

Empirical validity refers to the extent that scientific tests repeatedly generate findings that support the claims made in the theory. This evaluative dimension poses three questions.

First, has the theory stimulated empirical tests of all of the claims in its system of explanation? This question raises the issue of completeness. Second, are the research studies that claim to be tests of the theory really tests of the theory? This is a question that is often overlooked when scholars assume that researchers who say they are testing a particular claim in a theory have actually designed a valid test. In order to achieve validity, the design of a study that is purported to test a claim made in a theory must operationalize adequate measures of each concept as well as the relationship among those concepts as expressed in the proposition being tested. Bausell (1986) cautions that in order to test validity a researcher needs to ask: "Do the different components of the measurement procedure (which are usually items) match the different constituents of the attribute being measured?" (p. 156). Validity is "the extent to which an empirical measure adequately reflects the real meaning of the concept under consideration" (Babbie, 1998, p. 133). Thus validity is concerned with the "goodness of fit" between what the researcher has defined as a characteristic of a phenomenon and what he or she is reporting in the language of measurement.

In addition to operationalizing measures well, researchers also need to design their quantitative analyses to test relationships as expressed in the theory's set of propositions. For example, if a proposition says that X causes Y, then researchers need to conduct an experiment rather than a cross-sectional survey. Also, they need to run an asymmetrical test that shows that the influence is X onto Y and not Y influencing X.

The third question is: To what degree do the valid tests of theory support the claims of the theory? In determining support for claims, we need to think beyond statistical support and consider substantive support. Too often researchers will conclude that they generated significant support for hypotheses when they have achieved a p-value of less than .05 even when the statistic itself is weak. To illustrate, let's say a researcher designs a test of the relationship between X and Y and generates a finding of $r = .11, p < .01$. Researchers will typically claim that such a finding is significant, but the "significance" refers only to their confidence level (which in this case is less than one chance in 100 that $r = 0.11$ occurred by chance alone), not to the importance of the finding itself. Should a finding of $r = .11$ as an indicator of the strength of a relationship between X and Y be considered important? We could answer this question with a "no" based on the reasoning that even by social science standards, this is a weak indicator of a relationship. However, if the literature of previous tests was never able to find a relationship stronger than say $r = .06$, then this new finding might qualify as a "significant" breakthrough.

Openness

Does the theoretician recognize that his/her explanations are tentative, contextual, and qualified? If so, they are likely to demonstrate a continual willingness to adapt and grow the theory in response to criticism and patterns in the empirical literature. A quote from the Argentine poet Jorge Luis Borges captures a perspective that scholars should have in order to be a successful theoretician: "Nothing is built on stone; all is built in sand. But we must build as if the sand were stone." Scholars who introduce a system of explanation need to construct something substantial in order for it to make a contribution. To the extent that a theory appears equivocal or tentative, the theory lacks sufficient authority to guide thinking and research. However, as the theory captures the attention of scholars in the field, a literature of empirical testing and criticism grows, and there will inevitably be suggestions of areas where conceptualizations may be faulty and propositions are too broad so that they need to be scaled back. Scholars who ignore these suggestions and instead believe that their theory is rock solid will spend all their effort defending their initial speculations in the face of contrary evidence and their theory is likely to become irrelevant. In contrast, theoreticians who are comfortable with the tentativeness of their claims will be more open to altering elements within their systems of explanation to make them more useful.

Overall Utility

Does the theory provide a more compelling or more efficient explanation of the phenomenon? Degree of utility varies depending on who is making the judgment. For scholars and students of media effects, utility is keyed to the quality of thinking and writing. Theoreticians who have thought deeply about media effects, who have read the literature widely and critically, who have generated fresh and compelling insights about media effects, and who can express these ideas in a succinct and interesting manner deliver a high degree of utility.

For media effects researchers, utility is keyed to the extent the theory provides detailed guidelines about the most important claims to test, how to design studies to test those claims validly, and how to analyze data from those studies in order to find legitimate support for those claims or to identify why their studies do not find support. Thus theories with a more developed calculus will help researchers select the most valid measures and run the most appropriate statistical tests.

For the general public, utility is keyed to how well the theory provides an easy to understand approach to helping people deal with the media better in some everyday way. Within the general public of nonscholars and nonstudents are several publics, such as teachers, parents, consumer activists, and media regulators. For example, media regulators need benchmarks showing which media effects are the strongest, most widespread, and most harmful to both society and individuals; they also want to know if there are broad-scale strategies that have been proven to help protect people from harmful effects. In contrast, parents want to know what kinds of content they should expose their children to and how to talk to their children about issues and portrayals they experience in those media exposures.

The Evaluation Procedure

The evaluative procedure has three features. The first feature is that the evaluative procedure is not based on one characteristic of the theories but instead is multidimensional. Second, it uses a comparative strategy instead of a criterion-based strategy. And third, the assessment of value of each of the six theories is made both at the time it was introduced and then again after the theory has had a chance to develop.

Multidimensional Strategy

As you could see from the previous section that laid out the evaluative dimensions, each of these dimensions involved more than one characteristic and some involved as many as nine characteristics that were relevant for making an evaluative judgment on a dimension. Thus it is important to point out that the evaluative procedure is a complex one involving many characteristics. It is more complicated than merely comparing apples and oranges; instead it is like making fruit salad. Some readers might like more apples and others might like more pineapple. In this book, I must juggle various elements on each of the seven evaluative dimensions then arrive at summary judgments to position each of the six theories on each of the six evaluative dimensions. My intention here is not to claim that I am making the best fruit salad of all time that will appeal to all scholars. Instead, my intention is to illustrate the importance of conducting such analyses and evaluations of theories in order to stimulate insights about the nature of the most prominent theories that have been developed to explain media effects. I hope these insights will stimulate you to think more about how we can engage in the essential enterprise of theory construction and development in a continually better fashion.

Comparative Strategy

Evaluation is essentially the making of judgments about the value of something by comparing of an element to a standard. Elements that meet the standard are judged as adequate or acceptable; elements that exceed the standard are judged as outstanding or excelling; and elements that fall short of the standard are judged as inadequate. Therefore, standards are essential to conducting any evaluation.

Standards can be criterion based or comparison developed. Criterion-based evaluations rely on a clear *a priori* articulation of a standard. Given the nature of social science theories, there are no clearly established criterion standards. For example, there is no adequate standard that can be used for scope, that is, there is no scholarly consensus or authority-based designation for what constitutes the threshold for adequate scope. Of course, a scholar could develop such standards but the thresholds would appear as arbitrary. Instead, it appears to be much more useful to develop comparative standards during the application of the evaluation procedure. That is, theories will be compared with one another in a relative manner. Thus the evaluation procedure will not result in judgments about which theories meet—or fail to meet—some absolute standard; instead the evaluation procedure will result in an array of the theories such that some theories are revealed to be comparatively better than other theories. Thus the characteristics in the theories themselves set the comparative standards.

Comparison-based evaluation is conducted in a relative manner, that is, the elements to be evaluated are arrayed on an evaluative dimension so that their positioning on that continuum can be determined relative to the other elements. To illustrate, theories that are positioned on the broader end of the scope continuum can be regarded as superior on scope compared to the theories arrayed on the narrower end of the scope continuum. In essence, this task involves determining the relative worth of the six theories on each of the six evaluative dimensions.

Two Time Periods

The evaluation procedure will make relative judgments about the theories at two points in time. First we apply the evaluation procedure to the theory as it was originally presented at the time of its introduction. Then second, we evaluate the theory as it appears today. As McCombs (2014) writes, "Theories seldom emerge full-blown. They typically begin with a succinct insight and are subsequently elaborated and explicated over many years by various explorers and surveyors of their intellectual terrain. This has been the case for agenda-setting theory. From a parsimonious hypothesis about the effects of the news media on the public's attention to social and political issues, this theory has expanded to include propositions about the psychological process for these effects, the influences that shape communication agendas, the impact of specific elements in their messages, and a variety of consequences of this agenda-setting process. Expanding beyond the traditional news media, agenda-setting theory has become a detailed map of the effects of the flow of information about public affairs through a growing plethora of communication channels" (p. x).

Thus the comparison across theories at the time of their introduction shows how well developed the theory was when it was first presented. And a comparison of theories as they currently exist show how much they have changed over time. By making comparisons at these two time periods, we can generate greater insights about how active the theories have been over time, which leads to making relative predictions about those theories that are likely to increase in value into the future.

Conclusion

This chapter laid out the evaluative procedure that will be used in the next chapter. That procedure relies on three strategies of making comparisons across the six theories multidimensionally and at two points in time. Then evaluative judgments are made in a comparative, not absolute manner.

References

Babbie, E. (1998). *The practice of social research* (8th ed.). Belmont, CA: Wadsworth.

Bausell, R. B. (1986). *A practical guide to conducting empirical research.* New York, NY: Harper & Row.

Infante, D. A., Rancer, A. S., & Womack, D. F. (1993). *Building communication theory* (2nd ed.). Prospect Heights, IL: Waveland Press.

Littlejohn, S. W. (1999). *Theories of human communication* (6th ed.). Belmont, CA: Wadsworth.

McCombs, M. E. (2014). *Setting the agenda: The mass media and public opinion.* Cambridge: Polity Press.

Shoemaker, P. J., Tankard, J. W. Jr., & Lasorsa, D. L. (2004). *How to build social science theories.* Thousand Oaks, CA: Sage.

CHAPTER ELEVEN

Comparative Analyses

This chapter displays an evaluation of the six theories of media effects. This evaluation is a comparative one instead of an absolute one. An absolute evaluation is one that compares elements (the theories) to a clear standard in order to determine which elements meet, exceed, and fall short of that standard. An absolute evaluation is not possible with theories, because the standards used to evaluate them are not precise enough to be used as criteria. For example, scope is relevant to evaluating theories but there is no standard indicating what the appropriate scope of a theory should be in order for a theory to be considered adequate. Therefore, this chapter displays a comparative evaluation where theories are arrayed on a dimension to reveal which theories are better than other theories on that evaluative dimension.

This comparative evaluation of media effects theories uses six dimensions. Five of these dimensions are considered primary and are conducted first. These are the dimensions of scope, precision, heuristic value, empirical validity, and openness. Then using information about how the six theories are arrayed on these five primary dimensions, the theories are then arrayed on a summary dimension of overall utility.

Because theories are expected to change over time, the first two dimensions of scope and logical coherence are used twice to evaluate the theories. In the first usage, the theories are comparatively evaluated in their introductory stage, that is, this comparative evaluation relies on only the writings of their authors when the theories were first introduced into the scholarly literature. In the second usage, the theories are comparatively evaluated using all relevant publications in order to reveal changes to the theories up to the present day. The other four dimensions of heuristic value, empirical validity, openness, and overall utility consider all publications about the theory while giving greater weight to more recent publications.

Scope

The focal question in this section is: *Which of the six theories' systems of explanation covers broader amounts of the phenomenon of media effects?* To answer this question, we examine each of the six theories for breadth along three subdimensions: conceptualization of media, conceptualization of media effect, and breadth of factors of influence.

Conceptualization of Media

As for medium, each of the six theories provided a system of explanation that expressed no restrictions on channels when they were introduced (see Table 11.1). Also, five of the theories expressed no limits on type of message. The one exception is agenda setting. Agenda-setting theory initially had a focus on news type messages, but over time, agenda-setting theory expanded to consider all kinds of media messages.

Conceptualization of Media Effect

There is considerable variation on each of the subdimensions of function, timing, target level, type, valence, and intentionality. As for function, two theories (agenda setting and cultivation) regard media effects as long-term alterations in beliefs. Three theories (framing, third-person effect [TPE], and uses & gratifications) regard media effects as immediate, that is, something in people is triggered during the media exposures. The remaining theory—social cognitive—was introduced as having both immediate and long-term media effects. As for valence and intentionality, four theories were very broad (cultivation, framing, social cognitive, and third person). When agenda setting was introduced it was expressed as an unintended effect but over time it has incorporated intention. Uses & gratifications theory was introduced as a purely intentional effect and has remained the same as it has

Table 11.1. Evaluation of Scope

	Agenda Set	Cultivation	Framing	Soc Cognitive	3rd Per Eff	Uses & Grats
Original						
Medium						
By Channel	No limits	No limits	No limits	No limits	No limits	No limits
By Message Type	News	No limits	No limits	No limits	No limits	No limits
Media Effect						
By Function	Altering	Altering	Triggering	No limits	Triggering	Triggering
By Timing	Long term	Long term	Immediate	Both	Both	Both
By Target Level	Public	Population	Individual	Individual	Individual	Individual
By Type	Beliefs	Beliefs	No limits	No limits	Beliefs	Behaviors
By Valence	No limits	No limits	No limits	No limits	No limits	Positive
By Intentionality	Unintended	No limits	No limits	No limits	No limits	Intention
Factors of Influence	One	Two	One	Many	None	One
Over Time						
Medium						
By Channel	No limits	No limits	No limits	No limits	No limits	No limits
By Message Type	No limits	No limits	No limits	No limits	No limits	No limits
Media Effect						
By Function	Altering	Altering	Tr, Alt, Rein	No limits	Triggering	Triggering
By Timing	Both	Long term	Both	Both	Both	Both
By Target Level	Public	View Group	Individual	Individual	Individual	Individual
By Type	Bel, Att, Em, Beh	Bel, Beh	No limits	No limits	Beliefs	Behaviors
By Valence	No limits	No limits	No limits	No limits	No limits	Positive
By Intentionality	Both	No limits	No limits	No limits	No limits	Intention
Factors of Influence	Many	Two	Many	Many	Many	One

Highlighted cells in the bottom matrix indicate a change from the upper matrix.

maintained a focus on individuals as consciously selecting media exposures with the intention of achieving expected gratifications.

As for target level, four theories (framing, social cognitive, third person, and uses & gratifications) are all clearly focused on the individual both conceptually and operationally, and this focus has not changed over time. The other two theories—in their introductions—were clearly focused on large-scale aggregates. Agenda setting was focused on the public and has maintained that focus over time. Cultivation was focused on the entire population but when Gerbner started running his own tests of the theory, it became clear that the unit of measurement was the individual and the unit of analysis was the viewing level group (light viewers, medium viewers, and heavy viewers), not the entire public.

Factors of Influence

As for the scope of factors of influence, there is quite a bit of variation across theories. When they were introduced three theories specified only one factor of influence on the media effect. Agenda-setting theory focused on the single factor of influence of media agenda. Uses & gratifications theory focused on gratifications but a reciprocal process was integral to the system of explanation so that media usage was claimed to influence gratifications and expected gratifications were claimed to influence media usage. Similarly, framing theory claims a reciprocal process where people's schema influence their interpretation of meaning, which in turn reshapes their schema.

Cultivation claimed two factors of influence. One of these factors was that meaning was widespread through media messages and the other factor was the institutional practices in the media industries. But when Gerbner began testing his theory, the focus was on only one factor of influence—exposure level. Then after about a decade of testing, he added the factor of personal experience that was then used to test for a mainstreaming or resonance effect, which were variations from the general cultivation effect.

TPE specified no factors of influence, which is one of the major reasons why many scholars did not regard it as a theory. However, over time, third-person researchers have tested many factors of influence and found support for all of them, especially the cognitive factors of need for self-enhancement.

Changes

Looking across all the lines in Table 11.1, we can see that social cognitive theory started out as the broadest of all six and has done nothing over the years to limit its breadth. Framing also started fairly broad and with several changes over time—with function and timing—has increased its breadth.

On the other end of the scope spectrum, agenda setting started out as the least broad but it has made the greatest number of changes to scope over time and now is fairly broad. When it was introduced, agenda-setting theory claimed only a long-term effect focusing on beliefs that were unintentional by media producers, and the prediction of the public agenda was explained by only one factor—the media agenda. Now that theory recognizes that an agenda-setting effect can occur immediately or long term, manifest itself as a behavior or emotion in addition to a belief, can be intentional in additional to unintentional, and there are now many factors (especially need for orientation) that are used to explain the effect.

Comparison on Scope

Given the patterns displayed in Table 11.1, it appears that social cognitive theory exhibits the greatest scope among the six theories, because it has the fewest limiting characteristics. Social cognitive theory exhibits broad scope on 8 of the 9 dimensions. Then there is a step down in scope with agenda setting, framing, and third person each exhibiting four limits on scope, cultivation with five limitations, and uses & gratifications with six.

This broader scope is clear in the introduction of the theory and maintained over time. Bandura does not limit the scope of his theory to any one medium, vehicle, or message. Nor does he limit his explanation by effect. Bandura deals with a great many types of media effects across the traditional categories of cognitions, behaviors, attitudes, and beliefs. He is concerned with the media functions of acquisition and triggering but only in a minor way; he is much more concerned with alterations and reinforcements.

While none of these theories should be considered significantly narrower than the others, it appears that agenda-setting theory when introduced displayed the least scope among the six theories. It limited itself to explaining only one type of effect (belief) from one genre of content (news) in only the long term, only as an unintentional effect, and only using one factor of influence (media agenda). Over time, agenda setting has displayed the most growth in scope. It has expanded well beyond news to include other forms of content and explaining effects on attitudes, emotions, and behaviors in addition to beliefs. It has also developed explanations for immediate effects (in addition to only long term). And it has expanded on intentionality and the number of factors of influence featured in the theory.

The scope of cultivation theory is broad in terms of type of medium, targets, and situations. In its original conceptualization, the effects part of cultivation is not limited to any one medium; Gerbner conceptualized the influence coming from all media. However, in his testing of the cultivation effect, Gerbner and his team limited themselves to TV entertainment. In the original conceptualization, all people were affected, but the theory did not talk about media influence on larger aggregates, either to include or exclude them. However, when the cultivation team started testing the theory and especially when they added the concepts of mainstreaming and resonance, the theory still applied to all people, although it predicted that some people would be more cultivated than others. And the theory did not specify any conditions on situations.

Precision

The focal question in this section is: *Which theories exhibit a greater degree of precision as evidenced by completeness in addressing all the key features in their systems of explanation; clarity in the expression; and logical coherence?* To answer this question, we examine each of the six theories for degree of attention to detail along five subdimensions: scholarly foundation, key concepts, system of explanation, guidance for testing, and overall coherence.

Scholarly Foundation

To what extent have theoreticians acknowledged and analyzed relevant literatures in constructing their conceptual foundation? On this evaluative dimension there is a clear range from Bandura who provided an extensive scholarly foundation to Gerbner who presented almost none (see Table 11.2).

When Bandura introduced the first full version of the theory in 1977, he had already spent a quarter of a century assembling findings from psychological tests of human learning. *Social Learning Theory* (1977) cited over 200 empirical tests with 28 of the citations to his own empirical work. *Social Foundations of Thought and Action: A Social Cognitive Theory* (1986) included over 2,000 citations in its reference list with 65 references to his own empirical studies. In contrast, George Gerbner introduced cultivation theory into the scholarly literature with a relatively short essay with few citations. He published this essay in three different outlets with minor alterations across the three (1967, 1969a, 1969b). It appears that Gerbner was influenced by the ideas in several well-established scholarly literatures including European cultural studies, American sociological approach, public opinion research, the measurement of meaning, and models of media influence. It is important to note that Gerbner used the major ideas in these

Table 11.2. Evaluation of Precision

	Agenda Setting	Cultivation	Framing	Social Cognitive	3rd Person Effect	Uses & Gratifications
Original						
Foundation	Good	None	Good	Extensive	Good	Good
Key Concepts	Good	Good	Problem	Good	Good	Good
System of Explanation	Good	Good	Good	Good	None	Good
Guidance for Testing	Good	Partial	Good	Partial	Good	Partial
Coherence	Good	Good	Good	Good	Good	Good
Over Time						
Foundation	Good	Weak	Extensive	Extensive	Good	Extensive
Key Concepts	Good	Weak	Problem	Good	Good	Good
System of Explanation	Good	Weak	Good	Partial	Good	Good
Guidance for Testing	Good	Partial	Good	Partial	Good	Partial
Coherence	Good	Weak	Good	Good	Good	Good

Highlighted cells in the bottom matrix indicate a change from the upper matrix.

five well-established literatures so that his theory was able to build on the most significant scholarly concerns about macro social systems and how they gradually and continually influenced people in their everyday lives. However, it is curious that Gerbner never explained how his theory grew out of these ideas nor did he even credit any of these thinkers, despite working with many of them before introducing cultivation theory. His publications contain no citations to any of these ideas. Instead his publications introducing cultivation includes 11 references, 9 of which to his own nonempirical work, which makes his essay appear to be more a list of personal ruminations than a scholarly development of ideas. The closest he comes to giving credit is when he said, "Philosophers, historians, anthropologists, and others have, of course, addressed themselves to such problems before" (1969b, p. 139). In his many subsequent publications about cultivation, Gerbner never provided a detailed review of the literature of foundational ideas. When members of his research team published reviews of cultivation of empirical testing over the years, they often referred to how cultivation was similar as well as different from other contemporary media effects theories, but they too never acknowledged any foundational literature.

The other four theories were each introduced in a journal article or book chapter, so there was no space for those scholars to provide extensive reviews of foundational literatures. However, the introduction of each of these four theories clearly acknowledged foundational studies and literatures and gave credit to those thinkers. Over time, the authors of these four theories (with the exception of TPE) published numerous scholarly articles and book chapters refining their ideas and tying their system of explanation to other theories.

Key Concepts

To what extent have theoreticians highlighted their key concepts and presented each with a formal definition? Four of the theories did a good job with the precision of identifying key concepts and defining them in their introductions. The exceptions are framing and uses & gratifications. Framing theory was criticized early because there were many different definitions of framing in common usage and this created a good deal of confusion about what it really was (Chong & Druckman, 2007; Tewksbury & Scheufele, 2009). Entman (1993) called framing "a scattered conceptualization" that "is often defined casually, with much left to an assumed tacit understanding of the reader." The confusion arises from a question about the extent to which framing is attributable to characteristics in media messages or to receivers' schema. Until an answer to this question can be parsed with precision, the idea of framing itself remains ambiguous.

The other exception is uses & gratifications theory that was criticized for a lack of conceptual coherence (Blumler, 1979; McQuail, 1984) early on and this criticism continued (Rubin, 2009b; Ruggiero, 2000; Sundar & Limperos, 2013). Blumler (1979) and other critics have argued that the line between gratification and satisfaction is blurred, and Blumler wrote that "the nature of the theory underlying uses and gratifications research is not totally clear" (Sundar & Limperos, 2013).

System of Explanation

To what extent have theoreticians clearly identified their major propositions and make it explicit which concepts are related and the manner in which they are related? Five of the theories demonstrated a system of explanation at introduction that was good on precision. The exception is TPE, which presented no system of explanation—only the effect itself. Over time, TPE researchers have documented several factors that help explain the effect and now there is a system of explanation that is good.

Of the other five theories, four of them continued to refine their system of explanation in response to critics and empirical findings so that while the standards of precision increase as the theory ages, those theories have maintained a good level of precision. The exception is cultivation theory that has received a great deal of criticism that could have helped the theory grow but Gerbner has ignored almost all of it and continued to defend his original conceptualization as well as his team's practices established to test the theory. Although he added the constructs of mainstreaming and resonance in the 1970s, this was a fairly minor addition because it did little to increase the value of his system of explanation. Also, he began using control variables in his tests in response to early criticism (Hirsch, 1980), but he never dealt with this issue conceptually by providing an argument to justify the use of the particular control variables he chose to test.

Cultivation theory has continued to exhibit a troubling degree of ambiguity in all three areas of its system of explanation. As for institutional analysis, Gerbner continued to make his argument that television messages are mass-produced "to market specifications of industrial organizations for commodity and political markets" (Gerbner, 1990, p. 251). However, he did not develop this claim in enough detail to indicate what these market specifications might be or how those market specifications are revealed in the meaning embedded in media messages. Because he never conducted a test of this claim, there are no operationalizations of these ideas to guide researchers. As for message system analysis, Gerbner provided a fair amount of detail to specify how message analysts should begin the task of documenting widespread meanings. As for cultivation analysis, Gerbner provided little guidance to researchers in his theory's introduction but he published annual tests that clearly showed his vision of how to operationalize tests.

The precision Bandura exhibits with his concepts is high. The concepts are defined clearly. However, Bandura's conceptualization of media influence is fuzzy. He says there are a great many factors that work together in a reciprocal process. But he presents no propositions to detail his speculations about how that process works.

As for the TPE theory, the precision problems lie in the fuzzy use of terms such as perception, behavior, and estimations. There is fuzziness in the use of the word "perception." Scholars frequently refer to the "effect" in TPE as perceptions or social perceptions. This can lead to confusion because social perceptions are usually defined as attributions made by people when they observe particulars in social settings. Another faulty use of labeling is with behaviors. Most measures of behaviors are really behavioral intentions. And there is fuzziness in the meaning of estimations. Davison (1983) said, "In its broadest formulation this hypothesis predicts that people will tend to overestimate the influence that mass communications have on attitudes and behavior of others. More specifically, individuals who are members of an audience that is exposed to a persuasive communication (whether or not this communication is intended to be persuasive) will expect the communication to have a greater effect on others than on themselves" (p. 3). However, this claim lacks precision because he did not specify a standard for media influence. Without such a standard, it is impossible to determine if something is an "overestimation." The testing of this claim has defaulted to simply comparing the percentage of people who believe the media affect others with the percentage of people who believe the media affect them personally. Thus it is possible for both percentages to show an overestimation.

Guidance for Testing

To what extent have theoreticians laid out a calculus to guide designers of tests of theory? This evaluative subdimension reveals a split between theories that have provided good guidance from the beginning and continue to do so (agenda setting, framing, and third person). As for the other three, cultivation provided a good amount of guidance for testing the cultivation component but not the institutional or message components. Uses & gratifications theory has struggled with how to operationalize its concepts without being tautological. Social cognitive theory is built on findings from traditional social science methods, so researchers have no trouble designing individual studies; however, the theory's claim of reciprocal determinism makes it impossible to parse out the unique contributions of individual variables.

Coherence

Are there differences in definitions of key concepts, differences in the system of explanation, and/or differences in the calculus over time? These differences can be positive or negative. Differences can be positive if they are shown to be products of systematic reasoning and if they can be shown to improve the explanatory power of the theory over time. However, if the differences appear more as inattention to detail and editing flaws, then the theory's explanatory power atrophies over time. In other words, when theoreticians recognize a flaw in the initial version of their theories and make corrections to reduce those flaws, then the newer version is likely to display more logical coherence at that more recent point in time.

Which of the theories' systems of explanation exhibits higher degrees of consistency in the use of formal definitions; consistency in claims across propositions; and consistency in following through from assumptions in the use of concepts and propositions? In their introductions, five of the theories exhibited a good degree of logical coherence, that is, there were no obvious inconsistencies across definitions of concepts, systems of explanation, and calculus. The exception is uses & gratifications theory that has been criticized for a lack of conceptual coherence (Blumler, 1979; McQuail, 1984) early on and this criticism continued (Rubin, 2009b; Ruggiero, 2000; Sundar & Limperos, 2013). Blumler (1979) and other critics have argued that because the theoreticians have failed to make a clear enough distinction between gratifications and satisfactions, the meaning varies across each publication. It appears that this problem with a lack of clarity of central constructs has continued to allow researchers to attach different meanings to concepts such as motives and gratifications (Rubin, 2009b).

Over time as scholars designed research studies to test various parts of these theories, inconsistencies arose. With five of the theories, the theoreticians continually made adjustments to increase precision and maintain coherence. For example, with social learning theory, the consistency in labeling concepts and using the same definitions is high. Also, the consistency in listing the same concepts across writings is good. However, Bandura made some changes over time, especially in adding concepts, emphasizing self-efficacy much more, and even renaming the theory to social cognitive theory. Although there were changes in the theory over time, each new version of the theory displayed a high degree of coherence.

With cultivation theory, coherence was high in the introduction but was reduced throughout the years of testing as Gerbner continued to ignore problems as they arose. Gerbner's introduction of cultivation was elegant with its three components of media institutions that produced messages that reflected those institutional values and that these meanings were widespread across all messages in all media such that when people were continually exposed to these meanings in their everyday lives they would become cultivated to accept those meanings. His introductory essays were short, simple, and clear. The idea of institutional practices and values flowed well into the construction of messages which then flowed well into the effects component.

While there is high logical consistency among the various parts of Gerbner's original theory in its conceptualizations, disconnects start to appear when we look at how those ideas have been operationalized in empirical tests by his research team. As for message system analysis, Gerbner provided a fair amount of detail to specify how message analysts should begin the task of documenting widespread meanings. For example, Gerbner (1973) was clear that the meaning in messages typically does not reveal itself in a single symbol but that meaning lies in the relationship among the symbols in the messages. He cautioned that "the characteristics of a message system are not necessarily the characteristics of individual units composing the system. The purpose of the study of a system as a system is to reveal features, processes, and relationships expressed in the whole, not in its parts" (Gerbner, 1969a, p. 143). Furthermore, Gerbner (1990) directed message system analysts to look deeper than surface features such as plot configurations and look instead at "the underlying uniformity of the basic 'building blocks' of the television world: thematic structure, interaction patterns, social typing and fate," which lies in the consequences (p. 255). And to help guide message system analysts in this challenging task, Gerbner (1969a) laid out four questions: "(1) 'what is' (i.e., what exists as an item of public knowledge), (2) 'what is important' (i.e., how the items are ordered), (3) 'what is right' (or wrong, or endowed with any qualities, or presented from any point of view), and (4) 'what is related to what' (by proximity or other connection)" (1969a, p. 144). However, the message system analysis literature shows a pattern of counting the occurrence of manifest elements (such as acts of violence, gender of characters) and presenting those frequency counts as evidence of meaning, which is rather like trying to determine the meanings in a novel by counting the occurrence of different words.

While this equating frequency and meaning can often work well in constructing an answer to the first question of "what is," it is far too simple a method for constructing credible answers to the remaining three questions. Constructing an answer to the second question requires analysts to consider the position of information within messages. The answer to the third question requires analysts to recognize key contextual factors then assemble those factors in a way to reveal the meaning of an act or occurrence. And the answer to the fourth question requires analysts to look for patterns across messages.

When we look at the cultivation team's annual profiles of television content, the reported findings are based solely on arguments about the frequency of certain manifested elements, without considering patterns of contextual factors. While it is a challenging task to examine the web of context within which violence (or any other manifest occurrences) is presented, there are some examples of content analysis studies that have been able to move beyond the simple reporting of frequencies of acts and attempt to engage the more fundamental issue of the meaning that arises from the way those acts are portrayed. One example is the National Television Violence Study (1999), which examined 43 contextual variables and used patterns among those variables to make claims about meaning in the way violence was portrayed. This continued lack of precision is troubling because Gerbner (1969b) cautioned researchers that "I must stress that the characteristics of a message system are not necessarily the characteristics of individual units composing the system. The purpose of the study of a system as system is to reveal features, processes, and relationships expressed in the whole, not in its parts" (p. 128).

As for the cultivation analysis part of Gerbner's theory, there is a significant lack of precision concerning how exposure to messages leads to cultivation. Gerbner was initially unclear about how the meanings in media messages created or shaped the public's beliefs. In using a socialization perspective, it appeared that Gerbner conceptualized media influence as exerting a gradual but continuing influence. This is apparent in his use of metaphors like a glacier, which Gerbner used to illustrate how he believed that the steady flow of media messages slowly but constantly influenced beliefs. Also, Morgan and Signorielli (1990) argued that cultivation focuses on "long-term, cumulative consequences of exposure to an essentially repetitive and stable system of messages" (p. 18). The idea of accumulating influence is also in evidence when reviewers dismiss the persistently weak results in empirical tests by saying that while media influence appears weak at any given point in time, its influence is constant and therefore accumulates into something more substantial over time (Morgan, Shanahan, & Signorielli, 2014; Shanahan & Morgan, 1999). However, empirical findings from cultivation analyses do not support this assertion. To the contrary, the meta-analyses of Shanahan and Morgan (1999) show that elderly people exhibit less evidence of cultivation than do younger people, yet the authors ignored their findings and continued to make the claim for a cumulative effect (Morgan & Shanahan, 2010; Morgan et al., 2014); they indicated no recognition of this inconsistency between their claim and the findings of the research they review.

Comparison on Precision

When comparing the theories as they appeared when they were first introduced, it is fairly easy to determine that cultivation theory is the weakest on precision and that agenda setting is the strongest. Social cognitive is a close second in precision and the other three theories are about on par with each other.

When we look at where the theories are today, the precision of cultivation has not improved despite a great deal of testing and criticism that continues to reveal problems with precision. Agenda setting has remained high, and TPE has improved to tie it in second place. The other three theories have all improved in precision but still struggle with problems in defining key terms and providing adequate operational guidance.

Heuristic Value

The focal question in this section is: *To what extent has the theory attracted the attention of scholars in the field?* To answer this question, we examine the size of the literature that the theory has stimulated in terms of both total visibility and actual tests of a claim made by the theory.

Table 11.3 displays the six theories by date of introduction, with cultivation theory being listed first, because it is the oldest of the six. The middle eight lines in the table display the number of hits from each of eight separate searches using the name of the theory, with theory in the title surrounded by quotation marks so the search was conducted for the full phrase and not individual words in the phrase. For each theory, we added commonly used synonyms to guide the search. For example, with cultivation theory, we also used "cultivation hypothesis" and "cultivation analysis." With social cognitive theory, we also used "social learning theory."

The first two of these searches were in Google, with one being a general Google search and the second a search within Google Scholar. Given Google's personal algorithm, the results of these two searches are unstable, that is, they are sensitive to the searcher's browser history. I have tried to turn off this feature but even so, I got different numbers of hits each time I ran the same search over a period of several months. However, the fluctuations always clustered around the numbers reported in Table 11.3; so while these numbers should not be trusted as actual counts of all citation activity, they are useful indicators of the relative heuristic value established by the six theories.

The next six columns in Table 11.3 display the number of hits found in each of six academic databases that include primarily scholarly journals, books, and reports. Again the search was conducted with the full name of the theory in quotation marks and the range in years was for 1960 to 2017, with the exception of the search in Communication Abstracts that only allowed searchers back as far as 1980.

The numbers in these eight columns should not be equated with the number of empirical tests; instead they indicate the number of publications (including articles reporting on empirical tests but also review, critical, and summary articles) that have used the name of the theory in the title or as a keyword. Therefore, these numbers are useful indicators of each theory's relative heuristic value.

The final two columns in Table 11.3 display information about reviews of a theory's growing literature with an indicator of how large that literature was. I was able to find such reviews on only three of the six theories. TPE appeared to have attracted the attention of scholars and in the first decade and a half since its introduction, TPE had already created a literature of 45 published articles (Perloff,

Table 11.3. Evaluation of Heuristic Value

Theory	Year Intro	Hits Google	Google Scholar	Web of Science	Comm Abs	PoliSci Abs	Soc Abs	ERIC	Psyc Articles	# Studies Review	Year of Review
Cultivation	1969	90,600	7,570	108	172	21	164	43	37	500+	2010
Agenda Setting	1972	103,000	9,190	100	467	116	88	11	1	425+	2009
Uses & Gratifications	1974	56,700	7,720	161	257	12	54	18	19		
Framing	1974	72,900	11,000	239	491	177	186	17	17		
Social Cognitive	1977	551,000	148,000	2,933	194	105	1,428	457	2,184		
Third-Person Effect	1983	1,300	149	3	12	1	2	–	–	60	2008

1999). A year later Paul, Salwen, and Dupagne (2000) conducted a meta-analysis of this literature which was based on 32 empirical studies of TPE with 121 separate effect sizes reported. Then a few years later Sun, Pan, and Shen (2008) conducted a meta-analysis on 372 effect sizes from 106 studies described in 60 papers and publications.

Using the patterns in Table 11.3 to evaluate the heuristic value of these six theories, it seems that there are two outliers with social cognitive theory being superior to all others and the TPE theory being weaker than all others. The patterns of the middle four indicate that some are generally better than others, thus requiring the splitting of this group into two categories. The theories that are a bit stronger on heuristic value are agenda setting and framing, mainly within communication.

Empirical Validity

The focal question in this section is: *Which of the theories' systems of explanation has received the greatest degree of empirical support?* To answer this question, we examine the literatures generated by each of the six theories along three evaluative subdimensions: completeness, validity, and support. Completeness refers to the extent to which all the claims made in a theory have been tested. Validity refers to the extent to which the published tests that purport to test a theory's claims are adequate tests. Support for claims refers to the degree to which the empirical findings of adequate tests provide evidence to support the claims made by each theory.

Completeness

When considering completeness, it is important to identify what each theoretician promised in their introductions. Four of the theories were relatively modest in their introductions in terms of making claims; these are agenda setting, framing, third person, and uses & gratifications. Each of these theories began as a single claim then as the empirical research grew, the theoreticians added more claims. For example, agenda-setting theory started with the single claim that the public agenda was influenced by the media agenda. Then over time, the research testing agenda-setting theory began expanding its system of explanation by showing that there was growing evidence to support other claims beyond news coverage, telling people what to think about (basic agenda setting) and also telling people what to think on issues (attribute agenda setting). The research also suggested characteristics (need for orientation) about people that would make them more susceptible to the agenda-setting effect; expanded the outcome variable beyond beliefs to also include behaviors; and explained how the media agenda was shaped by factors both within the journalistic profession and from influences outside that profession. And it developed claims about network agenda setting and agenda melding. The addition of each of these claims served to elaborate the theory over time and make it a much more useful system of explanation. Thus the criterion for completeness expanded along with the theory.

In contrast to the four theories above, cultivation and social learning were more ambitious in their introductions in terms of claims made. Gerbner laid out three components of institutions, messages, and cultivated effects—each of which suggested a vast area of research. Bandura presented four components of attentional processes, retention process, motor reproduction processes, and motivational processes. Thus the criterion for completeness of these two theories required a great deal of empirical testing from the start. Bandura was able to meet this criterion of completeness right from the introduction because he had spent 25 years analyzing the already extensive literature on social learning and modeling then synthesized his set of claims from findings already in existence. Since then, he has kept up this monitoring and refining his theory over the past four decades, so there are no gaps between his system of explanation and empirical tests of those claims.

In contrast, when Gerbner introduced cultivation theory he presented very ambitious claims that (1) institutional practices exist in all media business that lead to the manufacture of messages with uniform meanings, (2) these standard meanings appear in all media messages regardless of medium or genre, and (3) mere exposure to these meanings is enough to cultivate beliefs about the real world among all members of the general audience. In his introduction Gerbner provided no empirical support for any of these claims. Over the next 25 years along with his research team, he conducted programmatic research attempting to provide evidence of widespread meanings and the cultivation effect on audiences. They also periodically published reviews of the growing literature of studies that purported to test cultivation and continually concluded that there was support for their claims of widespread meanings and cultivation effects. However, there is no evidence that Gerbner or his team published any research to test their claim that the mass production and rapid distribution of messages created new symbolic environments that reflect the structure and functions of the institutions that transmit them (Gerbner, 1969b). While reviewers of the cultivation literature (Morgan, 2009; Morgan & Shanahan, 2010; Morgan, Shanahan, & Signorielli, 2009; Shanahan & Morgan, 1999) continually acknowledge the importance of institutional analysis in the cultivation system of explanation, they rarely cite any research in this area, although there is a fairly well-developed literature on this very topic (for reviews of this literature, see Grossberg, Wartella, & Whitney, 1998;

McQuail, 2005). Furthermore, the scholars who produced these other literatures have displayed little interest in linking their findings with cultivation theory.

Even more troubling on this subdimension of completeness are the gaps in the research within message system analysis where that literature has yet to provide convincing evidence that there are meanings widespread across the television landscape, much less all mass media. While there are many studies that have examined content in mainstream commercial television, there are few studies that have looked at other kinds of television content such as news, informational programming, and especially advertising. This omission is especially glaring given Gerbner's argument that television has such a strong commercial interest so that we should expect those commercial values to show up strongest and most consistently in the great amount of advertising messages they present. Despite this lack of an adequate research basis, Gerbner, Gross, Morgan, Signorielli, and Shanahan (2002) continued to make claims that television's "drama, commercials, news, and other programs bring a relatively coherent system of images and messages into every home" (p. 44). And this claim is still being made today that multinational media conglomerates "dominate the cultural symbolic environment with stable and consistent messages about life and society . . . despite the emergence of so many specialized new channels and so many different types of programs that are often targeted to smaller and smaller audiences" (Morgan et al., 2014, p. 481).

Valid Tests

To what extent do the empirical literatures contain valid tests of the claims made by a theory? Five of the theories demonstrate a good pattern of validity in the empirical testing (see Table 11.4). Of course there are examples of weaker tests in each of these five literatures, but the overall patterns demonstrate that the tests of the claims made by these five theories are generally good.

The exception is cultivation theory, which has generated a literature with questionable validity in two areas—message system analysis and cultivation analysis. As

Table 11.4. Evaluation of Empirical Validity

Over Time	Agenda Setting	Cultivation	Framing	Social Cognitive	3rd Person Effect	Uses & Gratifications
Completeness	Good	Partial	Good	Extensive	Good	Good
Valid Tests	Good	Partial	Good	Good	Good	Good
Support for Claims	Strong	Weak	Good	Good	Strong	Weak

for the message system analysis literature, Gerbner in his introduction emphasized the documentation of meaning, not simply counting the occurrence of content elements. However, when he started his long line of empirical studies documenting violence, he created designs that ignored meaning and simplified the research to count only appearances of particular elements in the messages. Also, the content analysis of meaning would need to focus on message characteristics that can be attributed to production practices as documented through institutional analysis. It appears that none of the published studies in the message system analysis literature have met both these criteria.

As for the cultivation analysis literature, adequate tests of Gerbner's claims would require that at a minimum the cultivation indicator measures be constructed from the findings of a meaning analysis, as was pointed out above. Also, the stricter criteria would call for the use of macro measures of exposure over the long term and the use of longitudinal designs to examine the long-term influence of exposure in order to be considered an adequate test of Gerbner's claim about the influence of widespread meanings that are exhibited in cultivation indicators as a result of people's everyday exposures over the long term. Over the course of the past few decades, there has been a trend for researchers to publish what they refer to as "cultivation studies" but where the design of those studies failed to include elements (such as failing to test for the influence of widespread meanings) that Gerbner considered essential to cultivation theory (see Potter, 2014).

Support of Claims

To what extent do those valid tests of a theory generate findings that support the claims made by the theory? Two theories (agenda setting and third person) have literatures that show relatively strong support for their claims, and two other theories (framing and social cognitive) show patterns of good support.

Reviews of the TPE literature typically conclude that there is strong and continuing support for TPE in general but that there may be particular areas where the theory is weak or lacking support. In his review of TPE, Lasorsa (1992) said that about half of the members of any sample show a TPE while the others do not. This is typically enough to show overall support for the theory. However, this finding has led researchers to look for contingent factors to try explain why some people are susceptible while others are not. Also, researchers who have designed experiments can look for contingencies on the way the topic is presented in stimulus materials.

There have been two meta-analyses of the TPE literature and these both conclude that the literature shows strong support for TPE (relative to the support of other theories and other media effects) but that there are some important contingencies. Paul et al. (2000) conducted a meta-analysis of 121 separate effect sizes reported and converted these varied statistical indicators into a common metric of an r where a positive r indicated a TPE and a negative r indicated a first-person effect (i.e., greater perceived effects on oneself than on others). Their results indicate the perceptual component of the TPE hypothesis received robust support (r = .50), especially compared to meta-analyses of other media effects theories. They also tested eight factors (source, sampling, method, respondent, country, desirability, medium, and message) to see how stable the effect was. Source referred to published and unpublished studies. Method referred to surveys or experiments. Sampling referred to random and nonrandom. Respondent was either college students or noncollege people. Country was U.S. and other countries. Desirability had three values—desirable to believe, undesirable, and neither. Medium had four values (media in general, television radio, newspapers, and other). Message variable had seven values (message in general, pornography, television violence, commercial ads, politics, nonpolitical news, and other). Paul et al. (2000) reported that three of these characteristics (sampling, respondent, and message) were found to influence the strength of overall findings. As for sampling, samples obtained from nonrandom samples yielded greater TPE differences than samples obtained from random samples. As for respondent, samples obtained from student samples yielded greater TPE differences than samples obtained from nonstudent samples. And as for message, different types of content (e.g., general media messages, pornography, television violence, commercial advertisements, political content, nonpolitical news, etc.) were found to have differing effects on the size of the obtained third-person perceptions.

A few years later, Sun et al. (2008) conducted a meta-analysis on 372 effect sizes using a common metric of d, which is more traditionally used in meta-analyses. They tested the TPE for stability using 16 test factors. Of these 7 were research characteristics (study setting, data collection method, design, study population, sampling method, measure for perceived effects, and domain of perceived effects). Four were message characteristics (desirability of message, message topic domain, persuasive intent, and functional focus). Three were referent characteristics (referent other descriptor, geographical distance, and sociodemographic). They found an average effect size estimate of d = 0.646 (r = .307). They said, "The effect size, however, is significantly smaller than that reported in Paul et al.'s (2000) study, which, as we demonstrated, contained serious overestimation because they did not (a) apply the right effect size formula for within-subjects designs nor (b) address the statistical dependency among multiple effect sizes extracted from the same study" (p. 294).

Sun et al. (2008) also found the influence was not sensitive to five tested factors (research setting population, between- or within-subjects design, model of data collection, or whether single- or multiple-item measures were used). They wrote, "The perceptual discrepancy, however, is directional, depending on the desirability of presumed message influence. Contrary to Paul et al.'s (2000) conclusion, message desirability is found to be the most important moderator. The self–other perceptual gap is toward the direction of TPP for messages with undesirable or ambiguous social influences, whereas it is reversed for messages with presumed desirable influence. Although the evidence for FPP is not robust in part due to a much smaller number of effect sizes in the extant literature, it is clear that 'the negative influence corollary' (Gunther & Storey, 2003) specifies theoretical boundaries of TPP" (p. 294). They said in the abstract, "Results from a series of multi-level models show that the third-person perception is robust and not influenced by variations in research procedures. Desirability of presumed message influence, vulnerability of referent others, referent others depicted as being similar to self, and others being likely audience of the media content in question are significant moderators" (p. 280).

The two remaining theories (cultivation and uses & gratifications) have generated empirical literatures that consistently reveal weak support for the claims made by those theories. As for cultivation theory, the pattern of findings from studies labeled as tests of the cultivation system of explanation shows that support for Gerbner's claims is null (institutional analysis), partial (message system analysis), and weak (cultivation analysis). Support for the existence of widespread meanings across the television landscape is partial, because almost all of the message system analysis research is concentrated on looking for patterns within the narrow sampling frame of TV entertainment programming, which has been further reduced to focus on mainstream channels and limited dayparts. Although there are message system analyses of news and informational programming (e.g., Lee & Niederdeppe, 2011; Romer, Jamieson, & Aday, 2003), the findings from these studies have not been integrated with findings from other types of programming in a complete enough fashion to make the case for widespread meanings. As for cultivation analysis, the evidence that supports cultivation theory's explanation of television's influence on public beliefs has been persistently weak. This was pointed out by early critics of the theory (Hirsch, 1980; Hughes, 1980), and despite the huge growth in the literature since that time, the low ceiling of predictive power has not been raised. A meta-analysis of 5,799 separate findings derived from 97 studies/samples of tests of cultivation analysis reports that the average correlation across all those findings is .10 and that the average partial correlation is .09

(Shanahan & Morgan, 1999). This means television exposure predicts only about 1 % of the variation in cultivation indicators.

Gerbner was aware of these weak relationships and defended his system of explanation by saying that cultivation's effect was cumulative over time. However, this defense appears to be faulty because there is very little evidence that cultivation's influence is cumulative; to the contrary, the evidence suggests that the cultivation effect is not cumulative. In their meta-analysis, Shanahan and Morgan (1999) report that cultivation differentials are lower for older respondents than for younger ones. And longitudinal tests have found either no support (Morgan, 1982) or equivocal support (Morgan, 1987) for a cumulative influence. Although the findings of these two longitudinal studies challenge the validity of the cultivation explanation of media effects, cultivation researchers have let those findings stand unaltered for over three decades by not conducting additional longitudinal studies.

Furthermore, it appears that the cultivation effect is not widespread, but that it shows up in only a small percentage of the population. When examining the extent of evidence for cultivation in typical cultivation analysis studies, sizable percentages of respondents—even in the heavy viewing groups—do not choose the TV world cultivation indicator. For example, Hetsroni and Tukachinsky (2007) found that only 13 % to 28 % of their respondents showed evidence of a cultivation effect depending on the topic.

The empirical support of cultivation appears especially weak when we compare it to the level of support generated by other media effects theories. For example, agenda-setting theory is arguably the one media effects theory closest to cultivation in terms of its examination of patterns of meaning in media messages and the influence of those message patterns on large aggregates of people in the course of their everyday lives. Unlike cultivation theory, agenda-setting theory has been shown to have a relatively strong predictive power ($r = .53$) in a meta-analysis of its empirical literature (Wanta & Ghanem, 2007).

The strength of findings in the cultivation analysis literature also appears relatively weak when we compare them to the strength of findings determined by meta-analyses of other media effects such as the TPE ($r = .500$; Paul et al., 2000); inoculation effect ($r = .430$; Banas & Rains, 2010); hostile media effect ($r = .296$; Hansen & Hyunjung, 2011); effect of listening to popular music on mood and attitudes ($r = .210$; Timmerman et al., 2008); influence of sexually explicit materials on physiological and psychological reactions ($r = .212$ to $.248$; Allen et al., 2007); and engagement with media entertainment on knowledge, attitudes, and behaviors ($r = .270$; Tukachinsky & Tokunaga, 2013).

As for the topic of the effects of violence, which has been the most popular cultural indicator, cultivation analysis has been much weaker at predicting effects than have other systems of explanation. For example, Paik and Comstock (1994) conducted a meta-analysis of 217 studies examining the effect of exposure to television violence on antisocial behavior and reported that the average effect size is $r = .31$. Also, Anderson et al. (2010) conducted a meta-analysis on 130 research reports that presented over 380 effect-size estimates based on over 130,000 participants and found an average effect size of $r = .217$ on experiments testing the effect of playing violent video games on aggressive behavior. They also found an average effect size of $r = .183$ from cross-sectional surveys.

When researchers conduct tests to compare the explanatory power of cultivation with another media effects theory, they typically find cultivation to be the weaker explanation. For example, Diefenbach and West (2007) compared cultivation with the TPE and found the TPE to be a stronger explanation. Gross and Aday (2003) found that local news exposure accounted for an agenda-setting effect but did not cultivate fear of being a victim of crime. Martins and Harrison (2012) found that social identity theory was a stronger predictor of preadolescents' global self-esteem than was cultivation theory.

As for uses & gratifications theory, support is also weak. In an early review of the empirical literature testing the claims of the theory, McQuail (1984) concluded that there was little evidence of successful prediction or casual explanation of media choice and use. When McQuail (2005) again reviewed the growing literature, his conclusions did not change and he said that the theory failed to provide much successful prediction or causal explanation of media choice and use. He argued that the connection between attitude to the media and media use behavior is actually quite weak and the direction of the relationship is often uncertain. "Typologies of 'motives' often fail to match patterns of actual selection or use, and it is hard to find a logical, consistent and sequential relation between the three factors of liking/preference, actual choosing, and subsequent evaluation" (p. 426).

Openness

The focal question in this section is: *Which of the theories' systems of explanation exhibits higher degrees of openness?* To answer this question, we examine each of the six theories for how responsive theoreticians have been to scholarly criticism and to patterns of findings in the literature of empirical tests (see Table 11.5).

Table 11.5. Evaluation of Openness

Over Time	Agenda Setting	Cultivation	Framing	Social Cognitive	3rd Person Effect	Uses & Gratifications
Criticism Engaged	Engaged	Weak	Engaged	Engaged	Good	Engaged
Alterations to Theory	Extensive	Minor	Extensive	Intensive	Extensive	Extensive

Criticism Engaged

To what extent have theoreticians engaged with critical arguments either by convincingly defending their claims or by making alterations to their theory? Four of the theories (agenda setting, framing, social learning, and third person) have each received a relatively minor degree of criticism, typically by scholars trying to help improve the precision and scope of the theories more so than trying to challenge its fundamental claims. With each of these four theories, it appears the theoreticians have tried to use the criticism to improve various aspects of their systems of explanation. In contrast, cultivation and uses & gratifications have received substantially more criticism and those criticisms are much more serious challenges to their systems of explanation.

As for cultivation theory, soon after Gerbner introduced the theory and published his first few tests of the effects portion of the theory, critics began raising serious concerns (Doob & Macdonald, 1979; Hirsch, 1980; Hughes, 1980; Wober, 1978). These critics were bothered most by the weak findings that Gerbner was using to claim as evidence of a cultivation effect and suggested that there may be suppressor variables involved, such that if the influence of these suppressor variables were removed the correlations between TV exposure and cultivation indicators would be stronger. Gerbner and his team started reporting tests for some demographics as suppressor variables and found that those using those variables as controls made almost no change on the bivariate correlations between exposure and cultivation indicators.

Over time, the theory was criticized for other problems such as several dozen conceptual and operational problems (Potter, 1993, 1994, 2014) but Gerbner and his team have largely ignored all these critical issues.

As for uses & gratifications theory, it has been criticized for a lack of theoretical coherence (Blumler, 1979; McQuail, 1984; Ruggiero, 2000) and for lack of support for the assumption of an active audience (Severin & Tankard, 1997). While multiple critics have been critical of these problems over the years, there is little evidence of substantial improvement (McQuail, 2005; Sundar & Limperos, 2013).

Alterations to Theory

To what extent have theoreticians demonstrated an understanding of the patterns of findings in the empirical literature testing their claims and made alterations to their system of explanations to reflect those patterns? Four of the theories (agenda setting, framing, third person, and uses & gratifications) have made extensive alterations to the originally introduced version of the theory. By "extensive alterations" I mean that the theoreticians have added new concepts and propositions to the theory after its introduction in order to expand its system of explanation well beyond the original version. In contrast, social learning theory exhibited substantial intensive alterations, that is, it did not expand its scope or add to its original system of explanation but instead did considerable refinement and elaboration of the original ideas and propositions.

The one outlier is cultivation theory that substantially stayed with its original set of concepts and propositions with few exceptions. The most substantial addition to the original thinking was the creation of the concepts of mainstreaming and resonance in 1980.

Overall Utility

The focal question in this section is: *Which of the theories' systems of explanation exhibits higher degrees of overall utility?* To answer this question, we use the pattern of evaluative judgments on the previous six criteria to construct the overall summary judgment.

Table 11.6 presents a summary of the evaluation of all six theories on all evaluative dimensions. Those evaluations have been converted to quantitative scores to indicate the relative positioning of the theories on each of the evaluative dimensions. That is, the theory that was evaluated highest on a particular dimension was given a score of 6, the other point totals were determined relative to the highest rated theory on that evaluative dimension. For example, if the second and third rated theories on a dimension were very close to each other and close to the highest rated theory, then each of those two theories were given a 5; but if they were tied with each other but much lower than the highest rated theory, then they were both given a lower score (such as a 4 or a 3).

As Table 11.6 indicates, the evaluation procedure I display here shows that there are many reasons to regard social cognitive theory as the most useful of the six theories and cultivation as the least useful. In second place would be both agenda setting and framing. Then third person and uses & gratifications.

Table 11.6. Evaluation of Overall Utility

Theory	Year Intro	Years Since Intro	Scope	Precision	Heuristic Value	Empirical Validity	Openness	Totals
Cultivation	1969	48	3	1	3	1	1	9
Agenda Setting	1972	45	2	6	3	5	5	21
Uses & Gratifications	1974	43	3	3	2	2	4	14
Framing	1974	43	3	3	5	3	5	19
Social Cognitive	1977	40	6	5	6	4	5	26
Third-Person Effect	1983	34	3	3	1	5	4	16

Conclusions

This chapter displayed the evaluative judgments about the six analyzed media effects theories arrayed on five primary dimensions of scope, precision, heuristic value, empirical validity, and openness. The evaluative judgments from these five dimensions, which are each composed of several subdimensions, were used in a summary fashion to display an array on a big picture dimension of overall utility.

I expect that readers may disagree with some of the number values about overall utility as displayed in Table 11.6. Also, readers may disagree with some of the judgments on the five primary dimensions and their component subdimensions. In these cases, I ask readers to consider two things. First, I ask that readers think about the big picture and not focus too much on trivial differences arising from disagreements, such as me assigning a 3 rather than a 4, for example. Second, and more importantly, I ask that readers use disagreements as a motivation to conduct their own analyses and evaluations of these six theories as well as other theories. That is, my purpose is not to claim I have constructed the most author- itative, unchallengeable evaluations of these theories; instead, my purpose is to convince readers that rigorous scholarly analyses, evaluations, and comparisons of our theories is an important undertaking and to show them one way of undertak- ing this task.

References

Allen, M., Emmers-Sommer, T. M., D'Alessio. D., Timmerman, L., Hanzal, A., & Korus, J. (2007). The connection between the physiological and psychological reactions to sexually explicit materials: A literature summary using meta-analysis. *Communication Monographs, 74*(4), 541–560.

Anderson, C. A., Shibuya, A., Ihori, N., Swing, E. L., Bushman, B. J., Sakamoto, A., … Saleem M. (2010). Violent video game effects on aggression, empathy, and prosocial behavior in Eastern and Western countries: A meta-analytic review. *Psychological Bulletin, 136*(2), 151–173.

Banas, J. A., & Rains, S. A. (2010). A meta-analysis of research on inoculation theory. *Communication Monographs, 77*(3), 281–311.

Bandura, A. (1977). *Social learning theory.* Englewood Cliffs, NJ: Prentice-Hall.

Bandura, A. (1986). *Social foundations of thought and action: A social cognitive theory.* Englewood Cliffs, NJ: Prentice-Hall.

Blumler, J. G. (1979). The role of theory in uses and gratifications studies. *Communication Research, 6*(1), 9–36.

Chong, D., & Druckman, J. N. (2007). Framing theory. *Annual Review of Political Science, 10,* 103–126. doi:10.1146/annurev.polisci.10.072805.103054

Davison, W. P. (1983). The third-person effect in communication. *Public Opinion Quarterly, 47*(1), 1–15. doi:10.1086/268763

Diefenbach, D., & West, M. (2007). Television and attitudes toward mental health issues: Cultivation analysis and third person effect. *Journal of Community Psychology, 35,* 181–195.

Doob, A., & Macdonald, G. (1979). Television viewing and fear of victimization: Is the relationship causal? *Journal of Personality and Social Psychology, 37,* 170–179. doi: 10.1037/0022-3514.37.2.170

Entman, R. M. (1993). Framing: Toward clarification of a fractured paradigm. *Journal of Communication, 43*(4), 51–58. doi:10.1111/j.1460-2466.1993.tb01304.x

Gerbner, G. (1967). An institutional approach to mass communications research. In L. Thayer (Ed.), *Communication theory and research: Proceedings of the First International Symposium* (pp. 429–445). Springfield, IL: Charles C. Thomas Publisher.

Gerbner, G. (1969a). Toward 'cultural indicators': The analysis of mass mediated public message systems. In G. Gerbner, O. Holsti, K. Krippendorff, W. J. Paisley, & P. J. Stone (Eds.), *The analysis of communication content: Developments in scientific theories and computer techniques* (pp. 123–132). New York, NY: John Wiley & Sons.

Gerbner, G. (1969b). Toward 'cultural indicators': The analysis of mass mediated public message systems. *AV Communication Review, 17*(2), 137–148.

Gerbner, G. A. (1973). Cultural indicators: The third voice. In G. Gerbner, L. P. Gross, & W. H. Melody (Eds.), *Communication technology and social policy* (pp. 555–573). New York, NY: John Wiley & Sons.

Gerbner, G. (1990). Epilogue: Advancing on the path of righteousness (maybe). In N. Signorielli & M. Morgan (Eds.), *Cultivation analysis: New directions in media effects research* (pp. 249–262). Newbury Park, CA: Sage.

Gerbner, G., Gross, L., Morgan, M., Signorielli, N., & Shanahan, J. (2002). Growing up with television: Cultivation processes. In J. Bryant & D. Zillmann (Eds.), *Media effects: Advances in theory and research* (2nd ed., pp. 43–67). Mahwah, NJ: Erlbaum.

Gross, K., & Aday, S. (2003). The scary world in your living room and neighborhood: Using local broadcast news, neighborhood crime rates, and personal experience to test agenda setting and cultivation. *Journal of Communication, 53*, 411–426.

Grossberg, L., Wartella, E., & Whitney, D. C. (1998). *Mediamaking: Mass media in a popular culture.* Thousand Oaks, CA: Sage.

Gunther, A. C., & Storey, J. D. (2003). The influence of presumed influence. *Journal of Communication, 53*, 199–215.

Hansen, G. J., & Hyunjung, K. (2011). Is the media biased against me? A meta-analysis of the hostile media effect research. *Communication Research Reports, 28*(2), 169–179.

Hetsroni, A. (2007). Four decades of violent content on prime-time network programming: A longitudinal meta-analytic review. *Journal of Communication, 57*, 759–784. doi:10.1111/j.1460-2466.2007.00367.x

Hirsch, P. (1980). The "scary world" of the non viewer and other anomalies: A reanalysis of Gerbner et al.'s finding of cultivation analysis. *Communication Research, 7*, 403–456. doi:10.1177/009365028000700401

Hughes, M. (1980). The fruits of cultivation analysis: A reexamination of some effects of television watching. *Public Opinion Quarterly, 44*, 287–302.

Lasorsa, D. L. (1992). How media affect policymakers: The third-person effect. In J. D. Kennamer (Ed.), *Public opinion, the press and public policy* (pp. 163–175). New York, NY: Praeger.

Lee, C., & Niederdeppe, J. (2011). Genre-specific cultivation effects: Lagged associations between overall TV viewing, local TV news viewing, and fatalistic beliefs about cancer prevention. *Communication Research, 38*(6), 731–753. doi:10.1177/0093650210384990

Martins, N., & Harrison, K. (2012). Racial and gender differences in the relationship between children's television use and self-esteem: A longitudinal panel study. *Communication Research, 39*(3), 338–357.

McQuail, D. (1984). With the benefit of hindsight: Reflections on uses and gratifications research. *Critical Studies in Mass Communication, 1*, 77–93.

McQuail, D. (2005). *McQuail's mass communication theory* (5th ed.). Thousand Oaks, CA: Sage.

Morgan, M. (1982). Television and adolescents' sex-role stereotypes: A longitudinal study. *Journal of Personality and Social Psychology, 43*, 947–955.

Morgan, M. (1987). Television, sex-role attitudes and sex-role behavior. *Journal of Early Adolescence, 7*, 269–282.

Morgan, M. (2009). Cultivation analysis and media effects. In R. L. Nabi & M. O. Oliver (Eds.), *The Sage handbook of media processes and effects* (pp. 69–82). Los Angeles, CA: Sage.

Morgan, M., & Shanahan, J. (2010). The state of cultivation. *Journal of Broadcasting & Electronic Media, 54*, 337–355.

Morgan, M., Shanahan, J., & Signorielli, N. (2009). Growing up with television: Cultivation processes. In J. Bryant & M. B. Oliver (Eds.), *Media effects: Advances in theory and research* (3rd ed., pp. 34–49). New York, NY: Routledge.

Morgan, M., Shanahan, J., & Signorielli, N. (2014). Cultivation theory in the twenty-first century. In R. S. Fortner & P. M. Fackler (Eds.), *The handbook of media and mass communication theory* (pp. 480–497). Walden, MA: John Wiley & Sons.

Morgan, M., & Signorielli, N. (1990). Cultivation analysis: Conceptualization and methodology. In N. Signorielli & M. Morgan (Eds.), *Cultivation analysis: New directions in media effects research* (pp. 13–34). Newbury Park, CA: Sage.

National Television Violence Study. (1999). *National Television Violence Study.* Thousand Oaks, CA: Sage.

Paik, H. & Comstock, G. (1994). The effects of television violence on antisocial behavior: A meta-analysis. *Communication Research, 21*, 516–546.

Paul, B., Salwen, M. B., & Dupagne, M. (2000). The third-person effect: A meta-analysis of the perceptual hypothesis. *Mass Communication & Society, 3*(1), 57–85. doi:10.1207/s15327825mcs0301_04

Perloff, R. M. (1999). The third-person effect: A critical review and synthesis. *Media Psychology, 1*(4), 353–378. doi:10.1207/s1532785xmep0104_4

Potter, W. J. (1993). Cultivation theory and research: A conceptual critique. *Human Communication Research, 19*, 564–601.

Potter, W. J. (1994). *Cultivation theory and research: A methodological critique: Journalism Monographs.* Columbia, SC: Association for Education in Journalism.

Potter, W. J. (2014). A critical analysis of cultivation theory. *Journal of Communication, 64*(6), 1015–1036.

Romer, D., Jamieson, K. H., & Aday, S. (2003). Television news and the cultivation of fear of crime. *Journal of Communication, 53*, 88–104.

Rubin, A. M. (2009a). Uses and gratifications: An evolving perspective of media effects. In R. L. Nabi & M. B. Oliver (Eds.), *The Sage handbook of media processes and effects* (pp.147–159). Los Angeles, CA: Sage.

Rubin, A. M. (2009b). Uses-and-gratification perspective on media effects. In J. Bryant & M. B. Oliver (Eds.), *Media effects: Advances in theory and research* (pp. 165–184). New York, NY: Routledge.

Ruggiero, T. E. (2000). Uses and gratifications theory in the 21st century. *Mass Communication & Society, 3*(1), 3–37.

Severin, W. J., & Tankard, J. W. (1997). *Uses of mass media. Communication theories: Origins, methods, and uses in the mass media* (4th ed.). White Plains, NY: Longman.

Shanahan, J., & Morgan, M. (1999). *Television and its viewers: Cultivation theory and research.* Cambridge: Cambridge University Press.

Sun, Y., Pan, Z., & Shen, L. (2008). Understanding the third-person perception: Evidence from a meta-analysis. *Journal of Communication, 58*(2), 280–300. doi:10.1111/j.1460-2466.2008.00385.x

Sundar, S. S., & Limperos, A. M. (2013). Uses and grats 2.0: New gratifications for new media. *Journal of Broadcasting & Electronic Media, 57*(4), 504–525.

Tewksbury, D., & Scheufele, D. A. (2009). News framing theory and research. In J. Bryant, & M. B. Oliver (Eds.), *Media effects: Advances in theory and research* (pp. 17–33). New York, NY: Routledge.

Timmerman, L. M., Allen, M., Jorgensen, J., Herrett-Skjellum, J., Dramer, M. R., & Ryan, D. J. (2008). A review and meta-analysis examining the relationship of music content with sex, race, priming, and attitudes. *Communication Quarterly, 56*(3), 303–324.

Tukachinsky, R., & Tokunaga, R. S. (2013). The effects of engagement with entertainment. *Communication Yearbook, 37*, 287–321.

Wanta, W., & Ghanem, S. (2007). Effects of agenda-setting. In R. W. Preiss, B. M. Gayle, N. Burrell, M. Allen, & J. Bryant (Eds.), *Mass media effects research: Advances through meta-analysis* (pp. 37–51). Mahwah, NJ: Erlbaum.

Wober, J. M. (1978). Televised violence and paranoid perception: The view from Great Britain. *Public Opinion Quarterly, 42*, 315–321.

Big Picture

CHAPTER TWELVE

Patterns, Questions, and Challenges

Throughout the analyses and evaluations conducted in the previous chapters, some important questions have arisen concerning the development of knowledge about media effects. This chapter begins with highlighting of those questions then moves toward developing some tentative answers using the patterns developed thus far in the book. This final chapter concludes with a section that delineates the major challenges currently facing this field as it continues generating and sharing knowledge about media effects.

Fundamental Questions

While the analyses and evaluations have likely raised many fundamental questions, we will focus on what we think are the three most important ones: (1) What is a theory?, (2) Who is a theoretician?, and (3) With so many media effects theories, why is there so little usage of theory?

What Is a Theory?

This might seem to be a rhetorical question, because the term is commonly used by so many scholars without providing their definition, so it appears that scholars believe that there is a shared meaning for this term. However, when we look at how the term is used, there is reason to believe that the term "theory" does not exhibit a shared meaning; instead, it appears that there are various meanings in circulation.

This definitional "wobble" is seen clearly in the way this book's six systems of explanation were referred to when they were introduced, how their theoreticians have labeled them over time, and how subsequent scholars have treated them. For example, the creators of uses & gratifications, cultivation, framing, and third-person effects did not call their system of explanation a theory when they introduced it, but over time the creators and/or scholars who have tested these systems of explanation or reviewed the research sometimes refer to these systems as theories but sometimes not. To elaborate, uses & gratifications has often been referred to as an approach to thinking about the media rather than a theory (Katz, Blumler, & Gurevitch, 1974; McQuail, 2005; Rubin, 2009a, 2009b). Other scholars refer to it as a framework for understanding the processes (Katz et al., 1974), a perspective (Rubin, 2009b), or even a paradigm (Rubin, 2009b). Several scholars (Littlejohn, 2002; McQuail, 2005; Severin & Tankard, 1997) have published books on mass media and included uses & gratifications prominently in those books but have treated it less like a theory and more like an approach to analysis or a data-collecting strategy. Blumler (1979) argued "There is no such thing as the uses and gratifications theory, although there are plenty of theories about uses and gratifications phenomena" (p. 11). Palmgreen, Wenner and Rosengren (1985) seem to support this view and say that additional ideas contributed over the years may each be their own theory. These include expectancy-value relationships to gratifications (Babrow & Swanson, 1984; Palmgreen & Rayburn, 1982, 1983, 1984), transactional processes of gratifications and effects (McLeod & Becker, 1974, 1981; Wenner, 1982, 1983), and the dimensions of audience activity (Levy, 1983; Levy & Windahl, 1984; Windahl, 1981).

The same reluctance to label systems of explanation as a theory is also seen with cultivation. When Gerbner (1969a, 1969b) introduced his system of explanation, he continually referred to it as an approach. Then he commonly used the terms "cultivation hypothesis" and "cultivation analysis." Members of Gerbner's research team also seemed reluctant to apply the label "theory" to cultivation. Morgan and Signorielli (1990) called their book "cultivation analysis" and referred to cultivation as "a particular set of theoretical and methodological assumptions and procedures designed to assess the contributions of television viewing to people's conceptions of social reality" (p. 15). Then in their "State of Cultivation" essay for the *Journal of Broadcasting & Electronic Media* Morgan and Shanahan (2010) referred to cultivation as a theory, but also called it an hypothesis, an analysis, and even a paradigm.

When Goffman (1974) introduced framing as a system of explanation in his 576 page book, he never referred to it as a theory. Other scholars typically have referred to framing as an effect or a research area (McQuail, 2005; Shah, McLeod, Gotlieb, & Lee, 2009). But then in a major review, Tewksbury and Scheufele (2009) referred to it as a theory and showed how the research has suggested particular meanings for key terms and relationships among those key terms in a set of propositions.

Davison (1983) did not refer to third-person perceptions as a theory. Instead Davison referred to this pattern as "the third-person effect" and "the third-person hypothesis." Other scholars (Gunther, 1995; Hoornes & Ruiter, 1996; Huh, Delorme, & Reid, 2004; McLeod, Eveland, & Nathanson, 1997; Price, Tewksbury, & Huang, 1998; Shah, Faber, & Youn, 1999; Sun, Pan, & Shen, 2008; Tiedge, Silverblatt, Havice, & Rosenfeld, 1991) typically referred to it as an effect; however, it has also been referred to as "third-person conceptualization" (Cohen & Davis, 1991), "third-person effect model" (Gunther, 1995), and "third-person phenomenon" (Gunther & Thorson, 1992). Some scholars are careful not to refer to it as a theory. For example, in the first major review of TPE, Perloff (1999) said, "It is important to emphasize that the TPE is not a theory of public opinion, but rather a hypothesis or series of assertions about perceptions of public opinion and their effects" (p. 355) but he did not explain what he believed TPE was missing in order for him to avoid labeling it as a theory.

The two exceptions to this pattern of uncertainty in labeling are social learning theory and agenda setting. When Bandura introduced his system of explanation, he labeled it as social learning theory and used this term as the title of his book (Bandura, 1977). It is clear right from the beginning that Bandura regarded his set of ideas as a theory.

The other exception to this pattern is agenda setting, which started with uncertainty but appears to have outgrown that labeling uncertainty over time. In their classic "Chapel Hill Study" article, McCombs and Shaw (1972) never referred to their explanation as a theory. Instead they referred to it as a hypothesis. They said that their "analysis includes a juxtaposition of the agenda-setting and selective perception hypotheses. Comparison of these correlations too supports the agenda-setting hypothesis" (p. 185). Other scholars at the time were also reluctant to refer to agenda setting as a theory. In reviewing agenda setting, Kosicki (1993) claimed that "Although there is much informal writing and loose talk describing agenda setting as a hypothesis, empirical generalization, concept, metaphor, or even a full-fledged theory, it seems best to refer to agenda setting as a model of media effects" (p. 102), and he explains that the term model is a more modest and limited term than theory where a model "suggests that agenda setting is one type of complex media effects hypothesis linking media production, content and audience effects" (pp. 101–102). Edelstein (1993) repeatedly referred to agenda setting as a hypothesis. Rogers, Dearing, and Bregman (1993) referred to agenda setting as a phenomenon, not a theory or system of explanation. Two decades later, McCombs and Shaw (1993) were referring to it as a theory as evidenced by statements such as "Agenda setting is a theory about the transfer of salience" (p. 62). However, they were still using other terms such as theoretical approach, theoretical umbrella, theoretical metaphor, and perspective. By 2005 when McCombs published a review entitled "A look at Agenda-setting: past, present and future" he frequently referred to agenda setting as a theory over three dozen times in the short 13 page article.

If these theoreticians had presented their meaning for theory then showed how their system of explanation did not yet exhibit all the elements in that definition to qualify as earning the label of "theory," then we could understand why they used the labels they did as well as recognizing what changed in the system of explanation to lead some of these scholars to begin applying the label at a certain point in the maturation of the system of explanation. But none of the theoreticians have done this. Also, if critics and reviewers of these theories had presented their definitions, then their arguments about mislabeling would be more clear. The only exception to this pattern is Kosicki (1993) who argued that agenda setting is better called a model than a theory because the term model is "a more modest and limited term than theory" (p. 101) but he did little to explain what the agenda setting system of explanation was missing that disqualified it for being regarded as a theory.

Perhaps we can look at these patterns of labeling as a deep structure (Geertz, 1973) to infer the characteristics a system of explanation must have in order to be labeled as a "theory." Let's begin this examination by contrasting social learning with the other five theories. Why is it that Bandura was confident in calling his system a theory and media effects scholars did not challenge this labeling? One salient difference is that when Bandura introduced his system of explanation, it had already been elaborated to a high degree (i.e., composed of a great many concepts that were well defined and shown to be in relationship with one another) and had been built from a solid foundation of findings in the empirical literature. Bandura had spent 25 years analyzing and synthesizing the literature on social learning and modeling. His introduction of the theory presented dozens of concepts organized into processes (attention, retention, motor reproduction, and motivation). When reading through *Social Learning Theory*, one feels like Bandura is trying to avoid speculation as much as possible and instead build a system of explanation from patterns documented by well-established literatures. His theory is assembled from pieces we can trust because each piece comes from a trusted literature.

This would also explain why McCombs was reluctant to refer to agenda setting as a theory until it has been elaborated much more and had attained a great deal of empirical support. While the agenda setting explanation was intriguing in 1972, it had only one study to support it. Over the next four decades, it generated a literature of over 400 studies that not only found support for the original proposition but also expanded it into a system of explanation that elaborated the kernel idea by also providing propositions explaining who influenced that effect and how; what kinds of people were more susceptible to the effect and why; and expanded the effect beyond beliefs. Now agenda setting theory is on par with social cognitive theory in terms of the elaboration of its system of explanation and its base of empirical support for all of its major claims. Like social learning, agenda setting is now consistently regarded as a theory. Both present many claims about media effects and those claims are supported by a good deal of empirical testing.

It appears, however, that empirical support alone is not enough. Goffman's introduction of framing was every bit as detailed and grounded in the scholarly literature as Bandura's introduction of social learning. The only salient difference between Bandura and Goffman after introducing their elaborate systems of explanation is that Bandura continued to focus his scholarly energy on updating and refining his system of explanation by continually reviewing the growing literature of social modeling, conducting his own empirical tests, and publishing books, chapters, and articles on social learning theory. This maintained his credibility as a theoretician. Furthermore this credibility was concentrated on him, because there were no other scholars in his research area that demonstrated the degree of productivity and credibility anywhere near Bandura, so his ideas went largely unchallenged and even hardly ever criticized. In contrast, after Goffman introduced framing theory, he continued his scholarship in other areas such as social interactions, social construction of the self, and stigmas. His work was primarily focused on human interpersonal interactions, and media was only a peripheral interest. Also, he was very active in sociology, which had an overlap with communications but not as much of an overlap that the field of psychology did, which was Bandura's home area. And Goffman died less than a decade after he introduced framing theory, while Bandura continued active scholarship on social learning theory for more than four decades after its introduction. Therefore, compared to Bandura, Goffman left a vacuum surrounding framing theory within media effects studies.

Given the analysis above, it appears that the deep structure meaning of "theory" highlights three characteristics. First, there needs to be a relatively elaborate system of explanation that has been tested and supported by empirical findings. That is, it must present more than a handful of concepts and a single proposition. Second, speculation alone is not sufficient; there must be demonstrated evidence that the claims hold. And third, there needs to be an identifiable theoretician who is regarded with high degree of credibility, and this person needs to be visibly associated with the theory over a long period of time. This third characteristic brings us to our next question.

Who Is a Theoretician?

If we regard only social learning and agenda setting as the only "real" theories in the set of six, then the characteristic of scholarly credibility is central to determining who is a theoretician. A scholar builds credibility as a theoretician by displaying a long-term commitment to a system of explanation by continually mining elements from the relevant literatures. Some of those elements are findings of empirical studies; these are mined to demonstrate support for the theory's claims. Other elements are criticisms and findings that fail to support the claims of the theory; these are mined and used to forge alterations to the theory in order to achieve greater precision as well as to increase its validity. Thus theoreticians build credibility through demonstrating continuing commitment to the system of explanation as well as the willingness and the ability to make refinements that satisfy other media effects scholars.

The challenge of assessing a theoretician's credibility is relatively easy compared to the challenge of identifying who is a theoretician. One way to approach this task is to consider whether a theory needs to be identified with a single scholar or whether it can be identified by a team of scholars. For example, with agenda setting, McCombs and Shaw introduced the system of explanation but only McCombs consistently published reviews and updates of the system. Shaw was often a coauthor on reviews and revisions but not always. Also, Weaver was sometimes a coauthor on important publications refining and updating the theory. Therefore with agenda setting it could be argued that McCombs was the primary theoretician but that he was also part of a team with two other scholars guiding the development of that theory.

With cultivation theory, it is clear that George Gerbner introduced it and remained in control of theory for the first three decades by publishing annual tests of the effects part of his system of explanation. During those decades, he also published some review pieces by himself and with members of his research team (see Table 12.1). But by 1990, Gerbner appeared to be backing away as the central theoretician for cultivation and transferring that role to members of his research team, especially Nancy Signorielli and Michael Morgan who published a book on cultivation where they wrote a theory type introduction and Gerbner wrote a short

Table 12.1. Theories and Theoreticians

Theory	Introduction	Reviews	Other Reviews
Cultivation	Gerbner (1967)	Gerbner, Gross, Morgan, and Signorielli (1986)	Signorielli and Morgan (1990)
	Gerbner (1969a)	Gerbner (1990)	Shanahan and Morgan (1999)
	Gerbner (1969b)	Gerbner, Gross, Morgan, and Signorielli (1994)	Morgan, Shanahan, and Signorielli (2009)
		Gerbner (1999)	Morgan (2009)
			Morgan and Shanahan (2010)
			Morgan (2012)
Agenda Setting	McCombs and Shaw (1972)	McCombs and Shaw (1993)	Rogers and Dearing (1988)
		McCombs and Bell (1996)	Rogers et al. (1993)
		McCombs, Shaw, and Weaver (1997)	Wanta and Ghanem (2007)
		McCombs and Reynolds (2002)	Weiss (2009)
		McCombs (2004)	
		McCombs (2005)	
		McCombs and Reynolds (2009)	
		McCombs, Shaw, and Weaver (2014)	
Uses & Gratifications	Blumler and Katz (1974)	Katz (1987)	McQuail (1983)
	Katz et al. (1974)		Palmgreen (1984)
			Rosengren, Wenner, and Palmgreen (1985)
			Rubin (1986)

(Continued)

Table 12.1. *Continued*

Theory	Introduction	Reviews	Other Reviews
Framing	Bateson (1972) Goffman (1974)		Ruggiero (2000) Rubin (2009a) Rubin (2009b) Entman (1993) Fairhurst and Sarr (1996) Nelson, Oxley, and Clawson (1997) Scheufele (1999) Scheufele (2000) Druckman (2001) Chong and Druckman (2007) Tewksbury and Scheufele (2009) Scheufele and Iyengar (2015)
Social Cognitive	Bandura (1977)	Bandura (1986) Bandura (1997) Bandura (2002) Bandura (2009)	Parares, Prestin, Chen, and Nabi (2009)
Third-Person Effect	Davison (1983)		Lasorsa (1992) Perloff (1999) Paul, Salwen, and Dupagne (2000) Sun et al. (2008) Perloff (2009) Tal-Or, Tsafati, and Gunther (2009)

epilogue chapter. Since that time, Morgan has published key reviews by himself and with Signorielli and Shanahan.

All scholars will eventually retire and this raises a question about who will take over control of the theory. Because each of the six theories featured in this book were introduced at least three decades ago, and a few almost five decades ago, some of the theoreticians have already retired and others are likely to do so fairly soon. A vacuum of control over these systems of explanation could easily occur soon. With some of these theories, the theoretician has been working with a team so it is likely that one of those team members will take over control of the theory. But if this were to happen, other scholars would need to know that the "baton has been passed" to a particular successor. This appears to have already happened with cultivation.

What will happen with other theories where a single individual has been so strongly in control, such as with social learning theory? Bandura introduced social learning theory in 1977 and since that time has been exclusively identified as the theoretician of social learning. He has published many reviews and refinements over the years and all have been single authored. Bandura is now over 90 years old and still an emeritus professor at Stanford University. Because so much of this work has been single authored, it is not clear who will—or can—take over the theory. With agenda setting theory, it is clear that McCombs and Shaw introduced the theory. Over the next four decades, McCombs published eight major reviews either by himself or with other scholars closely associated with the theory. McCombs is almost 80 years old and still an emeritus professor at the University of Texas.

Some theories (uses & gratifications, framing, and third-person perceptions) have already exhibited an absence of control over the theory. The introduction of uses & gratifications theory has been credited to a book by Blumler and Katz (1974) that contained many chapters written by other authors associated with the theory—Gurevitch, McQuail, and Rosengren. Since that time, few of those authors have published reviews of the theory either by themselves or with other scholars. However, it appears that other scholars have become closely associated with the theory (especially Phillip Palmgreen and Alan Rubin) and each has published reviews that reflect on the theory and have suggested alterations to it. Now that more decades have elapsed, these "second-generation" scholars have retired or are nearing retirement with no easily recognizable "third-generation" scholar taking over the guidance of the uses & gratifications theory.

Framing theory had an ambiguous introduction with some scholars crediting Bateson and others crediting Goffman. Neither of these scholars were media effects researchers and neither published tests focusing on media influence as tests of their theory. However, an assortment of media scholars over the years have been attracted to the theory and have worked on elaborating it to fit the media effects area.

Third-person effect was introduced by Davison (1983) who then seemed to ignore this system of explanation. With both of these theories, other scholars have stepped into the vacuum and published scholarly reviews and even made elaborations to the original versions. Should these other scholars also be regarded as a system's primary theoretician?

This leads us to the question: Does there need to be a scholar recognized as being in control of the development of the theory? As we have seen with all of the six theories examined in this book, scholars beyond the theoretician will conduct tests of the claims made by the theory and publish their findings as tests of the theory. These researchers do not need the theoretician's permission to do so. And this work is necessary for the development of theories, so it is a positive thing. But what happens if there is a disagreement about how concepts should be defined, which assumptions should be altered, which propositions should be added or eliminated, and how the theory should be tested? With agenda setting theory, it appears that McCombs kept up with the literature of tests of the theory and periodically published reviews of that work, which resulted in agenda setting being elaborated to account for the findings in that literature. McCombs listened to criticism of the theory and made changes to overcome its weaknesses. He also added new propositions as suggested by findings in the literature. In contrast, Gerbner stuck to his original conceptualizations and operationalizations for tests of cultivation theory and dismissed almost all the criticism. For example, he regarded research that used less than macro-level measures of exposure to television (e.g., exposure to specific shows or types of programming) as not being valid tests of cultivation theory. However, Gerbner's ruling out of such studies did not discourage many researchers from continuing to use micro measures of exposure and publishing their research as tests of cultivation theory. And since Gerbner retired two decades ago, the research claiming to test cultivation theory has broken away from many of the claims Gerbner established when he first introduced cultivation (see Potter, 2014).

Having multiple researchers working on the same system of explanation can be an advantage if they all work together and produce more progress than any one scholar could. But what happens if they disagree over how the theory should be elaborated? Which scholar gets to say how these disputes are resolved? Or does the theory die at that point as each of the disagreeing scholars creates a different system of explanation from the original and giving each a different name?

These are important questions that will be answered over the next few decades as each of these six theories continues to generate tests with no single scholar mediating disputes for any one of these theories. Given the experience with framing, third-person perceptions, and uses & gratifications theories, the future does not look good when there is no single scholar identified as the controlling theoretician. Each of these three theories was introduced by theoreticians who left their theories in the hands of any researcher who was attracted to run a test of one of the theories' claims. While the literatures for all three theories continues to grow, so does confusion about the direction and current nature of each of these theories. And in the two decades since Gerbner retired, cultivation research continues to be a popular topic but most of the published research labeled as cultivation studies has ignored almost all of Gerbner's key ideas, especially the existence of widespread meanings throughout media messages and the macro-level nature of media influence. There are so many differences between the current designs of "cultivation theory" and what the theory claims that it seems that the theory has evolved into something so different than what Gerbner proposed that it is misleading to call current tests cultivation research (Potter, 2014).

Over the next few decades, we will see if these six theories survive as viable systems of explanation of media effects. And if they do survive, is it due to a charismatic researcher taking over leadership of the theory and guiding the research in a way that resolves disputes over meaning and testing to increase the theory's explanatory power? Or instead do theories thrive due to a community of researchers who work independently in providing continual testing and continually agree about a theory's alterations and extensions? Or do theories survive simply out of inertia?

Why so Much Theory Development Yet so Little Theory Usage?

Recall from Chapter 2 that there are many media effects theories but that most of the empirical literature is composed of studies that ignore them all. One content analysis of the media effects literature identified 144 theories (Potter & Riddle, 2007) (see Table 2.1) and another identified over 600 (Bryant & Miron, 2004). Both of these numbers are likely to be underestimates of the number of available media theories because both of these studies focused on relatively small samples of the very large media effects literature. Most of these theories are "one and done" mentions, that is, they are introduced in an empirical article (much like how agenda setting and third-person perceptions were introduced). But unlike those two theories, most of these other media effects theories never attracted any interest from media effects scholars. Potter and Riddle (2007) who analyzed media effects articles published in 16 journals from 1993 to 2005 found mentions of 144 theories, but that only 12 of these theories were mentioned in 5 or more studies in the sample of 936 published research articles. The remaining 132 theories were spread out over 168 articles.

Although there are many media effects theories in the literature, about two thirds of the published studies of media and effects acknowledge none of these theories (Kamhawi & Weaver, 2003; Potter, 2018; Potter, Cooper, & Dupagne, 1993; Potter & Riddle, 2007; Riffe & Freitag, 1997; Trumbo, 2004). Instead, the majority of this literature has always been and continues to be exploratory rather than theory driven. It is understandable why such a large proportion of the literature would not be theory driven in the decades of the 1940s, 1950s, and even the 1960s when there were few media effects theories. To be fair, there has been an increase in the proportion of the literature that is theory driven, but that proportion is still relatively low. The general trend appears to be an increase in theory-driven research from 34 % until 1990, then 42 % from 1990 to 2000, if we use a broad definition of theory. If we use a strict criterion for theory-driven research that requires authors to use an existing media effects theory, carefully deduce hypotheses from that theory, use the conceptualizations presented by the theoreticians, and test that system of explanation, then we can see that there appears to be a steady increase in the use of theory from 8.1 % (Potter et al., 1993) to 18 % (Trumbo, 2004) to 28.0 % (Potter, 2018).

Even if we concede that there is a growing use of theory, that level of use is still less than half, which leads scholars to regard this as a serious problem (Kamhawi & Weaver, 2003; McQuail, 2005; Nabi & Oliver, 2009; Potter, 2009). For example, Kamhawi and Weaver (2003) claimed that "theoretical development is probably the main consideration in evaluating the disciplinary status of the field. As our field grows in scope and complexity, the pressure for theoretical integration increases" (p. 20). Also, in their survey of major scholars in the field of mass communication, So and Chan (1991) reported that 63 % of respondents thought that the theoretical development should be a lot better. Journal reviewers have also been found to be critical of the use of theory. An analysis of reviewer comments for 120 manuscripts submitted to the *Journal of Communication* found that one of the most important concerns of those reviewers was a lack of theoretical integration (Neuman, Davidson, Joo, Park, & Williams, 2008, p. 220). But yet, about three quarters of published research in the field of media effects is *not* motivated by a theory and about half of the published research studies appear to ignore theories altogether.

It is indeed puzzling that with so many theories available, the majority of media effects studies continue to ignore theory. Recall from Chapter 2 that good theories can deliver a great deal of efficiency to researchers by giving them access to concepts with a higher degree of explication that provides a stronger basis for deducing hypotheses with greater precision; a history of measurement and data gathering procedures showing a progression of increasing validity; and a much stronger context for interpreting the findings of the research in a more conceptual and useful manner. With all these advantages that theories have to offer researchers, why do so many studies continue to be designed with no theory guidance?

Moving Toward Answers

As we move toward some tentative answers to the questions raised in the above section, it is useful to examine some patterns. First, we will look at how theories can be constructed, then second we'll examine patterns about how theories mature.

Theory Construction Patterns

The construction of a new theory requires a blend of identifying ideas from the existing literature along with at least one novel insight. When scholars simply list ideas from the literature, they are typically providing a descriptive review of the literature, and they have nothing new to contribute by way of explaining the phenomenon in a novel way. In contrast, when scholars provide only a novel insight without grounding it in an existing literature, they present only untethered ideas unpositioned in any flow of thinking. Thus in the process of theory construction, scholars experience a tension between building enough of a foundation from existing ideas in the literature and the creative urge to extend those ideas by providing novel insights.

Thus there are two fundamental tasks in constructing a useful theory. One task is for a scholar to critically analyze the literature on a topic to sort through all the findings in a way to discount faulty findings and highlight the most valid findings. The second task is to assemble all the valid findings generated by the first task into a system of explanation so that there is a coherence to the configuration of findings and that the system has the conceptual leverage needed to move beyond individual findings to make general statements about the nature of the phenomenon being explained as well as the working of the processes that determine that nature. This task requires considerable scholarly skill that relies on synthesis and creativity.

Let's take a look at the six theories to see what those theoreticians have produced in the way of a scholarly foundation supporting novel insights.

A balanced approach to theory construction was exhibited by McCombs and Shaw with agenda setting theory, Davison with third-person theory, and Blumler and Katz with uses & gratifications theory. The introduction of each of these theories was about 10,000 words, which is article length. These theoreticians all provided a short but adequate review of foundational ideas that were used as a support for a novel idea. The authors of the first two of these theories were presented in an unexpected finding in some research studies they had conducted and attempted to explain these unexpected findings with a novel idea. The authors of uses & gratifications presented a review of the literature as a way of demonstrating a shortcoming then called for a new approach to studying media effects.

The strongest foundations were created by Bandura in social learning theory and Goffman in framing theory. Both of these scholars conducted very detailed and extensive reviews of relevant literatures and published these reviews in single authored books. The contributions of these theoreticians were much more in the area of critical analyses of existing literatures than in providing novel insights.

When we look at the introduction of cultivation theory, we see many intriguing ideas that at first appear to be novel contributions made by Gerbner because those ideas are unattributed to anyone. At first cultivation appears as a highly creative theory. But scholars who are aware of the origins of the field of media effects studies will recognize all of these ideas as being already well developed in foundational literatures. So what at first appears as heavy on insights and light on foundation is actually the opposite.

The variety of these patterns tells us that there is no one way to develop a theory of media effects that will have high heuristic value.

Theory Maturation Patterns

Once a theory has been introduced into a scholarly literature, it seeks attention. Some theories attract a good deal of attention of both criticism and support mainly through empirical testing. There are two patterns about how media effects theoreticians have responded to this attention—closed system development and open system development.

Closed system development is a pattern where autocratic theoreticians exercise full control over their system of explanation. They periodically publish reviews of the empirical tests of their theory's claims where supporting evidence is emphasized and refuting evidence is either ignored or discounted as being faulty in some way. These theoreticians continually defend their initial assumptions, definitions, and system. If they present information about a calculus it is focused on how they conducted their own tests.

In contrast, open system development is a pattern where theoreticians allow other scholars to alter and elaborate their system of explanation. They consider criticism as well as findings that refute their original claims and use this information to alter their system of explanation to bring it more in line with current thinking.

Theoreticians feel a constant tension between these two patterns. If they are too closed and authoritarian, they risk attracting fewer scholars to their way of thinking and lower their willingness to test the claims of the theory. However, if they are too open, then they risk losing the identity of their theory.

Tentative Answers

The overriding question is why is such a small proportion of the empirical literature testing for media effects guided by a theory? In the physical sciences, research is typically guided by one dominant theory and perhaps several emerging theories that challenge that dominant theory. In social science fields, there are typically a larger number of theories but together they account for a high proportion of the research. So in the media effects field, which is a social science, we should expect more theories but we should also expect that the most tested theories should account for a relatively large proportion of the research. But the six theories analyzed in this book appear to account for only about 12 % of empirical studies that test for media effects. Bryant and Miron (2004) found that while these theories accounted for about 37 % of theory-guided published articles testing media effects, this number is only 12 % of all media effects research. This indicates that not only is the field of media effects predominately atheoretical, the most visible and enduring theories are infrequently used, that is, only about a third of the theory-driven research testing media effects is driven by any one of these six theories.

Why is the field of media effects so atheoretical? It is beyond the scope of this particular analysis to provide an answer for the entire field of media effects, where there are hundreds of theories available to provide guidance. However, we can use the analyses presented thus far to examine why these six theories may not be regarded as being useful by more researchers. Let's explore two possible reasons.

1. Marginal utility. One possible reason why these six theories have not generated a greater proportion of the empirical literature might be that many researchers perceive that these theories already have achieved a good deal of support so their efforts would have a greater payoff if they researched something different. While this might be the case with some researchers, there does not seem to be a pattern that supports this explanation. To illustrate, if the theories with the greatest published empirical support discouraged continuing research, then we should expect social cognitive theory to be the lowest on heuristic value among the six theories, but social cognitive theory is the highest on heuristic value.

2. Perception of inadequate guidance. Perhaps there is something about these particular theories that renders them as not very useful in the minds of many media effects researchers. If researchers are attracted to theories for purposes of efficiency in designing studies that can minimize design flaws, then researchers would look for those theories that have a long history of testing that has uncovered design flaws that have been corrected in subsequent testing. Therefore, the best theories would display a significant progression in their calculus.

While this explanation might hold for some researchers and some theories, there is no consistent support for this reason. For example, cultivation theory has been repeatedly criticized for major deficiencies in its calculus. Gerbner and his team have ignored the criticism and maintained their same procedures of sampling, measurement, and analysis. Not only has cultivation theory continued to attract researchers, those researchers have often ignored Gerbner's calculus, which led Gerber to question whether those studies qualified as tests of cultivation. Yet these studies successfully navigated peer review processes to get published in prestigious scholarly journals where they are displayed as tests of cultivation. This demonstrates that researchers often ignore guidance from theories to run their own versions of tests instead of choosing theories to test where they are provided with the greatest degree of guidance.

While the reasons explored in this section provided the beginning of an examination into the puzzling situation of atheoretical research in media effects, more thinking about the deep structure of research designs in this field is needed. This leads us to consider the major challenges that are currently facing the field of media effects.

Challenges

There are many challenges facing the field of media effects. In this section we will highlight the two fundamental sets of those challenges: generating knowledge and sharing knowledge.

Generating Knowledge

Theories can be valuable tools in generating knowledge about a field's focal phenomenon. A theory's value is linked to its precision in guiding researchers conceptually and operationally. Conceptual guidance comes in the form of (1) highlighting particular concepts, (2) providing clear, stable definitions for those concepts, (3) proposing a set of relationships as a system of explanation, (4) presenting those relationships as operative, and (5) highlighting the foundational axioms that form the support of the theory.

When theories are brand new, theoreticians are forced to rely more on speculation than on empirical support for the selection and definition of concepts as well as for claims in propositions and axioms. Also, with little or no history of measuring certain concepts or testing particular relationships, a newly introduced theory may not be able to offer much operational guidance.

As empirical tests are conducted, their findings stimulate the theoreticians to alter their selection of concepts and definitions. Also, empirical testing helps the theoreticians refine their set of propositions and axioms. And knowledge accumulates about which operational practices are more useful and which are faulty.

The development of a theory is marked by its increase in precision—providing better and more detailed definitions of concepts. The set of propositions becomes more detailed in terms of specifying relationships; it also becomes more useful as the system of explanation is shaped by the patterns of findings in the empirical literature.

Theories provide an efficient way of organizing the development of knowledge. Because theories are sets of propositions, reviewers of a literature can proceed much more efficiently by organizing their reviews to parallel the structure of a theory. First, they can access all relevant published work much more efficiently by using the keywords from the theory. Second, they can organize their reviews by propositions, bring readers up to date on the degree of support for each proposition and the explication of each concept.

Theoreticians develop more useful theories when they engage in sorting, calibrating, and elaborating. Sorting is distinguishing between useful and nonuseful findings. Calibrating is determining which findings are more valid and useful than others. Elaborating is incorporating patterns of findings into knowledge claims. When theoreticians do these tasks well, they more clearly define the cutting edge in the progression of knowledge about the focal phenomenon and thereby set the agenda for research. They direct research resources to the most important features of a phenomenon. Then they reinforce programmatic research so that the findings of earlier research have maximum impact on the design of the next round of studies that can push the cutting edge of knowledge forward.

Theories provide forums for critical analyses by attracting attention to their concepts, propositions, and axioms. This does not mean that all scholars need to accept all that a theory claims; instead, theories invite criticism as well as support. And when the criticism is written by scholars who understand the theory, their insights work to improve the theory by making sure that the progress of research findings reveals patterns about which claims are receiving valid support and which claims need scaling back or other forms of alteration.

Thus there are major challenges both with conceptualizations and with operationalizations. As for the first, we need clearer conceptualizations of media, effects, and the process of influence.

* Should the media be regarded as mass? If so, what about the newer media where users get on internet platforms to interact with other users and thereby create the content?
* What constitutes an effect? Does it have to be manifested or can it also be latent?
* What does it mean to assert the media are exerting an influence? If we move beyond direct and into indirect effects, we open up an almost infinite regress where everything possibly influences everything else; how can studies be designed to ferret out meaningful findings?

As for the operational challenges, we need more detailed assistance by theoreticians to guide researchers in translating their concepts into variables and their propositions into hypotheses. Also, researchers need more prescriptive guidance concerning issues of sampling, measurement, and analyses.

* Have we reached a limit with nonprobability samples such that research now needs to construct representative samples in order to generate findings that can advance knowledge about media effects?
* Which measures are no longer useful? Do self-reports of mundane behavior offer any value at all now that we know about the many heuristics people use that serve to invalidate self reports? Does it continue to make sense to use demographic measures as dichotomies?
* Have we reached a limit to the value of using classical statistics in our quantitative analyses? Is it time to stop using p-values as indicators of significance and instead think about other standards for conceptual and practical significance of findings?

Sharing Knowledge

It is not sufficient that a field only generates knowledge about its focal phenomenon, it also needs to share that knowledge to benefit people beyond the field in some way. Bandura (1977) in laying out the theoretical perspective of Social Learning Theory wrote that theories are "ultimately judged by the power of the procedures it generates" to develop knowledge "that lead to prediction and technical innovations using that knowledge" (p. 4). As examples, Bandura says, "Suppose, for example, aeronautical scientists developed certain principles of aerodynamics in wind tunnel tests; if in applying those principles they were never able to design an aircraft that could fly, the value of their theoretical assumptions would be highly questionable. The same judgment would be applied to theorizing in the medical field if certain theories about physiological processes never led to any effective treatments of physical maladies" (p. 4).

Sharing of useful knowledge is especially important in the field of media effects. This is because people in all cultures spend a great deal of time exposing themselves to media messages for information and entertainment. The more we understand about the effects of those constant exposures to such a wide variety of messages and the more we understand the process of influence, the more useful will be our knowledge. But in order for people to use that knowledge to protect themselves from unwanted risks and to amplify desired reactions, we need to translate that knowledge from academese into everyday language.

At the current time, there appears to be many faulty beliefs about the media and how they affect people and institutions. Third-person perception theory, agenda setting theory, and cultivation theory all show us the importance of heuristics in how people process information and create beliefs that are clearly faulty. The more the general public can use the wisdom generated by these theories, the more the public can avoid faulty beliefs and thereby make better decisions about how to live their lives.

As for nonscholarly publics, usefulness of knowledge is indicated by how much of a field's knowledge is understood and talked about in those publics—such as policymakers, citizen action groups, and laypeople—as well as how often they employ that knowledge in their everyday lives to heighten enjoyment of the media and avoid risks of negative effects. It is a huge challenge for us to provide the best knowledge we can to inform these discussions.

Conclusion

The field of media effects has achieved much through its century of growth. Each year it attracts more scholars who have conducted research documenting a wide variety of media effects and identified many important factors of influence that are associated with each of those effects. These scholars have produced a literature that is now likely to be well over 10,000 published studies.

Like all scholarly fields, media effects struggles with the challenges of producing better research designs that can generate knowledge that is more valid and more useful. With media effects, we have the additional challenge of understanding a phenomenon that is so large, so complex, and so dynamic. The mass media have changed more in the past several decades than they did in all the decades previous. The way people access media messages and how they navigate through all the overwhelming number of message choices has radically changed. Message formulas that were once fairly standard have been drastically altered with interactive media platforms. Media industries have morphed into new configurations of ownership and control that reflect demands of the changing markets for media messages. And all of this change is occurring at an accelerating pace.

If the field of media effects has a chance of remaining viable as a place where scholars produce insightful knowledge, researchers need to achieve greater efficiencies in the design and conduct of their research. The one tool that has the greatest potential to deliver such efficiency is a set of well-developed theories.

References

Babrow, A., & Swanson, D. L. (1984, November). *Disentangling the antecedents of media exposure: An extension of the expectancy-value analyses of uses and gratifications*. Paper presented at the Annual Conference of the Speech Communication Association, Chicago.

Bandura, A. (1977). *Social learning theory*. Englewood Cliffs, NJ: Prentice-Hall.

Blumler, J. G. (1979). The role of theory in uses and gratifications studies. *Communication Research, 6*(1), 9–36.

Blumler J. G., & Katz, E. (1974). *The uses of mass communications: Current perspectives on gratifications research*. Beverly Hills, CA: Sage.

Bryant, J., & Miron, D. (2004). Theory and research in mass communication. *Journal of Communication, 54*, 662–704. doi:10.1111/j.1460-2466.2004.tb02650.x

Cohen, J., & Davis, R. G. (1991). Third-person effects and the differential impact in negative political advertising. *Journalism Quarterly, 68*(4), 680–688. doi:10.1177/107769909106800409

Davison, W. P. (1983). The third-person effect in communication. *Public Opinion Quarterly, 47*(1), 1–15. doi:10.1086/268763

Edelstein, A. S. (1993). Thinking about the criterion variable in agenda-setting research. *Journal of Communication, 43*(2), 85–99.

Geertz, C. (1973). *The interpretation of cultures*. New York, NY: Basic Books.

Gerbner, G. (1967). An institutional approach to mass communications research. In L. Thayer (Ed.), *Communication theory and research: Proceedings of the First International Symposium* (pp. 429–445). Springfield, IL: Charles C. Thomas Publisher.

Gerbner, G. (1969a). Toward 'cultural indicators': The analysis of mass mediated public message systems. In G. Gerbner, O. Holsti, K. Krippendorff, W. J. Paisley, & P. J. Stone (Eds.), *The analysis of communication content: Developments in scientific theories and computer techniques* (pp. 123–132). New York, NY: John Wiley & Sons.

Gerbner, G. (1969b). Toward 'cultural indicators': The analysis of mass mediated public message systems. *AV Communication Review, 17*(2), 137–148.

Gerbner, G., Gross, L., Morgan, M., & Signorielli, N. (1986). Living with television: The dynamics of the cultivation process. In J. Bryant & D. Zillmann (Eds.), *Perspectives on media effects* (pp. 17–40). Hillsdale, NJ: Erlbaum.

Gerbner, G., Gross, L., Morgan, M., & Signorielli, N. (1994). Growing up with television: The cultivation perspective. In J. Bryant & D. Zillmann (Eds.), *Media effects: Advances in theory and research* (pp. 17–48). Hillsdale, NJ: Erlbaum.

Goffman, E. (1974). *Frame analysis: An essay on the organization of experience.* New York, NY: Harper & Row.

Gunther, A. C. (1995). Overrating the X-rating: The third-person perception and support for censorship of pornography. *Journal of Communication, 45*(1), 27–38. doi:10.1111/j.1460-2466.1995.tb00712.x

Gunther, A. C., & Thorson, E. (1992). Perceived persuasive effects of commercials and public service announcements: The third-person effect in new domains. *Communication Research, 19*(5), 574–596. doi:10.1177/009365092019005002

Hoornes, V., & Ruiter, S. (1996). The optimal impact phenomenon: Beyond the third person effect. *European Journal of Social Psychology, 26*(4), 599–610. doi:10.1002/(sici)1099-0992(199607)26:4<599::aid-ejsp773>3.0.co;2-7

Huh, J., Delorme, D., & Reid, L. N. (2004). The third-person effect and its influence on behavioral outcomes in a product advertising context: The case of direct-to-consumer prescription drug advertising. *Communication Research, 31*(5), 568–599. doi:10.1177/0093650204267934

Kamhawi, R., & Weaver, D. (2003). Mass communication research trends from 1980 to 1999. *Journalism & Mass Communication Quarterly, 80*(1), 7–27.

Katz, E., Blumler, J. G., & Gurevitch, M. (1974). Utilization of mass communication by the individual. In J. G. Blumler & E. Katz (Eds.), *The uses of mass communications: Current perspectives on gratifications research* (pp. 19–32). Beverly Hills, CA: Sage.

Kosicki, G. M. (1993). Problems and opportunities in agenda-setting research. *Journal of Communication, 43*(2), 100–127.

Levy, M. R. (1983). Conceptualizing and measuring various aspects of audience "activity." *Journalism Quarterly, 60,* 109–114.

Levy, M. R., & Windahl, S. (1984). Audience activity and gratifications: A conceptual clarification and exploration. *Communication Research, 11,* 51–78.

Littlejohn, S. W. (2002). *Theories of human communication* (7th ed.). Belmont, CA: Wadsworth.

McCombs, M. (2004). *Setting the agenda: The mass media and public opinion* (Repr. ed.). Cambridge: Blackwell. p. 198.

McCombs, M. (2005). A look at agenda-setting: Past, present and future. *Journalism Studies*, 6(4), 543–557. doi:10.1080/14616700500250438

McCombs, M., & Bell, T. (1996). *The agenda-setting role of mass communication: An integrated approach to communication theory and research* (pp. 93–110). Mahwah, NJ: Erlbaum.

McCombs, M. E., & Shaw, D. L. (1972). The agenda-setting function of mass media. *Public Opinion Quarterly, 36*(2), 176. doi:10.1086/267990. ISSN 0033-362X

McCombs, M. E., & Shaw, D. L. (1993). The evolution of agenda-setting research: Twenty-five years in the marketplace of ideas. *Journal of Communication, 43*(2), 58–67. doi:10.1111/j.1460-2466.1993.tb01262.x

McCombs, M., & Reynolds, A. (2002). News influence on our pictures of the world. In J. Bryant & D. Zillmann (Eds.), *Media effects: Advances in theory and research* (3rd ed., pp. 1–18). Mahwah, NJ: Erlbaum

McCombs, M., & Reynolds, A. (2009). How the news shapes our civic agenda. In J. Bryant & M. B. Oliver (Eds.), *Media effects: Advances in theory and research* (3rd ed., pp. 1–16). New York, NY: Routledge.

McCombs, M., Shaw, D. L., & Weaver, D. H. (1997). *Communication and democracy: Exploring the intellectual frontiers in agenda-setting theory.* Mahwah, NJ: Erlbaum.

McCombs, M. E., Shaw, D. L., & Weaver, D. H. (2014). New directions in agenda-setting theory and research. *Mass Communication & Society, 17*(6), 781–802. doi:10.1080/152054 36.2014.964871

McLeod, D. M., Eveland, W. P., & Nathanson, A. I. (1997). Support for censorship of violent and misogynic rap lyrics: An analysis of the third-person effect. *Communication Research, 24*(2), 153–174. doi:10.1177/009365097024002003

McLeod, J. M., & Becker, L. B. (1974). Testing the validity of gratifications measures through political effects analysis. In J. G. Blumler & E. Katz (Eds.), *The uses of mass communications: Current perspectives on gratifications research.* Beverly Hills, CA: Sage.

McLeod, J. M., & Becker, L. B. (1981). The uses and gratifications approach. In D. D. Nimmo & K. R. Sanders (Eds.), *Handbook of political communication.* Beverly Hills, CA: Sage.

McQuail, D. (1983). *Mass communication theory* (3rd ed.). Beverly Hills, CA: Sage.

McQuail, D. (2005). *McQuail's mass communication theory* (5th ed.). Thousand Oaks, CA: Sage.

Morgan, M. (2009). Cultivation analysis and media effects. In R. L. Nabi & M. O. Oliver (Eds.), *The Sage handbook of media processes and effects* (pp. 69–82). Los Angeles, CA: Sage.

Morgan, M. (2012). *George Gerbner: A critical introduction to media and communication theory.* New York, NY: Peter Lang.

Morgan, M., & Shanahan, J. (2010). The state of cultivation. *Journal of Broadcasting & Electronic Media, 54,* 337–355.

Morgan, M., Shanahan, J., & Signorielli, N. (2009). Growing up with television: Cultivation processes. In J. Bryant & M. B. Oliver (Eds.), *Media effects: Advances in theory and research* (3rd ed., pp. 34–49). New York, NY: Routledge.

Morgan, M., & Signorielli, N. (1990). Cultivation analysis: Conceptualization and methodology. In N. Signorielli & M. Morgan (Eds.), *Cultivation analysis: New directions in media effects research* (pp. 13–34). Newbury Park, CA: Sage.

Nabi, R. L., & Oliver, M. B. (Ed.). (2009). *Media processes and effects*. Los Angeles, CA: Sage.

Neuman, W. R., Davidson, R., Joo, S.-H., Park, Y. J., & Williams, A. E. (2008). The seven deadly sins of communication research. *Journal of Communication, 58*, 220–237.

Palmgreen, P. (1984). Uses and gratification: A theoretical perspective. In R. N. Bostrom (Ed.), *Communication yearbook* (Vol. 8, pp. 20–55). Beverly Hills, CA: Sage.

Palmgreen, P., & Rayburn, J. D. (1982). Gratifications sought and media exposure: An expectancy value model. *Communication Research, 9*, 561–580.

Palmgreen, P., & Rayburn, J. D. (1983). A response to Stanford. *Communication Research, 10*, 253–257.

Palmgreen, P., Wenner, L. A., & Rosengren, K. E. (1985). Uses and gratifications research: The past ten years. In K. E. Rosengren, L. A. Wenner, & P. Palmgreen (Eds.), *Media gratifications research: Current perspectives* (pp. 11–37). Beverly Hills, CA: Sage.

Perloff, R. M. (1999). The third-person effect: A critical review and synthesis. *Media Psychology, 1*(4), 353–378. doi:10.1207/s1532785xmep0104_4

Perloff, R. M. (2009). Mass media, social perception, and the third-person effect. In J. Bryant & M. B. Oliver (Eds.), *Media effects: Advances in theory and research* (3rd ed., pp. 252–268). London: Routledge. ISBN 9781135591106.

Potter, W. J. (2009). *Arguing for a general framework for mass media scholarship*. Thousand Oaks, CA: Sage.

Potter, W. J. (2014). A critical analysis of cultivation theory. *Journal of Communication, 64*(6), 1015–1036.

Potter, W. J. (2018). An analysis of patterns of design decisions in recent media effects research. *Review of Communication Research, 6*, 1–29. doi: 10.12840/issn.2255-4165.2018.06.01.014

Potter, W. J., Cooper, R., & Dupagne, M. (1993). The three paradigms of mass media research in mainstream journals. *Communication Theory, 3*, 317–335.

Potter, W. J., & Riddle, K. (2007). Profile of mass media effects research in scholarly journals. *Journalism & Mass of Communication Quarterly, 84*, 90–104.

Price, V., Tewksbury, D., & Huang, L.-N. (1998). Third-person effects on publication of a holocaust-denial advertisement. *Journal of Communication, 48*(2), 3–26. doi:10.1111/j.1460-2466.1998.tb02745.x

Riffe, D., & Freitag, A. (1997). A content analysis of content analyses: Twenty-five years of *Journalism Quarterly*. *Journalism & Mass Communication Quarterly, 74*, 873–882.

Rogers, E. M., Dearing, J. W., & Bregman, D. (1993). The anatomy of agenda-setting research. *Journal of Communication, 43*(2), 68–84. doi:10.1111/j.1460-2466.1993.tb01263.x

Rosengren, K. E., Wenner, L. A., & Palmgreen, P. (Eds.). (1985). *Media gratifications research: Current perspectives*. Beverly Hills, CA: Sage.

Rubin, A. M. (2009a). Uses and gratifications: An evolving perspective of media effects. In R. L. Nabi & M. B. Oliver (Eds.), *The Sage handbook of media processes and effects* (pp. 147–159). Los Angeles, CA: Sage.

Rubin, A. M. (2009b). Uses-and-gratification perspective on media effects. In J. Bryant & M. B. Oliver (Eds.), *Media effects: Advances in theory and research* (pp. 165–184). New York, NY: Routledge.

Severin, W. J., & Tankard, J. W. (1997). *Uses of mass media. Communication theories: Origins, methods, and uses in the mass media* (4th ed.). White Plains, NY: Longman.

Shah, D. V., Faber, R. J., & Youn, S. (1999). Susceptibility and severity: Perceptual dimensions underlying the third-person effect. *Communication Research, 26*(2), 240–267. doi:10.1177/009365099026002006

Shah, D. V., McLeod, D. M., Gotlieb, M. R., & Lee, N.-J. (2009). Framing and agenda setting. In R. L. Nabi & M. B. Oliver (Eds.), *Media processes and effects* (pp. 83–98). Los Angeles, CA: Sage.

Shanahan, J., & Morgan, M. (1999). *Television and its viewers: Cultivation theory and research.* Cambridge: Cambridge University Press.

So, C., & Chan, J. (1991, August). *Evaluating and conceptualizing the field of mass communication: A survey of the core scholars.* Paper presented at the annual meeting of the AEJMC, Boston.

Sun, Y., Pan, Z., & Shen, L. (2008). Understanding the third-person perception: Evidence from a meta-analysis. *Journal of Communication, 58*(2), 280–300. doi:10.1111/j.1460-2466.2008.00385.x

Tewksbury, D., & Scheufele, D. A. (2009). News framing theory and research. In J. Bryant & M. B. Oliver (Eds.) *Media effects: Advances in theory and research* (pp. 17–33). New York, NY: Routledge.

Tiedge, J. T., Silverblatt, A., Havice, M. J., & Rosenfeld, R. (1991). Discrepancy between perceived first person and perceived third-person mass media effects. *Journalism Quarterly, 68*(1/2), 141–154. doi:10.1177/107769909106800115

Trumbo, C. W. (2004). Research methods in mass communication research: A census of eight journals 1990 to 2000. *Journalism & Mass Communication Quarterly, 80*(2), 417–436.

Wenner, L. A. (1982). Gratifications sought and obtained in program dependency: A study of network evening news programs and 60 minutes. *Communication Research, 9*, 539–560.

Wenner, L. A. (1983, May). *Gratifications sought and obtained: Model specification and theoretical development.* Paper presented at the Annual Meeting of the International Communication Association, Dallas.

Windahl, S. (1981). Uses and gratifications at the crossroads. In G. C. Wilhoit & H. de Bock (Eds.), *Mass Communication Review Yearbook.* Beverly Hills, CA: Sage.

Index

H

hermeneutic process, of scholarship
 development 5, 31
heuristic value, of a theory x, 59, 197, 254,
 255, 286, 287
 and evaluation strategy 225–226, 228,
 234
human agency 182, 189, 193, 194, 204
human capabilities 179, 193–195
humanism xiv, 12, 37, 159
hypotheses, operationalization of 11, 15, 39,
 58, 290
hypotheticals 13

I

ideal type constructs 13
inadequate guidance, perception of 288
individual agency 182, 189, 193–194, 204
inductive method 16, 25–26
influence, process of 48, 88–89, 147–148,
 228, 290–291
institutional analysis 78, 81, 86, 249,
 258, 262
integration:
 of research findings xii
 theoretical 38, 126, 284
intention, growth of a scientific
 theory by 17
intentionality, of media effects 48, 54, 153
 and comparative analyses 243–245,
 and evaluation strategy 227–228, 230
internal coherence 217
Internet 24, 122–123, 126–127
interpretive beings, humans as
intervening variables 113, 147, 148

J

journalism 119, 122, 144, 202

K

Katz, Elihu 159
key concepts 48, 57, 79, 80, 139, 161,
 184, 205
 and comparative analyses 247–248
 and evaluation strategy 228, 230
knowledge,
 about the focal phenomenon of a
  scholarly field xiii, 5, 20, 289
 usefulness of 20, 291
knowledge building, in media research studies
 24–25, 26, 28, 228
knowledge generation 288, 290
knowledge sharing 290

L

learning, vicarious 193–194
life cycle, of scientific theories 16
limited synthesis, in media effects research
 32–33
limited translation, of ideas into media effects
 research 33–34
lines of research, major 59
Lippmann, Walter 76, 138
literature reviews 28, 31, 33, 234
locus of meaning 91, 93–94
logical coherence 228, 234, 242, 246,
 250, 251
logical consistency 252
longitudinal research 77, 90, 125, 150,
 259, 262
low elevation, of knowledge in media effects
 research 31

M

McCombs, Maxwell 64, 110
macro-level theory 28, 73, 74, 91, 93
mainstreaming 90, 244, 246, 249, 265